Beyond Law and Development

The book highlights new imaginaries required to transcend traditional approaches to law and development. The authors focus on injustices and harms to people and the environment, and confront global injustices involving impoverishment, patriarchy, forced migration, global pandemics and intellectual rights in traditional medicine resulting from maldevelopment, bad governance and aftermaths of colonialism. New imaginaries emphasise deconstruction of fashionable myths of law, development, human rights, governance and post-coloniality to focus on communal and feminist relationality, non-western legal systems, personal responsibility for justice and forms of resistance to injustices.

The book will be of interest to students and scholars of development, law and development, feminism, international law, environmental law, governance, politics, international relations, social justice and activism.

Sam Adelman is a Reader in the Law School at the University of Warwick. He was a student leader and was exiled during the struggle against apartheid in South Africa. His recent publications cover issues including climate change, climate justice, international environmental law, human rights, geoengineering, development and sustainable development. He has degrees from Wits University, Harvard University and the University of Warwick. He is a Research Associate at Nelson Mandela University and North-West University in South Africa and has been a visiting Professor in Ethiopia, Malawi, Kenya, Zimbabwe and South Africa and a visiting Fellow at the University of Rosario in Colombia. He has been involved in the founding of the global Law and Development Research Network (https://lawdev.org).

Abdul Paliwala is Emeritus Professor of Law at the University of Warwick where he was involved in the founding and teaching of Law in Development (renamed LLM International Development Law and Human Rights) since 1981. He has also been involved in the founding of the global Law and Development Research Network (https://lawdev.org). He previously taught at Queen's University of Belfast, the University of Dar es Salaam and the University of Papua New Guinea, where he also worked as the Secretary of the Law Reform Commission. He was Director of the CTI Law Technology Centre for UK Law Schools, the Law Courseware Consortium, the UK Centre for Legal Education and the Electronic Law Journals Project that published the *Journal of Information Law and Technology* and *Law, Social Justice and Global Development*.

Beyond Law and Development

Resistance, Empowerment and Social Injustice

Edited by
Sam Adelman and Abdul Paliwala

Routledge
Taylor & Francis Group
a GlassHouse Book

First published 2022
by Routledge
2 Park Square, Milton Park, Abingdon, Oxon OX14 4RN

and by Routledge
605 Third Avenue, New York, NY 10158

a GlassHouse book

Routledge is an imprint of the Taylor & Francis Group, an informa business

British Library Cataloguing-in-Publication Data
A catalogue record for this book is available from the British Library

Library of Congress Cataloging-in-Publication Data
A catalog record has been requested for this book

ISBN: 978-1-138-30032-3 (hbk)
ISBN: 978-1-032-25413-5 (pbk)
ISBN: 978-0-203-74529-8 (ebk)

DOI: 10.4324/9780203745298

Typeset in Bembo
by Taylor & Francis Books

We believe that young people in current and future generations can play a crucial role in constructing a just future for all species and the planet we live on. In this spirit we dedicate this volume to all young people and especially to our grandchildren Felix, Thea and Sophia in the hope that they will enjoy peaceful lives on a habitable planet.

Contents

PART II
Rights and Injustices 139

Contributors

Shaheen Sardar Ali holds the position of Rector at the National Academy of Higher Education (NAHE), operating under the auspices of the Higher Education Commission (HEC) of Pakistan. She is also Professor of Law at the University of Warwick (currently on leave) and has held professorial positions at the Universities of Peshawar and Oslo and was Vice-Chair of the United Nations Working Group on Arbitrary Detention (2008–2014). She has served as a cabinet minister for Health, Population Welfare and Women Development, Government of the Khyber Pukhtunkhwa Province of Pakistan. She was the Chair of Pakistan's first National Commission on the Status of Women (1999–2001). In 2012, she was named one of the 100 most influential women of Pakistan. Professor Ali has an LLB (Peshawar), LLM (Hull), MA (Peshawar) and PhD (Hull) and has published extensively in Islamic law and international human rights law including human rights of women and children and family law. She is the author of 9 books, 41 journal articles and 30 book chapters as well as a number of reviews and reports for national and international bodies. Her most recent monograph, *Modern Challenges to Islamic Law* (Cambridge University Press, 2016) has been widely acclaimed as a ground-breaking contribution to Islamic law scholarship.

Bill Derman is Professor Emeritus at Michigan State University and the Department of International Environment and Development Studies at the Norwegian University of Life Sciences. He holds a PhD in Anthropology from the University of Michigan and has carried out long-term field work in west and southern Africa. He is currently engaged in research on land restitution in South Africa and in water governance, human rights, gender and integrated water resources management in Zimbabwe. He has written extensively on land and water issues in southern Africa and on US development policy in Africa. He is co-editor of *Flows and Practices: The Politics of Integrated Water Resources Management in Southern Africa* (Weaver Press, 2017) and co-author of *United States Assistance Policy in Africa – Exceptional Power* (Routledge, 2017).

John Harrington is Professor of Global Health Law and Director of the ESRC Doctoral Training Programme in Wales. He holds degrees in law from Trinity College Dublin and Oxford University. Previous appointments include Liverpool, Warwick and the Free University of Berlin, as well as fellowships at the African Population and Health Research Center (Nairobi), University of Melbourne, European University Institute and University of Dar es Salaam. His books include *State Formation in Global Health: Development, Security and Sovereignty* (forthcoming), *Global Health and Human Rights: Legal and Philosophical Perspectives* (with M. Stuttaford eds., Routledge, 2010) and *Towards a Rhetoric of Medical Law* (Routledge, 2017).

Anne Hellum is professor at the Department of Public and International Law at the University of Oslo. She was awarded a dr. juris degree for her thesis *Women's Human Rights and Legal Pluralism in Africa* (Mond Books/TANO) in 1998. Since 1990 she has been involved in teaching and research at the Southern and Eastern African Regional Center in Women's Law (SEARCWL) at the University of Zimbabwe. She was also involved in setting up the European Doctorate in Law and Development (EDOLAD). As part of North/South university cooperation in the field of women's human rights and legal pluralism in Southern and Eastern Africa and has edited a number of books that are published by the Zimbabwean publisher Weaver Press. The most recent is *Water is Life: Women's Human Rights in National and Local Water Governance in Southern and Eastern Africa* which was co-edited with Barbara van Koppen and Patricia Kameri-Mbote (2016). Another important book is *Women's Human Rights: CEDAW in International, Regional and National Law*, which was co-edited with Henriette Sinding Aasen (2013).

Ambreena Manji is Professor of Land Law and Development at Cardiff. She was previously Director of the British Institute in Eastern Africa (2010–2014). She has held academic posts at the Universities of Warwick and Keele and has been a visiting fellow at the Faculty of Law, University of Cape Town and at Dar es Salaam Law School; a Global Teaching Fellow at Melbourne Law School; and Dame Lillian Penson Fellow at the Institute of Commonwealth Studies, University of London. Her research is focused on Law and Society in Africa. It is strongly interdisciplinary and includes work on law in African literature, African history, legal education and women and the law. Her most recent book is *The Struggle for Land and Justice in Kenya* (James Currey/Boydell & Brewer, 2020). Ambreena was president of the African Studies Association UK (2018–2020) and is currently a co-editor of *African Affairs*. She is a member of the Governing Council of the Arts and Humanities Council (AHRC). @AmbreenaManji

Oche Onazi is a Senior Lecturer in Law at the University of Northumbria and former Early Career Research Fellow of the Independent Social Research

Foundation. He holds degrees from the Universities of Edinburgh (PhD), Warwick (LLM) and Jos (LLB) and is a qualified (but non-practising) Barrister and Solicitor of the Supreme Court of Nigeria. Oche's research interests cover areas of legal philosophy, law and development and human rights. He is the author of *An African Path to Disability Justice: Community, Relationships and Obligations* (Springer, 2020) and *Human Rights from Community: A Rights-Based Approach to Development* (Edinburgh University Press, 2013).

Sharifah Sekalala is Associate Professor in the Law School at the University of Warwick. She is an interdisciplinary researcher whose work is at the intersection of international law, public policy, and global health. She is particularly focused on the role of human rights frameworks in addressing global health inequalities. She is currently principal investigator on a Wellcome funded project on the migration of data from health apps in SubSaharan Africa. Her relevant work includes, Sekalala et al. 'An intersectional human rights approach to prioritising access to COVID-19 vaccines', *BMJ Global Health* 2021; Sekalala, 'Categorising the gendered harms to caregivers during humanitarian emergencies: An analysis of law and practice during Ebola crises', *Social & Legal Studies*, December 2020; Sekalala et al., 'Analysing the human rights impact of increased digital public health surveillance in the wake of the COVID-19 crisis', *Health and Human Rights*, Volume 22 (2) *Special Issue on Human rights and Big Data* (2020).

Dallal Stevens is Professor of Refugee Law at the University of Warwick. Her research interests focus on refugee and asylum law and policy in the UK, EU and Middle East, areas on which she has published widely. Monographs include: *Reclaiming Migration: Voices from Europe's 'Migrant Crisis'* (authored with Vicki Squire, Nina Perkowski, Nick Vaughan-Williams; Routledge, 2021); *States, the Law and Access to Refugee Protection: Fortresses and Fairness* (ed., with Maria O'Sullivan; Hart, 2017); *Refugee Protection and the Role of Law: Conflicting Identities* (ed., with Susan Kneebone and Loretta Baldassar; Routledge, 2014) and *UK Asylum Law and Policy: Historical and Contemporary Perspectives* (Sweet & Maxwell, 2004). Dallal's work has been supported by external grants from AHRC-DFID, Norway Research Council, the Leverhulme Trust, the British Academy, the Arts and Humanities Research Board, and the ESRC. She is Book Review Editor with the *International Journal of Refugee Law* and on the Editorial Board of the *Journal of Immigration, Asylum and Nationality Law*.

Ann Stewart is a Professor at Warwick Law School. Her research interests relate to gender, law and development with a particular focus on Eastern and Southern Africa and South Asia. Her present research projects relate to gender and ageing in African plural legal contexts and gendered access to Higher Education in Haryana, India. She has a long-standing interest in social reproduction, care and care work with a focus on ageing both in the UK and within the global south in particular in Kenya. She teaches courses on Gender, Law and the Global Economy and Gender and the Law more generally. Her relevant works include 'Impoverishing care' in Beverley Clough and Jonathan Herring (eds), *Ageing, Gender and Family Law* (Routledge, 2018); 'Care or work: the tyranny of categories' in *Care, Migration and Human Rights: Law and Practice* (Routledge, 2015); *Gender, Law and Justice in a Global Market* (Cambridge University Press, 2011).

Monica Twesiime-Kirya is a Ugandan Law and Development Specialist, currently working as Senior Adviser at the U4 Anti-Corruption Resource Centre, Chr. Michelsen Institute in Bergen, Norway where she conducts research and provides advice on anti-corruption in public service delivery and mainstreaming gender in anti-corruption. U4 is an institutional partnership of eight bi-lateral development agencies from the UK, Germany, Norway, Sweden, Denmark, Switzerland, Finland and Canada, dedicated to sharing evidence on reducing the harmful impact of corruption on development.

Wouter Vandenhole is a human rights and law-and-development scholar. He holds the human rights chair at the Law Faculty of the University of Antwerp, and is a member of the Law and Development Research Group. Between 2007 and 2018, he also held the UNICEF Chair in Children's Rights. His research interests include the relationship between human rights law and development, children's rights, and economic, social and cultural rights. Among his many publications are: 'Children's Rights and Sustainable Development from a "Law and Development" Perspective', in C. Fenton-Glynn (ed.), *Children's Rights and Sustainable Development* (Cambridge University Press, 2019); 'De-growth and sustainable development: rethinking Human Rights Law and poverty alleviation', *Law and Development Review* (2018) 647–675.

Illan Rua Wall is a Reader at the Warwick Law School. He works on questions of protest and disorder, exploring sovereign orders, authority and policing. He is author of *Law and Disorder* (Routledge, 2021) and *Human Rights and Constituent Power* (Routledge, 2012). He co-directs the Warwick Centre for Critical Legal Studies, is on the editorial board of the journal *Law & Critique* and is a founding editor of the blog criticallegalthinking.com.

Andrew Williams is a Professor of Law at the University of Warwick. He is the author of *A Very British Killing: the Death of Baha Mousa* (Vintage, 2013) which won the George Orwell Prize for Political Writing in 2013. His latest book, *A Passing Fury: Searching for Justice at the end of WWII* (Jonathan Cape, 2016) examines the British investigations and trials of Nazi war criminals after 1945 and was shortlisted for the 2017 CWA Daggers Non-Fiction Award. He is currently co-director of the *Centre for Human Rights in Practice* and editor-in-chief of *Lacuna Magazine.*

Faqir Asfundyar Yousaf is a Litigation Solicitor at CTT Law Ltd. He is also a Member of the Chartered Institute of Arbitrators (MCIArb) and an Advocate of the High Court in Pakistan. In his years as an advocate and a legal practitioner in Pakistan and the UK, Mr Yousaf acquired experience in Civil and Commercial Litigation, International Arbitration, International Corporate Governance and Corporate and Commercial Law. Mr Yousaf has an LLM in International Corporate Governance and Financial Regulation from the University of Warwick and an LLB from the University of Punjab, Pakistan.

Preface

This is the second volume of essays in which contributors have been invited to consider whether discourses on development and law and development have outlived their usefulness and if so, what might replace them? Would it not be better to abandon such amorphous and contested concepts and focus instead on specific social injustices such as patriarchy, racism, impoverishment, national and international rights violations, the exploitation of peasants, workers and indigenous peoples, and global heating? The aim of the predecessor to this volume, *The Limits of Law and Development: Neoliberalism, Governance and Social Justice* (2021), was to problematise law and development orthodoxies and to outline the scope for new imaginaries to replace them. The contributors to this volume explore new approaches that focus on various injustices and harms and the potential to ameliorate or transcend them through forms of resistance.

This preface was written as the world is being transformed by the dual crises of Covid-19 and climate change. Addressing these crises has been made more difficult by dysfunctional national and global governance, authoritarian populism, democratic deficits, human rights violations, and the widespread perpetration of injustices. Although it is difficult to predict the future, history suggests that it is not illogical to expect that the peoples of the global South will continue to suffer from historical injustices and contemporary harms caused by maldevelopment. Although most of the chapters in this volume were written before the onset of the pandemic, we believe their authors make significant contributions to our understanding of problems that Covid-19 has thrown into sharp relief.

The urgent need to respond to these and other overlapping crises is being reflected in resistance by the people involved as is the case with the local resistance in Hong Kong, Myanmar, Brazil, India and global resistance movements such as Black Lives Matter and the Fridays for the Future climate strikes as well as academic analyses. It is noteworthy that a 2019 post-development dictionary combines academic as well as activist discourses driven by activism.[1]

1 Ashish Kothari, Ariel Salleh, Arturo Escobar, Federico Demaria and Alberto Acosta (eds), *Pluriverse: A Post-Development Dictionary* (Tulika Books, 2019).

The contributors to this volume take varying approaches to the problems of law and development but they all subscribe to the need for the interpenetration of academic discourses with activism in the struggles against social and ecological injustices. As Andrew Williams points out in his chapter, there is no room for bystanders in struggles for justice, peace, and human rights for current and future generations.

The Limits of Law and Development: Neoliberalism, Governance and Social Justice was dedicated to our late friends and colleagues Dwijen Rangnekar and Peter Fitzpatrick in acknowledgement of their contributions to struggles for global social justice. We reiterate our gratitude to our current and former students in Warwick Law School's LLM on International Development Law and Human Rights (formerly Law and Development) and the doctoral students who have contributed enormously to our understanding of local and global injustices. We are grateful to one of those doctoral students, Rohini Sen, for her work in the preparation of this book. We believe that young people in current and future generations, following the examples of Greta Thunberg, Malala Yusufzai and others, can play a crucial role in constructing a just future for all species and the planet we live on. In this spirit we dedicate this volume to all young people and especially to our grandchildren, Felix, Thea and Sophia.

Sam Adelman and Abdul Paliwala

Introduction

Sam Adelman and Abdul Paliwala

Introduction

The idea of development has engaged, influenced and frustrated the contributors to this volume and its predecessor, *The Limits of Law and Development: Neoliberalism, Governance and Social Justice* (Adelman and Paliwala, 2021a) and other post-development scholars (Esteva, 1992; Escobar, 2010; Kothari et al., 2019). In other contexts, development usually has positive connotations of healthy growth and progress, for example in relation to children. However, when it is applied to nation-states and their peoples today, in the Anthropocene, it is a misnomer.

Development became an object of desire after the Second World War, a siren call that lured its converts to believe that it paved the path to wellbeing, human rights, and social justice. Over time, development unfortunately often became the stuff of nightmares because it became synonymous with exploitation, corruption, inequality, bad governance, the extraction of rents and natural resources, and environmental devastation. Now in its eighth decade, development has been around long enough to entitle us to expect that such a ubiquitous idea might have delivered on its promises in a more consistent and less uneven manner.

Unthinking the Failures of Development and Law and Development

In *The Limits of Law and Development* (Adelman and Paliwala, 2021a), we suggested that the conceptual framework for law and development is flawed and that new imaginaries are required because development's promises have proved to be imaginary in much of the global South. The contributors to this volume seek to apply new imaginaries to a variety of social injustices.

Income levels and the standards of living of millions have improved in many countries, and China has demonstrated that extractive, growth-driven, carbon-based industrialisation can substantially reduce poverty. Measured by its GDP, a deeply problematic index of wellbeing, China is on the verge of becoming the wealthiest country in the world following unprecedentedly rapid development

DOI: 10.4324/9780203745298-1

that has produced the largest surveillance state in the world, extensive human rights violations in Xinjiang and elsewhere, and environmental degradation that facilitates the zoonotic transmission of deadly viruses.

At the same time, development has prevented millions elsewhere from escaping impoverishment. To the extent that development has succeeded, it has often done so by deepening injustices in much of the global South. In a world of plenty, impoverishment is a stark and unacceptable historical and structural injustice. Following Pogge (2002) and Baxi (2009), we use impoverishment rather than poverty to highlight the role of human agency in producing and perpetuating it. Impoverishment generally does not result from individual or national fecklessness but from an absence of resources and a denial of Senian capabilities or Nussbaumian flourishing (Sen, 1999; Nussbaum, 2011). It takes genius to survive on $1.90 per day, the World Bank's current measure of absolute poverty. Impoverishment is a direct consequence of capitalism and developmentalism. It is exacerbated by patriarchy, racism, and the oppression of peasants, workers and indigenous peoples.

Throughout the history of development, which is marked by neo-colonial structural inequalities, the immense wealth amassed by the global North and Southern elites has produced vast injustice.[1] Mainstream models of development have deepened the food, water, health and physical insecurity of all species. Maldevelopment is not a systemic bug but a logical corollary of developmentalism.

As appendages to development economics, law and development discourses have mirrored the conceptual failures of hegemonic models of growth-driven development. Law and development scholars distinguish the first phase of law and development, which commenced in the 1960s, from the New Law and Development movement that began in the 1990s with the advent of neoliberalism (Trubek and Santos, 2006; Adelman and Paliwala, 2021b). In the latter phase, significant aid funding has been provided to make legal systems more amenable to investors and other market actors, to increase access to justice, and to enhance the rule of law through constitutional amendments. Sadly, success has been limited (Tamanaha, 2011) because neoliberal dogma has consistently trumped social justice (Adelman and Paliwala, 2021b).

During the Great Acceleration, the pursuit of growth through extractive industrialisation degraded the material conditions for economic activity and the ostensible aims of development.[2] All economic activity is intrinsically destructive, but hegemonic models of development that know no bounds are tantamount to a war on nature. In 1987, the Brundtland Commission defined sustainable development as 'development that meets the needs of the present without

1 The world's 2153 billionaires have more wealth than the 4.6 billion people, who constitute nearly 60 per cent of the world's population (Oxfam, 2020).

2 The Great Acceleration describes the period which began in the decade after the Second World War and deposited traces in the Earth's stratigraphy of radionuclides from nuclear weapons testing and the exponential increase in the use of fossil fuels, concrete and plastic (Colvile, 2016).

compromising the ability of future generations to meet their own needs' (WCED, 1987: 43). By 1989 at least 140 definitions of sustainability existed (Johnston et al., 2006: 60), suggesting that the concept is so capacious and malleable that it can and does mean almost anything. States and corporations use it to claim they are promoting the Sustainable Development Goals with little fear of contradiction. Sustainable development rarely leads to ecological sustainability and far too often to unsustainability (Adelman, 2018; 2021). The Secretariat of the Convention on Biological Diversity (2020) noted that all of the 2010 Aichi biodiversity targets for protecting wildlife and ecosystems were missed during the preceding decade.[3] The ability of future generations to meet their own needs is increasingly imperilled.

Mainstream development theories also perpetuate the Enlightenment idea that history, modernity and progress unfold in a linear and irreversible direction (Adelman, 2020). This teleological notion of progress with its Darwinian undertones is reflected in colonial claims about the West's 'civilising mission' that denigrated the cultures of the colonised South as uncivilised (D'Souza, 2021). The cultural denigration of the South is a means of subordinating it (Said, 2003; Escobar, 2010; Esteva, 1992). Development as modernisation is its postcolonial avatar. Progress has been illusory for billions during both phases of law and development, with the contemporary phase initially tied to Cold War politics and then to the exploitation of Southern resources through neoliberal globalisation.

Two centuries after the Industrial Revolution, the idea of perpetual economic growth has comprehensively collided with planetary boundaries.[4] Capitalist development is a war on nature that is pathologically damaging to all forms of life. The gap between mainstream claims about the benefits of development, including sustainable development, and its actual consequences demonstrates the intrinsic unsustainability of both the concept and its implementation (Adelman, 2020). For example, a report commissioned by the UK Treasury warns that the world is at 'extreme risk' from the failure of mainstream economics to address the devastating effects of biodiversity loss (Dasgupta, 2021).

The Dasgupta review belatedly recognises what environmentalists have been arguing for at least half a century: that GDP is not merely an inadequate measure of wellbeing but positively dangerous because it is the yardstick by which national virility is calculated rather than wellbeing or justice.[5] Belated acknowledgement of the obvious is welcome, but the review remains trapped in green capitalist

3 Convention on Biological Diversity, Aichi biodiversity targets <https://www.cbd.int/sp/targets/> (accessed 21 June 2021).

4 Planetary boundaries <https://stockholmresilience.org/research/planetary-boundaries.html> (accessed 21 June 2021).

5 The world was alerted to the problem of growth in 1972 with the publication of *The Limits to Growth* (Meadows et al., 1972), the same year in which the UN Conference on the Environment took place in Stockholm – the foundational gathering for contemporary international environmental law.

assumptions that treat nature as capital or a set of commodities rather than offering a new imaginary commensurate with the scale and urgency of climate and environmental breakdown. The inability or unwillingness of neoclassical and neoliberal economists to jettison their orthodoxies brings to mind Upton Sinclair's observation that 'It is difficult to get a man to understand something, when his salary depends upon his not understanding it!' (Sinclair, 1994: 109).[6] The Dasgupta review is an attempt to rescue neoclassical and neoliberal economics from the axiological crisis into which it has descended but the climate and ecological crises cannot be resolved through the intellectual tools that created it.

Sustainable development is the latest mainstream incarnation of development. It replicates the predilection of economics for econometrics, mathematics, and the neoliberal dogma that value cannot be conceived unless it can be measured and priced.[7] Orthodox development economics vindicates Oscar Wilde's acid observation about knowing the price of everything and the value of nothing.

If the continuing problems of developmentalism provide the primary impetus for new imaginaries, this is reinforced by the withering of the certainties of Western modernism. These uncertainties have been counterpointed by recourse to an alternative relational paradigm. Mark Lupisella suggests that 'Relationalism is a broad fundamental conceptual umbrella that emphasizes a critical role for *relations in particular* and *relationality in general* as an important, perhaps central and fundamental, feature of the world' (Lupisella, 2020: 84; see also Rovelli, 2021; emphasis in the original). At a socio-economic level, the focus shifts from the individualism of neoclassical approaches to a concern with wider relationships among humans and their environment because only by taking these wider relationships into account does it become possible to promote well-being. Relational feminist ideas of care and indigenous approaches such as Pachamama and Ubuntu have come to the fore in struggles for social justice as counterpoints to possessive individualism and neoliberalism (Manji and Stewart, this volume; Onazi, this volume). Relationality also has roots in Greek philosophy and Eastern thought such as Buddhism (Lupisella, 2020; Rovelli, 2021). These changes are mirrored by shifts away from the fixed certainties of Newtonian physics to post-Einsteinian thinking on relationality in quantum theory (Lupisella, 2020; Rovelli, 2021).

Counter-hegemonic struggles against epistemologies of domination are a key source of new imaginaries in pursuit of cognitive justice. Boaventura de Sousa Santos (2015; 2018) describes the need to foster an ecology of knowledges to overcome the abyssal thinking that characterises modern Western thought. Walter Mignolo (2012) calls for border thinking to combat coloniality: the

6 This is of course not true of all economists but the general point holds.

7 See Mark Carney's (2021) attempt to distinguish values from value in an attempt to overcome the failings of neoclassical economics. Carney is in the vanguard of those who believe that climate breakdown can be fixed by green capitalism, but it appears that the putative magic of markets is slow to work. Carney is the UN's special envoy on climate action and finance.

material, immaterial, psychological, ideational, and ideological aspects of colonisation. Postdevelopment theorists have postulated alternatives to development rooted in subaltern epistemologies to replace the top-down imposition of mainstream models of development. Their aim is to find different ways of achieving justice without romanticising indigenous and other subaltern epistemologies and to heed Gayatri Spivak's warning about the dangers of facile acceptance of Southern voices (Spivak, 1999). New imaginaries usually emerge from suffering people engaged in resistance – formal and informal, legal and extra-legal – against harms and injustices. Voices of resistance offer imaginaries diametrically opposed to hierarchical, top-down ideological impositions such as the World Bank's construction of poverty and development. Resistance is a form of witness to injustice, a pointer to paths for action, and the prefiguration of a better future.

The form and role of resistance is explored by the authors in this volume, most of whom have long been engaged with discourses of development and law and development. Their contributions demonstrate that changing how injustices are framed to achieve a discursive paradigm shift is not an easy task. Critiques of development discourses have usually been immanent and involved reluctant acceptance of the idea of development in order to resist and go beyond it. Such critiques have had to overcome the fact that development is 'an amoeba-like concept, shapeless but ineradicable' (Sachs, 1992: 4) – as sustainable development demonstrates.

Development became hegemonic for several reasons. The West deployed it as a means of incorporating postcolonial states into the global economy on unequal terms and subjecting them to the discipline of markets and the international financial institutions. In the absence of alternatives, many postcolonial states engaged with the idea of development despite their misgivings. Development was a given on both sides of the divide. In successive incarnations such as the so-called Washington consensus and, latterly, sustainable development, it functioned as a driver of neoliberal globalisation. Development was enshrined in the international law of trade and investment, and hortatory, unenforceable and unfunded resolutions such as the Millennium Development Goals in 2000 and the Sustainable Development Goals in 2015.[8] New imaginaries demand resistance to hegemonic discourses in order to shatter orthodoxies and transcend epistemological and intellectual boundaries. As Upendra Baxi asked when considering whether it is possible to go beyond development:

> What leads to this new conception – is it merely old wine in new bottles? Or does it mark a qualitative conceptual change? If the latter, what are the circumstances/con-junctures that cause or condition this change, what are

8 Millennium Development Goals: https://www.un.org/millenniumgoals (accessed 3 June 2020); Sustainable Development Goals see Sustainable Development (un.org) (accessed 3 March 2021).

itineraries of planned global social change, and what may be the first stage of the future of whatever may be said to lie 'beyond development'?
(Baxi, 2021: 38).

Contributions to this Volume

This book is divided into two parts: *Towards New Imaginaries* and *Rights and Injustices*. The chapters reflect a variety of perspectives on development, a concept that all the contributors regard as problematic to varying degrees. Common themes are an overriding concern with injustices and harms to people and the environment, and the need to explore new approaches to development and human rights, preferably by going beyond development.

These perspectives on development are also paralleled by views on law and development. Wouter Vandenhole favours retaining law and development as a discourse, whereas other contributors explore ways of addressing harms and injustices such as impoverishment, displacement, (post-)coloniality, cultural and social exclusion, gender injustice and climate injustice, conflict, bad governance, and the structural inequalities in the global economic system. Most of the authors view resistance as an indicator and a result of injustice.

Towards New Imaginaries

The chapters in this part explore the nature of unjust development or maldevelopment, including the root causes of injustices, the role of resistance, and the scope for new imaginaries rooted in relationality. In our chapter on 'Social Injustices, Development and Resistance', we argue that confronting injustices arising from identifiable harms and suffering provides a framing that is more conducive to the wellbeing of all species and the biosphere than development because the latter cannot be conceived in isolation from destructive extractivism and endless growth. We suggest that the myriad injustices of maldevelopment and neoliberal globalisation, climate change, ecological destruction, pandemics and digitalisation provide the starting point for new imaginaries. These injustices are historic (slavery, colonialism, imperialism, patriarchy) and contemporary (impoverishment, inequality, racism, forced migration, climate change, pandemics and digital oppression). We draw a distinction between John Rawls's ideal theory of justice and Amartya Sen's more pragmatic approach based upon concrete injustices. We argue for the need to engage with the insistent, multitudinous voices of the marginalised, disempowered and disenfranchised, and describe the possibilities offered by relational alternative imaginaries such as *buen vivir*. Drawing on contemporary interpretations of Foucault such as Golder and Fitzpatrick (2009), we explore the nature of resistance and suggest that resistance can produce a basis for dethroning the dominion of destructive development and law and development.

One of the main challenges confronting development discourses is how to explain its absence or stalling in many Southern countries. While many scholars point to endemic injustices such violence, insecurity, and impoverishment as explanations, Raza Saeed argues against a version of developmentalist orthodoxy that suggests that maldevelopment results from the absence of a strong Hobbesian sovereign (Hobbes, 1909). In 'Post Hobbesian State, Sovereignty and Development', Saeed considers that this sovereign-centric perspective has lured institutions such as the World Bank and IMF into the idea that impoverishment is a direct consequence of Hobbesian anarchy and the absence of security, the solution to which is a strong developmental Leviathan. Saeed turns this argument on its head in his analysis of the role of the state in relation to social and economic insecurity, violence, and underdevelopment. For him, it is the presence rather than the absence of post-Hobbesian sovereigns in the global South that is responsible for these injustices. Saeed relies on Pearce's (2010) argument that the State in some Latin American countries does not resolve violence but instead forms alliances with corrupt and violent extra-state forces for the benefit of its power holders. Citing Baxi (2006) and Grear (2010) he suggests that the state can be both strong in its oppressive control of political institutions, citizens, and undesirables and permissively soft on national and global capital. Such states are dominated by private interests and exploit tribal, ethnic, religious, racial, patriarchal, and socio-economic tensions which lead to conflict and impoverishment. Saeed argues that if Hobbesian sovereignty is justified to secure peace, post-Hobbesian sovereignty is justified as a way of dealing with underdevelopment and impoverishment. However, instead of aligning the private interests of individuals with the public interest, the developmental state exploits socio-political contradictions for the benefit of the few. It is structured around an uneven distribution of fear, violence, and impoverishment. Post-Hobbesian sovereignty, in this light, is caught within a nexus of clientelism, tribalism, parochial politics, and global neoliberal capitalism. Saeed suggests the need to distinguish between two notions of Hobbesian sovereignty. Sovereignty by covenant or social contract assumes the existence of peace as a desirable common good with the sovereign acting as arbitrator of competing public and private interests. In contrast, sovereignty by acquisition or conquest, as in the continuity between colonial and post-colonial situations, is marked by a struggle for dominance. The resulting Leviathan is less concerned with the common goods such as peace, security, and order than with imposing its interests on the public for private gain. For Saeed, a legitimate sovereign cannot be imposed from the outside but has to emerge from the resistance of people themselves.

Jayan Nayar's chapter, 'Returning the Anti-Colonial to Philosophy', suggests a rejuvenation of anti-colonial philosophy as a basis for resistance to injustice. For Nayar, the main problem with postcolonial discourses is that they tend to take for granted the borders imposed by the colonial mentality that continues to shape the postcolonial present. Nayar argues that the sovereignty of contemporary postcolonial states is fractured by complex modes of territorial, extraterritorial, transnational, and global modes of law and governance. As a consequence, peoples are defined in ways that privilege the North while undermining the South. Northern transnational businesses are thus welcomed in the South as licensed privileged actors whereas others, such as Southern migrants to the North, are barred or controlled through legal and extra-legal measures. Finally, displaced persons are abandoned, made *persona non-grata*, and prevented from entering the North or forced to live in rightless modes in camps. Nayar challenges the notion of borders and border thinking used by Walter Mignolo (2012) because it enables external observers of domestic affairs to promote misleading depictions of reality at odds with the perceptions of internal observers. He argues that Mignolo's perspective accepts the legitimacy of national boundaries, a view that must be transformed by turning borders into the frontlines of 'audacious insurgent sites of struggle'. Struggles such as that of the Zapatistas in Mexico, become matrices for reimagination and the creation of a different world, and new structures and cultures in opposition to conventional postcolonial categorisations of peoples as developed or developing. Such struggles aim to reterritorialise, to redefine postcolonial boundaries in order to assert autonomy from institutionalised state political systems and affirm peoples' identities and cultures. For Nayar, the role of the insurgent intellectual or philosopher is to recover submerged knowledges and processes and use them to overturn the presumed normality, fixity, and universality of the postcolonial present.

Whereas Nayar deals with resistance as a phenomenon largely external to existing state and constitutional structures, Illan Rua Wall discusses how extra-systemic forms of resistance can be continued after they have been inscribed in constitutional structures. In his chapter on the 'Constitution of Turbulence' adopted by Bolivia in 2009, Wall describes how the election of the Movimiento al Socialismo (MAS) government in 2006 resulted in the inscription of a new constituent power involving extra-systemic social movements in parallel to the formal state structures. This was a radical attempt to prevent the tendency of states, particularly in Latin America, to neutralise popular power expressed through strikes and protests and to enforce new forms of obedience designed to prevent effective social transformation. The Bolivian Constitution introduced three innovations. First, the constitutional principle of *vivir bien/buen vivir* is a direction to all institutions to promote principles of life that promote ecology, pluralism, and relationality. Second, the Supreme Court is transformed from an elitist judicial body into a plurinational entity that enforces constitutional principles. Third, and most significant, the Constitution requires the state to provide spaces for social movements to challenge government at all levels. This latter provision resulted in the creation of a 'National Coordination for Change' coalition of major social movements. Wall describes the practical problems which ensued from this arrangement, including the right-wing coup that overthrew President Evo Morales in 2019 and its subsequent reversal by social movements. For Wall, the wider significance of the constitution of turbulence is not whether it succeeded in narrow constitutional terms, but the ways in which it sought to incorporate resistance in the Constitution as part of deeper social transformation.

The following two chapters emphasise the role of relationality as an alternative imaginary to that of individualist developmentalism. In '"I Built this House on my Back": A Historical Perspective on Care and Property in East Africa', Ambreena Manji and Ann Stewart link patriarchal injustice to the relational ethics of care. They use a feminist ethics of care perspective to illustrate the limitations of law and development orthodoxies rooted in neoliberal individualism and patriarchy. Manji and Stewart challenge development orthodoxies about the social and reproductive care provided by women and suggest that a relational ethos operates in African society exemplified by the ethic of care in the personal and property relationships between African women. They use the example of woman-to-woman marriage entered into by property-owning *malaya* sex workers in Kenya from colonial times to the present to challenge the idea in orthodox scholarship that the function of these marriages is to provide male heirs for the sex workers. In reality, Manji and Stewart argue, such marriages are complex devices for the women to escape the injustices of patriarchy. They categorise *malaya* women as care providers for their clients while simultaneously providing for their own care by having a wife with children who also receives compensation, in the form of upkeep and inheritance, for being a carer. They emphasise the negotiating skills of the sex workers and their resistance to colonial, traditional, and postcolonial patriarchal and legal structures. The grounding of marriages in customary ways is revealed to be more complex than a simplistic triumph of modernity over tradition.

The relationality ethos underlying the Manji and Stewart chapter is also used by Oche Onazi in relation to struggles by vulnerable communities. In 'The Role of Community in Human-Rights and Development Discourse: Resisting Apathy and Antipathy', Onazi argues that there is hostility or indifference to the role of communities in mainstream human rights discourses that focus upon and amplify individual autonomy. Although there are increasing references to groups in human rights instruments such as the African Charter on Human and Peoples' Rights, the ways in which these documents treat collectives suggest that the shift from individual to group rights is little more than a shift from antipathy to apathy. Onazi argues that the myriad projects in the World Bank's Community-Driven Development programmes have been limited to rural-based projects that have had little impact on overall community wellbeing. He links the concept of community to its relational roots in African culture based upon solidarity between people rather than essentialist, transcendental or metaphysical concepts such as tribes. Relationality also extends to the effective relationship between people and their environment. Onazi uses the Makoko settlement in Nigeria, one of the world's largest squatter settlements, as an example of the capacity of people from a wide range of backgrounds and localities to form a community through relations of solidarity developed in legal, regulatory and political struggles for the provision of resources such as sanitation, water, electricity, health care, and education, and against attempts to eradicate the community.

Rights and Injustices

This part focuses on the relationship between rights, injustices, and development. It covers issues such as whether rights discourse can provide an alternative imaginary to that of development, the interaction between national and global agencies, and the capacity of alternative social welfare systems, such as the Islamic, to confront global injustices such as impoverishment, patriarchy, forced migration, global pandemics, and intellectual rights in traditional medicine.

The section begins with chapters by Wouter Vandenhole and Andrew Williams that discuss the paradoxical role of human rights in dealing with global injustices. Baxi (2012) distinguished the modern human rights in the Universal Declaration of Human Rights from neoliberal, trade-related, market friendly human rights. For Issa Shivji, human rights 'constitutes one of the main elements in the ideological armoury of imperialism' and needs to be reconceptualised in the interest of peoples' struggles (Shivji, 1989: vii). Costas Douzinas critiqued the liberal conception of universal human rights as being inflected by coloniality, gender and class, and a neoliberal ethos (Douzinas, 2000). He later promoted the 'Other' of rights in the right to resistance and argues that rights can be revalidated only through such a right (Douzinas, 2007).

Human rights address injustice more effectively than development because they deal with harms or wrongs, but their focus on states as the primary duty-bearers limits their effectiveness in relation to non-state actors. Furthermore, human rights are constrained by narrow liberal and neoliberal conceptions of rights that prioritise civil and political rights over economic, social and cultural rights. In addition, human rights are threatened by authoritarian populism and China's outright hostility to any conception of human rights.

In 'Transnational Human Rights Obligations: Beyond Territory and State', Wouter Vandenhole considers the relationship between human rights, global justice, and development. Vandenhole suggests that global injustices can only be resisted by reformulating the dominant idea of development and linking it to global justice. He calls for a revivification of human rights through a focus on resistance to injustices in the struggles of social movements and peoples. In this way a top-down notion of human rights is transformed into a law from below that emerges from resistance against transnational actors such as corporations, armed groups, and state- and non-state-based global institutions. These struggles indicate the need to extend human rights duties and responsibilities to non-state actors.

In 'Beyond Development: Human Rights, Personal Responsibility and the Search for Meaning', Andrew Williams addresses the inability of contemporary human rights to deal with 'injustices, inequalities and sufferings on a massive scale'. Williams argues that being 'enraptured' by development is equally unsatisfactory because development perpetuates the developed-underdeveloped binary and reinforces colonial hierarchies in postcolonial states. Instead, he suggests 'a specific notion of human rights within or across borders in order to counter fundamental *injustices*'. This notion is based on the imperative of alleviating human suffering wherever it occurs, regardless of state boundaries. Vandenhole and Williams locate their analyses in injustice rather than statist international law, but Williams goes further in proposing personal responsibility as a supplement to existing human rights mechanisms to ensure that the responsibilities of states and international institutions are effectively enforced. The first step in his three-step approach is bearing witness or *temoinage*. This requires the presence of effective institutional mechanisms to ensure that the voices of those experiencing suffering can be heard first-hand or through observers of their suffering. The second step is calling to account public authorities, institutions, corporate and individual persons to explain how their responsibility for suffering has arisen. The third step is making wrongdoers accountable not only in formal institutions such as courts and tribunals but also in truth commissions, public inquiries and peoples' tribunals.

Bill Derman and Anne Hellum's chapter, 'The Human Right to Water and Beyond: Some Reflections on Water Justice and Water Reform in Zimbabwe', discusses the limitations of existing human rights discourses and the problems raised by gender and environmental injustices. They use Nancy Fraser's framework of recognition and redistribution to analyse how progressive sounding international human rights and policy frameworks disadvantage rural women in Zimbabwe. Following Baxi (2016), Derman and Hellum argue that an underlying problem causing African peoples, particularly women, to fare worst in water provision is the unexamined assumptions of global laws and policies. For example, the Integrated Water Resources Management developed by the UN through the Global Water Partnership[9] places too much emphasis on commercial cost recovery and thereby advantages industrial and capitalist agricultural use at the expense of peasant farmers and women subsistence croppers. Although the UN Committee on Economic, Social and Cultural Rights has recognised the human right to water as a part of the right to life, it focuses on water for personal and domestic use and is ambiguous on the water needs of women growing food crops. Derman and Hellum argue that Sustainable Development Goal 15 and the provisions of the Convention on the Elimination of All Forms of Discrimination Against Women, which are intended to address women's needs, have had limited effects.[10] They maintain that local implementation of international laws and policies tends to be skewed in favour of local and global neoliberal elites, resulting in continuing injustices for those who are doubly disadvantaged (in Nancy Fraser's terms) by identity and maldistribution – especially rural women farmers.

9 See Integrated Water Resources Management (IWRM), International Decade for Action 'Water for Life' 2005–2015 <https://www.un.org/waterforlifedecade/iwrm.shtml> (accessed 22 June 2021).

10 The aim of SDG Goal 15 is to 'Protect, restore and promote sustainable use of terrestrial ecosystems, sustainably manage forests, combat desertification, and halt and reverse land degradation and halt biodiversity loss'.

Neoliberal globalisation, armed conflict and climate change have displaced millions of people and forced them to become migrants, asylum seekers or refugees who suffer myriad injustices. In 'Access to Justice for Refugees', Dallal Stevens describes the failure of law and global governance to deal with repeated and ongoing humanitarian crises caused by displacement. Many countries that have ratified the Geneva Conventions and the 1951 Refugee Convention ignore their provisions, express reservations, or dump responsibility onto inadequately resourced UN agencies and non-governmental organisations. Stevens argues that new imaginaries for redressing the injustices of displacement require a principle of access to justice which includes physical access to territory, to just and effective procedures, and to social justice in the form of fairness and equality of liberties and opportunities. She critically assesses whether initiatives such as the Sustainable Development Goals and the New York Declaration on and the Global Compact on Refugees of 2018 or the World Bank's shift to a 'development' strategy are adequate. Stevens suggests that rhetorical promises or a shift from a rights-based approach to one encompassing rights and social justice are too easily undermined by neoliberalism. One of the biggest problems in constructing coherent responses to displacement is that the views of the displaced are rarely reflected.

Can the idea of social welfare in Islam provide an alternative imaginary to existing approaches to development and injustice? In 'Islamic Epistemologies, Law, Social Justice and Injustices: The Case for Islamic Welfare Systems', Shaheen Ali and Fakir Yusaf outline the notion of welfare in Islamic theology and the unsatisfactory contemporary practices it produces. A duty of welfare is contained in Islam's foundational texts. In contrast to contemporary capitalism, the duty of welfare is integral to classical Islamic finance as well as charity. The prohibition of *riba* or usury is a cornerstone of classical finance because it ensures that transactions between lenders and borrowers are joint ventures in which both parties are affected by successful or unsuccessful outcomes. Equally significant is the *qard hasan* loan system that makes it a religious obligation to award loans to those in financial difficulties and to forego foreclosures in cases of distress. The system of *zakat* is a personal religious obligation to provide relief for the poor and needy. Ali and Yusaf's analysis of contemporary Islamic practice describes how the modification of these ideas by states, Islamic financial institutions, and, most significantly, by ordinary Muslims results in the dilution of social justice principles as *riba* and *qard hasan* are influenced by neoliberal economic practices. *Zakat* is either converted into a state tax whose charitable aspects are questionable or subject to haphazard performance by individual Muslims.

The Covid-19 pandemic highlighted the injustices hardwired into the global political-economy, for example the ways in which maldevelopment affects public health provision and access to vaccines. The chapter by Monica Twesiime Kirya and Sharifah Sekalala, 'Countering Corruption to Promote Social Justice in the Global Fund to Fight AIDS, Tuberculosis and Malaria: The Case of Uganda' examines the record of the Global Fund to Fight AIDs, Tuberculosis and Malaria in Uganda. In principle, the Fund (which foreshadows Covax, the international initiative to provide Covid-19 vaccines to the global South) is an innovative global approach for dealing with the injustices of global diseases that confirms the need for coherent and effective transboundary solutions – a message rammed home by the coronavirus pandemic. Large pharmaceutical corporations have largely failed to develop cures for diseases such as malaria that inflict harms primarily on the global South or, when they have done, made them inordinately expensive and, in the case of the Covid vaccine, unconscionably lucrative for most of them. The Fund made a concerted effort to supply medicines to the South by involving the private sector, global public institutions, civil society organisations, and state agencies in the North and South. Kirya and Sekalala argue that the Fund's structures and processes have been utilised by corrupt Southern institutions to undermine disease control and in ways that exacerbate social injustices. They criticise an ostensibly participatory model that is easily captured by elites due to little involvement by those affected, reliance on global consultancies primarily interested in profit, the role of local agents who prioritise personal interest, and inadequate mechanisms of accountability and transparency. Kirya and Sekalala conclude that the Fund's mission to save lives is undermined by the unjust socio-political environment in which it operates. Global injustices are as much a creature of exploitative Southern rulers and capitalists as of the Global North.

One of the great injustices of colonialism was the denigration of the cultures of the colonised. To the extent that they were acknowledged, recognition of these cultures took bastardised and subordinated forms. In medicine, this involved the imposition of Western knowledge and the suppression of indigenous knowledge. At the same time, denigrated knowledges were resources that could be exploited to benefit colonisers, as in the 'discovery' of quinine as a remedy for malaria. These hierarchies of knowledge persist in the postcolonial era in complex ways that confine the traditional to a subordinated mode while the global South is exploited for valuable medical resources. John Harrington's chapter, '"In My Own Village": Chronotopes, Governmentality and the Changing Regulation of Traditional Medicine in Kenya', uses the concept of chronotopes to illustrate continuities and changes in the regulation of medicine in the transition from the colonial to the postcolonial period. A chronotope represents the form in which the ideological, political, legal, social, and economic context of a phenomenon such as the regulation of medicine, is perceived in geographical space and historical time. Harrington uses the explanatory example of the gradual reclassification of smoking from a social habit into an epidemic in the global North, the spread of this categorisation to the South and the consequent regulatory responsibility of the World Health Organization (WHO). In the past, traditional medicine was treated as non-dynamic knowledge, and confined to village or tribal chronotopes. This prevented it from obtaining universal acceptance and gave Northern pharmaceutical companies free rein to pillage its beneficial qualities. In Kenya, this resulted in resistance against local, national, and international institutions. The Protection of Traditional Knowledge and Cultural Expressions Act

(2016) created a new class of intellectual property rights enabling communities to prevent the use of local herbal remedies without their consent or to license these remedies for a fee or a percentage of profits. In addition, section 74 of Kenya's 2016 Health Act was enacted to support and regulate traditional medicines. Harrington discusses international initiatives on traditional knowledge such as the Convention on Biological Diversity and the WHO's Traditional Medicine Strategy 2014–23. He argues that currently, there is co-existence of the chronotope of modernisation, which historically restricted traditional medicine in favour of modern Western medicine with the reaffirmation of the value of traditional knowledge and medicine. This leads to contradictory and complex approaches to regulation. Harrington describes how modernisers believe the way forward is to combine both and emulate China's development of traditional medicine as an exportable commodity and an engine for economic growth.

Beyond Development?

Upen Baxi asked whether the idea of moving beyond development is 'merely old wine in new bottles? Or does it mark a qualitative conceptual change?' (Baxi, 2021: 38). In our opinion, the old wine of development itself consistently finds new bottles to fill. Unfortunately, every new incarnation has failed to produce significant results. During the years in which we have taught Law in Development, we have come to realise that it is more important to address the underlying causes of maldevelopment and injustices than the putative panaceas of development and law and development. In the past, development has been a handmaiden to Western neo-imperialism, and now to emergent Chinese imperialism. In their own way, each of the contributors to this book explores new approaches that can be broadly categorised under three headings: (i) examining forms of oppression and injustices; (ii) seeking new imaginaries based on relationality or new approaches to social justice; (iii) exploring forms of resistance to locate the voices of the oppressed and subjects of injustice. We believe that asking whether it is possible to move 'Beyond Development' has liberated the authors from the straitjacket imposed by developmentalism and enabled them to engage in a wider exploration of the domains of their expertise from the problem of refugee displacement to human rights, gender justice, constitutionalism, and the flaws of global and national regulatory systems.

References

Adelman, S. 2018. The Sustainable Development Goals, Anthropocentrism and Neoliberalism. In French, Duncan and Kotzé, Louis (eds), *Sustainable Development Goals: Law, Theory & Implementation*. Edward Elgar.

Adelman, S. 2020. Modernity, Anthropocene, Capitalocene and the Climate Crisis. In Bollier, D. and Grear, A. (eds), *The Great Awakening: New Modes of Life Amidst Capitalist Ruins*. Punctum Books.

Adelman, S. 2021. Beyond Development: Towards Sustainability and Climate Justice in the Anthropocene. In Adelman, S. and Paliwala, A. (eds), *The Limits of Law and Development: Neoliberalism, Governance and Social Justice*. Routledge.

Adelman, S. and Paliwala, A. 2021a. *The Limits of Law and Development: Neoliberalism, Governance and Social Justice*. Routledge.

Adelman, S. and Paliwala, A. 2021b. Beyond Law and Development? In Adelman, S. and Paliwala, A. (eds), *The Limits of Law and Development: Neoliberalism, Governance and Social Justice*. Routledge.

Baxi, U., 2006. *The Future of Human Rights*. Oxford University Press.

Baxi, U. 2009. *Human Rights in a Posthuman World*. Oxford University Press.

Baxi, U. 2012. *The Future of Human Rights*. Oxford University Press.

Baxi, U. 2016. Towards a Climate Change Justice Theory? *Journal of Human Rights and the Environment*, 7: 7–31. Available online at DOI: https://doi.org/10.4337/jhre.2016.01.01 (accessed on January 8, 2020).

Baxi, U. 2021. Ameliorating Human Futures through Postdevelopment? In Adelman, S. and Paliwala, A. (eds), *The Limits of Law and Development: Neoliberalism, Governance and Social Justice*. Routledge.

Carney, M. 2021. *Value(s): Building a Better World for All*. Penguin Random House.

Colvile, R. 2016. *The Great Acceleration: How the World is Getting Faster, Faster*. Bloomsbury.

Dasgupta, P. 2021. *The Economics of Biodiversity: The Dasgupta Review*. HM Treasury.

D'Souza, R. 2021. International Law and Development: From 'Company Raj' to Global Governance via Indirect Rule. In Adelman, S. and Paliwala, A. (eds), *The Limits of Law and Development: Neoliberalism, Governance and Social Justice*. Routledge.

Douzinas, C. 2000. *The End of Human Rights: Critical Thought at the Turn of the Century*. Bloomsbury Publishing.

Douzinas, C. 2007. *Human Rights and Empire: The Political Philosophy of Cosmopolitanism*. Routledge.

Escobar, A., 2010. *Encountering Development: The Making and Unmaking of the Third World*. Princeton University Press.

Esteva, G., 1992. Development. In Sachs, W. (ed.), *The Development Dictionary: A Guide to Knowledge as Power*. Zed Books.

Golder, B. and Fitzpatrick, P. 2009. *Foucault's Law*. Routledge-Cavendish.

Grear, A., 2010. *Redirecting Human Rights: Facing the Challenge of Corporate Legal Humanity*. Palgrave Macmillan.

Hobbes, T., 1909. *Hobbes's Leviathan, Reprinted from the edition of 1651 (With an essay by the late W. G. Pogson Smith)*. Clarendon Press.

Johnston, J., Gismondi, M. and Goodman, J. eds. 2006. *Nature's Revenge: Reclaiming Sustainability in an Age of Corporate Globalization*. Broadview Press and Garamond Press.

Kothari, A., Salleh, A., Escobar, A., Demaria, F., and Acosta, A. eds. 2019. *Pluriverse: A Post-Development Dictionary*. Tulika Books.

Lupisella, M. 2020. *Cosmological Theories of Value: Science, Philosophy and Meaning in Cosmic Evolution*. Springer.

Meadows, D.H., Meadows, D.L., Randers, J. and Behrens, W.W. 1972. *The Limits to Growth: A Report for the Club of Rome's Project on the Predicament of Mankind*. Universe Books.

Mignolo, W. 2012. *Local Histories/Global Designs: Coloniality, Subaltern Knowledges, and Border Thinking*. Princeton University Press.

Nussbaum, M. 2011. *Creating Capabilities: The Human Development Approach*. Harvard University Press.
Oxfam. 2020. *Time to Care: Unpaid and Underpaid Work and the Global Inequality Crisis*. Oxfam.
Pearce, J. 2010. Perverse State Formation and Securitized Democracy in Latin America. *Democratization* 17, 286–306.
Pogge, T. 2002. *World Poverty and Human Rights*. Polity Press.
Rovelli, C. 2021. *Helgoland*. Allen Lane.
Sachs, W. ed. 1992. *The Development Dictionary: A Guide to Knowledge as Power*. Zed Books.
Said, E. 2003. *Orientalism*. Penguin.
Secretariat of the Convention on Biological Diversity. 2020. *Global Biodiversity Outlook 5*. Secretariat of the Convention on Biological Diversity.
Sen, A. 1999. *Development as Freedom*. Oxford University Press.
Shivji, I. 1989. *The Concept of Human Rights in Africa*. African Book Collective and Codesria.
Sinclair, U. 1994. *I, Candidate for Governor: And How I Got Licked*. University of California Press.
Spivak, G. 1999. *A Critique of Postcolonial Reason: Toward a History of the Vanishing Present*. Harvard University Press.
Santos, B. de S. 2015. *Epistemologies of the South: Justice against Epistemicide*. Routledge.
Santos, B. de S. 2018. *The End of the Cognitive Empire: The Coming of Age of Epistemologies of the South*. Duke University Press.
Tamanaha, B. 2011. The Primacy of Society and the Failures of Law and Development. *Cornell International Law Journal*, 44 (2), 216–244.
Trubek, D. and Santos, A. 2006. *The New Law and Economic Development: A Critical Appraisal*. Cambridge University Press.
WCED, 1987. *Our Common Future: Report of the World Commission on Environment and Development*. United Nations.

Part I

Towards New Imaginaries

Chapter 1

Shifting the Frame from Law and Development to Ending Injustice

Sam Adelman and Abdul Paliwala

Unthinking Development

History is always perched on the shoulders of scholars, but we are seldom aware that we are writing at an epoch defining inflexion point produced by the confluence of climate change and Covid-19. In Paul Klee's famous painting, the *Angelus Novus*, the face of the angel of history is turned towards the past but, in Walter Benjamin's words, 'a storm drives him irresistibly into the future, to which his back is turned, while the pile of debris before him grows toward the sky. What we call progress is *this* storm' (Benjamin, 2006: 392; emphasis in original).

As the scale of the pandemic became apparent in the early months of 2020, it soon became clear that the *status quo ante* cannot be restored after this storm because the intertwined coronavirus and climate calamities signify a broader and deeper civilisational and existential crisis that cannot be resolved by returning to the unjust world before coronavirus (BC). Returning to normal is not an option because what was considered to be normal was the problem. As Antonio Gramsci wrote, the 'crisis consists precisely in the fact that the old is dying and the new is yet to be born. And in the interregnum, a great variety of morbid symptoms appear' (Gramsci, 1971: 276).[1] Transboundary threats cannot be solved through anachronistic mainstream, neoliberal models of development that are broken beyond repair. Mainstream models of development have exacerbated the long-standing systemic inequalities that exploded the global economy in 2008 and accelerated the destruction of habitats that facilitated zoonotic transmission of Covid-19 (Leach et al., 2021). We call this maldevelopment. After coronavirus (AC), change is necessary to protect current and future generations from new pandemics and intensifying climatic harms.

The idea of development has long engaged us, the contributors to these two volumes, and other post-development scholars. Development has positive connotations of healthy growth and progress, for example in relation to child development but, applied to nation-states in the Anthropocene, it is a misnomer.

1 Isabelle Stengers (2015: 47) distinguishes catastrophe from crisis on the basis that the former is a crisis from which there is no recovery. Global heating may be a catastrophe.

DOI: 10.4324/9780203745298-3

Development became an object of desire after the Second World War. It was a siren call that lured its converts to believe that it paved the path to wellbeing, human rights, and social justice. Over time, however, development too often became the stuff of nightmares, especially for indigenous peoples because it facilitated exploitation, corruption, inequality, bad governance, and environmental devastation. Now in its eighth decade, development has been around long enough to entitle us to expect that it would have delivered on its promises. In 1992, Wolfgang Sachs wrote that 'The last 40 years can be called the age of development. This epoch is coming to an end. The time is ripe to write its obituary' (Sachs, 1992: 1). More recently, Sachs has argued that:

> Twenty-five years later, in 2018, none of its promises have materialized. On the contrary, disarray, even chaos reign, fear and anger are widespread contrasting sharply with the triumphalism of the 1990s. If one had to find a word for the current atmosphere in the northern, as well as parts of the southern hemisphere, it would be: fear of the future, a fear that life prospects are shrinking and that children and grandchildren will be less well off.
>
> (Sachs, 2019: xiv–xv)

The fact that development is still so widely embraced is a testament to its zombie-like capacity to survive (Gudynas, 2011: 441).

In *The Limits of Law and Development: Neoliberalism, Governance and Social Justice* we wrote:

> law and development concepts and discourses – orthodox, reformist or critical – create a risk of shifting our gaze away from concrete social injustices because they are preoccupied with models of development, institutions and economic and political factors such as growth and governance. For this reason, we argue that new imaginaries that focus on harms and injustices are required.
>
> (Adelman and Paliwala, 2021b: 16)

The chapters in that volume explore the problems of the discourses of development, law and development, and their unsuccessful attempts to address their underlying defects. In the introduction to this volume, we discuss the link between the failure of development and the need for new imaginaries. and develop that argument in this chapter by arguing that shifting the focus from development to the elimination of injustices offers a better way of framing the problems confronting us.

Justice and Injustice

The confluence of Covid-19 and climate change once again exposes the limitations of liberal theories of justice, including John Rawls's influential *Theory of Justice*

(Rawls, 1971). Our bottom-up approach, in which the experience of suffering injustice defines forms of resistance and potential solutions, seeks to address two central flaws in Rawls's hypothesis. First, Rawls argues that an optimal framework for justice can be constructed by abstract, rational individuals in the original position and behind a veil of ignorance. Rawls contends that their deliberations will produce a document similar to the US Constitution. South Africa's post-apartheid constitution – one of the most liberal in the world – perhaps most closely approximates Rawls's ideal, but it is proving to be compatible with many injustices including the racial stain it is designed to eradicate. This is inevitable because liberal constitutional protections of individual rights occlude the structural causes of the injustices they are supposed to eliminate. A second, related problem is that even if we concede Rawls's assertion that a polity's common values are what enable it to give law to itself, the limits of liberal constitutionalism made him unable to extend his theory beyond the bounded territory of the nation-state and thereby reconcile the sovereign obligations of decent peoples with the cosmopolitan rights of all peoples (Rawls, 1999).

In *The Idea of Justice,* Amartya Sen addressed the deficiencies in Rawls's theory through a focus on injustice and an extension of his capability theory (Sen, 2009). He rejects Rawls's restriction of justice to polities with ostensibly common cultures because 'there are few non-neighbours left in the world today' (Sen, 2009: 173). Sen contends that social justice should not be evaluated in binary terms (justice/injustice) because justice is a spectrum rather than a definitive, stable condition. In Sen's view, an abstract, transcendental idea of justice is not necessary to enable us to evaluate the fairness of different institutions. He is therefore more concerned with 'actual realizations and accomplishments rather than the right institutions and rules' (Sen, 2009: 10). Nonetheless, like Rawls, Sen's theory of justice is rooted in Enlightenment rationality and *a priori* constitutional and institutional requirements that seldom reflect reality. Unlike Rawls, he accepts that there is not a single conception of a just society, which enables him to acknowledge the significance of resistance to injustices of the kind advocated by subaltern voices such as Gandhi, Mandela and Martin Luther King (Sen, 2009: 18, 332).

Sen's idea of freedom as the means and end of development is a significant advance on economistic approaches and his theory of justice is more attentive to concrete, quotidian injustices than Rawls, but he does not provide a sustained critique of the structural and systemic injustices of global capitalism.[2] Equally troubling is Sen's view that justice and human rights are moral entitlements rather than legally enforceable obligations.[3] In contrast, Thomas

2 'One of the questions that has been repeatedly put to the advocates of the capability approach has been that of structural injustice: does the capability approach address sufficiently the extent to which lack of human flourishing can be attributed to unjust social, political and economic structures and can it be deployed to bring about their transformation?' (Deneulin et al., 2006: 3).

3 See Sen's debate with Upendra Baxi about human rights (Sen, 2004; Baxi, 2009, ch. 2).

Pogge's theory of global justice is predicated upon an obligation to prevent injustice – *primum non nocere*, first do no harm – which is also imperative for climate justice (Pogge, 2002). Pogge's overly technicist approach focuses upon international law obligations and solutions at the expense of the role of struggle and resistance.

Human rights provide an ethically elevated grammar that enjoys greater legitimacy than domestic law and politics and they are an important bulwark against oppression. Unsurprisingly, however, rights-based approaches to maldevelopment and other harms replicate the flaws of liberalism because they tend to focus upon possessive individualism at the expense of collective wellbeing (Adelman and Paliwala, 2021b). Despite this, human rights can be reimagined in ways that development cannot, for example in relation to the structural and systemic causes of global heating (Grear, 2012). Hegemonic models of development cannot be reimagined because they are inextricably linked to extractivism and infinite growth.

Relationality, Vulnerability, Thinking Injustice

Like economics, law and development is a discourse that is undermined by the resistance of corporeal, embedded human beings to the injustices of market discipline and biopower. Feminist thinkers such as Martha Fineman and Anna Grear have cogently argued that justice should be conceived from the perspective of vulnerable individuals embedded in nature rather than the invulnerable, fictitious Kantian subject of liberal legality – the bounded autonomous, sovereign, possessive individual of Enlightenment rationality (Fineman, 2013; Grear, 2017). Much can also be learned from feminist and indigenous thinking about relationality (Weir, 2017; Seck, 2019). Jennifer Nedelsky argues that a relational approach regards 'the person whose rights and well-being are at stake' as 'constituted by their relationships' and 'it is only in the context of those relationships that one can understand how to foster their capacities, define and protect their rights, or promote their well-being' (Nedelsky, 2011: 121). Relationality highlights the influences of economic, social and political institutions and structures. As Mackenzie (2014: 33) argues, 'despite the importance of the notion of ontological vulnerability, many forms of vulnerability are caused or exacerbated by social and political structures'.[4] Ontological vulnerability, interconnected corporeality and relationality are closely tied to wellbeing and in/justice. There are continuities between vulnerability and relationality, Sen's capabilities approach, and Nussbaum's concept of flourishing (Nussbaum, 2006). Relationality and vulnerability theory are diametrically opposed to neoliberal conceptions of resilience

4 We take heed of Catherine Mackenzie's warning that vulnerability can be used to justify paternalistic social relations (Mackenzie, 2014: 34) and Angela Harris's that universalising conceptions of vulnerability may inadvertently perpetuate social injustice (Harris, 2014).

that occlude sovereign and corporate structures of injustice and devolve responsibility to adapt to systemic harms from the state to society and individuals.[5]

Judith Shklar argues for a shift in focus from justice to injustice and the way we relate to injustices, including the relationship between private and public injustices:

> Most injustices occur continuously within the framework of an established polity with an operative system of law, in normal times. Often it is the very people who are supposed to prevent injustice who, in their official capacity, commit the gravest acts of injustice, without much protest from the citizenry.
>
> (Shklar, 1990: 19).

Shklar argues that a great deal is missed by looking only at justice. 'The sense of injustice, the difficulties of identifying the victims, and the many ways in which we all learn to live with each other's injustices tend to be ignored, as is the relation of private injustice to public order' (Shklar, 1990: 15).

Injustices result from harms. Feinberg describes three types of harm. First, damage to an object or thing. Second, 'the thwarting, setting back, or defeating of an interest' that is more substantial than a desire or want and undermines an individual's wellbeing. Third, 'One person *wrongs* another when his indefensible (unjustifiable and inexcusable) conduct violates the other's right, and in all but certain very special cases such conduct will also invade the other's interest' (Feinberg 1987: 34; emphasis in original).

Framing problems from the perspective of injustice broadens our understanding of its causes and the range of potential solutions. For example, viewing climatic harms as the result of the capitalist imperatives of growth and profit enables an understanding of their impacts on human rights, and on cultural, economic and psychological loss and damage to vulnerable corporeal beings. It also facilitates understanding of the links between human rights and resistance. Similarly, resilience should be understood not merely as the capacity to withstand economic and financial reverses but as the capacity to respond to them. In relation to an irreversible threat such as global heating, it is important to differentiate unfairness and ill-luck from structural injustice and human agency. Exposure to climatic harms may, for example, be an unfair accident of geography whereas the West's history of carbon colonialism is an injustice caused by human agents acting within complex structures (Hornborg, 2019).

Our core argument is that focusing on injustice facilitates analysis of the structural harms of global capitalism and the violations that accompany it. Other scholars have adopted different points of departure such as capabilities or

5 Chandler and Reid (2016) argue that neoliberalism produces degraded subjects whose resilience and adaptability skills may be enhanced, but whose autonomy and individual agency are shrunken.

flourishing (Sen, 1999; Nussbaum, 2006), needs (Doyal and Gough, 1991) and vulnerability (Fineman and Grear, 2013). Injustices are linked to these approaches, as we argue below in relation to vulnerability.

Focusing on injustice at this historical conjuncture highlights the indivisibility of justice. For example, climate justice is not attainable without environmental, distributive, gender, global, procedural and reparative justice, none of which is achievable while the structural injustices of Covid-19 and climate change put lives at risk. These existential transboundary threats epitomise vulnerability on an interconnected planet and the fact that injustice anywhere is an insult to justice everywhere. In short, we believe that our focus upon social injustice offers a framework that facilitates analysis of socio-political and socio-legal structures, the systemic harms of neoliberal globalisation, and Foucauldian approaches to discipline, biopolitics and power (Mezzadra, Reid and Samaddar, 2013).

An obvious retort to our suggestion that injustices should define the way in which we ought to address suffering is that human rights already does this or that democracy is the best way of preventing them. Today, few struggles are not framed in human rights terms. Our concern is that, as with development, and discussed by Williams in this book, hegemonic interpretations of human rights are too often complicit in reproducing injustices – particularly the Western tendency to prioritise civil and political rights over economic, social, and cultural rights while paying lip service to the indivisibility of human rights. Democracy is increasingly threatened by the authoritarian populism of Bolsonaro and Modi, Putin's 'managed' democracy, Orban's 'illiberal' democracy and the United States' near-death experience under Trump. Liberal democracy is also compatible with a wide range of social injustices because it tends to empower the powerful rather at the expense of the majority (Santos, 2007). Like justice, democracy and human rights are terrains of continual struggle rather than points of arrival.

Naming Injustices

Injustice is subjectively experienced but emerges from the institutions and structures that make it possible. Because perceptions of injustice are subjective, it is unlikely that an overarching theory of justice to which everybody can subscribe is attainable.

It may be possible to agree that certain harms are always unacceptable but not about how to eradicate them. Genocide is a universally proscribed crime against humanity that has taken place in China and Rwanda within living memory. The problem is compounded in the absence of a *jus cogens* prohibition on deforestation. There might be wide agreement that deforestation is an existential threat but not that commodifying and monetising forests is the solution.[6] The fact that there appears to be cross-cultural agreement about the Sustainable Development Goals

6 This is the underlying neoliberal premise of the REDD+ framework (Reducing emissions from deforestation and forest degradation) (Adelman, 2017).

says more about global power structures and hegemonic ideas of development than ecological sustainability (Adelman, 2018). Acknowledging that a meta-theory of justice is unattainable does not entail a collapse into relativism. As Sen argues:

> The recognition of evident injustice in preventable deprivation, such as widespread hunger, unnecessary morbidity, premature mortality, grinding poverty, neglect of female children, subjugation of women, and phenomena of that kind does not have to await the derivation of some complete ordering over choices that involve finer differences and puny infelicities.
>
> (Sen, 1999: 254)

Injustices are material and non-material, economic and non-economic, and direct and indirect but invariably involve systemic violence, physical and mental oppression, and rights violations. They may also involve epistemicide, ecocide or genocide. Impoverishment and forced migration are systemic. Injustices are frequently interlinked. For example, warfare causes loss of life, rape, pillage, destruction, and impoverishment as well as dehumanisation and physical and mental scarring. It creates waves of refugees who suffer in limbo in camps or perish in pursuit of asylum and safety (Kneebone, Stevens and Baldassar, 2014) while sustaining the necropolitics of the arms trade.

Climate change and the coronavirus pandemic are linked by biodiversity loss and unsustainable development: there appears to be strong correlation between ethnicity, poverty and susceptibility to Covid-19 in all countries (Pan et al., 2020). The poor and vulnerable are most exposed to Covid-19 by maldevelopment and the inequalities that result from distributive injustice. The pandemic exposes the different levels of risk faced in the global North and the South by the socially distanced rich in gated communities and the inhabitants of favelas and slums forced to choose between eating and dying (Egger et al., 2021). If we are all in this together, it is only in tenuous ways. Lockdowns increased the debt burden on Southern countries and deprived them of resources for public health (Kose et al., 2020). As the pandemic began, the IMF and the World Bank were warning about mounting debt and deepening impoverishment in the global South.[7] The gulf between the quality of disease control mechanisms and public health systems in the South and North is unfair because it is unjust, as is Northern vaccine nationalism exacerbated by intellectual property regimes which have made countries in the global South dependent upon global pharmaceutical companies and limited initiatives akin to charity such as the Covax project.[8]

7 Larry Elliott, 'World Bank calls for debt relief programme as amounts owed hit record levels', *The Guardian*, 12 October 2020. Available online at: https://www.theguardian.com/business/2020/oct/12/world-bank-debt-relief-record-levels-covid (accessed 20 January 2020). The amount owed by the poorest countries was at record levels before the onset of the Covid-19 crisis.

8 Kai Kupferschmidt, 'Unprotected African health workers die as rich countries buy up COVID-19 vaccines', *Science*, 17 February 2021. Available online at: https://

Global heating and biodiversity loss inflict a plethora of injustices on the poor and vulnerable in the global South, who are most at risk from harms for which they are least responsible. The threat of rising sea levels is experienced in very different ways on small island states in the Pacific Ocean, in delta states such as Bangladesh and Vietnam, or megacities such as New York and Shanghai. Global heating will displace millions in the years ahead, destabilise neighbouring states, and fuel xenophobic populism in the North. People displaced by climatic harms currently have no protection under international environmental, human rights or refugee law – an injustice that will be compounded as Northern states treat displacement as a national security issue rather than an urgent humanitarian problem. If law is too often an obstacle to climate justice, climate displacement demonstrates the paradox that its absence can be equally problematic. For the 39 member states in the Alliance of Small Island States whose survival is threatened by rising sea levels, a right to relocation and resettlement is a precondition for climate justice (Adelman, 2016). Ecological catastrophe is linked to global capitalism and neoliberal models of development in a vicious cycle that undermines democracy and violates human rights. The intersecting and overlapping nature of these harms diffuses resistance and complicates the search for solutions. Viewed from a different perspective however, the fact that they are entwined in a Gordian knot means that the climate and ecological crisis provides an opportunity – perhaps the last – as an imperative to deal with a range of injustices. Since anthropogenic hyper-agency occurs within the structures, disciplines and ideological straitjacket of global capitalism, Capitalocene is a more appropriate term than Anthropocene to describe the current era (Adelman, 2021).

The persistence of historic injustices demonstrates how difficult they are to overcome. They combine primordial injustices such as patriarchy and discrimination against indigenous peoples with the depredations of colonialism and imperialism which have left postcolonial scars and neocolonial deformations that are difficult to uproot in a global economy designed to perpetuate inequality through the disciplinary techne of markets and international economic institutions. A quarter of a century after the formal end of apartheid, South Africa is still one of the most unequal countries in the world. The persistence of gender injustice has many causes, including liberalism's emphasis on individual equality and exploitation in global care chains (Stewart, 2011). Feminist critiques of patriarchy oppose these injustices by relying on an ethic of care based on the

www.sciencemag.org/news/2021/02/unprotected-african-health-workers-die-rich-countries-buy-covid-19-vaccines (accessed 18 February 2021). The Covax initiative for equitable global access to Covid-19 vaccines expects about 1.8 billion doses to be available to the 92 participating countries. This suggests that poor Southern countries will not be fully vaccinated before the middle of this decade. World Health Organization, 'COVAX publishes first interim distribution forecast', 3 February 2021. Available online at: https://www.who.int/news/item/03-02-2021-covax-publishes-first-interim-distribution-forecast (accessed 3 February 2021).

principles of relationality (Gilligan, 1993; Tronto, 1993). International responses ameliorate some injustices to a degree. For example, the Convention on the Elimination of Discrimination Against Women is designed to achieve gender justice, as legal measures adopted by Northern and Southern countries to prohibit gender discrimination and enhance equality and inclusivity, but women remain systemically disadvantaged everywhere in areas such as equal pay for equal work, reproductive health, etc. (Young, 2009). Similarly, while progress has been made in relation to LGBTQ+ issues, homosexuality is still a crime across much of the South.

Indigenous peoples continue to suffer from the historic injustices of colonialism, especially settler colonialism. Global heating is a threat multiplier that exacerbates historical injustices such as genocide and land grabbing. Indigenous communities have achieved piecemeal victories in courts, but settler states have never made meaningful restitution or delivered reparative justice despite truth and reconciliation processes in countries such as Canada and South Africa. In non-settler states such as Botswana, the San people continue to suffer under neocolonial policies. The non-binding UN Declaration of the Rights of Indigenous Peoples reflects the international 'community's' level of concern about ongoing indigenous struggles for social justice (Alfred, 2005; Bargh, 2007).[9] The injustices of racism and orientalism remain pervasive (Said, 1993; 1994).

As Foucault demonstrated, governmentality and power are not top-down, unilinear processes but diffuse and capillary (Foucault, 1980: 81–2). Neopatrimonial elites consistently seek to evade democratic accountability through nepotism and parallel governmentality (Erdmann and Engel, 2007). Silent empires built on market ideology underpin postcolonial imperialism (Fitzpatrick, 2021). In neoliberal doxa, market efficiency ostensibly promotes individual freedom from overweening state regulation. In Douglass North's New Institutional Economics, institutions exist to promote market efficiency (Faundez, 2016). But institutions are rarely neutral and invariably facilitate transnational corporate interests at the expense of relatively weak, formally sovereign developing countries. One consequence of four decades of neoliberal hegemony has been the prioritisation of corporate rights – which Upendra Baxi termed trade related market friendly human rights (Baxi, 2012) – over those of citizens.[10] The Panama Papers reveal the labyrinthine nature of the economic injustices perpetrated by the wealthy through complex networks (Obermaier and Obermayer, 2017) – injustices resulting from the deprivation of welfare resources and the financing and sustenance of oppressive regimes (Cheeseman, 2020). The structural nature of contemporary economic injustices deeply penetrates societies through unsustainable natural resource

9 Presumably, the global 'community' is similar to the 'Global Partnership' repeatedly referred to in *Transforming Our World: The 2030 Agenda for Sustainable Development*, both of which are as rare as unicorns.

10 Covid-19 prompted prognostications about deglobalisation or even the demise of full-blown neoliberal globalisation. Time will tell.

extraction, land grabs, and exploitative globalised production chains (Suwandi, 2019; Bair, 2014). Global capital pits countries against each other in races to the bottom that intensify inequality within and between them. Global commons are under siege everywhere as tropical forests and the oceans are privatised or exploited by sovereign states. The resources extracted or stolen – crops, minerals, media, digital, pharmaceutical, bio- and nano-technologies, and biological resources – are protected under newly dominant property regimes imposed through unjust intellectual property rights (Liang, 2009; Rangnekar, 2010; Kleba and Rangnekar, 2013). Global capitalism is doubly extractive of natural resources and rents (Burchardt and Dietz, 2014).

Many of the socio-economic and cultural processes that drive neoliberal globalisation are made possible by digitalisation through social media, commodity chains, 'platform' capitalism, and robotic, bio- and nano-technologies (Baxi, 2009; Paliwala, 2013; Srinicek, 2016). As Hornborg (2019: 9) argues, 'Technologies may locally replace, reorganize, and control labour, increase rates of profit, serve as tools of military conquest, and generally shape human mentalities and perceptions of reality'. Technology and injustice are linked in contradictory ways. Technology is never neutral. It saves lives through vaccines and destroys lives through the weaponry that enriches many developed countries. Digitalisation has loosened the North-South metaphor as global firms have outsourced production to the South while retaining intellectual property rights. The growth of information technologies has produced digitally connected people in the South with aspirations to Northern forms of consumption. Software developers in Bangalore may have more in common with their counterparts in Silicon Valley than the urban poor in their own metropolis. Technology's promises are eroded in the walled gardens of states such as China and Iran, and quasi-states exercising hitherto sovereign powers such as the nihilistic, unregulated Silicon Valley giants (Zuboff, 2019). Surveillance states, the most intensely intimate form of biopolitical control, are made possible by appropriation of personal data in the name of security. Techno-redemption will remain a mirage as long as the poor suffer absolute or relative digital exclusion. Techno-fetishists dangle the promise that geoengineering can solve climate breakdown (Gates, 2021). Yet, revolutionary new technologies based on artificial intelligence threaten to reorganise our lives in ways which threaten existing political, social and economic institutions. Shoshana Zuboff's response to this threat is for us all to say: '"No More!" We too can be the authors of many "great and beautiful" new facts that reclaim the digital future as humanity's home' (Zuboff, 2019: 525).

Cartographies of Injustice

Whereas orthodox approaches treat underdevelopment as a failure of the nation-state, we believe that its predations are better understood as a combination of domestic, regional and international elements even if, in Baxi's words, 'It is often enough difficult, if not impossible, to locate the *distinctively* "local" within the "global"' (Baxi, 2012: 282; emphasis in original).

Like the First and Third Worlds, North and the South are political and ideological concepts rather than territorial maps. There have always been parts of the South in exploited and racialised parts of the North, and Southern elites are increasingly surrounded by impoverishment. Northern wealth was built upon slavery and indentured labour. Colonial movements between North and South involved racial or ethnic oppression, cultural suppression, epistemicide, and genocide.[11] These movements take new forms in the contemporary world. Whether as refugees, economic migrants escaping social injustices in their land, or invited or uninvited 'care' workers, people from the global South are present in the North in ways best described as repressive tolerance and are generally excluded from full citizenship. The Northward flow of skilled workers contributes to the further impoverishment of the South, as the scarcity of health workers in the South during the pandemic illustrates. While flows of remittances ameliorate impoverishment in the South, they do not discharge Northern colonial and ecological debts through reparative justice (Khory, 2012). Moreover, the Northern incursions into the South continue in new forms. Whereas during colonialism, permanent settlers were accompanied by temporary administrators and traders, today the movement is largely that of temporary businesspeople, consultants, aid workers, global administrators, and tourists.

The nature of the injustices outlined above suggests complex postcolonial relationships between the local and the global, evident in landgrabs, mineral exploitation, deforestation and persistent impoverishment.

Resistance

It is not possible to comprehend resistance to injustices outside structures and context. Baxi identifies the authors of human rights as rightless people in struggle rather than theorists writing about ethereal yet inherent, inalienable, and universal rights (Baxi, 2009; 2012) – their authorship 'lies scattered amongst people in resistance, and communities in struggle' (Baxi, 2012: 282). This approach gives primacy to the contexts in which injustices occur, the structures that facilitate them, and the ways in which they are resisted.

Michel Foucault described why resistance is intrinsic to power (Foucault 1990: 94; Simons, 2013). As Golder and Fitzpatrick write:

> Power is not, as Foucault emphasized … 'an inescapable fatality at the heart of societies, such that it cannot be undermined'. Instead, formations of power are constitutively lacking, always in the process of ruination and being undermined and reformed by resistance.
>
> (Golder and Fitzpatrick, 2009: 76)

11 For a graphic account of the physical and cultural annihilation of aboriginal peoples see Pascoe (2007).

Counterintuitively, this suggests that the antidote to injustice is not justice from above but resistance from below. Since justice is in the eyes of the sufferer, it is contested and disparate rather than homogenous. Liberal theories of justice rooted in possessive individualism and sovereign-centric rationality have created or perpetuated injustices against individuals, particularly those deemed to be alien others (Heinze, 2013). Racism and patriarchy may transcend time and space, but they manifest differently in local contexts and are suffered in uniquely personal ways by embedded, connected, corporeal beings.

Paradoxically, although intersecting and overlapping injustices are experienced by individuals, justice is indivisible. For Nancy Fraser (2003), distributive justice is inextricably linked to recognition, participation, and procedural justice. And as we argue above, climate justice is unattainable in the absence of environmental, distributive, gender, global, reparative, and procedural justice, all of which emerge through resistance from below.

Structural, systemic injustices are never corrected without sustained resistance. Resistance takes many forms, both legal and extra-legal, ranging from reactions against quotidian injustices to civil disobedience and violence when other alternatives are foreclosed – as in struggles for self-determination and human rights. Resistance ranges from campaigns by civil society and social movements such as Black Lives Matter, #MeToo, Fridays for Future and numerous global South based movements such as Lok Adhikar Manch (LAM) analysed by Caouette and Kapoor (2016). Resistance takes the form of struggles against the structural inequalities of the global political-economy, unfairness in the distribution of medicines and vaccines, debt relief, and democratic accountability and transparency, and the struggles of indigenous peoples and environmental defenders against ecological destruction and unsustainable development (Caouette and Kapoor, 2016; Kothari et al., 2019). As Jayan Nayar points out in this volume, resistance is always at risk of institutional capture by the unjust institutions it seeks to change. Injustice may be part of the human condition but not inevitably in forms that cannot be changed. The ending of apartheid and slavery, and full female suffrage demonstrate the power of resistance, which will always be necessary because there is no plateau on which it is possible to arrive secure in the knowledge that democracy, human rights, justice, and the rule of law have been achieved. As Nelson Mandela put it, 'I have discovered the secret that after climbing a great hill, one only finds that there are many more hills to climb' (Mandela, 1995: 751).

Law is a focus for all forms of resistance that seek to delegitimise, destabilise or destroy power regimes. Law is implicated because, together with capitalism, it is a discourse of knowledge-power designed to reduce the need for physical coercion and generally imposes violence at a distance. Paradoxically, law and development constitute both a vehicle for resistance, for example in the demand by the global South for a New International Economic Order and a right to development, and a means of anaesthetising struggles against injustice. History suggests that extra-legal resistance that asserts a higher legitimacy or morality has a greater likelihood of success because of the gap that commonly exists between law and justice. Civil disobedience succeeded in overthrowing the Raj in India but failed to dislodge apartheid and has a mixed legacy in the United States. Martin Luther King Jr's civil rights campaign had many commonalities with Mohandas K. Gandhi's Satyagraha (King, 1963; Gandhi, 2001).[12] To the perplexity of many of their followers, both believed that the citizen who disobeys unjust laws nevertheless has a duty to accept punishment as a witness to the truth of injustice in order to transform the soul of the perpetrator. In contrast, the progenitor of India's Constitution, Babasaheb Ambedkar, suggested that merely refusing to fight an oppressive regime when attacked was insufficient: 'To abolish war, you must win war and establish a just peace' (Kuber, 2017: 236). Mandela's African National Congress reached the same conclusion in the struggle against apartheid.[13] Demands for climate justice are rooted in the suffering and injustices inflicted by climatic harms. The central lesson of the Anthropocene/Capitalocene is that relying on law, human rights, and sovereign-centric decision making is not enough. Climate justice will not be achieved without resistance from below.

Because the circumstances of justice are always in flux, new forms of resistance using new technologies continuously emerge, although digitalisation raises questions about the relationship between clicktivism by netizens and politics on the ground by citizens (Paliwala, 2013; Jordana and Leidner, 2018). Information technology has facilitated connectivity, organisation, and loose structures of resistance such as Hacktivism that enable what Jean-Luc Nancy would term singular pluralities (Wall, 2011) without eliminating injustices. It has given rise to new, amorphous structures and ideas of cosmopolitan netizenship that enable millions to interact in cyberspace (Paliwala, 2013) but twenty-five years after the inception of the internet, the implications of these new structures on injustice remain unclear (Morozov, 2011; Zuboff, 2019).

Towards Alternatives

The first requirement in the search for alternatives is decolonising our minds. Santos (2014: 26) argues that the persistence of the colonial mentality makes it 'as difficult to imagine the end of colonialism as it is to imagine that colonialism has no end'.

12 Compare King, M. L. Junior, Letter from Birmingham Jail 1963. Available online at: http://www.huffingtonpost.com/brian-penny/just-laws-vs-unjust-laws_b_3737765.html (accessed 5 January 2021) and Gandhi (2001).

13 Nelson Mandela's statement from the dock at the opening of the defence case in the Rivonia Trial. Pretoria Supreme Court, 20 April 1964. Available at: https://www.un.org/en/events/mandeladay/court_statement_1964.shtml (accessed 5 February 2021).

> Coloniality encompasses the material aspects of colonisation as well as its immaterial, psychological, ideational and ideological aspects – the worms that epistemologies of mastery seek to burrow into our consciousness. Coloniality is an outlook that deploys these epistemologies that define reality and legitimises their power to do so: coloniality seeks to obliterate resistance to dominant discourses such as patriarchy, colonialism and neoliberalism.
>
> (Adelman, 2015: 18)

Walter Mignolo (2012: xvi–xvii) suggests that coloniality can be resisted through border thinking. 'Engaging in border thinking is tantamount to engaging in decoloniality; that is, in thinking and doing decolonially'. Mignolo writes that 'Border thinking is an epistemology, an ethic and politics that emerge from the experiences of people taking their destiny in their own hands and not waiting for saviors' (Ibid.: xxii). It is a form of epistemic disobedience that:

> points toward a new way of thinking in which dichotomies can be replaced by the complementarity of apparently contradictory terms. Border thinking could open up the doors to an other tongue, an other thinking, an other logic superseding the longer history of the modern/colonial world.
>
> (Ibid.: 338)

In this volume, Nayar goes further in suggesting that 'border thinking' still ties itself to colonial borders when what is needed is resistant anti-colonial thinking. Reimagining law and development through injustice is a form of epistemic resistance – a refusal to remain mired at the level of consciousness that brought us to this conjuncture. It requires openness to alternative ways of seeing, being, and knowing, replacing hubristic epistemologies of dominance and mastery with epistemologies of humility (Adelman, 2015).

This opens our eyes to the nature of actual and potential colonial, imperial, and contemporary postcolonial and neoliberal injustices and forms of resistance against them. We have outlined a variety of forms of resistance by global South states, activist organisations, and subaltern struggles but it is a mistake to construct a hierarchy of the legitimacy of struggles. Calls for a New International Economic Order and subaltern struggles against mining and land grabbing operate on different planes. Governments who call for global economic justice are often in league with mining companies whose extractivism is part of the problem. It is therefore necessary to assess the best strategy in each context that might benefit people suffering harm and injustices. Legal strategies are important but seldom without contradiction (Rajagopal, 2005).

Hannah Arendt provides an important guide to action through her concept of personal responsibility not as a legal or moral concept of citizenship but as a political idea of the person as someone who becomes fully human through interaction with others in the public sphere within a political community

(Arendt, 1977). This notion imposes responsibility on each person to oppose injustice. The oppressed who resist such as indigenous peoples struggling against maldevelopment in the Amazon are rendered silent and invisible in the absence of solidarity from a larger political community in which personal responsibility is pooled.

We have argued that we need alternatives to development, to law, and to law and development. Adelman (2021) and Philippopoulos-Mihalopoulos (2011) are amongst the growing number of legal scholars calling for a legal paradigm shift commensurate with the scale and urgency of the current climate and eco crises. The authors in *Pluriverse: A Postdevelopment Dictionary* explore resistant and alternative approaches to development and formal positive law such as the Zapatista movement, feminism and older religious and indigenous, cosmovisions (Kothari et al., 2019). They suggest non-hierarchical ways of thinking rooted in the material experiences of embedded, interconnected, vulnerable, corporeal beings.

One example is the way in which indigenous peoples in the Andes have understood climate for millennia without Western science and farmed without herbicides and pesticides. They have lived in harmony with nature, which is regarded as a living entity, *Pachamama*, rather than an inert collection of resources yet to be commodified. In Bolivia, Colombia, and Ecuador, giving constitutional rights to nature makes sense to the extent that Andean cosmologies embrace Western ideas of rights. In countries pursuing extractive development, engaging with Western legal concepts is a form of defence against maldevelopment and injustice. The concept of *buen vivir* (living well) is at the centre of Andean cosmovisions that oppose mainstream models of development as inimical to indigenous onto-epistemologies. In contrast to linear Western ideas of progress in which a country emerges from an underdeveloped to a superior, modernised state, life is understood to be in permanent flux and society always under construction. Economic growth and the pursuit of profit for their own sakes are alien, especially when they are accompanied by environmental destruction and inequality. It follows that capitalism is hostile to the central idea of well-being, which flows from harmonious relationships with nature that enable collective standards of living to rise consistent with the idea of 'good living' or 'living well'. Science is accepted as one way of seeing and knowing amongst others. Holism and relationality are favoured over possessive individualism and exclusionary rights.

It is both easy and facile to romanticise indigenous onto-epistemologies that are not uncontradictory; for example, the compatibility of varieties of *buen vivir* with patriarchy or other social injustices (Cochrane, 2014). We point to them because they demonstrate that it is possible to live well without destroying the planet, and because the failure of Western forms of law and development have created the urgent need for alternatives. Moreover, these onto-epistemologies are congruent with a range of contemporary alternative movements that oppose dominant global orthodoxies that demand that we do the same thing again and again while watching the planet burn – the necropolitics of green capitalism, ecological modernisation, and sustainable development. Using development rather than injustice to frame the problems confronting us has resulted in crisis. The UN Environment Programme, a longstanding proponent of green capitalism, has finally accepted that 'The current mode of development degrades the Earth's finite capacity to sustain human well-being' (UNEP, 2021: 51). Capitalism is now literally a matter of life and death. As Frederic Jameson observed, 'it is easier to imagine the end of the world than to imagine the end of capitalism' (Jameson, 2003: 76). The struggle for climate justice is the biggest – and perhaps the final – opportunity we have to address the myriad of intertwined and overlapping injustices.

The pandemic demonstrates the scale of transboundary harms, the speed with which they can erupt, and the injustices they cause. Global heating may unleash sudden, irreversible feedback loops caused, for example, by a tipping point in Amazon deforestation driven by Brazil's maldevelopment policies. We know what the problem is and what needs to be done, and that we have the tools to do it. The problem is a failure of political will to tear down structures of injustice: racism, patriarchy, and capitalism. Boaventura de Sousa Santos maintains that humanity tends to find weak answers to strong questions. Santos argues that the deeply entrenched separation of nature from society in Western thought will soon:

> reach its ultimate, ecological limits, that the insatiable exploitation of nature must have an end, lest human life on the planet become unsustainable. This is perhaps the strong question that raises the most perplexity, since all Western thinking, whether critical or not, is grounded on the Cartesian idea that nature is a *res extensa* and, as such, an unlimited resource unconditionally available to human beings.
>
> (Santos, 2014: 198)

Conclusion

We have suggested that confronting injustices arising from identifiable harms and suffering provides a framing that is more conducive to the wellbeing of all species and the Earth itself than development because development cannot be conceived apart from destructive extractivism and growth fetishism. Postdevelopment thinkers have long abjured Western models of development, but the fact that we are still writing about its dangers indicates the Sisyphean nature of the task. In the end, development will die because it is literally unsustainable. Resistance can hurry its extinction along with the injustices it produces. Justice involves hearing the insistent, multitudinous voices of the marginalised, disempowered, and disenfranchised, and the way they conceive injustice and resistance. If we cannot reimagine social justice now, it is unlikely we ever will. In David Graeber's words, 'The ultimate, hidden truth of the world, is that it is something that we make, and could just as easily make differently' (Graeber, 2015: 89). We can be the authors of a more just future.

References

Adelman, S. 2015. Epistemologies of Mastery. In Grear, A. and Kotzé, L.J. (eds), *Research Handbook on Human Rights and the Environment*. Edward Elgar.

Adelman, S. 2016. Climate Justice, Loss and Damage and Compensation for Small Island Developing States. *Journal of Human Rights and the Environment* 7(1), 32–53.

Adelman, S. 2017. Tropical Forests, Climate Change and Neoliberal Environmental Governmentality. In Tan, C. and Faundez, J. (eds), *Natural Resources and Sustainable Development: International Economic Law Perspectives*. Edward Elgar.

Adelman, S. 2018. The Sustainable Development Goals, Anthropocentrism and Neoliberalism. In French, D. and Kotzé L.J. (eds), *Sustainable Development Goals: Law, Theory & Implementation*. Edward Elgar.

Adelman, S. 2021. A Legal Paradigm Shift towards Climate Justice in the Anthropocene. In S. Adelman and L. Kotzé (eds), *Oñati Socio-Legal Series* 11(1): *Climate Justice in the Anthropocene*, 44–68.

Adelman, S. and Paliwala, A. 2021a. *The Limits of Law and Development: Neoliberalism, Governance and Social Justice*. Routledge.

Adelman, S. and Paliwala, A. 2021b. Beyond Law and Development? In Adelman, S. and Paliwala, A. (eds), *The Limits of Law and Development: Neoliberalism, Governance and Social Justice*. Routledge.

Alfred T. 2005. *Wasase: Indigenous Pathways of Action and Freedom*. Toronto University Press.

Arendt, H. 1977. *The Life of the Mind, Vol.* II. Harcourt Brace Jovanovich.

Bair, J. (ed). 2014. Editors Introduction: Commodity Chains in and of the World System. *The Journal of World Systems Research* 20(1), 1–10.

Bargh M. 2007. *Resistance: An Indigenous Response to Neo-Liberalism*. Huia Press.

Baxi, U. 2009. *Human Rights in a Posthuman World*. Oxford University Press.

Baxi, U. 2012. *The Future of Human Rights*. Oxford University Press.

Benjamin, W. 2006. On the Concept of History. In Benjamin, W., *Selected Writings*, Volume 4, 1938–1940. Belknap Press of Harvard University Press.

Burchardt, H. J., & Dietz, K. 2014. (Neo-)extractivism – a New Challenge for Development Theory from Latin America. *Third World Quarterly* 35(3), 468–486.

Campbell, M. 2018. *Women, Poverty, Equality: The Role of CEDAW*. Bloomsbury.

Caouette, D. and Kapoor, D. eds. 2016. *Beyond Colonialism, Development and Globalisation*. Zed Books.

Chandler, D. and Reid, J. 2016. *The Neoliberal Subject: Resilience, Adaptation and Vulnerability*. Rowman & Littlefield.

Cheeseman, N. 2020. How Western Companies Undermine African Democracy. *The Africa Report*. 16 November 2020. Available online at: https://www.theafricareport.com/50500/how-western-companies-undermine-african-democracy/ (accessed 20 November 2020).

Cochrane, R. 2014. Climate Change, Buen vivir, and the Dialectic of Enlightenment: Toward a Feminist Critical Philosophy of Climate Justice. *Hypatia* 29(3), 576–598.

Deneulin, S., Nebel, M. and Sagovsky, N. 2006. *Transforming Unjust Structures*. Springer.

Doyal, L. and Gough, I. 1991. *A Theory of Human Needs*. Guilford.

Egger, D. et al. 2021. Falling Living Standards during the COVID-19 Crisis: Quantitative Evidence from Nine Developing Countries. *Science Advances* 7(6), eabe0997.

Erdmann, G. and Engel, U. 2007. Neopatrimonialism Reconsidered: Critical Review and Elaboration of an Elusive Concept. *Commonwealth and Comparative Politics* 45(1), 95–119.

Escobar, A. 2011. *Encountering Development: The Making and Unmaking of the Third World.* Princeton University Press.

Esteva, G. 1992. Development. In Sachs W. (ed.), *The Development Dictionary: A Guide to Knowledge as Power.* Zed Books.

Faundez, J. 2016. Douglass North's Theory of Institutions: Lessons for Law and Development. *Hague Journal on the Rule of Law* 8: 373–419.

Feinberg, J. 1987. *The Moral Limits of the Criminal Law Volume 1: Harm to Others.* Oxford University Press.

Fineman, M.A. 2013. Equality, Autonomy, and the Vulnerable Subject in Law and Politics. In Fineman, M. and Grear, A. (eds), *Vulnerability: Reflections on a New Ethical Foundation for Law and Politics.* Ashgate.

Fineman, J. and Grear, A. eds. 2013. *Vulnerability: Reflections on a New Ethical Foundation for Law and Politics.* Ashgate.

Fitzpatrick, P. 2021. In Search of Nothing: Silent Empires and the Law Beyond Development. In Adelman, S. and Paliwala, A. (eds), *The Limits of Law and Development: Neoliberalism, Governance and Social Justice.* Routledge.

Foucault, M. 1980. *Power/Knowledge: Selected Interviews and Other Writings, 1972–1977.* Pantheon Books.

Foucault, M. 1990. *History of Sexuality.* Volume 1. Penguin.

Fraser, N. 2003. Social Justice in the Age of Identity Politics: Redistribution, Recognition and Participation. In Fraser, N. and Honneth, A. (eds), *Redistribution or Recognition? A Political-Philosophical Exchange.* Verso.

Gandhi, Mahatma. 2001. *Non-violent Resistance (Satyagraha).* Dover.

Gates, B. 2021. *How to Avoid a Climate Disaster: The Solutions We Have and the Breakthroughs We Need.* Knopf.

Gilligan, C. 1993. *In a Different Voice: Psychological Theory and Women's Development.* Harvard University Press.

Golder, B. and Fitzpatrick, P. 2009. *Foucault's Law.* Routledge-Cavendish.

Graeber, D. 2015. *The Utopia of Rules: On Technology, Stupidity, and the Secret Joys of Bureaucracy.* Melville House.

Gramsci, A. 1971. *Selections from the Prison Notebooks of Antonio Gramsci.* International Publishers.

Grear, A. 2012. Human Rights, Property and the Search for Worlds Other. *Journal of Human Rights and the Environment* 3(2), 173–195.

Grear, A. 2017. Foregrounding Vulnerability: Materiality's Porous Affectability as a Methodological Platform. In Philippopoulos-Mihalopoulos, A. and Brooks, V. (eds), *Research Methods in Environmental Law: A Handbook.* Edward Elgar.

Gudynas, E. 2011. Buen Vivir: Today's Tomorrow. *Development* 54(4), 441–447.

Harris, A. 2014. Vulnerability and Power in the Age of the Anthropocene. *Washington and Lee Journal on Energy, Climate and Environment* 6(1), 98 (UC Davis Legal Studies Research Paper No. 370).

Heinze, E. 2013. *The Concept of Injustice.* Routledge.

Hornborg, A. 2019. Colonialism in the Anthropocene: The Political Ecology of the Money-energy-technology Complex. *Journal of Human Rights and the Environment* 10 (1), 7–21.

Jameson, F. 2003. Future City. *New Left Review* 21, 65–79.
Johnston, P. et al. 2007. Reclaiming the definition of sustainability. *Environmental Science and Pollution Research International* 14 (1), 60–66.
Jordana, G. and Leidner, D. 2018. Why Marginalized Groups Struggle to Leverage Digital Activism. *Association for Information Systems*. Available online at: https://lup.lub.lu.se/record/7aa443a1-272d-4098-8273-331875a7230a (accessed 20 February 2021).
Khory, K. ed. 2012. *Global Migration: Challenges for the 21st Century*. Palgrave Macmillan.
King, M.L. Jr. 1963. Letter from Birmingham Jail. Available online at: http://www.huffingtonpost.com/brian-penny/just-laws-vs-unjust-laws_b_3737765.html (accessed 5 January 2021).
Kose, M., Ohnsorge, F., Nagle, P. and Sugawara, N. 2020. Caught by a Cresting Debt Wave, *Finance & Development* 57(2), 40–43.
Kleba, P. and Rangnekar, D. eds. 2013. Special Issue: Fairness in Biodiversity Politics and Law: Interrogating the Nagoya Protocol. *Law, Environment and Development Journal* 9 (2).
Kneebone, S., Stevens D. and Baldassar, L. eds. 2014*Refugee Protection and the Role of Law: Conflicting Identities*. Routledge.
Kothari, A., Salleh, A., Escobar, A., Demaria, F., Acosta, A. eds. 2019. *Pluriverse: A Post-Development Dictionary*. Tulika Books.
Kuber, W.N. 2017. *Builders of Modern India: Dr. B. R. Ambedkar*. Publications Division, Information & Broadcasting Ministry, Govt. of India.
Leach, M., MacGregor, H., Scoones, I. and Wilkinson, A. 2021. Post-pandemic Transformations: How and Why COVID-19 Requires us to Rethink Development. *World Development*, 138, 105233.
Liang, L. 2009. Piracy, Creativity and Infrastructure: Rethinking Access to Culture. (July 20). Available online at: https://ssrn.com/abstract=1436229 (accessed 5 March 2021).
Mackenzie, C. 2014. The Importance of Relational Autonomy and Capabilities for an Ethics of Vulnerability. In Mackenzie, C., Rogers, W. and Dodds, S. (eds), *Vulnerability: New Essays in Ethics and Feminist Philosophy*. Oxford University Press.
Mandela, N. 1995. *Long Walk to Freedom*. Little Brown and Company.
Mezzadra, S., Reid, J. and Samaddar, R. 2013. The Biopolitics of Development. In Mezzadra, S., Reid, J. and Samaddar, R. (eds), *Reading Michel Foucault in the Post-colonial Present*. Springer.
Mignolo, W. 2012. *Local Histories/Global Designs: Coloniality, Subaltern Knowledges, and Border Thinking*. Princeton University Press.
Morozov, E. 2011. *The Net Delusion: How Not to Liberate the World*. Penguin.
Nayar, J. 2019. The (Non)Perplexity of Human Rights. *Theory & Event*, 22(2), 267–302.
Nedelsky, J. 2011. *Law's Relations: A Relational Theory of Self-Autonomy, and Law*. Oxford University Press.
Nussbaum, M. 2006. *Frontiers of Justice: Disability, Nationality, Species Membership*. Belknap Press.
Obermaier, F. and Obermayer, B. 2017. *The Panama Papers: Breaking the Story of How the Rich and Powerful Hide Their Money*. Simon & Schuster.
Paliwala, A. 2013. Netizenship, Security and Freedom. *International Review of Law Computers and Technology* 27(1–2), 104–123.
Pan, D. et al. (2020). The impact of ethnicity on clinical outcomes in COVID-19: a systematic review. *EClinicalMedicine* 23 (2020): 100404.
Pascoe, B., 2007. *Convincing Ground*. Aboriginal Studies Press.

Philippopoulos-Mihalopoulos, A. 2011. Towards a Critical Environmental Law. In Philippopoulos-Mihalopoulos, A. (ed.), *Law and Ecology: New Environmental Foundations*. Routledge.
Pogge, T. 2002. *World Poverty and Human Rights*. Polity Press.
Rajagopal, B. 2005. Limits of Law in Counter-hegemonic Globalisation: The Indian Supreme Court and the Narmada Valley Struggle. In Santos, B. de S. and Rodríguez-Garavito, C.A. (eds), *Law and Globalization from Below*. Cambridge University Press.
Rangnekar, D. 2010. Special Issue on Geographical Indications. *Journal of World Intellectual Property*, 13(2),
Rawls, J. 1971. *A Theory of Justice*. Harvard University Press.
Rawls, J. 1999. *The Law of Peoples with The Idea of Public Reason Revisited*. Harvard University Press.
Reid, J. 2013. Interrogating the Neoliberal Biopolitics of the Sustainable Development-Resilience Nexus. *International Political Sociology* 7(4), 353–367.
Sachs, W. 1992. Introduction. In Sachs, W. (ed.), *The Development Dictionary: A Guide to Knowledge as Power*. Witwatersrand University Press and Zed Books.
Sachs, W. 2019. Foreword: The Development Dictionary Revisited. In Kothari, A. et al. *Pluriverse: A Post-Development Dictionary*. Tulika Books.
Said, E. 1993. *Orientalism*. Penguin.
Said, E. 1994. *Culture and Imperialism*. Vintage.
Santos, B. de S. 2005. Beyond Neo-Liberal Governance: The World Social Forum as Subaltern Politics and Legality. In Santos, B. and Rodriguez-Garavito C. A. (eds), *Law and Globalization from Below: Towards a Cosmopolitan Legality*. Cambridge University Press.
Santos, B. de S. ed. 2007. *Democratising Democracy: Beyond the Liberal Democratic Canon*. Verso.
Santos, B. de S. 2014. *Epistemologies of the South: Justice against Epistemicide*. Paradigm Publishers.
Seck, S. L. 2019. Relational Law and the Reimagining of Tools for Environmental and Climate Justice. *Canadian Journal of Women and the Law* 31(1), 151–177.
Sen, A. 1999. *Development as Freedom*. Oxford University Press.
Sen, A. 2004. Elements of a Theory of Human Rights. *Philosophy & Public Affairs* 32(4), 315–356.
Sen, A. 2009. *The Idea of Justice*. Harvard University Press.
Shklar, J. N. 1990. *The Faces of Injustice*. Yale University Press.
Simons, J. 2013. Power, Resistance, and Freedom. In Falzon, C., O'Leary, T. and Sawicki, J. (eds), *A Companion to Foucault*. Wiley-Blackwell.
Spivak, G. 1999. *A Critique of Postcolonial Reason: Toward a History of the Vanishing Present*. Harvard University Press.
Srinicek, N. 2016. *Platform Capitalism*. Polity Press.
Stengers, I. 2015. *In Catastrophic Times: Resisting the Coming Barbarism*. Open Humanities Press.
Stewart, A. 2011. *Gender Law and Justice in the Global Market*. Cambridge University Press.
Suwandi, I. 2019. *Value Chains: The New Economic Imperialism*. Monthly Review Press.
Twining, W. and Paliwala, A. 2021. Southern Voices: Extending a Project. In Adelman, S. and Paliwala, A. (eds), *The Limits of Law and Development: Neoliberalism, Governance and Social Justice*. Routledge.

Tronto, J., 1993. *Moral Boundaries: A Political Argument for an Ethic of Care*. Psychology Books.

UNEP. 2021. *Making Peace with Nature: A Scientific Blueprint to Tackle the Climate, Biodiversity and Pollution Emergencies*. United Nations Environment Programme. Available online at: https://www.unep.org/resources/making-peace-nature (accessed 5 March 2021).

Wall, I rua. 2011. Anonymous Hacktivism and the Discourse of Human Rights from Human Rights in Ireland. Available online at: http://humanrights.ie/tag/resistance/ (accessed 10 February 2021).

WCED (World Commission on Environment and Development). 1987. *Our Common Future*. Oxford University Press.

Weir, A. 2017. Decolonizing Feminist Freedom: Indigenous Relationalities. In McClaren, M.A. (ed.), *Decolonizing Feminism: Transnational Feminism and Globalization*. Rowman & Littlefield.

Young, I.M. 2009. Structural Injustice and the Politics of Difference. In Gaus, G.F., Christiano, T. and Christman, J.P. (eds), *Contemporary Debates in Political Philosophy*. Blackwell.

Zuboff, S. 2019. *The Age of Surveillance Capitalism: The Fight for a Human Future at the New Frontier of Power*. Profile Books.

Chapter 2

Post-Hobbesian State, Sovereignty and Development

Raza Saeed

Introduction

In 2003, Bruce Bueno de Mesquita et al. proposed an intriguing set of indicators to gauge the 'social welfare' of the people of a given country (Iqbal and Starr, 2016: 25; Bueno de Mesquita et al., 2003). Termed as the *Hobbes Index*, the indicator was premised on a rather literal interpretation of Thomas Hobbes's notion of the life of the individual in the so-called state of nature being 'solitary, poor, nasty, brutish and short' (Hobbes, 1909: 132). The Index proposed to calculate various potential 'miseries' for people, calculating how people's daily lives in a given country fared against the Hobbesian schema (Bueno de Mesquita et al., 2003: 461). It measured 'brutishness' in terms of domestic and external violence, 'shortness' with regard to mortality and life expectancy rates, and categorised 170 countries from around the world based on data gathered across almost two decades. One of the key stated aims of the Index was to establish the distance some countries had travelled from the so-termed 'state of nature' by way of providing security, economic development and public goods to their people (Rothstein, 2007: 159). As is the case with many other such matrices and indices, North America, Japan and Western European countries seized the top tier while the so-called developing countries trailed them, with postcolonial African states at the bottom. The implication of this ranking was to convey that the lower tiered states had travelled the least distance from the 'state of nature' and that they continued to dwell in a rather primitive socio-political context marked by violence, insecurity and underdevelopment.

Much has been written in the last two decades about the rise of such indices, rankings and quantification exercises as tools of global governance, which aim to govern 'at a distance' (Broome and Quirk, 2015) by creating normative environments to shape the behaviour of states and other actors (Davis et al., 2015; Saeed, 2020). It has also become increasingly acknowledged that such 'indicatorology' attempts to reduce complex social phenomena to a set of quantifiable numbers at the expense of nuance and interconnectedness (Paliwala and Kamchedzera, 2013), which is especially problematic because these measurements cannot completely escape the issues of selection bias and subjectivity. But while these

DOI: 10.4324/9780203745298-4

conceptual critiques are certainly valid and important, this chapter aims to take the discussion towards a different direction. The nominative and conceptual peculiarity of the 'Hobbes Index' shows, at the very least, the continued import of Hobbesian terminology within the development discourse (broadly construed) to talk about insecurity, violence and underdevelopment within certain socio-political orders.

It is the transplantation of Hobbesian logic to the language of development over the last few decades that offers the departure point for the current chapter. The import of a Hobbesian approach within the current development discourse rests on the equation of underdevelopment, insecurity and violence with the notional state of nature. As discussed below, it is considered a ready formula by various commentators to apply to current conflict-ridden and impoverished societies. Simply put, the argument is based on the premise that the lack of socio-economic welfare and the associated presence of insecurity and violence carries the same undertones as the pre-political state of nature that Hobbes spoke about, with a perpetual war of all against all precluding arts and industry. With the problem constructed in a certain way, the solution also follows the same thread – it proposes a strong political setup at the centre, the absence of which is considered to be the root cause of these social ills. What is demanded then is a strong sovereign power, a Leviathan, as the panacea for multifarious societal issues.

It is intriguing that although the terminologies have morphed into what is more relatable for disparate audiences in the current age, the underlying logic behind the application of the Hobbesian schema has remained unchanged for five centuries. It involves the theoretical construction of a notional *lack*, attributed to the absence of a strong and capable sovereign, which results in the justification of the institution of sovereignty as the solution. While Hobbes's formulation identified this *lack* with the absence of peace and the presence of perpetual violence, the various connected threads within the development discourse conflate it with factors such as economic fragility, socio-political instability, and their impact on security and violence. This then suggests that what is generally considered as an old 'fiction of the state of nature' (Veitch et al., 2019: 16) is construed by some as far less fictional today than we should readily assume.

However, a key contradiction emerges from this conflation of development discourse with Hobbesian logic, which requires a re-reading of their interplay. This conflation not only ignores, but actively hides the role of the Leviathanesque state in the creation and sustenance of problems pertaining to impoverishment, underdevelopment, insecurity and violence. The assumption that connects these societal problems to the absence of a centralised political authority does not hold true for many conflict-prone countries, especially those grappling with their post-conflict and postcolonial trajectories. It is argued here that the perversity of this logic only becomes apparent when we flip the frame and consider problems of violence and underdevelopment as deeply entrenched within the postcolonial political framework – the underlying assumption is challenged when we realise that these problems may not emanate from the pre-political state of nature, but from the political nature of the state.

It is this paradoxical and predatory political and sovereign power that the current chapter understands as Post-Hobbesian Sovereignty. There are many other names by which a Post-Hobbesian state is recognised – it has been called a 'predatory state' (Evans, 1989), a 'cunning state' (Randeria, 2003) or a 'perverse state' (Pearce, 2010), with each of the terminologies emphasising some specific facet of this particular manifestation of the state. This chapter suggests the terminology of 'Post-Hobbesian State' for two reasons. First, it is proposed to counter some development practitioners' insistence on using Hobbes as a frame of reference to understand present-day situations of underdevelopment and insecurity. Second, and more importantly, the term is used here to refer to the creation or sustenance of violence and impoverishment, leading to a situation that conceptually echoes the Hobbesian state of nature, for the sovereign's own continued survival and legitimacy. In this case, the argument for the return of a Leviathan is an error of political-theoretical judgement, as it fails to understand the complexity behind the contradictions and problems already present in the society. It is argued below that this theoretical insight can also be read into Hobbes's own writings with reference to the difference in his two notions of sovereignty – the conceptual difference between constitutive sovereignty and acquisitional sovereignty.

This chapter, therefore, proposes an alternative theoretical understanding of the interplay between development discourse and the Hobbesian paradigm. It proceeds in three steps. First, it relies on accounts within contemporary development discourse to highlight the link between the framing of developmental issues and the Hobbesian approach. Second, it discusses how the formulation does not account for those scenarios where violence is generated or perpetuated by some states. Finally, the chapter develops the link between violence, sovereignty and development through an analysis of the Hobbesian account of sovereignty. It is argued that re-reading Hobbes shows, both in theory and its applicable practice, how the strengthening of predatory, cunning or perverse states exacerbates the contradictions of underdevelopment and violence rather than solving them. The discussion is followed by a conclusion.

This chapter speaks about development in the context of the critiques of traditional notions of development that focus primarily on economic growth and linear progress (see, for instance, Rist, 2014). Development or underdevelopment are therefore not adopted here as unproblematic or uncontested categories. Although it is not possible to outline the contours of the paradigm in its entirety here, the chapter adopts the term development here as an idea that does not but *should* lead to social justice, human dignity, substantive equalities, physical and psychological security, at least a bare minimum of socio-economic resources, agency, and political and epistemic freedoms. Underdevelopment, then, is taken here as impoverishment – as the absence of any or all of these social goods. Based on this understanding, the aim of the chapter is not to rescue or rehabilitate the non-critical account of development. Rather, it furthers the critique against one-size-fits-all approaches within development (of which the Hobbesian import is one amongst many) based on superficial understanding of societal trajectories, and which have been the hallmark of the development discourse since its emergence.

The Search for a Leviathan

Hobbes's theoretical formulation is one of legal-political philosophy's most recognised propositions. The starting point for Hobbes's discussion on sovereignty is the notion of equality – the equality in the power, ability and desire of each man to attain his ends (Tuck, 2015: 86–89). He wrote about the equality of fear, which compels the war of each man with every man, and about the fear of equality, which leads men to vainglory, diffidence and ultimately pride, which becomes the undoing of natural law. This equality also applies to men's desire to acquire wealth, attain power, accumulate resources, achieve fame, and preserve their families. Minor differences in mental or physical abilities between individuals conceded, he suggests that the strategies, tactics, and confederacies of men are enough to keep every individual on par with the other (Hobbes, 1909: 92). But in a world where each man has the same goals and abilities, there also exists the impossibility for all to attain or sustain their possessions.

It is inevitable in this formulation that the competition over resources, the fear of losing out and equality of ability to inflict harm leads to constant internecine conflict. In the absence of a central political authority – a 'common Power to keep them all in awe' – man's penchant for personal interest and private gain leads to perpetual conflict, a condition of war 'as if of every man, against every man' (Hobbes, 1909: 96). The dominant behavioural instinct that guides an individual in Hobbes's bleak world, apart from power and vainglory, is the desire for self-preservation. It is this most basic of interests, as the basis of other interests, which Hobbes considers one of the key laws of nature. But the life of the individual in this warlike scenario is devoid of all art or industry and said to be divested from collectivities and the important aspect of socialisation. What exists instead is 'continuall feare, and danger of violent death; and the life of man, solitary, poore, nasty, brutish, and short' (Hobbes, 1909: 99).

This pre-political state of nature – pre-political because there is no political society or sovereign authority assumed to exist prior to this situation of perpetual conflict; and state of nature, because it is said to exist a priori within nature – is not only full of violence but also devoid of any possibility of justice (Hobbes, 1909). With justice inextricably linked to law which in turn is an essential attribute of the sovereign, the absence of a sovereign and consequently of law means that the whole paradigm of justice and injustice falls away. However, for Hobbes, even during this state of conflict, there are certain laws of nature and inclinations that create the possibility for peace. The fear of death, a desire for peace and self-preservation, aided by reason which guides men to identify common grounds of agreement, provide a course for resolution. The individuals' realisation that the solution to their predicament lies in men's curbing of their own liberties and in making themselves subject to a higher authority, leads to the creation of a corporate being – 'that great Leviathan called a Common-Wealth, or State' (Hobbes, 1909: 132). Through this *pactum societatis*, or societal contract, individuals create an artificial political entity, vested with utmost power, which then becomes the ultimate arbiter of justice, power, and individual rights and the ultimate guarantor and provider of security.

Hobbes's framework is relevant to the argument of this chapter in two ways. First, as noted previously, is the idea of the lack – the absence of security, industry, peace, and progress – that is said to emerge due to the absence of a sovereign political authority. The second aspect, which is more intriguing and significant for our purposes, is that it is precisely this premise that is adopted by the development commentators and is found woven through the strands of the current development discourse. A look at the literature on development, sovereignty, and state fragility highlights that this link is not incidental, as commentators writing about different countries make specific references to the Hobbesian logic in their prognosis and prescriptions.

This Hobbesian terminology, for example, has been used to describe the situations in Bangladesh and the situation of 'millions in Eastern Ukraine, in Syria, in Iraq, in much of the Middle East' (Milam, 2015). Braithwaite and Wardak show how the international community's analysis and response to the crisis in Afghanistan in and around 2001 was largely based on a Hobbesian approach (Braithwaite and Wardak, 2013: 181). This notion has also been adopted to describe the conditions in Libya with regard to the post-2011 crisis (Tripathy, 2013), the conflict-ridden Democratic Republic of Congo (Autesserre, 2009), and even Western Europe, especially in terms of the emergence of the far right (Gray, 2015). The reach of the term is even more evident when we also include the states of 'Bosnia, Burundi, Liberia, Rwanda [and] Kosovo' (Avant, 2004), among many others. However, the problem here is not about making references to a seventeenth-century political theory but about the logic underlying and propagated by these perspectives.

Pakistan too is cited as a key example of a country caught within Hobbesian contradictions. Since its independence in 1947, successive political regimes have been caught within clientelism, parochial politics, ethnic struggles, insurgencies, religious militancy, socio-economic inequality, and democratic deficit. For the past four decades, it has spent almost half its life under military regimes, has been plundered by dynastic parties and corrupt elites and, despite being one of the world's most populated countries and its eighth nuclear power, has a damning record when it comes to human rights violations and lack of social development (see Jaffrelot, 2015). Some commentators have attributed this to the collapse of the social contract between the state and the citizen. I. A.

Rehman, one of the country's most notable civil society activists and until recently the head of the Human Rights Commission of Pakistan proclaimed that the 'indifference with which loss of life is treated in Pakistan suggests that it was for people like us that Hobbes wrote' his ideas on sovereignty (Rehman, 2012).

These linkages become more pronounced as we delve deeper into development literature. Leeson and Williamson, for instance, suggest rather definitively that 'nearly all social scientists have concurred with Hobbes's characterisation of anarchy and his prescription of government as the solution to the social dilemma' posed by insecurity and violence (Leeson and Williamson, 2009: 77). In the same vein, Sorensen argues that socio-economic impoverishment in a given country is a direct result of the 'Hobbesian' conditions resulting from a lack of security for all, which means that all economic and material development is ultimately dependent on the security situation of a country (Sorensen, 1996: 903–916). He suggests that an insecure society is not only unable to progress economically and materially but is also liable to lose all its material progress and resources because of the insecurity. We can also find this Hobbesian framing creeping into development projects and law and development initiatives. Borner and others, for instance, understand contract enforcement as akin to anarchy – 'violent, warlike and poor', giving rise to the supposed 'ideal state as the solution' (Borner et al., 1995: 23).

The Economist wrote in 1997 with regard to the World Bank's World Development Report that 'Hobbes, it appears, has found some improbable disciples at the World Bank' and that the report in question 'has one central point: that an effective state is essential for a prosperous economy' (*The Economist*, 1997). Robin Bunce in his masterful work on Hobbes writes about the continued relevance of Hobbes to the development discourse and suggests that the World Bank emphasises the case for a strong state as the main factor leading to development. He argues that this approach was 'explicitly linked to Hobbes in [a] 1999 paper, again for the World Bank, on Judicial Reform and Economic Development' (Bunce, 2009: 113).

Hobbes's analogy has also informed the work of economists working for the IMF, such as Raghuram Rajan, who was at one time IMF's Economic Counsellor and Director of IMF's Research Department and later became IMF's Chief Economist. It is indeed significant although perhaps not that surprising that a development policy influencer, such as Rajan, makes direct references to the Hobbesian analysis:

> And there is hope, supported by a growing body of research, that more students of development are realizing that a better starting point for analysis than a world with only minor blemishes may be a world where nothing is enforceable, property and individual rights are totally insecure, and the enforcement apparatus for every contract must be derived from first principles – as in the world that Hobbes so vividly depicted. Not only

> will this kind of work more closely approximate reality in the poorest, conflict-ridden countries, but it could also lead to more sensible policy.
>
> (Rajan, 2004: 57)

This statement is problematic not because of its references to the Hobbesian logic, but because it evidently suggests that the scholars of development should disregard historical, contextual, political and local factors and return to the supposedly pre-political state of nature in order to make sense of fragile and weak states, in order to create a more 'sensible policy'. Similarly, in a 2011 paper on failed states, Rajan advocated that in order for failed states to escape the state of nature, they require an economically empowered citizenry by the election of a central 'neutral and foreign power', outside the electorate, to provide stability (Rajan, 2011).

There are two aspects that we can infer from these examples. First, that the employment of Hobbes's analogy is not incidental to development discourse, but that there is evidence of it being invoked expressly in various discussions. This lens looks at developing countries and postcolonial societies – places which generally portray characteristics categorised as the state of nature in Hobbes – as pre-political and caught within a primitive state of nature. This is not far from the ideas of linear development, modernisation theories and other older and problematic assumptions which have been challenged at length by many development scholars (see, for instance, Escobar, 1997). The second aspect is that the Hobbes-development analogy treats violence or underdevelopment as resulting from the absence or weakness of the state and therefore traces the solution within the claim for a strong state. The Hobbesian logic adopted within development operates in three steps: one, the identification of a lack or a deficiency; second, the attribution of this lack to the absence of a political entity; and finally, the consequent proposition of the strong sovereign as a solution. It brings underdevelopment and violence and the sovereign together within one frame, without understanding the complexity of their links and without uncovering the theoretical assumptions behind these. It is to the state's role within this complex framework that we now turn.

Capturing the Leviathan

There are several notable critiques levelled against the Hobbesian proposition. That it is a work of fiction and a thought experiment with no relevance to reality is a criticism often forwarded within political literature. Another perspective suggests that it provides a justification for absolutist rule, where subjects do not hold any real power to challenge the governing structure (Ryan, 2016: 93). Important as these critiques are, they are not sufficient to dismiss the claims that connect Hobbes's approach to current debates on development. In order to understand the contradiction created by the import of a Hobbesian schema within development discourse, it is important to delve deeper into the interplay between violence, development, and sovereignty.

Fear of violence is the key factor that both constitutes and sustains sovereignty for Hobbes (Newey, 2014: 86–144). It is the fear of violence at the hand of another that compels one to seek peace through the construction of a sovereign power. At the same time, it is the fear of violent destruction by the sovereign that forces people to obey the rules of the sovereign and not harm other constituents and citizens. This two-step approach, that justifies the sovereign as a safeguard against civil conflict and legitimises the sovereign's ability to harness that same violence, is replicated within the development paradigm. If the idea that 'security derives from the state' (Sorensen, 1996: 903) is readily accepted as a starting position and that the main indicator of the success or stability of the state is the Weberian notion of its monopoly over legitimate violence (Anter, 2014), it then inevitably follows that the insecurity and violence present in certain societies necessarily implies the absence or fragility of state infrastructure. In this way, security becomes a 'precondition of development' (Sorensen, 1996: 903), while also being one of development's main goals. This is precisely why the Hobbesian logic is seen to apply to various political contexts such as Afghanistan, Congo, Balkans, Somalia, among many others – regions trapped in a cycle of violence and insecurity and consequently said to be unable to meet their socio-economic development needs.

The intricacy of the relationship between violence and underdevelopment, however, goes much deeper than security being a prerequisite for socio-economic development. That violence and insecurity lead to underdevelopment has been an insight widely accepted by development organisations. But the idea that underdevelopment itself is a form of violence has also come to the fore in the last few decades. This expands the notion of violence beyond physical and immediate harm that is generally included in our understanding of violence (Galtung, 1969). It expands to include structural causes connected with the creation or sustenance of conditions which harm the physical or mental well-being of individuals, especially those that belong to societies' margins. The idea of structural violence, then, transcends direct physical insecurity and focuses on 'social injustice' by problematising the structural causes and factors that contribute to insecurity, whether it is physical, mental, emotional, political, social or economic (Galtung, 1969: 171).

The notion of 'slow violence' is a further extension of the idea of structural violence. Although more generally applied to environmental concerns and climate justice, slow violence is a useful concept to understand the predicament of those who are gradually impoverished or brutalised by the lack of socio-economic opportunities and absence of political-cultural resources (Nixon, 2011). It highlights how violence creeps in on people by virtue of wealth inequality, environmental issues, and individuals' capabilities, among other things. The idea of slow violence, then, calls for a deeper understanding of the relationship between violence and development, and suggests that underdevelopment (as the absence of structural conditions to help people realise their potential) itself leads to or even counts as violence.

But while 'underdevelopment as violence' discourse allows us to look at violence as a broader social category than immediate and physical violence, it creates a logical contradiction for development discourse in its interplay with Hobbesian presuppositions. This is because even if Hobbesian logic about violence as the natural state of society in the absence of a dominant political authority is assumed as correct, the same cannot be said for underdevelopment as violence, or its manifestation as structural violence. Scholars have been arguing for many decades about the role that certain states have actively played in the creation or sustenance of insecurity (Pearce, 2010) or socio-economic divides within their own borders (Evans, 1989). While immediate or apparent violence may mask these factors, the concept of structural violence alerts us to the foundational, structural, and political (rather than the pre-political) causes behind this violent inequality. The role of the state within this sphere is marked not just by absence but especially by its presence within the domain in the construction of structural violence. Based on this, the expanded understanding of violence or the idea of underdevelopment as violence, should pave the way for an alternative form of questioning. It should compel us to question the role of the state in relation to the concepts of fragility, violence, and underdevelopment. What if we were to momentarily consider that, rather than an anomaly, the presence of violence, impoverishment, and human rights violations is connected to the political structure of particular states? What if we assume that certain states' inability to deal with these problems is a feature of the design rather than a flaw?

Some scholars have highlighted this conundrum within specific political and geographical contexts. For instance, Jenny Pearce's notion of 'perverse state formation' voices an important perspective in support of this idea. Through an insightful study of Latin American countries, Pearce argues against the commonly held view that these problems depict 'failed state[s] threatened by urban social violence' (Pearce, 2010: 286). She suggests on the contrary that in the Latin American scenario, the state has not sought to find solutions to violence or to monopolise it; rather the 'state gains huge political capital from its ongoing confrontations at the same time as it allies with pathological and corrupt violent actors outside the state in order to gain temporary victories' (Pearce, 2010: 299). Even if the state is not solely responsible for these confrontations and contradictions, it benefits from the consequences and plays a role in the 'multiplication of deadly personal interactions and private violence' (Pearce, 2010: 300).

Other similar voices warn us against considering the Leviathan as an unproblematic panacea for all (pre)political problems. Shaffer, for instance, considers violence as a specific product of the imposed order, rather than an absence of order as assumed by those applying the Hobbesian terminology to modern state and development debates (Shaffer, 1975). Ikelegbe critiques the over-reaching of the state in Nigeria – a 'ravaging leviathan' – by virtue of its entrapment within the ethnic and tribal politics (Ikelegbe, 2005). The Nigerian state, in his view, is not based on the premise of providing security and socio-economic protection to the people but rather feeds off them in order to further its own survival. Similarly, Braithwaite and Wardak, in their detailed study of the Afghan conflict, highlight the limitations of Hobbesian solutions in transitional countries and societies recovering from conflict (Braithwaite and Wardak, 2013; Wardak and Braithwaite, 2013).

Somalia is another key example of a postcolonial state caught in this cycle of violence, underdevelopment, clientelism, and parochial power politics. Emerging from decades of civil wars and unrest, the country is criticised as a 'failed state' or a 'collapsed state' on the one hand (Pham, 2013: 1), and praised through slogans of 'Somalia Rising' on the other (Hammond, 2013: 183). After unsuccessful experiments of dictatorship, socialism, de-colonisation, constitution-making, and dealing with a fragile democracy, and 'over a dozen unsuccessful attempts' at establishing and maintaining a unified state authority, Somalia's recent constitutional experiments have tried to use federalism as the solution to the problems of politics based on clan-linkages, traditions, religious struggles, and disparities in power and resources. But the clan, religion, and tradition-based identities and politics, which are rooted in Somali societal structures, have proven difficult to eradicate from the representative assembly. This problem is exacerbated when we look at the inequality of power, resources, and influence between different clans and different regions and its impact on constitutional negotiation and marginalisation of certain groups (Menkhaus, 2007: 360). The state is therefore unable to escape the political and socio-economic contradictions present in the society.

It is important to note that underdevelopment in such contexts – both as an act as well as a description – operates on local as well as transnational or supranational scales. For instance, consider a developing country caught in the midst of globalisation, neoliberal capitalism, and transnational corporations. Baxi and Grear suggest how a number of states attempt to negotiate their positions within the movement of global capital by becoming simultaneously hard and soft (Baxi, 2006: 249–250; Grear, 2010: 14). These states are hard with regard to border control and keeping dissent in check, but soft when it comes to re-distributive capacities, movement of capital, regulation of corporations, implementation of labour standards, and socio-economic welfare of the citizenry. If underdevelopment results from the exploitative and appropriating conditions at the structural level, then the violence that results from this cannot be said to exist because of the absence of a strong political authority. Here, in relation to global capital, the contradictory nature of the state vis-à-vis underdevelopment and violence is more apparent.

It is, therefore, suggested here that the violence, chaos, and underdevelopment that we witness in such conflict-ridden and impoverished countries cannot be readily attributed to *the state of nature* but are inevitably linked to *the nature of state*. When the identification of underdevelopment and conflict in societies is met with the assertion of a stronger state, there is an underlying assumption about starting from scratch – that either there was no effective state structure or that there was no strong state which could implement its writ on the society. On the other hand, if we suggest that the issue is not the presence or absence of the state but the specific structure of state institutions, it compels us to focus on the predatory nature of certain conflict-ridden, developing or postcolonial states.

It is this particular category of state that is here referred to as the Post-Hobbesian sovereign, in order to emphasise the differences between the generally recognised Hobbesian sovereign and the specific sovereign power that is solipsistic and self-serving. Hobbesian sovereignty is characterised by a strong sovereign – it is presented as a resolution to the problem of perpetual violence and the war of all against all; the Post-Hobbesian sovereign, in contrast, is characterised by a strong sovereign that gains legitimacy from the discourse of underdevelopment and insecurity resulting from it. The Post-Hobbesian sovereign is not there to resolve the contradictions that emerge from a conflict-prone society; rather, contrary to the logic of the development discourse, it is part of these very contradictions and often exacerbates them for its own survival and justification.

The use of 'post' here is not just a temporal marker to denote what comes after, but to differentiate this specific notion of sovereignty from the commonly recognised model of Hobbesian sovereignty. It refers to the type of sovereign authority that is partial, clientelist, caters to private interests, and divides the society along tribal, ethnic, religious, racial, patriarchal or socio-economic lines. From societies embroiled in civil wars and internecine conflicts, to those troubled by impoverishment and socio-economic crises, we see instances of this type of sovereignty across different continents. While Hobbesian sovereignty is justified through the lack of peace, the Post-Hobbesian sovereignty in its modern manifestations is justified as a mechanism to address underdevelopment and impoverishment. However, its aim is not to align the private interests of individuals with the public interests of society, but to exploit the socio-political contradictions for the benefit of the few. It is a state structured around uneven distribution of fear, violence, and impoverishment in society. Post-Hobbesian sovereignty, in this light, is caught within the nexus of clientelism, tribalism, parochial politics, and even global neoliberal capitalism.

Clientelism and private interests at the helm of the state mean that violence and fear (including underdevelopment, conflict, and power politics) impact some sections and people more than others (Pearce, 2010: 286). In Post-Hobbesian sovereign formations, the sovereign emerges when private and parochial interests align and attain power where they can acquire the mantle of the public good; in many postcolonial societies, still marked by coloniality and factionalism, the state or the sovereign or the polis precisely follows this trend. Tribalism, ethnic and religious alliances, claims of epistemic superiority, and parochial politics in the guise of statesmanship hide the fact that the state remains partial and aligned to private interests. And the presence, as well as the inequality, of this protracted violence is a key outcome of such partisan politics.

Post-Hobbesian sovereignty can therefore be known by a variety of different names – a cunning state (Randeria, 2003), a perverse state, or a predatory state (Evans, 1989) – all of these terminologies referring to the exploitative, partial, and parochial nature of this sovereign. This is different from the labels of fragile, failed, weak or collapsed states that focus on the (in)ability of the state to achieve certain ends, but do not problematise the reasons leading to the so-called state fragility. The category of Post-Hobbesian sovereignty is conceptualised to suggest that the problems of violence and underdevelopment are often a direct outcome of structural causes and calls into question the intentions behind the political framing and decision-making. The terminology of Post-Hobbesian sovereignty, more importantly, highlights the creation of the state of nature as a political exercise rather than a pre-political natural occurrence. The state of nature, in this manifestation, is not just about an all-out individualism and a war of all against all, but about the generation of fear of violence for the justification, creation or sustenance of parochial sovereign authority. This is done through amplification of ethnic or religious divides, artificial depletion or scarcity of resources, subjection of one section or the entire populace to violence, or ineffective handling of problems of security.

The Political Nature of the 'Pre-political' State of Nature

An important question then arises whether this category of Post-Hobbesian sovereignty can be located within Hobbes's own theoretical framework. Furthermore, is the application of Hobbesian logic completely inadequate to understand the current development discourse and therefore to be disregarded completely? It is granted that Hobbes's work, significant as it is, could not have foreseen the categories of fragile states, development, violence or colonialism as we understand them today. It was firmly rooted in violence which he regarded as pre-political. However, it is suggested here that the possibility of the capture of the Leviathan by a predatory state is present within Hobbesian theory itself, when we contrast the two types of sovereignty proposed by him. This is not meant to safeguard Hobbes's theory from possible critiques, but to alert development practitioners and commentators against uncritical application of Hobbesian logic to the theoretical and practical complexities of current situations.

Robert Fine suggests that the primary question for classical jurists, including Hobbes, was the analysis of the contradictions and regulation of private interests (Fine, 2002: 11). Private right was a revolutionary idea of equality of 'every man', which would emerge within Western philosophy only once the bonds of religion and of status quo linked to natural law and natural right began to fade after the Renaissance. But while this was prior to the emergence of Marxist analysis of the contradictions of private rights, the classical jurists were not uncritical of the problems that private rights and interests raised. They were aware of the 'dark side' of private gains, and the issues of individual 'egoism' and 'self-interest', along with their role in the emergence of violence (Fine, 2002: 12). But the central question that these accounts addressed was how to align the private rights of the individual with collective interests for the benefit of the public.

Conscious of the paradoxes of private right and arguing against the constructions of divine order that preceded it, classical jurisprudence focussed on the presence of an earthly authority – the sovereign. Sovereignty was the institution that would be able to resolve these contradictions and align the interests of the individual with the interests of the collective. For Hobbes, the Leviathan is an entity that emerges from the societal pact of individuals – it represents the will of the collective as well as public interest. The business of the state, as Hobbes suggested, is the safety of individuals – keeping order and providing force to keep the original covenant in place, to align the private interest with the common good and ensure that the pact is not revoked or broken – an exchange of protection and loyalty (Agamben, 2015). Peter Fitzpatrick writes that despite the claims of absolutism and positivism, Hobbesian sovereign was dutybound to ensure 'the well-being and improvement of the people' and could be 'utterly resisted' if it threatened the individual citizen's right to self-preservation and attain prosperity (Fitzpatrick, 2001: 94).

Hobbes took the idea of private interest, along with its associated egoism, self-interest, and violence to its logical breaking point. He conceptualised a society where individual interest became the ultimate rationale which would create perpetual conflict, constant fear, and never-ending violence. It should be acknowledged that, when superficially analysed, the problems of parochial politics, tribalism, self-interest, and consequent violence in certain postcolonial societies, such as Somalia and others described above, are not too dissimilar to this. The need for the state or the political entity arises because, when the pursuit of private rights becomes excessive, it endangers society and the wider humanity. But this is a line that the conventional approach to conflict, underdevelopment, and state failure fails to follow to its logical conclusion. If certain private interests become powerful enough to impinge on the private interests of others, if certain non-state actors gain enough strength so as to threaten others, or if the private interests impoverish others for the sake of their own enrichment, the sovereign *should* emerge as the key redressal mechanism. But if the sovereign is partaking in creating or sustaining this imbalance – as in the case of perverse, predatory or Post-Hobbesian sovereignty – or if inequality is embedded within the structure of state institutions, then mere strengthening of the central structures will not resolve these issues but further exacerbate the problems.

This insight can be read within the two categories of sovereign formulations that Hobbes conceptualised – sovereignty by institution, and sovereignty by acquisition (Tuck, 2015: 117–144). The more recognised and dominant accounts of Leviathan in our understanding refer to the instituted sovereignty where individuals enter into a societal contract to evade continuous war and the danger of destruction. Sovereignty by acquisition, on the other hand, is sovereignty by war and conquest – where the sovereign authority subdues all other actors. In this case, a sovereign power, already in existence, forces individuals to submit, with the threat of death for non-submission. For Hobbes, once the sovereign is instituted by either means, there is no distinction between sovereignty by acquisition or by institution. But there are crucial differences between the two categories, which commentators do not devote enough attention to. Sovereignty by covenant or contract assumes the existence of peace as a desirable common good. Private interest is thus to be sacrificed for the public good of many as well as the private good of each. It assumes a reconciliation of the contradiction between the competing public and private interests. But in contrast, sovereignty by acquisition is marked by a struggle for dominance within a geographical or political sphere, and the emerging state does not make any inherent claims about provision of peace as a public good (Ryan, 2016: 93).

Sovereignty by acquisition, as Hobbes explains in *De Corpore*, is the expansion of property and sovereignty by a master (Hobbes, 1994). And it is precisely this manifestation of sovereignty that resembles our conceptualisation of the Post-Hobbesian sovereign or the cunning, predatory or perverse state. The creation of the sovereign or the public revolves around the dialectic between two spheres: the subsuming of the oikos (biological sphere, the household or that which represents private interest) becomes the foundation of the polis or the sovereign authority (the collective or the sovereign, that refers to public interest). It is the dissolution of clan solidarities, family linkages, and parochial self-interests that gives rise to the political fraternity of the city (Agamben, 2015: 4–11). But the Post-Hobbesian sovereign, that emerges and operates through acquisition rather than constitution, is not focused on the dissolution of the private for the interest of the collective; rather, it represents the expansion of the private to the extent that it assumes the mantle of the public. Agamben suggests that stasis (civil war or violence) 'marks the threshold through which the unpolitical is politicised and the political is "economised"' (Agamben, 2015: 17). Violence, both physical and structural, is a necessary outcome as well as the means by which the political is captured and the private is publicised.

Regardless of the reasons why this insight is not elaborated on within Hobbes's own work, the problem here is that this blind spot is replicated within development discourse. Although both sovereignty by constitution and sovereignty by acquisition may operate in the same manner, the key difference lies in terms of their logic and it is the latter that provides us with the theoretical roots for a Post-Hobbesian sovereign. The main logic of this sovereign is not to bring peace to an otherwise violent world by assuming all conflict unto itself; rather, it is to appropriate this violence in the service of whatever interests that it holds dear. Many colonial and postcolonial states, at least conceptually, exemplify this phenomenon – they were formulated through war, genocide, and annihilation of local cultures and, in moving towards the postcolonial situation, they wielded their place and power to an entity that took over this space without changing its politics (Saeed, 2018). With sovereignty itself an artifice, sovereignty by acquisition creates an artificial state of nature by offering individuals a choice between submission and sovereign violence, and consequently justifies itself through the imposition of violence. This violence is decidedly political, for the sovereign already exists at the juncture where the choice between destruction and submission is offered to the individual. And this cycle of violence-submission-justification continues unchallenged and unproblematised for many political orders.

Conclusion

The solution to a problem cannot escape the confines put in place by the identification and framing of that problem. Unfortunately, this is the situation within orthodox global political discourse with regard to problems of extremism, state fragility, insurgencies, democratic deficit, and legitimacy crises faced by states across all continents and socio-political contexts. The solution generally proposed for most of these issues is strikingly similar – the strengthening of the state and the creation of a Leviathanesque political structure. It is as if the coming of the Leviathan will resolve every problem that we locally and globally face, from persistent violence to underdevelopment. The uncritical acceptance of this reasoning is what this chapter has striven to challenge.

I have argued that the problems of impoverishment and violence, which we normally attribute to the state of nature, are actually products of the political structures present in postcolonial contexts. Hence, the solution that entails a move towards a stronger state is paradoxical and a false remedy. What we see in the contexts of many conflict-ridden, underdeveloped, and democratically deficient states is not just the failure of the states but an expansion of private interests in the guise of public interest. The violence and clientelism that we see within Post-Hobbesian sovereign situations means that this kind of sovereignty is always partial towards some sections and some individuals compared to the entire population. I have also suggested that the Post-Hobbesian sovereignty can also be examined as akin to sovereignty by acquisition within Hobbes's own framework. Although for Hobbes there is no difference between his two variants of sovereignty, the gap between the two categories comes to light when we analyse sovereignty by acquisition from the lens of the Post-Hobbesian conflict-ridden state and as constitutive of the state of nature. The Leviathan that emerges through acquisition, or the imposition of the state of nature, is not inherently premised on any notion of the common good (peace, security or order), but takes private interest (expansion or survival) to the point where it can be imposed as a public good.

Three main corollaries of this argument need emphasis. First, the category of Post-Hobbesian sovereign is not something reserved for postcolonial or developing states, although they are more likely to reflect this category due to the greater likelihood of their capture or the problematic histories of their formulation. Predatory states or states that are prone to be hijacked by private interests, many of which are also present within the western or northern hemisphere, may also fall into this category. Second, the critique offered in this chapter has not been put forward with the intent of dismissing the public or weakening the idea of the state altogether, a perspective that may be favoured by some neoliberal economic commentators. On the contrary, it is a call for the politicisation and democratisation of the public, rather than mere strengthening of the enforcement or regulatory capacities of the state which can exacerbate the contradictions already present within the system.

Finally, the more significant problem is the uncritical adoption of the Hobbesian paradigm by social and political commentators to identify, interpret, and resolve issues of governance. I have sought to suggest that the Hobbesian logic and its application to development discourse becomes more problematic than the problem it tries to resolve. If impoverishment, underdevelopment, and violence are key tactical components of the formation and continuation of certain categories of the state, that means that a strengthening of the sovereign for its own sake is also an exacerbation of the contradictions it is trapped in and the fissures it generates. A solution for physical or structural violence perpetrated by Post-Hobbesian sovereignty, then, does not lie in the creation of yet another political authority or in the strengthening of predatory states. The creation of legitimate political authorities might go some way to resolve the situation – but taking the lead from the Hobbesian paradigm, a legitimate sovereign cannot be imposed from the outside and has to emerge from within the constituents. Therefore, the main task for the development practitioners and scholars who uncritically adopt the Hobbesian framework is to recognise that an unreflective assertion of the conventional paradigm may actually be contributing to the detriment of the societies that they are allegedly trying to assist.

References

Agamben, G., 2015. *Stasis: Civil War as a Political Paradigm*. Stanford University Press.

Anter, A., 2014. *Max Weber's Theory of the Modern State: Origins, Structure and Significanc*. Palgrave MacMillan.

Autesserre, S., 2009. Hobbes and the Congo: Frames, Local Violence, and International Intervention. *International Organization* 63, 249–280.

Avant, D., 2004. Conserving Nature in the State of Nature: The Politics of INGO Policy Implementation. *Review of International Studies* 30, 361–382.

Baxi, U., 2006. *The Future of Human Rights*. Oxford University Press.

Borner, S., Weder, B. and Brunetti, A., 1995. *Political Credibility and Economic Development*. St Martin's Press.

Braithwaite, J. and Wardak, A. 2013. Crime and War in Afghanistan Part I: The Hobbesian Solution. *British Journal of Criminology* 53, 179–196.

Broome, A. and Quirk, J., 2015. Governing the World at a Distance: The Practice of Global Benchmarking. *Review of International Studies* 41, 819–841.

Bueno de Mesquita, B., Smith, A., Siverson, R., et al. (2003) *The Logic of Political Survival*. MIT Press.

Bunce, RER., 2009. *Thomas Hobbes*. Continuum.

Davis, K.E., Kingsbury, B., and Merry, S.E., 2015. The Local-Global Life of Indicators: Law, Power, and Resistance. In Merry, S.E., David, K.E., and Kingsbury, B. (eds), *The Quiet Power of Indicators: Measuring Governance, Corruption and the Rule of Law*. Cambridge University Press, pp. 1–24.

Escobar, A., 1997. The Making and Unmaking of the Third World through Development. In Rahnema, M., and Bawtree, V. (eds), *The Post-Development Reader*. Zed Books.
Evans, P.B., 1989. Predatory, Developmental, and Other Apparatuses: A Comparative Political Economy Perspective on the Third World State. *Sociological Forum* 4, 561–587.
Fine, R., 2002. *Democracy and the Rule of law: Marx's Critique of the Legal Form*. Blackburn Press.
Fitzpatrick, P., 2001. *Modernism and the Grounds of Law*. Cambridge University Press.
Galtung, J., 1969. Violence, Peace, and Peace Research. *Journal of Peace Research* 6, 167–191.
Gray, J., 2015. Islamist Terror, Security and the Hobbesian Question of Order. *New Statesman*. 144 (5290), 26–31.
Grear, A., 2010. *Redirecting Human Rights: Facing the Challenge of Corporate Legal Humanity*. Palgrave Macmillan.
Hammond, L., 2013. Somalia Rising: Things Are Starting to Change for the World's Longest Failed State. *Journal of East African Studies* 7, 183.
Hobbes, T., 1909. *Hobbes's Leviathan, Reprinted from the edition of 1651 (With an essay by the late W. G. Pogson Smith)*. Clarendon Press.
Hobbes, T., 1994. De Corpore Politico. In Gaskin, J.C. (ed.), *The Elements of Law, Natural and Politic: Human Nature and de Corpore Politico with Three Lives*. Oxford University Press.
Ikelegbe, A., 2005. The Construction of a Leviathan: State Building, Identity Formation and Political Stability in Nigeria. In Fawole, W.A., and Ukeje, C. (eds), *The Crisis of the State and Regionalism in West Africa: Identity, Citizenship and Conflict*. Council for the Development of Social Science Research in Africa (Codesria).
Iqbal, Z., and Starr, H., 2016*State Failure in the Modern World*,. Stanford University Press.
Jaffrelot, C., 2015. *The Pakistan Paradox: Instability and Resilience*. Random House India.
Leeson, P.T., and Williamson, C.R., 2009. Anarchy and Development: An Application of the Theory of Second Best. *The Law and Development Review* 2, 77–96.
Menkhaus, K., 2007. The Crisis in Somalia: Tragedy in Five Acts. *African Affairs* 106, 360.
Milam, W., 2015. A Paper Leviathan. *The Friday Times*. Available online at: http://www.thefridaytimes.com/tft/a-paper-leviathan/ (accessed 20 March 2020).
Newey, G., 2014. *The Routledge Guidebook to Hobbes' Leviathan*. Routledge.
Nixon, R., 2011. *Slow Violence and the Environmentalism of the Poor*. Harvard University Press.
Paliwala, A. and Kamchedzera, G., 2013. Justice Indicatorology: A New Theatre for Justice? *Law, Social Justice & Global Development*, 2013. Available online at: https://warwick.ac.uk/fac/soc/law/elj/lgd/2013_2/paliwala_kamchedzera/ (accessed 30 November 2019).
Pearce, J., 2010. Perverse State Formation and Securitized Democracy in Latin America. *Democratization* 17, 286–306.
Pham, J.P., 2013. *State Collapse, Insurgency, and Counterinsurgency: Lessons from Somalia. Report for US Army War College*. US Army War College Press.
Rajan, R., 2004. Assume Anarchy? Why an Orthodox Economic Model May Not Be the Best Guide for Policy. *Finance and Development*, 44 (3), 56–57.
Rajan, R.G., 2011. Failed States, Vicious Cycles, and a Proposal. 2 March. Center for Global Development Working Paper.
Randeria, S., 2003. Cunning States and Unaccountable International Institutions: Legal Plurality, Social Movements and Rights of Local Communities to Common Property Resources. *European Journal of Sociology / Archives Européennes de Sociologie / Europäisches Archiv für Soziologie* 44, 27–60.

Rehman, IA., 2012. A Dehumanised Horde. *Dawn*. Available at: http://www.dawn.com/news/713520/a-dehumanised-horde (accessed 20 March 2020).

Rist, G., 2014. *The History of Development: From Western Origins to Global Faith*. Zed Books.

Rothstein, B., 2007. The Quality of Government Institute at Goteborg University. *Statsvetenskaplig Tidskrift* 109.

Ryan, A., 2016. *On Hobbes: Escaping the War of All Against All*. Liveright.

Saeed, R., 2018. Law and Coloniality of Empire: Colonial Encounter and Normative Orderings in the Indian Sub-Continent. *Yearbook of Islamic and Middle Eastern Law* 19, 103–133.

Saeed, R., 2020. The Ubiquity of State Fragility: Fault lines in the conceptualisation and categorisation of Failed and Fragile States. *Social & Legal Studies* 29 (6), 767–789..

Shaffer, BD., 1975. Violence as a Product of Imposed Order. *University of Miami Law Review* 29, 732–763.

Sorensen, G., 1996. Development as a Hobbesian dilemma. *Third World Quarterly* 17, 903–916.

The Economist. 1997. It's the government, stupid. *The Economist*, 28 July, 113–114.

Tripathy, D., 2013. Back to the State of Nature. *Aljazeera*. Available online at: http://www.aljazeera.com/indepth/opinion/2013/10/back-state-nature-201310168252312131.html (accessed 25 March 2020).

Tuck, R., 2015. *Thomas Hobbes: Leviathan*. Cambridge University Press.

Veitch, S., Christodoulidis, E.A. and Farmer, L., 2019. *Jurisprudence: Themes and Concepts*. Routledge.

Wardak, A., and Braithwaite, J., 2013. Crime and War in Afghanistan: Part II: A Jeffersonian Alternative? *The British Journal of Criminology* 53, 197–214.

Chapter 3

Returning the *Anti-Colonial* to Philosophy

Jayan Nayar

The Problem of the (Post)Colonial Present

Once upon a not so distant past, much of the human population rose in celebration with utterances, in so many midnight hours, of 'Freedom', of 'Independence', of 'Sovereignty'.[1] Thus was proclaimed: out of colonialism, 'decolonisation'; out of rightslessness, equality; out of silence, a defining voice; indeed, out of wretchedness, as Franz Fanon (2001: 252) affirmed (in hope), a 'whole man'.

Today, we commonly speak of decolonisation in terms of betrayals (Davidson, 1992; Chatterjee, 1993; Ayittey, 1994; Mamdani, 1996; Mbembe, 2001; Memmi, 2006; Ndlovu-Gatsheni, 2013), and of the 'Third World', once a symbol of the dream of a post-colonial new humanity, as jaded if not defeated (Escobar, 1995; 2004; Berger, 1994). Notwithstanding the many repeated promises of development and human rights, growth and democracy, through the many vision statements, 5-year development plans and policy prescriptions, much of what was promised as liberation through decolonisation never came to pass. For most, decolonisation remains defined by the interconnected national realities of inflicted impoverishment and international enforcement of the underlying structural injustices of the global political, legal, economic and knowledge systems. The 'post-colonial' experience, as a global systemic actuality, has been one where national elites continue to collude with transnational capital to facilitate and manage the processes of dispossession and accumulation for private profit; the 'comprador' phase of the 'Second Scramble for Africa' as Issa Shivji (2006) calls it. This is far from the exaltations of new beginnings portended by the flag, the anthem and the constitutional document that marked the birth of the

1 In this essay the many terms that are part of the normalised lexicon of political-legal discourse are explicitly refused a givenness of meaning and application, instead their apparent givenness itself, and the implications that flow from such normalisations of categories, will be the subject of our attention. To avoid the clumsiness of repeating the use of quote marks to demonstrate this questioning, I will simply do so for its first usage, assuming that the reader will understand that any subsequent use is not intended to suggest an acceptance of their meanings. Occasionally, where a word such as World is used in a special sense it is capitalised to differentiate it from a more general meaning.

DOI: 10.4324/9780203745298-5

'post-colonial' into the global imaginary, so distant from the portent of the new heralded by those many midnight hours. The harsh truth is this: the post-colonial world remains, as Fanon (2001: 29) so evocatively described, 'cut in two': ostentatious privilege and abject suffering is the abiding situation. Once, the post-colonial imagination of 'development' promised the 'new humanity' of decolonisation.[2] Now the question that confronts us is this: how to think past/beyond the post-colonial when it is the post-colonial actuality that perpetuates and enforces the continuities of violence and dispossession, still the 'Black Man's burden' (Davidson, 1992)?[3] Which brings us to the here and now, to our collective labours to 'think resistance' (again), as this volume of essays invites us to do, 'beyond law and development'.

I begin with the following observations:

1 Notwithstanding the countless exposés of the problems of development, and the many post/decolonial repudiations of its colonial antecedents, phenomenological consequences and its associated colonial-modern epistemologies, the violence of law and development continues apace, the

2 There is abundant critical literature on the violence of development that ranges from the early days of the critique of economic growth, to subsequent critiques of the many adjectives attached to development reconceptualised – sustainable development, social development, human development etc. – to more recent critiques which question its very Eurocentric ontological and epistemological foundations; for a broad flavour of such critiques, see (Sachs, 1992; Escobar, 1995; Rahnema and Bawtree, 1997; Petras and Veltmeyer, 2007; Krishna, 2008; Adelman and Paliwala, 2021).

3 Indeed the 'post-colonial' has been an enduring problem for us thinkers of the South; post-colonial theory, decolonial theory, Third World Approaches to International Law (TWAIL), are all responses to this underlying problematic. As an illustration of approaches and concerns, these in their different ways have sought to correct the colonial legacy in the post-colonial situation: by revealing the continuing matrices of the coloniality of power/being/knowledge (Quijano, 2000; Mignolo, 2000; Wynter, 2003; Maldonado-Torres, 2004; Lugones, 2010); by excavating silenced epistemologies and philosophies (Santos, 2014; Connell, 2007; Gordon, 2000; Dabashi 2015); by thinking 'liberation/freedom', from 'exteriority', as 'excess' (Dussel, 2003; Neocosmos, 2016); by reinserting the continuities of colonialism into the normalising narratives of international law (Anghie, 2005; Rajagopal, 2008); by excavating voices and phenomenologies of being invisibilised by (post)colonial erasure (Spivak, 1988; Lugones, 2010; Anzaldua, 1987) etc. This rich and varied literature has no doubt contributed much to unworking the assumptions and normalities of Eurocentric claims to epistemological primacy, universality, objectivity, and in exposing the various undersides – philosophical and experiential – of colonial-modernity, thereby affirming critically a pluriverse of Beingness otherwise than 'White'. But for all this, for all the critical insights, exposés and corrections, for all the repudiations of colonial-modernity, for all the knowledge we have gained through these postcolonial/decolonial intellectual labours, we remain firmly entrenched in the ever tightening hold of a colonial-modern rationality of neo-liberal global capitalism as it continues to lay waste to our social and natural worlds. Global coloniality, it would appear, sits comfortably with post/decolonial critique. A different orientation of thought is necessary and urgent.

civilisational-developmental rationality remains the entrenched shared language of post-colonial ultra-nationalists and their neoliberal globalist allies alike.

2 Notwithstanding the totalising claims of (post-colonial) developmental rationalities and their consequent violence, communities of struggle persist in resisting the destruction of their life-worlds and in regenerating their socialities of the 'commons' (Esteva and Prakash, 1998; Figlan et al., 2009; Zibechi, 2012; Esteva et al., 2013).

How might we read these signs? The first points to the continuing colonial inheritance of the post-colonial 'inter-national' settlement, and of the subsumption of the post-colonial state into the structures and processes of the globalised order of predatory neoliberal capitalism. The second, that indeed, the 'poor' do think and act (Guha, 1988; Figlan et al., 2009; Neocosmos, 2016), even if they – in accordance to the grammars and speech-rules of colonial-modern languages, cannot 'speak' (Spivak, 1988). Critical here is the actuality that, attempts towards the enforced totalisation of (capitalist, neoliberal) developmental rationalities notwithstanding, on-going everyday struggles that refuse obedience to the closures of the present persist across the world. It is precisely to this *encounter* between the assertion of closure and the disobedience of repudiation that my chapter is directed.

Underpinning my arguments is a view of thinking – of the doing of philosophy – as a praxis of *anti-colonial encounter.* Through this perspective of encounter we bring to view the opposition between the two locations of being-thinking corresponding to the two actualities described above: (1) the *(post)colonial* location from which are (re)presented and enforced *(b)orders of subjectification;*[4] (2) the *anti-colonial* locations from which are confronted *frontlines of desubjectification.*

Such a counterposing of the (post)colonial *border* and the anti-colonial *frontline* serves to demarcate the (post)colonial and anti-colonial as incommensurable philosophical orientations as they stand in enunciative and interpretive confrontation; the function of the 'post-colonial' as a discursive category is to normalise the (b) orders of contemporary global coloniality. As such, to think from anti-colonial frontlines is to repudiate the assumptions of authority inherent in colonial philosophies that continue to organise and narrate the post-colonial World as a (b) ordered totality. From this re-appropriation of philosophical authority, we might affirm the many insurgent struggles for the material transformation of worlds as continuing the legacy of anti-colonial hope and imagination – to 'be-otherwise' – in the face of (post)colonial closure.

4 The notion of the (post)colonial as distinct from the asserted 'post-colonial' is central to my argument. The (post)colonial signals a shift in orientation that departs from the assumption of an ontological rupture marked by the 'Declaration of Independence' which defines conventional understandings of political-legal onto-epistemology. I provide a fuller explanation of this point below.

On Encounters, Borders and Frontlines.

A long time ago was invented the notion of 'discovery'. The so-called *conquistadors* 'discovered' the 'Americas' and named her inhabitants 'Indios'. Thus begins the story of the 'World' in 'History' (Mignolo, 2000; Chakrabarty, 2000; Nandy, 1995), universalised by colonial philosophies of (b)ordering as an artefact of coloniality. (B)ordering is:

> a system of inscriptions and emplacements which define the structures that regulate and enforce 'Human'-beingness-in-the-world. (B)ordering in this sense is the combined operation of both discursive disciplines (the invention/discoveries of categorical names, 'theories' of associational meanings, vocabularies of (un)belonging and government, etc.) and physical practices (the erection and policing of borders/fences/walls, etc.) that configure the World as known and understood as being.
>
> (Nayar, 2019: 271)

We know this story well, and it has oft been told. For our purposes, it is critical to remember that the philosophical invention of discovery was an act of naming and rationalising an *encounter*. The assertion of discovery inscribed name and meaning upon a place encapsulated – the New World – and a population defined – Indios. Thus was inscribed 'nothingness' upon the being of the 'discovered', a Non-Being now created by the philosopher's name, (b)ordered and *made-subject* to a rationalisation of difference as heathens/children of God, savage/infantile, inside/outside, included/excluded, belonging/non-belonging. And along with these names of differentiated subject-beingness were constructed and enforced structures of physical delineations of differentiation – fences, cages, churches, schools, territories – which situated the Other-ed within regimes of subjugation-subjection. All this, it is clear to see, was 'thought' from the location of the discoverers. And from these (philosophical) beginnings all else follows.

The colonial-modern imaginaries of the 'Human', 'sovereignty', 'State', 'subjectivity', 'political-belonging', are all words born out of this original, authorial discovery. They are also names that (b)order and enforce the World, now normalised and universalised as the foundational categories of post-colonial political-legal philosophy, and the institutionalised structures of rationalised and enforced governmentality. But here is the thing: none of the aforementioned names pertain to any inherent, intrinsic or interminable truth as such; they are but philosophical inventions that ascribe meaning-to-the-world that are sought to be naturalised through assertions of universality and eternality. They are, simply put, names invented by the discoverers enforced as (b)orders of coloniality upon the bodies and territories of the conquered, the contained, made-subject (Nayar, 2014). This is precisely the work of colonial philosophies to do, as in the colonial past, so in the post-colonial present, to colonise the thinking-beingness of the conquered,[5] to name 'subjects', to define the universal terms of 'civilisation' and 'Humanity', to set the possibilities and limits of critical imagination and action under the orders of 'legality', in short, to prescribe and enforce (post)colonial borders. Against such normalised (b)orders of making-subject persist *anti-colonial* philosophies of *desubjectification*.

Anti-colonial philosophies, in my use of the term, are articulations of a confrontation which opens to incommensurability the rationalisations of colonial philosophies which define and emplace subject-ed beingness, on the one hand, and the rejections of communities of resistance and recovery on the other; it is the praxes of *thinking-being-otherwise*. From the very origins of namings which rationalised and enforced racial slavery and colonial subjugation have such anti-colonial refusals persisted, the 'maroon thinking' of rebellious slaves in their liberated territories (Walsh, 2012) being early assertions of what I term 'desubjectification': the refusal to *be* as inscribed by the *names* and ascribed into the *places* assigned by (post)colonial rationalisations of beingness. Resistance to being-made-subject, in this sense is a pervasive presence that ruptures the assertions of totality that inhere in dominant political-legal re-presentations of (un)belonging;[6] thus we might understand, in recent experience, the powerful

5 I make a distinction here between conquest-colonialism and colonisation. Colonialism is a political-legal order. It is the structural normalisation and bureaucratisation of regimes of conquests and appropriations; it is a regime therefore that *subjugates* the encountered 'other' and makes the other subject *to* government. Colonisation, on the other hand, is the closure of the meaning-of-being within a bounded Totality. It involves the transmogrification of (already-)being – through the philosophical negation and material subjugation of the encountered Other-ed as Non-Being (without name, meaning, cosmologies, pasts) – into a subject-being of colonial (b)ordering; it is a process therefore that *subjectifies* the encountered 'Other-ed' and makes the other a subject *of* a totalised order of governmentality. We see colonisation at work in this regard in the phenomenological accounts that have come to serve as central to much of contemporary 'postcolonial' and 'decolonial' thinking: this is the (non-)being that Fanon spoke of as the 'Negro' in his *Black Skins and White Masks* (Fanon, 1986), that Memmi (2006) described as the 'colonised' in the *Colonizer and the Colonized*, that Biko referred to as the 'Black Man' (Biko, 1978: 28–32), for example. For my purposes what is critical is the disconnection, as a matter of assumption, that the conquered-within-colonialism were indeed 'colonised'. My argument relies on the counter-position that colonialism notwithstanding, the majority of the globally subjugated – as subjects of colonialism – remained *uncolonised*.

6 And so, we might read Douglass's (1852) repudiation of the call to liberty attached to the US celebrations of the 4th of July ('This 4th of July is yours, not mine. You may rejoice, I must mourn.'), Gandhi's (1938) proclamation of *Swaraj* that denies the coloniser's claim to legitimate subjection; Fanon's (1986) account 'concerning violence' on the transformation of the 'native' in overturning the coloniser's world; Biko's (1978) affirmation of 'Black Consciousness' as a reclaiming of thought and being from White denials and subordination; Freire's (1974) intent of 'conscientisation' as a pedagogy of refusal to abide by the namings and emplacements of extant regimes of oppression; Anzaldua's (1987) rebellious courage of being 'mestiza' in the 'borderlands', amongst many others.

political reverberations of the Zapatistas' 'Ya Basta' and their subsequent regeneration of their life-worlds through the maxim 'to govern by obeying' – a 'theoretical revolution' as Walter Mignolo (2002) called it – and in South Africa, of the defiant affirmations of the 'living politics' of the *Abahlali base-Mjondolo* (*AbM*) shack-dwellers movement (Figlan et al., 2009), as examples also of this same collective refusal to *be-subject*.

Against the many contexts of oppression, therefore, anti-colonial philosophies serve to overturn the assumptions of the fixity of the enforced 'post-colonial' present as (b)ordered by the extant colonial-modern political-legal categories. Specifically, they (1) deny the totalising claims of the (post)colonial inscriptions of subject-names and meanings of human being-ness, (2) repudiate the enclosures of political-legal (b)orders of rule and obedience, belonging and unbelonging, and crucially (3) name the 'encounter' from the locations of communities of refusal that stand against the assertions of colonising power. If colonial-modern philosophies invented 'nothingness', 'inexistence', or 'Non-Being', as categories of negation in defining the encountered Other-ed, anti-colonial philosophies begin with affirmations of beingness, with their memories and their imaginations.[7] Those subjugated to conquest and colonialism, and attempted to be made-subject to (post)colonial rationalisations of negations and differentiation, therefore, appear in that encounter already with name, meaning, cosmologies, pasts, consciousness, voice; they do not 'become' into some idealised space of 'the political' as Vivienne Jabri (2012) understands it, but rather recover their Beingness within their own totalities of meaning (Nayar, 2013) to assert their authority of thinking being-otherwise as non-subjects to extant orders of dispossession.[8]

I intentionally stress the *anti*-colonial quality of the philosophical encounter. I do this to emphasise the contingent and contextual nature of all thinking, as well as the incompleteness, and unknowability – in the abstract, out of time and place – of the substantive actualities of being-otherwise that rely upon located experience and experimentation, not professionalised intellectual presumptions. The anti-colonial perspective therefore asks the questions that de-normalise the colonial assertion even as it does not promise ready answers to questions of the

7 For an interesting comparison between modern-'technological' and 'native' (American) cosmologies in this connection, see Mander (1991: 21–19). Also generally, Anzaldua, 1987; Kohn, 2013; Vaughan, 2007.

8 In this connection I want to make a further distinction between what I understand as *ontological philosophies of (Already-)Being* and *praxiological philosophies of Being (-Otherwise)*. By the former I mean affirmations of human-beingness that are derived from cosmologies other to the defining constructions of colonial-modernity: *ubuntu, buen vivir, dharma, the dreamtime*, for example (and I concede my ignorance on these and countless others). These are the 'pluriversal' onto-epistemologies that make-up the uncountable presence of beingness-as-human in the world. I have no ability to speak of these wisdoms; I stress simply that these presences abound and persist uncolonised even if conquered. What is important to me however is that the recognition of such cosmological pluriversality serves as a point of departure for the subsequent encounter with colonial philosophies.

future. As an example, the Zapatistas state it simply as 'asking we walk'. This encapsulates best the *anti*-colonial orientation as struggle to recover life-spaces and re-make social relations from (post)colonial negation and appropriation (Zibechi, 2012: 127–158). Thus are imagined and created different possible journeys and worlds, with different regimes of names and meanings, to stand against colonial philosophies that seek universality, dominance and fixity. It is useful in this connection to contrast the *frontline* perspective advanced here with the 'border-thinking' of 'decolonial' theory.

Mignolo and Tlostanova (2006: 206) define 'border thinking' as 'the epistemology of the exteriority; that is, of the outside created from the inside'. But the 'border' in this sense is already a discursive and material artefact of colonial philosophies, it is already a categorical inscription upon the world, making sense in the world only because of the colonial ascriptions of naming and fixing, demarcation and differentiation, acknowledgements and repudiations, permissions and prohibitions. The border thus is a technology of subjectification. It is inherently 'conservative', its intent to contain and manage the regime of meanings which enforce the differentiated conditions and possibilities of subject-beingness as a statement of the present, fixed and final. To border-think, therefore, is to already think as 'subject-ed' upon the demand at the border: 'Who goes there? Name thyself!', with the appropriate response for re-cognition. Despite Mignolo's (2007: 459) rightful intention to 'de-link' – to change not simply the content of the 'conversation' but its terms – the 'border' remains foundationally the term upon which the conversation is deemed possible, permissible, towards translation, commensurability, accommodation. As such are epistemological variances permitted to add adjectives of 'alterity' to the categories of the normal, to exoticise extant categories of bordered-Beingness: 'indigenous rights' being a much-negotiated example. As such also are we, as 'border-thinkers', invited to-Be commensurate, comprehensible, polite and civilised, towards accommodation and recognition, to pursue epistemic projects that celebrate pluriversality within (b)ordered regimes and institutions of knowledge production and distributions, rewards and censure. Whilst 'conversation' is permitted, therefore, the border – as the foundational 'term' on which the encounter is defined – remains secure as a marker on the world.

The *frontline* opens a different conversation. *Frontlines* are sites, both philosophical and material, of audacious and insurgent repudiation of the assertions and assumptions of (b)orders. The anti-colonial frontline – a question opened up by an assertion of encounter – marks a refusal; it is an enactment of de-naming the border, of refusing totalising orders of subject-beingness and emplacements. It is a praxiological space of desubjectification; it is disruptive in intent and rebellious in imagination. The de-naming of borders enables us to open up the closure of the post-colonial settlement to continuing anti-colonial interrogations. And so we come to the crux of the matter. How might we begin to rupture the fixed and enclosed (b)orders of the (post)colonial through an anti-colonial praxis of frontlines?

On the *Post-Colonial* and the *International* in the *Global*

The names that are inscribed upon the world, of peoples and of geographical places, the meanings and imaginations attached to them, the hopes and possibilities that emanate and flow from them, none of these are fixed, none of these can be conquered and trapped within a totality of names, meanings and imaginations, yet, they are the very philosophical ground from which the material regimes of (b)orders of the post-colonial world are constructed. And it is precisely the enforcement of these 'political-legal' categories of (b)ordering and subjectification – state (sovereignty), territorial borders, citizenship (and all other categories of '(un-)belonging'), 'democracy' and constructs of 'representative' authority – that we confront when we assert an imagination of 'Another World' to be possible. More than an epistemological question, this is a material concern that defines the conditions of subject-beingness in the world and the factual borders that police and enforce them. Underpinning this (b)ordering is the asserted philosophical situation of the 'post-colonial' in the 'international'. Understood in its entirety the first challenge for an anti-colonial philosophy is precisely, therefore, to repudiate the fixity of the 'post-colonial' in the 'International'.

This we know: the post-colonial stands implicated within an international that remains constituted by colonial-imperial logics of differentiation, inequalities and subordination (Krishna, 2008; Ndlovu-Gatsheni, 2013; Jabri, 2012). The implications of this realisation however are less certain and much contested: ranging from the repudiations of the national project (Esteva et al., 2013; Chatterjee, 1993; Mbembe, 2001), to affirmations of a liberatory nationalism rescued from the 'disavowals' of *post-modern-postcolonial* and *post-structuralist* critiques (Lazarus, 1999; Zeleza, 2003), to assertions of a need to revive and renew 'insurrectionary' transnational political imaginations of the post-colonial, such as that of Pan-Africanism (Shivji, 2006). As I read it, what is apparent in much of the scholarly preoccupation with the (post-colonial) state is that, although diverse in their prescriptions for possible futures, they retain essentially the givenness of the architecture of the *international* as the point of reference for *post-colonial* imaginations. The post-colony in other words is defined *vis à vis* the international, its coming into being heralded by the declaration of independence as the instantiation of decolonisation (Jabri, 2012: 84–85). The international is thereby assumed to be an *external* inter-state organisational structure of global (b)ordering. From this moment are the state and the international, as distinct spheres of governance, understood to be in conflictual co-constitutive tension, the post-colonial aim being to transform the contours of the international through reformulation of underlying principles and laws of international relations.[9] However a curious circularity of analysis and argument

9 This we understand as the past and present of the TWAIL project; see for example Anghie and Chimni (2003); Anghie (2006). For a more historical perspective on the Third World imagination of international law and its contemporary implications, see Baxi (2006).

surrounds a seemingly inescapable fate: the post-colonial condition of the international is intrinsically and structurally subject to coloniality; for those inclined to postmodern/post-structuralist/postcolonial readings this recognition serves to disavow the dream of decolonisation; for others such structural implicatedness serves as an impetus to further assert the structuralist project, be it national or transnational. Neither approach pauses to question the givenness of the 'post-colonial-in-the-international'.

A different reading of global (b)ordering would view the post-colonial-in-the-international – as an organised space of bordered state units – as a configuration of the *global*. In this different light a more complex regime of relationalities becomes plain to view. Contrary to the reification of the state as a realm of 'sovereignty-citizenship' in colonial-modern mythologies, the (post-colonial) state may be better understood as a composite entity which enables the operation of differentiatedly regulated *licence, containment* and *bans* (Nayar, 2014). It is not simply the negotiation of a sovereign-citizen 'constitution' therefore that defines the politics of the state as it is conventionally understood but that of a transnational constitutedness of the state-space; old, and incessantly repeated, categories such as sovereignty, the constitution, citizenship, and the like may still fill our textbooks and serve as rationalising ideologies of political rhetoric, but they do not operate quite as the regulatory logics of the (b)ordered present. As Saskia Sassen (2008) describes, the political-legal geography of the (post-colonial) state is instead both constituted by, and constitutive of, global 'assemblages of territory, authority and rights'. The (b)ordered state is thus revealed as a fractured, fragmented, contested territorial and regulatory locus of transnational global relationalities and its myriad regimes of 'global law' (Fischer-Lescano and Teubner, 2004; Backer, 2012) rather than the foundational bounded unitary entity of a coherent sovereign order of constitutional (un)belonging as fetishised by colonial-modern political-legal philosophy. The essential 'reason' that defines the global architecture of bordered states therefore is not – as is commonly assumed and asserted – the making of citizen-subjects as the critical category of subjectification, but, through the myriad functions of the 'privatisation of sovereignty' (Mbembe, 2001: 78), the enforcement and regulations of a global biopolitical regime of differentiated 'subject'-beingness (Vaughn-Williams, 2009; Hindess, 1998; 2000; Nayar, 2014). Thus we see the actuality of global (b)ordering: for a small 'globalised' minority, the full privileges and impunity of supraterritorial *licence*; for many subjected to the regulation of a labouring 'citizenship', the rights and obligations of precarious territorialised *containment*; and for a large section of the global population deemed disposable, the violence of de/re-territorialised a(*ban*)donment (Nayar, 2014; 2019).

Thus we understand the post-colonial reconfiguration of coloniality. By instantiating a *past* and *present* of colonialism-decolonisation the declaration of independence serves as the philosophical gesture of (b)ordering which re-rationalises the state-in-the-international within the geography of *(post)coloniality*. The organisation of territoriality through its various historical manifestations – from the colonial to the post-colonial and now (under the conditions of late-modernity) the globalised-privatised-disaggregated state-form – all correspond, therefore, to the underlying rationality of global coloniality; a 'decentralised despotism' of 'native authorities' (Mamdani, 1996) remains the underlying logic and organisational structure of the post-colonial global order. For this reason, it is critically important to reframe the 'state-in-the-international' itself as a colonial frontline. What implications follow?

Quite simply, we foreclose the imagination and praxis of the anti-colonial when we mistake the *frontline* – that is the state-in-the-international – of a unitary structural global regime for the *border* which purportedly marks a separation between the state and the international. A border-perspective would assume the givenness of the state-form and of the essential architectural design of a territorially-demarcated international system of states; it would locate the 'nationalist project' and the post-colonial international struggle as movements towards subjectification-recognition-redistribution. An *anti-colonial* perspective is less fixated with reifications of 'post-colonial' grand designs. Instead, it would question precisely this assignation of the post-colonial moment in the becoming-into-the-international as a categorical rupture.

This is not to wish away either the post-colonial state or the international as actualities of (b)ordering. Their oppressive regimes of cruelty are all too real. My argument is that they remain contingent inventions open to interrogation. From an anti-colonial lens what is sought to be rationalised as the normalities of post-colonial (b)orders has only a claim to existence subject to the judgements of peoples in struggle. This renders precarious and contingent the 'post-colonial' settlements – of (b)ordering, (un)belonging, representational and regulatory authority – purportedly fixed by the 'declaration of independence'. We are thus able to locate more concretely the 'national-liberation struggle mode' (Neocosmos, 2016: 124–130) of anti-colonial desubjectification in its historicity, minus its subsequent ossification in mythologies of liberation whereby its anti-colonial content is domesticated and contained to serve as the stuff of commemoration in museum displays and extravagant national day theatrics. There is no reification, in this understanding of the *anti-colonial*, of the 'post-colonial' state. It is important to remember in this connection that historical context and contingency matter; that the particular philosophies of collective re-affirmation – of nation and nationalism – significant as they were (and remain) within the elite public spaces of anti/colonial posturing and diplomacy, did (and do) not quite encapsulate the whole, or even main, story of anti-colonial aspirations and struggle as effected by the 'politics of the people' (Guha, 1988: 40).[10] Basil Davidson (1992: 185) makes the point plainly:

10 See Neil Lazarus's interesting interpretation of Fanon. Lazarus argues for 'a retention of the categories of 'nation' and 'universality' towards an anti-imperial

> Down the line of agitation and organization, among the mass of rural and urban supporters of the anti-colonial movements, there was small sign of any developing loyalty or attachment to this or that colony-turned-nation. What the multitudes wanted, by all the evidence, was not a flag for the people or an anthem for the people, nearly so much as they wanted bread for the people, and health and schools for the people, while caring precious little, as these same multitudes would overwhelmingly prove in the years ahead, about winning frontiers for the people. The jubilant crowds celebrating independence were not inspired by a 'national consciousness' that 'demanded the nation,' … They were inspired by the hope of more and better food and shelter.

It was then and it remains so now. Even as the post-colonial regime of meanings fix and define the public discourse of national and international law and politics, the 'multitudes' remain inspired by imaginations not so enclosed as they continue to rise up against policed post-colonial pacifications of 'freedom'. An *AbM* movement press release (21 April 2008) as a 'mourning' of 'UnFreedom day', is eloquent (Figlan et al., 2009: 30):

> On Sunday it will be Freedom Day again. Once again we will be asked to go into stadiums to be told that we are free. Once again we will not be going into the stadiums. We will, for the third time, be mourning UnFreedom Day. Since the last UnFreedom Day we have been beaten, shot at and arrested on false charges by the police; evicted by the land invasions unit; disconnected from electricity by Municipal Security; forcibly removed to rural human dumping grounds; banned from marching by the eThekwini City Manager; slandered by all those who want followers not comrades; intimidated by all kinds of people who demand the silence of the poor; threatened by new anti-poor laws; burnt in the fires; sick in the dirt and raped in the dark nights looking for a safe place to go to the toilet.

These words are significant not simply because they protest the inflictions of the post-colonial violence upon the communities of the dispossessed, but rather because they articulate and reveal an anti-colonial assertion of *desubjectification* against the (b)orders of 'UnFreedom' which enforce the post-colonial reconfiguration of coloniality. When judged from the *frontline* it is not in the author-ity of (post)colonial elites therefore to foreclose the imaginations of the anti-colonial; the names and meaning

intellectualism, to construct a standpoint that is socialist, nationalitarian, liberationist, internationalist …' (Lazarus, 1999: 143). Although I agree with the underlying concern to return the post-colonial imagination to continuing anti-imperialist struggles which motivates Lazarus's arguments, I am less convinced that it is possible to do so by (re)capturing the 'nation' as a formation of anti-colonial praxes; see below.

of the post-colonial settlement remain always subject to judgement and repudiation. Of concern is the actual operation of the here and now of the state-in-the-international. The relevant question is: to what extent is the continuing anti-colonial struggle enabled by any particular post-colonial organisation of the state as a frontline in the encounter against colonial-global constellations of power?

Encounters Along Two Frontlines

So we return to the continuing struggles against the materiality of the post-colonial everyday. Two *encounters* elucidate the present-day implications of anti-colonial philosophy. Firstly, the encounters of resistance and renewal against the appropriations and dispossessions of inflicted development within the enclosed sovereign borders/frontlines of the (post)colonial state; and secondly, the transnational encounters against the incarcerations and expulsions of *bans* based on assertions of the borders/frontlines of '(un)belonging'.

The Post-Colonial State and the (B)ordering of Obedience

With respect to the first, the philosophical repudiation here involves the (post)colonial claim to sovereign authority, and its inscriptions of (subjected-)citizenship. Such repudiations begin the world over with the articulation of the much repeated 'No!' Raul Zibechi (2012: 14–16) in surveying the diverse social movements in Latin America identifies four common characteristics of refusal and renewal:

- the reterritorialisation of the movements: the recovering of spaces from state-capital enclosures for the regeneration of social and economic (re) production
- the assertion of autonomy from the state and institutionalised political systems; the recovering of social organisation and decision-making practices
- the valorisation of culture and the affirmation of identities and differences: the recovering of (dangerous) names of being(otherwise) from the emptiness of 'citizenship'
- the formation of independent intellectuals: the recovering of knowledge-systems and its processes.

We might choose to understand these characteristics of social movements as pertaining to the politics of 'civil society' within the state, as being therefore wholly within the political-legal rationalisations of (post)colonial philosophies of sovereignty and democratic participation. That is, if we remain enchanted by the philosophical sophistry of the assertion of sovereignty as a performative of decolonisation-after-colonialism and thereby as a command to obedience. Alternatively, we might read such struggles differently, understanding the 'politics of the governed' – to borrow from Partha Chatterjee (2004) – as having an altogether different philosophical significance.

Everyday experiments of 'insurrections against the market' and the reclaiming of the 'commons' (Esteva et al., 2013: 100, 121) bear witness to the regeneration of the material conditions and organisational forms of social-beingness in negation of colonial-modern rationalities of civilisation-development. Such recoveries involve the very matter of life lived otherwise than commanded, peoples' refusals to be subjected to the names and emplacements of (post)colonial developmental/civilisational rationalities exemplifying what Ghassan Hage (2012: 292) termed 'alter-politics' as the 'alternative to the political order'. These transformations of beingness-in-the world can be understood as precisely the 'seismic ethico-epistemo-ontological shift' that Cornell and Seely (2016: 130) urge. The spirit of rebellion, to *be* otherwise than *subject* to the state, is well nurtured in the everyday (Zibechi, 2012; Esteva et al., 2013; Nayar, 2017). Esteva et al. (2013: 112) put it well:

> While academia continues with the exploration, conceptualization, and interpretation of social reality, tending time and again to reduce it to the 'old truths' of modernity, people by the millions are creating new social realities with corresponding social paradigms, leaving behind the social paradigm within which they were colonized, enclosed, exploited, marginalized, and oppressed.

Indeed, it must be the continuing function of anti-colonial philosophies to overturn the old truths of colonial modernity. By reclaiming the names, places and social organisation which enable a living together in ways otherwise than as objectified subjects for development we affirm that these grassroots re-appropriations of human beingness are to be read and understood as *anti-colonial* assertions of *desubjectification*. Thus, the post-colonial becomes a contingent category of (b)ordering, ever open for anti-colonial interrogation, repudiation, and recovery as necessary. The 'living politics' of the *AbM* movement, a 'Third Force' they called it (Zikode, 2006: 186), is an example of just such a praxis of the frontline:

> We need to get things clear. There definitely is a Third Force. The question is, what is it and who is part of the Third Force? Well, I am the Third Force myself. The Third Force is all the pain and the suffering that the poor are subjected to every second in our lives. The shack dwellers have many things to say about the Third Force. It is time for us to speak and to say, 'this is who we are, this is where we are, and this is how we live'.[11]

Such statements of course portend no immediate solution to the problems of law and development, they are not cited to indicate a different developmental path, nor epistemological journey. Rather they demonstrate thinking-being against the

11 See also, Zikode's (2014) denunciation of South African 'democracy'. For discussions on the significance of the *AbM* movement, see Pithouse (2006); Patel (2008); Gibson (2008); Neocosmos (2016: 229–40).

closures of colonial inscriptions and emplacements. To engage in philosophy at the frontline in this way – to do a 'living politics' in the words of the *AbM* movement – is to think dangerously (Cesaire, 2000; Speed, 2005); it is to embrace a seditious philosophy that ruptures the (b)orders of command and obedience so that lives, in all the uncertainties of struggle, may be reclaimed from (post)colonial violence and violations to be lived otherwise than as subjected by the (post)colonial state.

The Post-Colonial International and (B)ordering of (Un)Belonging

The world as we know it is a world defined by the cartographic map drawn over the centuries with human blood. This invention, born out of rationalisations of 'rightful' expansion – as a 'natural' and unfettered right to travel and trade – now, in its post-colonial variant, represents a closed and unimpeachable fixity of named territorial truths of emplacement where inscriptions of nationality-citizenship serve as tethering devices to secure named bodies to identifiable territories. The right to an exclusionary national-belonging is now the order of the present, the sanctity of national borders is rationalised as constituting the fundamental democratic precept of the 'spheres of justice' (Walzer, 1983), of providing the essential protection of national culture and association (Miller, 2005; Miller, 2016), of defining the political reason of (b)ordering '(un)belonging' (Nagel, 2005; Risse, 2005; Sangiovanni, 2007). So go the various arguments for defining differentiated subject-beingness so that the 'stranger' may be named, and kept out. In these thoughtful philosophical deliberations, justice, it seems, warrants the rightful (b)ordering of exclusions. In response, we find well-intentioned arguments for a preferred global regime of movement defined by 'cosmopolitan' openness and generosity (Carens, 1987; Riley, 2008). Thus are the philosophical arguments on the 'justice' of post-colonial (b)orders rehearsed.

But the actual practice of bordering works somewhat differently. We note that the purported sanctity and inviolability of 'territoriality' does not quite apply to certain categories of privileged cross-border movement; indeed the global regime of borders is replete with facilities that serve as preferential gateways for the movements of capital and its agents (Sparke, 2006; Salter, 2006). For such hyper-citizens of the 'transnational capitalist class' (Sklair, 2001), the condition of subject-beingness is not defined by territorial boundedness, not contained by a national political-belonging; they are quite the *exemptional* bearers of *licence*, free still to travel and trade across expedited channels of border-gateways. The arguments of cultural dilution or the erosion of the national democratic fabric pose no impediment to their transboundary mobility. Such anxieties surface only when what is at issue is the movement of those who appear at the border (many from territories formerly-conquered, and still subjugated and plundered) who, in abjection, audaciously claim the 'right' to travel. Against their 'dangerous bodies' are the biopolitics of borders and human movement effected and enforced (Vaughn-Williams, 2009; Amoore, 2006), their-subject-beingness defined by expulsions, incarcerations, *bans*.

Indeed, the discourses on borders are manifestly now conducted through the imaginaries of frontlines against the invading hordes that must be repulsed (Brown, 2010).

Let us instead frame the problematic of injustice differently, now from the other side of the *frontline*. We do this by disposing of the nonsense that the 'accident of history' – the particularities of pasts that have birthed the international order as presently divided by state borders – is a moral irrelevance to the 'political' conception of justice as Nagel (2005) proclaims. Instead we recall with Nikolas Rose (1999: 253) that 'abjection' is an 'act of force', not a natural state of deprivation. It is an inflicted condition of the world as it has been intentionally, not accidentally, constituted, rationalised, (b)ordered. Post-colonial philosophies of political separation – of borders of (un)belonging, of citizenship as political-affiliation/association – are all inventions of convenience, rationalisations of denial and violence; it is a fundamental function of the post-colonial 'inter-national' settlement to enforce regimes of containment and managed mobility of subjected bodies for a global regulation of 'racialised capitalism' (Smith, 2016). This said, bodies subjected to abjection are less inclined to remain in their places of containment. They assert their presence to appear out of their prescribed (b)ordered place. (Post)colonial philosophies are quick to name and emplace 'subjects' yet again: 'refugee', 'asylum-seeker', 'illegal migrant' are all re-inscriptions of subjectivity. And in the face of this 'crisis' of the unwanted appearance of abjection, in the face of the abject suffering (and deaths) of these 'cast-offs' (Nyers, 2003) of (in)humanity, is the best we can do to appeal for 'registration' and the dispensation of a modicum of humane accommodation and protection?[12] By what 'truth' has the dispossessed acquiesced to this (b)ordering and parcelling out of the World?

We might assert an audacious anti-colonial recovery of political geography instead. What this involves is a repudiation of the very global architecture of containment and separation of the purportedly (b)ordered post-colonial settlement. As I make this argument, Cesaire's (2000: 1) denunciation comes to mind: '*Europe is indefensible* … morally, spiritually indefensible'. This served to articulate in its time the powerful premise for a 'nationalist' mode of desubjectification against the colonial present, but a revision is needed today. I would add to Cesaire's formulation the following assertion, reflective of the present (post)colonial problem: 'Europe', as a naming upon the world, bordered upon the conquests of those Other-ed, now boarded-up against those Other-ed, is *conceptually* indefensible; the idea of 'Europe', named, bordered, rationalised, rendered into 'the international' as a post-colonial abomination of (un)belonging, is *indefensible*! And with this

12 A corrective to the more common literature, which centres around 'Human Rights'-based appeals to protection of displaced persons, is provided by Franke (2008) who argues that the Human Rights framework with its rootedness in rationalities of territoriality is incapable of addressing the 'problem' of displacement and movement.

repudiation of the idea of 'Europe' might the materiality of 'Europe' be reinserted within an anti-colonial register.[13]

On Thought, 'Illegality', and an Anti-Colonial Proposition

But this is all just so much talk, conducted amongst 'ourselves', isn't it? Ours is not – let us be frank – the site of anti-colonial transformation. Or might it be? It depends of course. If we merely add to the mountain of literature that is already available, repeating analyses and prescriptions of all that has gone wrong and all that *should* be done to correct the problems of 'development', then I doubt we contribute anything different. The problems of the present – the problems of inflicted 'development' – are not the result of inadequate knowledge, imagination, political direction, awaiting only enlightened prescriptions for change, to be offered by our critical intellectual labours. If instead we understand that the cruelties of the present persist not by oversight, neglect or misguidedness but rather by design, effected and enforced with full knowledge and intent as the normality of the colonial present, then as we talk among ourselves so must we carry the burden to reflect upon our purpose here. We arrive back at that initial question: what might it mean for us to 'think resistance'? Let me conclude with some reflections on the implications of thinking being otherwise as anti-colonial praxes.

To name struggle as *anti-colonial* in a post-colonial situation is by itself an originary act of naming the *frontline*; it is a refusal to interpret the encounter in the present through the philosophical lenses and vocabulary of the 'border' and to accept the normality and interminability of the post-colonial settlement as indeed *post*-colonial. And this raises from the outset an uncomfortable, even dangerous, post-epistemological realisation – uncomfortable, that is, to institutionalised critical thinkers thinking from within borders, dangerous, however, to all concerned: the collective struggle against colonial (b)orders is necessarily a

13 This was a rare attempt by Aime Cesaire and Leopold Senghor, for all of their limitations, to reconfigure the meaning of the post-colonial through 'departmentalisation' and transnational 'federalism' respectively; the implications on the present if such imaginations had not 'failed', as Gary Wilder (2015: 244) tells us, are poignant:

> … African *sans papiers* in metropolitan France would not be foreigners demanding hospitality but citizens whose rights of mobility, family reunification, social security, and political participation were legally protected. Africans would not be outsiders appealing for economic aid from a *foreign* French state nor targets of dehumanizing humanitarianism. …West African peoples would be integral members of an expanded European Union. … I am not suggesting that Senghor's programme to reconstitute France as a democratic socialist federation would have necessarily led to a happy outcome. But there are no a priori grounds for dismissing it as any less plausible than the territorial national solutions to colonial freedom the world did embrace.

It is no 'accident of history' that such alternate 'frameworks' of (b)ordering were not so embraced.

struggle of *affirmative illegality*, or in the terms of Enrique Dussel (2008: 105), the illegal but legitimate 'compulsion' of liberation praxis. The confrontation of present coloniality of development and its co-constitutive law requires this explicit affirmation of illegality in encounter. It is delusional to think that the governmental regimes of global coloniality, in their manifold private/corporate and public/state constellations, will otherwise be shifted by some enlightened border-dialogical persuasion of global human solidarity. In the present time when everything, even post/decolonial theory can be packaged into commodities for supply- and demand-based consumption, more than a celebration of 'ecologies of knowledges' is necessary to de-normalise the violence and cruelties of the present; indeed it is not 'lazy reason' as Santos (2014: 164) tells us, that defines the philosophy and practice of coloniality past and present, but a very diligent, interventionist and penetrative reason of subjectification and subjugation that entrenches (post)colonial desires as material and structural normalities. Better we explicate the very intentionality of (post)colonial philosophies in making-subject differentiated beings, better we might read and articulate anti-colonial struggles to be otherwise. *Desubjectification*, as being-out-of-order, is by definition an act of illegality.

This recovering of the anti-colonial vocabulary of affirmative illegality, as a reaffirmation of anti-colonial resistance, refusal and regeneration, therefore, is critical. We need to be mindful that the violated – as owners of their sense of violation – will claim and do as they wish, if and when they wish, without need for any acknowledgement or permission from institutionalised philosophers of 'resistance'; such everyday struggles of rejection and renewals for livelihoods, for dignity, for hope, are commonplace the world over (Zibechi, 2012; Figlan et al., 2009; Esteva et al., 2013). Whilst it is common for critical thinkers to celebrate these instances of resistance and regeneration, the inherent fact and danger of their 'illegality' is seldom explicitly addressed; resistance in this sense is a safer term of art for intellectual exchange. Even if we might attempt to deflect our attention from the essential illegality of the anti-colonial, it is necessary to confront the inconvenient fact that such encounters are so named by colonial philosophies. As Arundhati Roy (2011) recounts in the context of India, (post)colonial powers in the present have no qualms of naming their suppressions against the rebellious-impoverished as 'encounters' at the frontline! The question for us here is how *we*, as 'thinkers of resistance', choose to assign a different meaning to these normalities of the post-colonial present.

So, philosophy as anti-colonial praxis indeed matters. It matters precisely because it constructs the categories which frame and interpret the encounter of imaginations and actions, and which thereby define, as an aspect of struggle, the registers within which names, places, and meanings are inscribed upon bodies and territories; it matters because it *encounters* the naming of 'illegality' and refuses those that so name their assertion of 'sovereignty'. Philosophical work in this respect de-names the normalising categories of colonial rationalisations of (b)orders and names anew the authority of resistance and renewal against the apparent interminability of post-colonial reorganisations of coloniality. It is, simply put, philosophy against the political-legal (b)orders of the World as presently asserted and enforced.

It is important to state this explicitly as what is thought as 'anti-colonial' in this connection is not intended merely to serve as an accommodation of the Other-ed, of the 'excluded', into the (reformed) totalities of the present; it is thought that seeks not to remain enframed by the familiar ontological categories of (b)ordering deemed to be the only permitted, or possible, pathways to imagining the worlds of being, and being-ness in the world. What we are concerned to do here – if we are concerned to indeed think resistance to the post-colonial problems of development and law beyond commonplace appeals for greater compassion and largesse towards the impoverished, the wretched, the damned – is to overturn the presumed 'universality', fixity and normality, of the post-colonial present. This is precisely the work of anti-colonial philosophy: to think the *unthinkable* as the *impermissible* is done. I suggest the following as a philosophical proposition for a continued anti-colonial praxis: *if it is not the actuality that no life matters any less than any other life, then so be it that no lives shall matter any more than any other life.*

References

Adelman, S. and Paliwala, A. eds., 2021. *The Limits of Law and Development: Neoliberalism, Governance and Social Justice*. Routledge.

Anghie, A. and Chimni, B., 2003. Third World Approaches to International Law and Individual Responsibility in Internal Conflicts. *Chinese Journal of International Law*, 2 (1), 77–103.

Anghie, A., 2006. The Evolution of International Law: Colonial and Postcolonial Realities. *Third World Quarterly*, 27 (5), 739–753.

Anghie, A., 2005. *Imperialism, Sovereignty and the Making of International Law*. Cambridge University Press.

Anzaldua, G., 1987. *Borderlands/La Frontera: The New Mestiza*. Aunt Lute Books.

Amoore, L., 2006. Biometric Borders: Governing Mobilities in the War on Terror. *Political Geography*, 25, 336–351.

Ayittey, G.B.N., 1994. *Africa Betrayed*. Palgrave Macmillan.

Backer, L.C., 2012. The Structural Characteristics of Global Law for the 21st Century: Fracture, Fluidity, Permeability, and Polycentricity. *Tilbury Law Review*, 17, 177–199.

Baxi, U., 2006. What May the Third World Expect from International Law? *Third World Quarterly*, 27 (5), 713–725.

Berger, M.T., 1994. The End of the Third World. *Third World Quarterly*, 15 (2), 257–275.

Biko, S., 1978. *I Write What I Like*. Edited by Aelred Stubbs. Heinemann.

Brown, W., 2010. *Walled States, Waning Sovereignty*. Zone Books.

Carens, J.H., 1987. Aliens and Citizens: The Case for Open Borders. *Review of Politics*, 49, 251–273.

Cesaire, A., 2000. *Discourse on Colonialism*. Translated by Pinkham, J.Monthly Review Press. Available online at: <http://www.rlwclarke.net/Theory/SourcesPrimary/CesaireDiscourseonColonialism.pdf> (accessed 3 July 2017).

Chakrabarty, D., 2000. *Provincializing Europe: Postcolonial Thought and Historical Difference.* Princeton University Press.

Chatterjee, P., 1993. *The Nation and its Fragments: Colonial and Postcolonial Histories.* Princeton University Press.

Chatterjee, P., 2004. *The Politics of the Governed: Reflections on Popular Politics in Most of the World.* Columbia University Press.

Connell, R., 2007. *Southern Theory: The Global Dynamics of Knowledge in Social Science.* Polity.

Cornell, D. and Seely, S., 2016. The Spirit of Revolution: Beyond the Dead Ends of Man. Polity Press.

Dabashi, H., 2015. *Can Non-Europeans Think.* Zed Books.

Davidson, B., 1992. *The Black Man's Burden: Africa and the Curse of the Nation State.* Boydell & Brewer.

Douglass, F., 1852. The Meaning of July Fourth for the Negro. Available at <http://www.historyisaweapon.com/defcon1/douglassjuly4.html> (accessed 26 September 2017).

Duffield, M., and Waddell, N., 2006. Securing Humans in a Dangerous World. *International Politics*, 43 (1), 1–23.

Dussel, E., 2003. *Philosophy of Liberation.* Translated by Martinez, A., and Morkovsky, C. Wipf and Stock.

Dussel, E., 2008. *Twenty Theses on Politics.* Translated by Ciccariello-Maher, G.Duke University Press.

Escobar, A., 1995. *Encountering Development: The Making and Remaking of the Third World.* Princeton University Press.

Escobar, A., 2004. Beyond the Third World: Imperial Globality, Global Coloniality and Anti-Globalisation Social Movements. *Third World Quarterly*, 25 (1), 207–230.

Esteva, G., and Prakash, M.S., 1998. *Grassroots Post-Modernism: Remaking the Soil of Cultures.* Zed Books.

Esteva, G., Babones, S., and Babcicky, P., 2013. *The Future of Development: A Radical Manifesto.* Policy Press.

Fanon, F., 1967 (2001 reprint). *The Wretched of the Earth.* Translated by Farrington, C. Penguin Books.

Fanon, F., 1986. *Black Skin, White Masks.* Translated by Markmann, C.L.Pluto Press.

Figlan, L., Rev. Mavuso, Ngema, B., Nsibande, Z., Sibisi, S., and Zikode, S., 2009. *Living Learning.* Abahlali baseMjondolo and Rural Network. Church Land Programme. Available at <untitled (churchland.org.za)> (accessed 12 February 2021).

Fischer-Lescano, A., and Teubner, G., 2004. Regime Collisions: The Vain Search for Legal Unity in the Fragmentation of Global Law. *Michigan Journal of International Law*, 25, 999–1046.

Frank, A.G., 1969. *Latin America: Underdevelopment or Revolution.* Monthly Review Press.

Franke, M.F.N., 2008. The Displacement of the Rights of Displaced Persons: An Irreconciliation of Human Rights between Place and Movement. *Journal of Human Rights*, 7 (3), 262–281.

Freire, P., 1974. *Pedagogy of the Oppressed.* Penguin Books.

Gandhi, M.K., 1938. *Hind Swaraj.* Navajivan Publishing House. Available at <http://www.mkgandhi.org/ebks/hind_swaraj.pdf> (accessed 20 August 2016).

Gibson, N.C., 2008. Upright and free: Fanon in South Africa, from Biko to the shackdwellers' movement (Abahlali baseMjondolo). *Social Identities*, 14 (6), 683–715.

Glover, J., 2001. *Humanity: A Moral History of the Twentieth Century.* Pimlico.

Gordon, L.R., 2000. *Existentia Africana: Understanding Africana Existential Thought*. Routledge.

Gordon, L.R., 2015. *What Fanon Said: A Philosophical Introduction to His Life and Thought*. Hurst & Co.

Grosfuguel, R., 2008. Transmodernity, border thinking, and global coloniality: Decolonizing political economy and postcolonial studies. *Eurozine*. Available at <http://www.eurozine.com/transmodernity-border-thinking-and-global-coloniality/> (accessed 4 July 2017).

Guha, R., 1988. On Some Aspects of the Historiography of Colonial India, in Guha, R. and Spivak, G.C. (eds), *Selected Subaltern Studies*, p. 37. Oxford University Press.

Hage, G., 2012. Critical Anthropological Thought and the Radical Political Imaginary Today. *Critique of Anthropology*, 32 (2), 285–308.

Hindess, B., 1998. Divide and Rule: The International Character of Modern Citizenship. *European Journal of Social Theory*, 1 (1), 57–70.

Hindess, B., 2000. Citizenship in the International Management of Populations. *American Behavioural Scientist*, 43 (9), 1486–1497.

Hindess, B., 2002. Neo-liberal Citizenship. *Citizenship Studies*, 6 (2), 127–143.

Jabri, V., 2012. *The Postcolonial Subject: Claiming Politics/Governing Others in Late Modernity*. Routledge.

Kohn, E., 2013. *How Forests Think: Towards an Anthropology Beyond the Human*. University of California Press.

Krishna, S., 2008. *Globalization and Postcolonialism: Hegemony and Resistance in the Twenty-first Century*. Rowman & Littlefield.

Lazarus, N., 1999. *Nationalism and Cultural Practice in the Postcolonial World*. Cambridge University Press.

Lugones, M., 2010. Towards a Decolonial Feminism. *Hypatia*, 25 (4), 742–759.

Maldonado-Torres, N., 2004. The Topology of Being and the Geopolitics of Knowledge. *City*, 8 (1), 29–56.

Mamdani, M., 1996. *Citizen and Subject: Contemporary Africa and the Legacy of Late Colonialism*. Princeton University Press.

Mander, J., 1991. *In the Absence of the Sacred: The Failure of Technology and the Survival of the Indian Nations*. University of California Press.

Mbembe, A.J., 2001. *On the Postcolony*. University of California Press.

Mbembe, A.J., 2016. Decolonizing the University: New Directions. *Arts & Humanities in Higher Education*, 15 (1), 29–45.

Memmi, A., 2006. *Decolonization and the Decolonized*. Translated by Bononni, R.University of Minnesota Press.

Mignolo, W.D., 2000. *Local Histories/Global Designs: Coloniality, Subaltern Knowledges, and Border Thinking*. Princeton University Press.

Mignolo, W.D., 2002. The Zapatistas's Theoretical Revolution: Its Historical, Ethical, and Political Consequences. *Review (Fernand Braudel Center)*, 25 (3), 245–275.

Mignolo, W.D., 2007. Delinking: The Rhetoric of Modernity, the Logic of Coloniality and the Grammar of Decoloniality. *Cultural Studies*, 21 (2–3), 449–514.

Mignolo, W.D. and Tlostanova, M.V., 2006. Theorizing from the Borders: Shifting the Geo- and Body-Politics of Knowledge. *European Journal of Social Theory*, 9 (2), 205–221.

Miller, D., 2005. Immigration: The Case for Limits, in Cohen, A.I. and Wellman, C.H. (eds), *Contemporary Debates in Applied Ethics*, pp. 193–206. Blackwell Press.

Miller, D., 2016. *Strangers in Our Midst: The Political Philosophy of Immigration*. Harvard University Press.
Nagel, T., 2005. The Problem of Global Justice. *Philosophy & Public Affairs* 33 (2), 113–147.
Nandy, A., 1995. History's Forgotten Doubles. *History and Theory* 34 (2), 44–66.
Nandy, A., 2003. *The Romance of the State: And the Fate of Dissent in the Tropics*. Oxford University Press.
Nayar, J., 2013. The Philosopher's Elusive Subject: On the Problem of the 'Present' in the 'Political'. *Journal of Critical Southern Studies*, 1, 23–59.
Nayar, J., 2014. On the Elusive Subject of Sovereignty. *Alternatives: Global, Local, Political*, 39 (2), 124–147.
Nayar, J., 2017. Some Thoughts on the '(Extra)Ordinary': Philosophy, Coloniality and Being Otherwise. *Alternatives: Global, Local, Political*, 42 (1), 3–25.
Nayar, J., 2019. The Non-Perplexity of Human Rights. *Theory & Event*, 22 (2), 267–302.
Ndlovu-Gatsheni, S.J., 2013*Coloniality of Power in Postcolonial Africa: Myths of Decolonization*. CODESRIA.
Neocosmos, M., 2010. Analysing Political Subjectivities: Naming the Post-developmental State in Africa Today. *Journal of Asian and African Studies*, 45 (5), 534–553.
Neocosmos, M., 2016. *Thinking Freedom in Africa: Toward a Theory of Emancipatory Politics*. Wits University Press.
Nyers, P., 2003. Abject Cosmopolitanism: The Politics of Protection in the Anti-Deportation Movement. *Third World Quarterly*, 24 (6), 1069–1093.
Patel, R., 2008. A Short Course in Politics at the University of Abahlali baseMjondolo . *Journal of Asian and African Studies*, 43 (1), 95–112.
Petras J. and Veltmeyer, H., 2007. The 'development state' in Latin America: Whose development, whose state? *The Journal of Peasant Studies*, 34 (3–4), 371–407.
Pithouse, R., 2006. The Promised Land and the University of Abahlali baseMjondolo. *African Sociological Review*, 10 (1), 102–142.
Pogge, T., 2007. *World Poverty and Human Rights: Cosmopolitan Responsibilities and Reforms*. 2nd edition. Polity Press.
Quijano, A., 2000. Coloniality of Power and Eurocentrism in Latin America. *Nepantla: Views from South*, 1 (3), 533–580.
Rahnema, M. and Bawtree, V., eds., 1997. *The Post-Development Reader*. Zed Books.
Rajagopal, B., 2008. *International Law from Below: Development, Social Movements and Third World Resistance*. Cambridge University Press.
Randeria, S., 2007. The State of Globalization: Legal Plurality, Overlapping Sovereignties and Ambiguous Alliances between Civil Society and the Cunning State in India. *Theory, Culture & Society*, 24 (1), 1–33.
Riley, J.L., 2008. *Let Them In: The Case for Open Borders*. Gotham Books.
Risse, M., 2005. What We Owe to the Global Poor. *The Journal of Ethics*, 9 (1–2), 81–117.
Rose, N., 1999. *Powers of Freedom*. Cambridge University Press.
Roy, A., 2011. *Walking with the Comrades*. Penguin Books.
Roy, A., 2015. *Capitalism: A Ghost Story*. Verso.
Sachs, W., ed., 1992. *The Development Dictionary: A Guide to Knowledge as Power*. St. Martin's Press.
Salter, M., 2006. The Global Visa Regime and the Political Technologies of the International Self: Borders, Bodies, Biopolitics. *Alternatives: Global, Local, Political*, 31 (2), 167–189.

Sangiovanni, A., 2007. Global Justice, Reciprocity, and the State. *Philosophy & Public Affairs*, 35 (1), 3–39.

Santos, B.S., 2014. *Epistemologies of the South: Justice Against Epistemicide*. Routledge.

Sassen, S., 2008. Neither Global nor National: Novel Assemblages of Territory, Authority and Rights. *Ethics & Global Politics*, 1 (1–2), 61–79.

Shivji, I., 2006. Pan-Africanism or Imperialism? Unity and Struggle towards a New Democratic Africa. *African Sociological Review / Revue Africaine de Sociologie*, 10 (1), 208–220.

Sklair, L., 2001. *The Transnational Capitalist Class*. Blackwell.

Smith, A.A., 2016. Migration, Development and Security Within Racialised Global Capitalism, *Third World Quarterly*, 37 (11), 2119–2138.

Sparke, M., 2006. A Neoliberal Nexus: Citizenship, Security and the Future of the Border. *Political Geography*, 25 (2), 151–180.

Sparke, M., 2009. On Denationalization as Neoliberalization: Biopolitics, Class Interest and the Incompleteness of Citizenship. *Political Power and Social Theory*, 20, 287–300.

Speed, S., 2005. Dangerous Discourses: Human Rights and Multiculturalism in Neoliberal Mexico. *PoLAR: Political and Legal Anthropology Review*, 28 (1), 29–51.

Spivak, G., 1988. Can the Subaltern Speak? In Nelson, G. and Grossberg, L. (eds), *Marxism and the Interpretation of Culture*, pp. 271–313. Chicago: University of Illinois Press.

Vaughan, G., 2007. *Women and the Gift Economy: A Radically Different Worldview Is Possible*. Inanna Publications.

Vaughn-Williams, N., 2009. *Border Politics: The Limits of Sovereign Power*. Edinburgh University Press.

Walsh, C., 2012. 'Other' Knowledges, 'Other' Critiques: Reflections on the Politics and Practices of Philosophy and Decoloniality in the 'Other' America. *TRANSMODERNITY: Journal of Peripheral Cultural Production of the Luso-Hispanic World*, 1 (3), 11–27.

Walzer, M., 1983. *Spheres of Justice*. Basic Books.

Wilder, G., 2015. *Freedom Time: Negritude, Decolonization, and the Future of the World*. Duke University Press.

Wynter, S., 2003. Unsettling the Coloniality of Being/Power/Truth/Freedom: Towards the Human, After Man, Its Overrepresentation – An Argument. *The New Centennial Review*, 3 (3), 257–237.

Young, I.M., 2006. Responsibility and Global Justice: A Social Connection Model. *Social Philosophy & Policy*, 23 (1), 102–130.

Zeleza, P.T. 2003. *Rethinking Africa's Globalization, Volume 1: The Intellectual Challenges*. Africa World Press.

Zibechi, R., 2012. *Territories in Resistance: A Cartography of Latin American Social Movements*. AK Press.

Zikode, S., 2006. The Third Force. *Journal of Asian and African Studies*, 41 (1–2), 185–189.

Zikode, S., 2014. *Twenty Years of Hell in Shacks*. Presentation to the DDP Conference on 'Twenty Years of Local Democracy in South Africa', Durban, 20 & 21 October 2014. Available at <http://abahlali.org/node/14413/> (accessed 2 October 2017).

Chapter 4

The Constitution of Turbulence

Zavaleta, Linera and Constituent Power in Bolivia

Illan Rua Wall

Introduction

When the left-wing indigenous candidate Evo Morales was elected as President of Bolivia in 2006, the movement he led was faced with a significant problem. The political and legal structures established over the previous 40 years were inimical to the radical platform that swept him to power. The constitutional structures inscribed the state as the site of market stability, and a business-as-usual exclusion of the indigenous majority of Bolivia. The *Movimiento al Socialismo* (MAS) government represented the antithesis of the political elites that had fashioned the Bolivian state for well over a century. If their coming to power was to have any lasting significance, the old state had to be overcome. This chapter argues that of the many novelties developed in the 2009 Bolivian constitution, one of the most intriguing was the generation of a radically new form of separation of powers. Where the conventional separation of powers internally divides power within the state apparatus, ensuring that no one arm of the state can overpower the others, the Bolivian model actively encouraged extra-systemic social movements. The constitution envisioned an active and continuing constituent power that counter-balanced the tendency of state structures to become 'recursive' in their power. In this way, the 2009 Bolivian experiment is a 'constitution of turbulence', something that would have important effects on the trajectory of the Bolivian state over the decade that followed its adoption. This would culminate in the 2019 coup and its subsequent defeat.

Conventional wisdom demands that popular unrest is bad for states because it runs the risk of releasing forces that may lead to violent conflict, civil war and even the dreaded failed-state status. Turbulence is a state of open social and political antagonism. It reveals rifts among the populace that take a long time to heal. Even in its most minor forms, it causes serious economic harms. Events like revolutions, assassinations, military coups and political unrest have negative effects on growth, external borrowing and inflation (Renn, Jovanovic and Schröter, 2011; Knight, 2013). There are myriad reasons for this, not least the fears of foreign investors for the security of their property rights or risk-averse

DOI: 10.4324/9780203745298-6

domestic economic agents who may 'hesitate to take economic initiatives' in the face of instability (Alesina et al., 1992). Given this conventional wisdom, it seems obvious that the constitution should foster a restful population, and the state should quell disorder. It would seem very strange that a constitution and its primary theorists should pose instability, contestation and contradiction as the key elements of a new order. But Morales, Álvaro García Linera (his Vice-President), and many of the delegates in the constituent assembly saw this as a necessary way of checking the intensification of state power that a more traditional separation of powers often entails. This chapter focuses on the function of constituent power in the 2009 constitution, examining the material constellation of state power imagined by the new constitutional structure. It examines the types of political and legal agency proposed by the major theorists of the constitution, insisting that the extra-systemic constitutionalisation of resistance is a key dynamic of Bolivia's attempt to move beyond hegemonic notions of development. In short, the constitution of turbulence entails a rendering of constituent power that is supposed to drive popular innovation within *and without* the constitutional structure.

The Bolivian State and Society

For many on the left of development studies the Andean constitutional experiments in Venezuela, Ecuador and Bolivia (Schilling-Vacaflor, 2011: 3) were the manifestation of the much longed for alternative to hegemonic development models (Gudynas, 2011; Cubillo-Guevara et al., 2016). Of particular note were three key elements: the plurinational recognition of multiple cosmologies, particularly gathered as *vivir bien* [1]; the rights of *Pachamama* (Mother Earth); and the constitution of direct and multiscalar democratic forms. It is useful initially to understand Bolivia's 2009 constitution through the lens of 'vivir bien'. This was meant to orient the constitution to the sense of 'living well', rather than living better (see also Augusto Baldi, 2013 and Mattison and Mignolo, 2012). Instead of the comparative and competitive Western approach to the good life, *vivir bien* was rooted in a non-market-oriented politics of living-together or living in common. In the Bolivian constitution it signifies a web of connections. Perhaps most importantly, it connects to the idea that the state is plurinational rather than monocultural. In this sense, the text goes further than recognition of the presence of indigenous populations (although we should not dismiss the symbolic significance of recognition for populations that have been subjugated since colonisation). Measures were introduced to support 'communitarian' democracy in indigenous-campesino territories and municipalities, including forms of autonomy (Constitution of the Plurinational State of Bolivia: Articles 289–296). Alongside this are the enhanced human rights norms, enforced by new popular

1 A variety of terms are used to describe living well in the Andean countries interchangeably, including *Buen Vivir* as well as terms in indigenous languages.

judicial and administrative rights of action (Ibid.: Articles 13–76). *Vivir bien* also signifies an immanent political and economic principle of administrative function, judicial decision making and economic planning, perhaps most evident in the repositioning of environmental rights and norms in the constitution. No longer a matter of micro-regulation of air quality or river pollutants, *Pachamama* takes centre stage, at once signifying a new environmental regime, the new position of indigenous peoples and a new political imaginary of the state.

At the core of these novelties was the attempt to make the Bolivian state adhere more closely to its society. Drawing on the work of Bolivian sociologist René Zavaleta Mercado, García Linera and other primary theorists of the new constitution insisted that Bolivian society was 'motley' in nature (Augsburger, 2021: 2). Zavaleta's description of Bolivian society was *abigarrada* or *abigarramiento*, which is a difficult term to translate. It is generally rendered as motley, but could also be disjointed or multicoloured. It contains hints of chaos, disorder, mess and being muddled and it has a close connection to colour or pattern. Zavaleta sought to describe a society in which 'incomplete capitalist structures coexist with social and juridical structures proper of pre-capitalism' (Hesselroth, 2015: 63). It was socially, economically, politically, ethnically and geographically fragmented. Bolivia's motley society meant that what development discourses still tended to understand as linear stages were actually all mixed up. García Linera describes it as 'the multiplicity of cultural, temporal, technological, political and productive systems that are structurally differentiated from the civilisational constitution of dominant capitalism' (García Linera, 2008: 310, cited in Williams, 2015: 299). A motley society is an unassimilable multiplicity that cannot be homogenised as an organic unity.

Zavaleta argued that to think about development in a 'motley' society, it was necessary to avoid economism altogether and understand development as the emergence of a correspondence between state and society. Anne Freeland explains that this meant both the emergence of 'the nation-state as such, as a collectivity that recognizes itself in the state' and 'as the development of self-determination, which, for Zavaleta, was the practical extension and realization of self-knowledge, the epistemic construction of the self and the collectivity as political subject' (Freeland, 2014: 67). Freeland describes these two modes of power as constituted and constituent power (see also Colon Rios, 2012). Constituted power is the identification of the collectivity with the state, where constituent power is the realisation of self-knowledge of the collectivity. Crucially, for Zavaleta, the question posed by these two modes of power was 'legibility' and intelligibility. The problem with the motley society was that it remained unintelligible or illegible to the state. This illegibility would remain except when society unified from below to express its difference from the constituted order. In other words, society was unintelligible to the state, except when it revolted. But when it did constitute a counterpower to the state, it could begin to emerge as a new hegemony, manifested as a resistance to the form of state power. Freeland says that in a crisis produced by the popular unrest of a constituent moment, society might begin to gain a coherence. This legibility is not one that could be given by a state or an economic order, but instead emerges from the radical demands of a moment of contestation.

> It is as the ground of the general crisis that Zavaleta's concept of *abigarramiento* works against the reification of representation, against the ossification of the constituted order and in the service of collective constitutive action. It is the persistence of an incommensurability that precludes the total closure of the constituted and therefore guarantees the possibility of de- and re-constitution.
> (Freeland, 2014)

For García Linera, this moment of social legibility emerged with significant force between 2000 and 2005 when social movements contested privatisation of water and development of extractivist infrastructure.

In the 1990s, Bolivia had been subject to intense structural adjustment, with extensive privatisation, individualisation and other neoliberal strategies of governmentality. This process gave birth to an increasingly strong set of social movements. Two events in particular were essential to the manifestation of their power: the 2000 Cochabamba water war, in which social movements prevented the privatisation of the water supply, and the 2003 gas war in which contestation over a wider variety of economic policies from coca growing to the building of a gas pipeline through Chile led to an intensification of the power and agility of the social movements (Olivera, 2004). The forms that emerged from this activism solidified around MAS, leading in 2006 to the election of Evo Morales' government. For Williams (2015: 299; emphasis added), the period of 2000 to 2005 was not a matter of forging hegemony '*over* the disjointed, but *from within* the disjointed by means of the hegemonic articulation of social diversity'.

In this context, García Linera moved in a different direction, developing what he called the 'multitude form'. He explains that unlike the union form that gathered diverse interests and combined them with a mode of policing the common line, the multitude form 'lacks a stable structure of control and mobilization of its members. It appeals above all to justice and a conviction in the cause being fought as its way of guaranteeing a mass turnout at mobilizations' (García Linera, 2004: 76). Understood through the Cochabamba water war, the multitude is held together by a common organisation:

> Unlike the 'crowd' – which gathers together individuals who have no group affiliation or organisational dependence and who are united rather simply by the euphoria of immediate action – the decisive characteristic of the multitude is that it overwhelmingly represents a gathering of 'collective' or collectivized individuals.
> (García Linera, 2004: 72)

The multitude which emerges is a manifestation of the unintelligibility of society, as viewed from the position of the old state. It emerges precisely as the crisis of the old state form, and the common demand for something that accords to the motley society. And it is this that MAS sought to use to resolve the disarticulation of state and society.

For García Linera, after Cochabamba these social movements began to develop a sort of parallel power to the state. He claimed that at several times during 2000:

> this dense web of assemblies and plebeian democratic practices not only demanded rights from the state within a system of parties and parliament, but also replaced the state as the mechanism of government, as the system of mediation and as the culture of obedience. The multitude … possesses an organising force capable of challenging the relevance of the prevailing systems of government … and of erecting (up to now provisionally) alternative systems for the exercise of political power and the conduct of legitimately democratic life.
>
> (García Linera, 2004: 82)

This is the process described by Lenin in his 1917 essay 'The Dual Power'. There he explained that in the days between February and October 1917 the emergent Workers' and Soldiers' Soviets were parallel institutions to the state. They would gradually develop their material power while the bourgeois provisional government was concerned only with the appearance and projection of power. Brought to fruition, the dual power strategy ultimately led to the final revolutionary break in October (Lenin, 1917).

According to García Linera, the Bolivian gas wars of 2003 represented 'the maximum expression of plebeian dissidence in relation to the state' (García Linera, 2008: 344). At that point, Bolivia was 'faced with the specter of an emergent dual power' and this revolutionary threat presented two possibilities: 'The path of gradual institutional change via electoral means, with Evo Morales as the main candidate' or 'The insurrectional path of the revolutionary retransformation of the State' (Williams, 2015: 305, citing García Linera, 2008: 349). Importantly, Morales and MAS represent a *non-revolutionary* route through the crisis. As Webber (2015a: 200) observes, MAS turned a social revolution into the beginnings of a political revolution. Despite turning away from dual power and the possibility of a revolutionary event, MAS continued to rely on the parallel structures of the social movements. We might say that these 'shadowed' the state, both before and after the election.

MAS relied on this extra-systemic organisation initially for its negotiating power, and subsequently for its electoral success. Organisations of campesinos, coca growers, feminist organisations, urban unions and indigenous groups demonstrated, supported and campaigned for MAS. However, given their extra-systemic politics, the question was what would become of these resistant groups after the 2006 election of MAS and later for the new constitution. Did the new government signify a fundamental shift of mode from the mutual illegibility of state and society, or would the old disarticulations re-emerge in new forms? MAS would rely on these extra-systemic movements after the election, claiming to become a government *of* the social movements (instead of a government *for* social movements). The 'government *of* social movements' has to be understood in a double sense: the movements would never simply be incorporated into the state but nor would they simply be expelled or repressed.

For García Linera, because of the motley or disjointed nature of society, Bolivian sovereignty is 'always subject to the spontaneity of plebeian dual power – rather than being an expressive synthesis of society as a whole' (Williams, 2015: 306). Bolivia would always run the risk of dual power until a state could be constituted as hegemony *of* diversity, rather than hegemony *over* diversity (see also Moreiras, 2015). But in practical terms, the way that the new government would relate to the constituent power manifested by the social movements would be crucial. Would it crush resistance, strikes and protest, signaling the continuance of the old state form, or would MAS remain faithful to the movements that took it to power? Even though MAS had not gone all the way with dual power to the revolutionary break, the problem that it generated, one that had been resolved in the bloodiest way by Lenin when the Kronstadt revolt was suppressed, began to manifest itself explicitly within months of the new constitution. If the non-governmental power was allowed to continue in parallel, it would begin to weaken the new executive power as new modes of antagonism appeared. Thus, while the multitude form was crucial to the rise of MAS, the question now became its role in relation to the new state under the new constitution.

The Constitution and Beyond

It is important to situate the question of constituent power in its traditional sense, in order to see the novelty of the Bolivian constitution of turbulence. In most modern written constitutions we find a nod to the originating power of the people that is supposed to be expressed within particular governmental institutions. In constitutional theory, the power of the people is called constituent power, and this is generally thought of as the popular power to tear down the state, reorder society and generate new ways of organising political life (Loughlin, 2003; Wall, 2012). Constituent power is a way for law to give form to the violent moment where the old legal order is overthrown and a new order is established. This power is figured in the constitutional order, but at the same time it is transformed. The once destructive revolutionary power of the people is now apprehended through institutions which take on the mantle of the people. The people's disorderly rejection of the previous regime needs to be appropriated as the moment of origin and authority. However, the process of appropriation is not straightforward because it is important, particularly for liberal constitutional orders, to separate the revolutionary violence from the new political order. The revolutionary event contains an affective dynamics that runs counter to the state. Instead of a habitual obedience, the populace are bound to an idea or practice of another state. The new state must distinguish itself from this violence, because it too must rely ultimately upon a habitual obedience. It must train its populace once again to be restful.

We can therefore identify a double desire at work in Western constitutionalism, to appropriate constituent power and firmly differentiate it from the constitutional order. This results in particular constitutional forms that underscore the popular will while insisting upon its legitimate expression exclusively or primarily through constitutional political forms and institutions. This is the classical Western approach (one largely shared by liberals and conservatives alike). The turbulence of the origin is appropriated and disassociated to generate an apparently stable order. The result is a government empowered to repress popular disorder, protest and even revolution; a government which claims to act to protect the people created and constituted by the constitution, and against the people who manifest themselves in protest. In this way, conventional Western constitutionalism privileges the present state against the potential of a different, future state. Dussel (2008) calls this 'self-referential' power – a power that ultimately refers to itself to justify its actions. The Bolivian constitutional experiment seeks to unwork precisely this development of recursive state power.

Morales' and García Linera's constitutional thinking on this was formed between the experience of radical left resistance in the five years previous to MAS electoral success (2000–2005), and the threats presented by the right-wing former elite after the election of MAS in 2006. For Morales and García Linera, it was important that society should not, once more, become unintelligible to the state. Therefore it was essential that the state remained highly responsive to the social movements. Without this there was a continuing danger of a recurrence of dual power. However, this openness to extra-state social forces could not be unlimited. This was a project under sustained assault from the right and it was therefore essential that the state was strong enough to see off the concerted assault. However, these are two contradictory imperatives. How can a state remain simultaneously defensive against sabotage *and* open to extra-systemic forces that seek to change it? It is best to approach this concretely, as a process whereby contradictions emerge at particular points – what García Linera calls 'creative tensions' – and are resolved. We will look at the two sites of contradiction that were contained within the constitutional apparatus, and one that exceeded it, thereby threatening the entire edifice.

When Morales took power, two issues quickly became apparent – from the constitutional apparatus and the social elite. The first threat manifested itself in the form of the state. While the constitution originated in 1967, it had over and again existed in the shadow of military dictatorships. What is more, the constitutional reforms of 1994 were driven by President Gonzalo Sánchez de Lozada's neoliberal agenda of decentralisation (Hammond, 2011: 663), and so would prove inimical to the MAS platform. The state is a site of conflict and contradiction. Just because new politicians are elected does not mean that the entire state bureaucracy will readily effectuate their wishes. In Greece, Syriza found that bureaucrats and functionaries resisted their new approach to politics (Varoufakis, 2017; Douzinas, 2017). Documents were lost, policy briefings were incomplete or delayed, and processes and protocols were used to slow or block change. In Bolivia, there was administrative resistance, but more than that, the constitution of the state itself was materially and symbolically bound into the neoliberal regime that preceded the election, so that reconstituting it would prove essential to Morales' government.

The second major threat to the Bolivian experiment was the rise of a different sort of dual power, the force of the *media luna* region – the conservative half-moon shaped lowland region starting from the north through to the eastern region of Santa Cruz and the southern province of Tarjia. The *media luna* region began to assert itself against the largely indigenous and poor *altiplano* Central and Western regions. The resulting tension took a number of forms, perhaps most important being increasingly strident separatist demands bankrolled in part by USAID, as Wikileaks revealed (Beeton & Main, 2015). This was very different to the activism of the pre-2006 period in that it was now the former political, social and economic elite who took to the streets in numbers, performing major acts of sabotage on gas pipelines, taking control of airports and government offices across the *media luna* and generally challenging the hegemony of the state and including plans for the assassination of Morales (Evans, 2008; Garcia, 2009). The *media luna* resistance was in effect the old state seeking to reassert itself. Liberal accounts of this antagonism, voices that were often absent during moments of repression before 2006, complained that the state was responding in a way that undermined the promised rights of free speech and association. But the two threats from the right underline precisely the type of problems that the left in power faces (Douzinas, 2016).

In 2010, García Linera quoted Robespierre: 'The objective of a constitutional government is to conserve the Republic; the objective of a revolutionary government is to found it ... The revolutionary government needs extraordinary activities, precisely because it is in a situation of war' (Schilling-Vacaflor, 2011: 13, citing García Linera, 2010).[2] MAS had the role of founding a new state from the remnants of the old one. With Morales, García Linera argued for a strong executive that could resist attempts to return former elites to power. A government *of* social movements should not be conceived in liberal terms, as a neutral arbiter whose function is to facilitate plural political views competing to convince a disinterested population. Such an idealised view always hid a commitment to perpetuate the inequality and indignity of the majority under the status quo. In Bolivia, these were political forms that until 2006 had been used to continue domination by the wealthy, reactionary elite. Schilling-Vacaflor (2011) is correct when he

2 For a fuller discussion of this Jacobin politics see Monzón, 2014.

complains that the strong executive power provided for in the constitution and cemented by MAS was polarising and exclusionary. But more important is his subsequent comment that 'perhaps the debilitation of the existing order and the corresponding institutions was a necessary precondition to constructing a new social and institutional order' (Schilling-Vacaflor, 2011: 14). In other words, the strong executive presented significant threats, but nonetheless it may have been necessary to shift such ingrained social inequality, as well as economic and political exclusion. As Hugo Moldiz put it, 'on the one side, we are creating a new state and, on the other, the old state continues. Therefore … if it is constructed badly, this state is going to end up re-consolidating the old state. It is going to undermine the new state.'[3]

According to conventional separation of powers logic, the strong executive needed to be 'balanced' against other institutions. In particular juridical and legislative institutions could hold a strong executive in check (see, for example, Loughlin, 2003). In terms of juridical power, the Bolivian Constitution sought to destabilise extant state forms. It replaced the Constitutional Tribunal (Constitution of the Republic of Bolivia, 1967: Articles 119–121) with a Plurinational Constitutional Court (Articles 196–204). This sought to generate a creative tension within the state. The reconstitution of the Bolivian judiciary, from a juridical elite to a body that reflects the plurinational population, sought to shed light on the monocultural and elitist nature of the judiciary under the liberal, neoliberal and conservative iterations of the Bolivian state. By reconstituting the judiciary, the process of adjudication itself becomes more visible. Law and judgment become a question rather than a neutral and invisible form of power. The state itself becomes more clearly visible. But this is not just, or perhaps not only about the demystification of power relations. A plurinational supreme court brings plural traditions of judgment, which bring the *process* of decision, and the *normative frameworks* of decision to the centre of the question. Instead of a unitary sense of law, which claims the tradition of European Enlightenment as its object and method, this introduces a turbulence within the juridical rationality. Pluralising the cosmologies at the heart of law can disturb its established forms, but it also reflects the 'motley' nature of society (Augsburger, 2021: 10–13). However, because the new 'plurinational' judiciary would largely be appointed in the Morales era, and would be part of the new constitutional structure, inevitably there is a suspicion that they would lack the strength necessary to restrain a strong executive.

In terms of governmental power, the executive was strengthened against the judiciary and legislature (Constitution of the Plurinational State of Bolivia, Article 172). As in Venezuela and Ecuador, this should be understood not as a

3 He was commenting upon the usefulness of Marx and Lenin in making the revolution: 'We are not going to find in Marx or Lenin, nor in the reading of small stones, nor in the wrinkles of grandparents, the recipe to go forward. We will only find this recipe in the course of the journey. There are no recipes for socialism' (Wynter and McIlroy, 2013).

rejection of the idea of countervailing powers and forces providing a check to the executive, but rather as a problematisation of the liberal separation of powers. The constitution allows other modes of contestation that would be more likely to act with the interests of the poor and excluded in mind than traditionally constituted political parties and judiciary. We might see the parallels with Venezuela's attempt to harness what Chavez called 'communal democracy' in the final speech before his death (Ciccariello-Maher, 2016). The communal experiment in Venezuela consolidated more than 45,000 local communal councils into an increasing number of communes. The communal experiment was not an attempt to decentralise power, as imagined in certain neoliberal schemas. As George Ciccariello-Maher explains, in Venezuela communal democracy 'was never about decentralising power but organising power in the barrios and the country from the bottom up' (Ciccariello-Maher, 2016: 23; see also Wilde, 2017: 140). This is *not* the state trying to create a forum in which groups traditionally excluded from power can be heard by those in power. It is *not* about the powerful having a space to hear the poor, acting as a final arbiter of what constitutes a legitimate demand, and deciding which (market) mechanisms should be used to ameliorate their concerns. Instead Venezuela's communal democracy was an attempt to turn the state inside out, to push actual power out of its confines without simply ceding it to 'the market'. Ciccariello-Maher (2016: 18) explains that the 'state did not create the communes, what the state has done is legally recognize the existence of the first councils and later the communes, formalizing their structure – for better and for worse – and even encouraging their expansion'. Local communal councils are a form of power that was recognised by the Chavez regime as a continuing local manifestation of political consciousness and power. The reforms in the Chavez legislation were designed to legally empower the collectives and to give local communities genuine social and economic power.

While local councils were not introduced or recognised in Bolivia, we might instead see two moves which parallel this. In the most straightforward, the constitution sought to establish 'new spaces for participation and social control' (Constitution of the Plurinational State of Bolivia, 2009: Articles 241 & 242, see also Schilling-Vacaflor, 2011: 4). This includes both a constitutional mandate for civil society to challenge governance, and an obligation on the state to support and provide spaces for this contestation (Article 241.V and 241.VI). In particular, the 'National Coordination for Change' group draws together major social movements into a coordinating mechanism. This mechanism relies on existing social mobilisations and their coordination groups that had taken shape in the Gas and Water wars. The role for these groups in the state was designed to ensure that the constituted power did not become self-referential. However, as we have seen, the danger with this sort of power is that it simply incorporates the social movements *within* the state. The Venezuelan Council experiment also entailed a sort of counter-power beyond the state. The significance of this extra-systemic balancing would become clear with the TIPNIS crisis.

From TIPNIS to the Coup

If the initial threats to MAS in power came from the bureaucracy and the *media luna*, the third challenge came from the social movements that were once at the heart of its popular base. In 2010 a deep division emerged between MAS and the lowland indigenous group the *Confederación de Pueblos del Oriente Boliviano* (CIDOB). In 2011, Morales sought to push through a stretch of highway in the Isiboro-Secure National Park and Indigenous Territory, known as TIPNIS. The road had been planned for at least a decade, but MAS sought to use it to deprioritise the interest of the *media luna* region of Santa Cruz through which goods had to flow from Beni in the north to Cochabamba in the south. The Beni–Cochabamba road instead was to travel through the centre of the country, cutting travel times in half and opening the central region to development. It was part of a network of roads being built in the region, funded by President Lula's Brazil, which would ultimately connect the Amazon region to the Pacific. Webber (2012) suggests that the road was designed to 'promote the flow of Brazilian commodities, particularly soyabeans, to Pacific ports for export'. However, with the road would come capitalist development, in the form of ranchers, loggers and *cocaleros* (coca farmers). This is precisely what the indigenous people of the TIPNIS aimed to resist because it would destroy their ways of life. In August 2011, just under 2000 indigenous people in the TIPNIS park began a march from Trinidad in the Amazon Basin to the capital, La Paz. The protestors marched for a month before arriving in Yucumo – a very small pro-government town just under 100 miles from La Paz – where they were met with significant police violence, with several injured and four dead. The repression led the main trade union, the Bolivian Workers Centre (COB), to call a 24-hour strike on the 28th of September. Two days later Morales suspended the TIPNIS highway project.

Morales had initially called the marchers 'enemies of the nation' because of the significance of the highway for economic and political developments, but by the time he suspended the highway at the beginning of October, he had asked for forgiveness. He disavowed the police violence and claimed that his government would not have ordered it. Following high profile resignations, the TIPNIS resistance gradually subsided. But after the TIPNIS crisis, many national and international left-wing critics insisted that the Bolivian socialist experiment was at an end, and that MAS had begun to pursue policies antithetical to part if not all of its constituency of the poor and excluded (Webber, 2012). These critics suggested that this was not a movement to socialism, but a new type of reformist capitalism. They pointed to the increasing proximity between the *media luna* politicians and MAS (Webber, 2015b). If this was correct, it would signify both the diversion of MAS's political project and the flowering of a 'self-referential' power that would lead to the re-emergence of the illegibility or unintelligibility between state and society. It is important to remember at this point that the purpose of this chapter is not to evaluate the politics of MAS, but rather to understand the constitutional apparatus in the terms suggested by its theorists. For this reason, it is important not to reduce the constitution to the policies of MAS, despite how intricately bound they are to the constitution. It is a mistake to identify what a particular government does within the constitutional framework as the inevitable outcome of that framework itself. A constitution is neither an all-powerful text that can magically transform the nature of political contestation, nor an empty form of words (mere symbolism or empty legalism) that has no effect. It was important for MAS to overcome the old state by way of a constituent assembly and a new constitution precisely because it had material and symbolic effects. A new constitutional apparatus establishes different forms, sites and modes of disagreeing. It imagines particular types of subjects and discursively produces heterogeneous subjectivities that are in excess of those it imagined. It privileges particular modalities of power, but also begets different (unimagined) sites of resistance. In short, constitutional structures have predictable and unpredictable effects as they are received by the populace, as new contradictions emerge and as new practices become conventional. A new constitutional structure has a role in generating these, but it also does not determine them. There are always a myriad of other forces at play.

After 2011, the social base upon which MAS relied began to gradually dwindle, as Morales began to rack up a growing number of significant political mistakes, gradually alienating important allies and parts of its popular base (Santos, 2020). This came to a head in 2019 when Morales failed to reach 51% of the vote in the national election, and the coalition of the 'old middle class' seized their opportunity to overthrow him (García Linera, 2021). A contested election re-ignited the simmering protest of conservative anti-Morales movements. The MAS government began to lose their grip on the state soon after the initial election results emerged. Large scale protests were swift, with escalating violence directed against MAS offices, communities and activists. In a matter of days the police mutinied (García Linera, 2019), the Head of the Army 'suggested' that Morales should step down. On the 12th of November, 2019, Morales fled to asylum in Mexico and the following day the conservative deputy head of the Senate, Jeanine Áñez, took over the position of 'interim' President.

Reflecting on these events, García Linera explained that 'the military threw their weight behind the coup because, as the days passed, there was no social mobilization. It didn't seem like a big issue at the time – we had seen plenty of similar attempts over the years' (García Linera, 2021). But this miscalculation allowed the plotters to convince the police and military that mobilisation would not follow their disobedience. When they made their support for the coup clear, Morales was faced with an impossible decision to call for a full mobilisation of the social movements and risk significant bloodshed, or resign (García Linera, 2021). Once in power, the leaders of the new government sought to strengthen the hand of the military and police, initially giving them full immunity from prosecution over any deaths that occurred while suppressing any social unrest.[4] At the same time, they sought to re-establish the special position of the Catholic Church for the state. One of the leaders, Luis Fernando Camacho, infamously insisted during the coup that 'Bolivia for Christ, Pachamama will never again enter this [presidential] palace' (Casey, 2019). Áñez initially selected a cabinet that was entirely free of any indigenous people, before buckling to pressure and adding two indigenous ministers. Together, they set to work undermining the social policy and constitutional structures established since 2009. They sought to change the symbolic and normative orientation of the state, shifting the gradual 'indianisation' of the state and destroying its plurinational symbols. For our purposes, it is Áñez's vow to pacify the country and 'reconstruct democracy' (Collyns, 2019) that is of particular importance. This was not simply a matter of shifting social policy; the new state would attempt to 'pacify' its populace. In other words, they aimed to un-work the continuing potential of a disruptive constituent power, to destroy the extra-systemic counter-power that the constitutional theorists described.

As in the Water and Gas wars, La Paz's reliance on water, food, power and fuel which ran through El Alto – the working class and indigenous city just above the capital – was once more critical. Soon after the coup, barricades were established and connections cut. These forced Áñez to promise swift elections in January, albeit without Morales, whom the coup charged with various crimes. The pressure also forced her to revoke the immunity of the police and army, and these concessions led to the lifting of the first blockade. Fresh elections were the central plank of the coup's international claim for legitimacy. Áñez was only supposed to act as a transitional leader who would hold elections on the 22nd of January, and then step aside. But the elections did not materialise, initially because of delays within the government and later for Coronavirus-related reasons. By the end of July of 2020, there was a growing demand from below for fresh elections. The problem for the right was that polls suggested that MAS would again win in the first round of the election with over 40% of the vote. The coup leaders – now fragmented into three or four political constituencies – baulked at the possibility of losing power to MAS once more, even if Morales was no longer directly in power.

In early August 2020, following a fourth suspension of elections a general strike began: social movements began a national blockade of roads; key Andean passes (essential for the movement of goods and services around the country) were dynamited; and major protests broke out. García Linera (2021) remarked that the social movements took territorial control of key zones as they had done in 2000. What's more, there was evidence to suggest that the state apparatus that had been so essential in the coup was beginning to turn. For instance, Ollie Vargas reported that the absence of police from many of these protests in August may have been connected to reports that in certain areas the police were refusing to be mobilised to defend the coup (Democracy Now! 2020). The strike appeared to show the popular base that had become more passive

4 Supreme Decree No. 4078. 15/11/2019. Bolivia.

under Morales, once more returning to the streets. And this finally forced Áñez's hand. The election took place on the 18th of October 2020, and Luis Arce of MAS was swept to power in the first round with 55% of the vote.

With the defeat of the coup, the question becomes how it should be conceptualised in constitutional terms. Very clearly, the Áñez government sought to unwork the 2009 constitutional apparatus. Pachamama and plurinationality were a key focus for them, but the coup-government also sought to pacify the social movements. There were massacres, extensive state repression and vindictive prosecutions. The government was hostile to the very constitutional apparatus itself. However, what is fascinating is that it is exactly the extra-systemic living constituent power that the theorists of the 2009 constitution point to, that guaranteed the constitutional apparatus itself. The coup was a failure, not simply in the sense that Áñez was forced into elections that the right lost. It was also a failure in the sense that the constitutional apparatus – with its intra-systemic forces *and* its extra-systemic 'living' constituent power – was maintained even in its suspension. If the constitutional apparatus creates the sites and forms of contestation, then the coup demonstrates both its weakness (that the coup was initially possible) and strength (that it was ultimately defeated). But it also underscores the inadequacy of simply focusing on the constitution, as a rarefied document. The constitution did not organise the popular mobilisation, it did not generate and maintain the living solidarity that made such resistance possible. The constitution is not magic. But if we understand the constitutional apparatus as combining an intra-systemic organisation of power *and* an extra-systemic check on that power from the social movements, then we can begin to grasp its importance.

The Constitution of Turbulence

I argue that we should understand this combination of intra-systemic and extra-systemic modes of contestation as the 'constitution of turbulence'. That is, the 'constitution' of a series of forces that can challenge the state as its power becomes recursive. I mean 'constitution' here not in the sense that it 'creates' the extra-systemic constituent power, but rather that it recognises these extra-systemic forces (like the Venezuelan communal system) and accepts their importance to the entire constitutional apparatus. It is a constitution of turbulence because it goes beyond Western constitutionalism's tendency to absorb and pacify constituent power, instead adopting the ongoing role of a form of constituent power that lives beyond the state structure. Early liberal constitutionalism proposed a strong set of institutional forms *in which* political antagonism could take place. More recent generations of constitutional experiments have often sought to democratise governmental processes through localism, participatory planning and other mechanisms. The Andean constitutional experiments in Venezuela, Ecuador and Bolivia are a radicalisation of these attempts that seeks to place meaningful social and economic power into the hands of the poor and excluded while retaining a strong central power capable of seeing off threats to the constitutional settlement. This constitutionalisation of power was always going to struggle not to become self-referential by overemphasising the executive form over all others. Extra-systemic contestation is, by its very nature, a challenge to state order. In most situations, the first response of public power to extra-systemic contestation is likely to be a mix of grudging tolerance and careful policing of the bounds of action. States enter into a calculation about how and when they can legitimately suppress extra-systemic contestation. Liberal accounts claim that Bolivian constitutionalism is authoritarian because it has strengthened the executive and weakened the judiciary and the legislature. I suggest that this misses the basic principle upon which the constitutional apparatus is understood by its theorists.

In *Las Tensiones Creativas de la Revolución*, García Linera (2013b) argues that there were five stages in the revolutionary process between 2000 and 2010, from Cochabamba to the subordination of *media luna* autonomism. These stages would be progressively overcome, transforming into creative tensions within a national-popular bloc that underlies the institution of the state. What is important here is less García Linera's historicisation of state power, than the basic method that underlies it (Webber, 2016). At the outset, the executive formulates a policy. In a neoliberal model, this would be analysed as risk or cost/benefit, which can be assuaged or massaged through transnational and national expert intervention. In the Bolivian model, it is instead put through internal processes of contestation and challenge from social movements and other interests as they operate within the state, thus involving the operation of an internal participatory model. However, crucially, this is not the end point. Despite this internal contestation, there can never be any guarantee that the new policy is actually in the best interests of the poor and excluded, or for that matter, that it is supported by them. There is always a significant risk that those in power will succumb to the recursive 'logic of the state' which Abensour (2011) contrasts with the 'logic of democracy'. Social movements have long been aware of the dangers of 'participation', through which they can be co-opted, bought off or become overly-reliant on the state. As MacNelly (2016) explains in the Bolivian context, 'Many protagonists of the struggles of 2000–05 were given positions within the government, decapitating local civil society leadership and cementing the government's official channels as the legitimate route for change'. By encouraging only intra-systemic contestation the government seeks to bring political contestation onto its own terrain. The ultimate danger as MacNelly underlines is the decapitation of social movements which might close 'off alternative avenues to enact change from below' (MacNelly, 2016). However, what García Linera's method underlines is that one of the primary theorists of the new constitution envisages that there will always be extra-systemic contestation. The Bolivian constitution is an invitation to dissensus (Ranciere, 1999). The government embarks upon a course of action, which drives contestation from below as social forces reconstitute themselves through new modes of coordination within the multitude-form. This is the process in which the relation of intelligibility or legibility between the state and society breaks down and is reconstituted. When the crisis comes to a head, the disarticulation is at its most extreme before coming to some sort of resolution. While the disorder of this disarticulation appears to signal a failure of the constitutional structure, I contend that it is essential to the vibrancy of the Bolivian experiment. Ironically, the rise and fall of the coup is the ultimate expression of this structure.

The Bolivian Constitution of 2009 is based on a theory of constitutions in which the necessity of extra-systemic contestation is essential. The state neither rolls over in the face of disagreement nor instantly represses it. In place of the standard managerial understanding of politics against which constitutional settlements are measured, the constitution becomes a genuinely political point of contestation. This is essential because if this argument is correct, success should be measured by the extent to which the population remains engaged in the contestation of political policies. This means that it should encourage schisms and political spats, social movements combining in ever novel forms while breaking with MAS and reformulating agreements, engaging in lively protests, strikes and blockades. In this perspective, success is measured in turbulence, dissensus and disagreement. If 'creative tensions' are managed away, if they never become apparent on the streets, if they are hidden in backroom agreements and uncontested expert interventions, the system merely returns to a managerial constitutionalism. Failure may be measured by pacified docility of the population, even in the face of measures clearly against their interests, whereas success is to be found in the arguing of the state to a standstill. As García Linera put it in the context of the economic planning of mining: 'You have to argue over it. In plebeian language, [this means] … work stoppages, marches, threats, reconciliation. And it produces a more complicated, more conflictive, riskier outcome but it is the people deciding about a common resource' (García Linera, 2013a). This, then, is a constitution of turbulence.

References

Abensour, M., 2011. *Democracy against the State*. Polity.

Alesina, A., Ozler, S., Roubini, N., and Swagel, P., 1992. Political Instability and Economic Growth. *National Bureau of Economic Research Working Paper 4173*. http://www.nber.org/papers/w4173 (accessed 31 July 2018).

Augsburger, A., 2021. The Plurinational State and Bolivia's Formación Abigarrada. *Third World Quarterly*, 42 (7): 1566–1582, DOI: doi:10.1080/01436597.2021.1899803.

Augusto Baldi, C., 2013. Sumak Kawsay, Interculturality and Decolonialization. *Critical Legal Thinking*15/04/2013, http://criticallegalthinking.com/2013/04/15/sumak-kawsay-interculturality-and-decolonialization/ (accessed 31 July 2018).

Beeton, D. and Main, A., 2015. The Latin America Wikileaks Files. *Jacobin* (29/09/2015) available at https://www.jacobinmag.com/2015/09/latin-america-wikileaks-hugo-chavez-rafael-correa-obama-venezuela-intervention/ (accessed 2 May 2017).

Buchanan, R., 2006. Legitimating Global Trade Governance: Constitutional and Legal Pluralist Approaches. 57*Northern Ireland Legal Quarterly*, 1–19.

Casey, M., 2019. Old Religious Tensions Resurge in Bolivia after Ouster of Longtime Indigenous President. *The Conversation*, 19 November. https://theconversation.com/old-religious-tensions-resurge-in-bolivia-after-ouster-of-longtime-indigenous-president-127000 (accessed 12 January 2021).

Ciccariello-Maher, G., 2016. *Building the Commune*. Verso.

Collyns, D., 2019. Bolivia President's Initial Indigenous-free Cabinet Heightens Polarization. *The Guardian* (14 November). https://www.theguardian.com/world/2019/nov/14/bolivia-president-jeanine-anez-cabinet-indigenous (accessed 12 January 2021).

Colon Rios, J., 2012. *Weak Constitutionalism: Democratic Legitimacy and the Question of Constituent Power*. Routledge.

Constitution of the Plurinational State of Bolivia, 2009. Available at http://www.parliament.am/library/sahmanadrutyunner/Bolivia.pdf (accessed 2 May 2017).

Constitution of the Republic of Bolivia, 1967. Available at http://pdba.georgetown.edu/Constitutions/Bolivia/consboliv2005.html (accessed 31 July 2018).

Cubillo-Guevara, A.P., Hidalgo-Capitán, A.L., and García-Álvarez, S., 2016. El Buen Vivir como alternativa al desarrollo para América Latina. *Iberoamerican Journal of Development Studies*, 5(2): 30–57.

Democracy Now!2020. General Strike & Blockade in Bolivia Enter Day 11 as Protesters Condemn Delayed Vote by Coup Government. *Democracy Now!*13 August. https://www.democracynow.org/2020/8/13/bolivia_general_strike_ollie_vargas (accessed 12 January 2021).

Douzinas, C., 2016. The Left in Power. *Critical Legal Thinking*, 11/04/16. Available at http://criticallegalthinking.com/2016/04/11/left-in-power-syriza-possible-second-rise/ (accessed 2 May 2017.)

Douzinas, C., 2017. *Syriza in Power*. Pluto Press.

Dussel, E., 2008. *Twenty Theses on Politics*. Duke University Press.

Evans, D., 2008. Bolivia 'Uncovers' Plot to Assassinate President Evo Morales. *The Telegraph*, 23 December.

Freeland, A., 2014. Notes on Rene Zavaleta: Abigarramiento as Condition of Constitutive Power. *Alternautas* 1 (1): 65–70. http://www.alternautas.net/blog/2014/8/31/k1gjjqvwi5c2eqc5hl3ckgm3i4fdyp (accessed 31 July 2018).

García Linera, A., 2004. The 'multitude'. in Olivera, O. with Lewis, T. *Cochabamba: Water War in Bolivia*. South End Press.

García Linera, A., 2008. *La Potencia Plebeya: Acción colectiva e identidades indígenas, obreras y populares en Bolivia*. Edited by Pablo Stefanoni. Buenos Aires: Prometeo Libros.

García Linera, A. 2010. El Estado en Transición. Bloque de Poder y Punto de Bifurcación. In García Linera, Á., Prada, R., Tapia, L. and Vega Camacho, O. (eds), *El Estado. Campo de Lucha*. La Paz: Muela del Diablo, pp. 9–43.

García Linera, A., 2013a. There Is No Exclusive Model. *Bolivia Rising*. 4 June. http://boliviarising.blogspot.co.uk/2013/06/alvaro-garcia-linera-there-is-no.html (accessed 31 July 2018).

García Linera, A., 2013b. *Las Tensiones Creativas de la Revolución: La Quinta Fase del Proceso de Cambio en Bolivia*. Luxemburg.

García Linera, A., 2019. The Military Coup that Overthrew Our Government Was Revenge Against Indigenous Bolivians. *Jacobin Magazine*. Available at https://jacobinma

g.com/2019/11/evo-morales-coup-indigenous-bolivia-alvaro-garcia-linera (accessed 10 June 2021).

García Linera, A., 2021. Former Bolivian VP Álvaro García Linera on How Socialists Can Win. *Jacobin Magazine*. Available at https://jacobinmag.com/2021/04/interview-alvaro-garcia-linera-mas-bolivia-coup (accessed 9 June 2021).

Garcia, E., 2009. Plot to Kill Bolivia's President Foiled. *Reuters*, 16 April 2009.

Gudynas, E., 2011. Buen Vivir: Today's Tomorrow. *Development* 54 (4): 441.

Hammond, J. L., 2011. Indigenous Community Justice in the Bolivian Constitution of 2009. *Human Rights Quarterly* 33(3): 649.

Hesselroth, A., 2015. The Decolonization of Bolivia's Antinarcotics Policy. *Bolivian Studies Journal* 21: 63.

Knight, J., 2013. The Economic Causes and Consequences of Social Instability in China. *China Economic Review* 25: 17.

Lenin, V. I., 1917. The Dual Power. *Pravda* (no. 28), available at https://www.marxists.org/archive/lenin/works/1917/apr/09.htm (accessed 31 July 2018).

Loughlin, M., 2003. *The Idea of Public Law*. Oxford University Press.

MacNelly, A., 2016. Evo Morales and the Limits of Twentieth Century Socialism. *Roar Magazine*, 02/03/2016, https://roarmag.org/essays/bolivia-referendum-morales-lost/ (accessed 31 July 2018).

Mattison, C. and Mignolo, W., 2012. Delinking, Decoloniality & Dewesternization: Interview with Walter Mignolo (Part II). *Critical Legal Thinking* (02/05/2012), available at http://criticallegalthinking.com/2012/05/02/delinking-decoloniality-dewesternization-interview-with-walter-mignolo-part-ii/ (accessed 31 July 2018).

Monzón, J., 2014. The Constitution as a Post-Colonial Discourse: An Insight into the Constitution of Bolivia. *The Seattle Journal for Social Justice* 12 (3), available at http://digitalcommons.law.seattleu.edu/cgi/viewcontent.cgi?article=1712&context=sjsj (accessed 21 April 2017).

Moreiras, A., 2015. Democracy in Latin America: Álvaro García Linera, an Introduction. *Culture, Theory, Critique*, 56 (3): 266–282.

Olivera, O., with Lewis, T., 2004. *Cochabamba: Water War in Bolivia*. South End Press.

Ranciere, J., 1999. *Dis-agreement – Politics and Philosophy*. University of Minnesota Press.

Renn, O., Jovanovic, A., Schröter, R., 2011. Social Unrest. *OECD/IFP Future Global Shocks Program*. IFP/WKP/FGS(2011)5. Available at http://www.oecd.org/gov/risk/46890018.pdf (accessed 21/04/17).

Santos, B. de, S., 2020. Evo Morales: An Indian Out of Place. CADTM. Available at https://www.cadtm.org/Evo-Morales-An-Indian-out-of-place (accessed 8 June 2021).

Schilling-Vacaflor, A. 2011. Bolivia's New Constitution: Towards Participatory Democracy and Political Pluralism. *European Review of Latin American and Caribbean Studies* 90: 3.

Varoufakis, Y., 2017. *Adults in the Room*. Farrar, Strauss and Girard.

Wall, I. R., 2012. *Human Rights and Constituent Power*. Routledge.

Webber, J., 2012. Revolution Against "Progress": The TIPNIS Struggle and Class Contradictions in Bolivia. *International Socialism: A Journal of Socialist Theory*2012 (January): 133. Available online at http://www.isj.org.uk/?id=780 (accessed 1 January 2015).

Webber, J., 2015a. Dual Powers, Class Compositions, and the Venezuelan People. *Historical Materialism* 23 (2): 189–227.

Webber, J., 2015b. Bolivia's Passive Revolution. *Jacobin* (29/10/15). https://www.jacobinmag.com/2015/10/morales-bolivia-chavez-castro-mas/ (accessed 24 April 2017).

Webber, J., 2016. Evo Morales and the Political Economy of Passive Revolution in Bolivia, 2006–2015. *Third World Quarterly* 37 (10): 1855–1876.

Wilde, M., 2017. Contested Spaces: The Communal Councils and Participatory Democracy in Chavez's Venezuela. *Latin American Perspectives* 44 (1): 140.

Williams, G., 2015. Social Disjointedness and State-Form. *Culture, Theory and Critique* 56 (3): 297–312.

Wynter, C. and McIlroy, J., 2013. There are no recipes for socialism: Interview with Hugo Moldiz, Bolivian Marxist. *Links: International Journal of Socialist Renewal.* Available at http://links.org.au/node/3318 (accessed 2 May 2017).

Chapter 5

'I Built this House on my Back'

A Historical Perspective on Care and Property in East Africa

Ambreena Manji and Ann Stewart

> ... the most aggressive prostitution, conducted from windows and stoops, was performed by the most dutiful of daughters. The women who walked the streets were working for their families. It was the women who waited decorously and discreetly in their rooms, peaceful and isolated, deferential and polite, who were in fact entirely out for themselves, eager to disinherit fathers and brothers and to establish themselves as independent heads of households ... they believed in independent accumulation.
>
> (White, 1990: 20–21)

Introduction

The substantive content of this chapter revisits Luise White's groundbreaking study on prostitution in colonial Nairobi, which brought feminist scholarship to bear on development studies. It is an example of the way in which feminist analysis has opened new perspectives and challenged accepted scholarship in the field of development studies as well as in the narrower field of law in development, although 'law' proved to be resistant to a gender analysis for longer than many other disciplines. The chapter begins therefore with a brief reflection on how feminist scholarship has provided a critique of law in development scholarship. It then moves on to demonstrate how the critiques offered relate to our re-reading of Luise White's work from a contemporary feminist perspective and contributes to setting agendas for the future.

East African history is used to explore care labour, its performance, and its recognition. In recent years there has emerged a growing literature on care and social reproduction, in particular their meaning, content, and quantification (Stewart, 2015; Stewart, 2017; Hoskyns and Rai, 2007; Rai, Hoskyns & Thomas, 2014). The World Bank (2011) has stated that recognising and redistributing the burden of care is 'smart economics' because it promotes gender equality but also addresses economic exclusion. International campaigners and human rights policy makers have asserted, in the context of the post 2015 Sustainable Development Goals (SDG) that a rights approach should be adopted (Sepulveda Carmona, 2013).

DOI: 10.4324/9780203745298-7

This literature has tended to focus on contemporary manifestations of (unpaid) care work (Sustainable Development Goals, Equality Goal 5, target 4). In this chapter our aim is to explore the recognition of care labour in historical perspective before reflecting more briefly on a present example which has roots in East African history. We ask: how might using historical material as a source, and thus *going back* to look for care, cast light on our thinking about care giving and care compensation? What do historical accounts of women's reproductive labour, for example, tell us when viewed anew through a care lens? How has reproductive labour been rewarded historically? Specifically, what are the connections between care labour and property as a form of compensation?

We revisit Luise White's path-breaking book on prostitution in colonial Nairobi and reread it for care. We focus on two themes. Firstly, we explore the 'labour forms' of prostitution in colonial Nairobi uncovered by White and consider them as forms of care labour, focusing on the provision of care and its receipt. Secondly, we look at how the strategies of property accumulation of *malaya* women in colonial Nairobi facilitated their accumulation of significant 'bequeathable assets' (Bernheim et al., 1985). We argue that this allows us to explore the operation of a care-property nexus (Sloan, 2013) both upstream and downstream. Upstream, the work of *malaya* women reproduced male labour cheaply for the colonial state (in their subdued, respectful form of prostitution they were 'like wives' (White, 1990: 65)). They were important care workers. At the same time, the practice of *malaya* prostitution enabled women to engage in rapid independent property accumulation. Determined to deny their patrilineal kin and to disinherit fathers, brothers and uncles, propertied women adopted independent kin ('pseudo-kin' in Bujra's (1975) formulation) to whom they left their accumulated property, often through 'woman to woman' marriages. These new kin were often young women who in their turn provided care to the *malaya* woman in old age. We argue that, downstream, the choice to take on new women kin constituted bequest strategies based on care considerations (Bernheim et al., 1985; Kalabamu, 2014). *Malaya* women bequeathed their accumulated property in return for care received. What might these strategies of accumulation and bequest tell us about care and its compensation historically? This chapter thus seeks to understand bequest strategies (Bernheim et al., 1985; Deininger et al., 2010) and care claims in their historical specificity.

We continue to use insights from a historical perspective to reflect on contemporary connections between care labour and the use of property as a form of compensation. Our focus shifts to an examination of what is known colloquially as woman-to-woman marriages (WTW) to reread them from a care perspective. White's account of the way in which the *malaya* women used this practice breaks with the mainstream historical anthropological literature, which saw WTW in East Africa as a means of addressing infertility and supporting patriarchal lineage systems. We review the colonial and post-colonial literature from a care perspective and explore its contemporary use to assess the extent to which the practice is being recognised, as for the *malaya* women, as a means of caring by and for older propertied women. To what extent are claims by the care-giving younger women being recognised in the plural legal context of Kenya? We argue that reviewing *malaya* sex working and WTW from a care perspective sheds interesting light on the relationship between care labour and property. Women who have accumulated some assets are able to use this bequeathable wealth in older age to secure care for themselves. The arrangement adopted, which is rooted in an accepted customary practice, enables the younger care-givers to secure a better future for themselves as 'wife/care givers' rather than 'domestic servant/care givers'. We therefore see the way in which women recast these relationships as responses to the injustices of patriarchy.

Looking Back to Look Forward

White (1990: 21) argues that her research established that in colonial Nairobi, '[t]he work of prostitutes was family labor' and that prostitutes' patterns of reinvestment reproduced families: some 'inaugurating [a new] cycle of family and lineage formation in literal, concrete terms' (White, 1990: 16; see also Shrage, 1994). She is aware that this finding contradicted 'prevailing perceptions of the place of prostitution and the exploitation of prostitutes in capitalist societies' which centre on degradation and victimisation. She asks: is this because prostitution in Nairobi was unique, incomparable with anything in the West or is it because scholarship has focused on the ways in which prostitution has been regulated in Europe and America? Is it because Africa is completely different? Or because her findings result from interviews from the women themselves who tell their own story (White, 1990: 8)? Her frame of reference is informed by conceptual understandings of the contribution of what has been defined as social reproduction (SR) to production.[1] 'If prostitution is one of the forms domestic labour takes, where it takes place merely describes the site of the reproduction of male labour power' (White, 1990: 12). White's perspective is 'political economy written with women's words' rather than 'women's history' (White, 1990: 21). She was writing at a time when 'African historians were beginning to privilege participants' accounts over those of colonial rulers' (White, 1990: 28).

The debates over how to understand prostitution have intensified greatly since White asked her questions but these questions have far wider resonance for the way in which feminist scholarship, particularly in the area of law, has addressed 'development'. First because of feminism, women's experiences have formed the basis for critiques of prevalent understandings and informed new

1 Rai and Hoskyns describe SR as: 'biological reproduction; unpaid production in the home (both goods and services); social provisioning (by this we mean voluntary work directed at meeting needs in the community); the reproduction of culture and ideology; and the provision of sexual, emotional and affective services (such as are required to maintain family and intimate relationships)' (Hoskyns & Rai, 2007: 300).

ways of thinking in huge swathes of scholarship and activism, perhaps most obviously in relation to international human rights law. Secondly and more importantly for present purposes, women have become less 'hidden from history'. The work of Mbilinyi (1988), Bujra (1975), White (1990), and Chanock (1982), informed by gender perspectives, revealed the contradictions and understandings of colonialism. Customary law was understood as a product of complex power relationships, involving contests and alliances between dominant men often keen to keep women in their place. It was thus malleable and open to change. The nature of the colonial state was re-evaluated from a gender perspective (Parpart and Staudt, 1989). Women emerged as actors who both experienced the impact of the state, and exploited opportunities available, in different ways to men, as we see in the present study (Stewart, 1996; Manji, 1999).

Thirdly, these insights informed analysis of the post-colonial state and, in particular, the enduring importance of understanding the implications of legal pluralism from an African gender perspective (Hellum et al., 2007). Both men's and women's identity and subjectivity are moulded within complex 'semi-autonomous social fields' (Falk Moore, 1978). However, women experience their subjectivity as clanspersons and citizens differently (Merry, 2006). They, along with women globally, are expected to undertake a disproportionate amount of SR necessary to support families, communities, and society. This labour tends to be located within the family and community, the institutions that are regulated through customary and religious (often now described as 'non-state') norms and are responsible for the allocation of resources. Thus, claims for recognition of the work of care are primarily contested within this domain, as recently illustrated by Nyamu Musembi's (2013) critique of the way in which the CEDAW committee understands 'harmful cultural practices' in legally pluralist African states.

Once customary law is understood as contestable, it becomes important to find out who has the power to contest and under what conditions. What is the impact of socio-economic change and the spread of equality and rights ideologies on customary law? What 'truths' are heard in dispute resolution fora including courts? Ground breaking socio-legal research from a gender/women's perspective to privilege participants' accounts, in White's words, opened new perspectives and critiques. This included the research undertaken by the Women and Law in Southern Africa and subsequently by the Southern and Eastern African Regional Centre for Women's Law in collaboration with the University of Oslo Women's Law Institute and Anne Hellum (1999) in particular, along with other scholars such as Anne Griffiths (1997), which sought to find out what was happening 'on the ground' from a gender/women's perspective. Their many and varied findings included understanding the normative basis for practices: that a relational subjectivity, reflected in such concepts as Ubuntu, challenges the highly autonomous individualism enshrined in neoliberal rule of law ideology and enriches feminist ethics of care scholarship and feminist discussions related to relational autonomy, responsibility and vulnerability (Fineman, 2008). Anne Hellum's (1999) study of infertility, presaging subsequent interest in WTW practices, revealed the nuanced ways in which this issue was addressed within the legally pluralist context of Zimbabwe.

At the level of practice, these findings challenged the truth relating to customary practices presented in courts. Is it still the case, as we explore later, that daughters do not inherit under many customary systems and that WTW are solely concerned with ensuring male inheritance when a wife is 'barren'? Are women adapting practices to provide for their needs? Are these changes recognised and forming the basis for claims?

Feminist scholars brought the 'private', understood in an African context, into critical scholarship because it matters to women. This perspective shone a different light on the developmental state and its responses to women's claims for equality. One of the present authors questioned in 1996 whether 'women should give up on the state in Africa' in her analysis of high profile/infamous court cases involving such claims (Stewart, 1996). The other argued that the phallocentric legal centralist paradigm had hindered women's engagement with legal pluralism in Africa and that state law has been at best ambivalent and at worst physically and symbolically coercive (Manji, 1999).

White's work is set within a political economy framework but adds a gender perspective. She understands prostitution as a form of domestic labour. Since her work in 1990, materialist analysis of law has lost its resonance within feminist legal scholarship (contra Conaghan, 2013; Fudge, 2013; Rittich, 2002). Nonetheless, there has been a resurgence of interest within what can broadly be defined as the political economy of development for understanding the way in which the relationship between socially reproductive and productive labour is being recast under present conditions of globalisation. To put it simply: care matters. Millions of women (and some men) migrate internally and internationally, often under very poor social and labour conditions, to provide it as domestic workers/carers. Women's continuing responsibility for its provision deeply affects the way in which they are incorporated into global labour markets (Stewart, 2011; Pearson, 2014). The burden of care traps the poorest in a life of drudgery and deprives them of the ability to engage with the labour market (World Bank, 2011; Sepulveda Carmona, 2013).

Feminist scholars and activists are developing new ways of understanding SR and tackling the inequalities associated with it. They focus on its depletion and the role of families, communities, and states in its replenishment (Rai, Hoskyns and Thomas, 2014). Pearson (2014) argues that the state has a key role in providing 'social infrastructure' to relieve the burdens of care. Activist organisations have been developing ways of quantifying the burden of care on the bodies of individual women and on communities (Bibler & Zuckerman, 2013; Oxfam, 2016). International policy makers have been arguing for a right to care – in effect a right of the individual to be relieved of excessive care through the provision of additional resources (Sepulveda Carmona, 2013). These claims have been organised around the need to recognise, reduce, and redistribute care – the 3Rs agenda (Elson, 2008). They have met with some success. Target 5: 4 of the SDG equality goal requires all to: recognise and value unpaid care and domestic work through the provision of public services, infrastructure and social protection policies, and the promotion of shared responsibility within the household and the family as nationally appropriate. This critique of much of the mainstream policy discussions focuses on how care affects an ability to labour productively and efficiently (World Bank, 2011). However, the focus of this chapter, reflecting that of White, is on how the labour of care relates to the accumulation and transfer of property assets.

Labour Forms, Care and the Colonial State

White (1990: 20) sought to 'conceptualis[e] prostitution through its labour forms'. Arguing that the different labour forms taken by colonial prostitution in Nairobi between 1920 and the late 1950s are connected with 'strategies of reproduction not with personality', White showed how each form of prostitution had its own characteristics, as well as its own 'rate of accumulation, and organisation of labour time' (ibid.). White's work distinguishes between *Watembezi, Wazi Wazi* and *Malaya* prostitution. In the *Watembezi* form, which derives its name from the Kiswahili verb, Kutembea, to walk, women solicited on the street. In the Wazi Wazi form, women sat outside their doors, calling out to men and engaged in brief sexual encounters in which they provided sexual, but rarely other, services to men. The origins of the name *Wazi Wazi* have been debated: some suggest it is taken from the Kiswahili word open, to suggest the open porches and windows of the women, others that they take their name from their origins in the Waziba clans of northwest Tanganyika (now Tanzania). The *Malaya* form, in which we are most interested in this chapter, was a stable form of prostitution, offered by women – often converts to Islam – from their rooms and later houses. Beginning life as 'urban tenants', these women practised a slow and steady form of accumulation, establishing themselves over time as independent heads of households with their 'healthy respect for the value of real estate' (White, 1990: 17). These forms can also be related to kinship. Wazi Wazi women, originating in the Bukoba district of northwest Tanganyika, came to colonial Nairobi to accumulate money to send back to their fathers in order to help them to cope with their recent integration into the world economy by the colonial compulsion to grow cash crops such as coffee. This was the 'prostitution of daughters'. These women 'saved a generation of indebted cash crop producers' (White, 1990: 20) when they came home to Tanganyika in the 1940s bearing their earnings from Nairobi and handed them over to their male kin. As White beautifully shows, it was the labour of the streetwalking, aggressive prostitutes widely condemned in Nairobi for their shameful public behaviour which had the most loyal and familial of ambitions: earnings were returned to father and brothers in order to stabilise them and to provide for male kin, for example by establishing them as farmers on their smallholdings or as shopkeepers. In contrast, *Malaya* women practised a slow, Islam-inflected form of prostitution in which concealment, honour, and demure behaviour were expected. Yet these women 'were in it for themselves' (White, 1990: 16), their outward propriety masking the reality that they fully intended to disinherit their male kin. In doing this, they 'were inaugurating the cycle of family and lineage formation in literal, concrete terms, and taken in aggregate, they were involved in class formation; they were joining the ranks of the urban petty bourgeoisie' (ibid.).

The centrality of domesticity to forms of prostitution in colonial Nairobi is richly suggestive. In Kenya, the colonial state explicitly recognised the constructive role that *malaya* women played in reproducing male labour for a state structured around a migrant labour economy. Citing a report by Eric Davies, the Municipal Native Affairs Officer, White shows that the colonial authorities were clear sighted in their recognition that these women 'could reproduce male labour power cheaply and effectively enough for the state' (White, 1990: 94). For example, the colonial state was, through the labour of *malaya* women, saved the costs of providing housing to migrant workers. Women's sexual and reproductive labour enabled the state to depress wages because migrant men did not have to maintain families in urban Nairobi. It was not necessary to pay them a family wage.

Malaya women formed a feminised, urban, 'intimate-labour class' (Hochschild, 1983) who through their work subsidised the colonial state. Of what did this work consist? White is clear that *malaya* women provided both sexual services and care. She writes: '*Malaya* women provided the amenities working men needed' (White, 1990: 56). Women told White: 'you talk, you make tea for him, and you keep your house clean…no one could tell they were … not my husband just by looking' (ibid.). White points out:

> poor men could purchase fleeting domesticity while skilled and self-employed men could afford night-long imitations of married life … bathwater, bread, cleanliness, respect … not only did these reproduce labour power but they did so in a gendered vision of service that working men could purchase.
>
> (White, 1990: 226)

In *malaya* prostitution, a woman is being paid not just for the task-based labour she will perform but also for her emotional commitment and intimacy. 'They wanted loyalty, and personal attention, and greetings in their own language – they wanted the reproduction of intimacy' (White, 1990: 227), as captured by the feminist SR concept (Hoskyns and Rai, 2007).

But *malaya* women's property accumulation pointed out one of the contradictions of the colonial state. To the extent that it needed women to assist in the reproduction of labour, it was also ambivalent about their work: the result of their work was property accumulation and class formation (Bujra, 1975; White, 1990). It is to these implications of women's property accumulation that we now turn.

The Care:Property Nexus

What then might be the relationship between care and property? In this section, we explore what we know about how care might be being recognised and compensated through the mechanism of bequest and at the moment of inheritance. Deininger et al. (2010) have argued in relation to new inheritance laws in India that 'at low levels of development, land is not only a key asset but inheritance also constitutes the main avenue for accessing it.' In his work on peri-urban Gaborone, Kalabamu (2014) has focused on new practices of inheritance by daughters that avoid discriminatory customary rules that formally disbar them from inheriting property from their parents. Kalabamu has argued that there has been an increase in parents choosing to endow their daughters with property after their death in recognition of the care investment made by the daughter (which is often supplemented by financial contributions to building new houses such as purchasing building materials). He has described this recognition of care work done by daughters – for example, by residing with their parents, remaining unmarried and 'looking after them in their old age' – as an emerging 'duty-beneficiary principle'. Kalabamu has argued that there is in consequence an emerging gender equality, although the recognition of care provided to parents is not uncontested by male kin.

Kalabamu's work builds on a rich seam of African feminist socio-legal scholarship identified above which has recognised that customary rules are products of and reflect complex power relations (Griffiths, 1997). As a result, they are contestable: they can adapt and can absorb new norms including those relating to gender justice. Few of these claims appear in formal courts. Most are resolved in informal dispute resolution contexts and, as Nyamu Musembi (2013: 211) points out, are only revealed through empirical investigation. Herein lies the value of those studies undertaken, often but not always, under the aegis of women's law scholarship which emphasised the context-specific way in which such property claims emerge in pluralist settings (see, for example Odgaard and Bentzen, 2007; Stewart and Tsanga, 2007; Armstrong, 1992; Nyamu Musembi, 2002). This grounded research revealed the way in which daughters use forms of entitlement recognised within the customary domain to claim a share of the family resources. 'These claims are not made in the language of equal entitlement with their brothers' but 'made in the restricted language of "use rights" (as opposed to outright ownership)' (Nyamu Musembi, 2013: 210). These 'use rights', reflecting a 'right of return' to natal homes for married/widowed daughters, are rewards for a caring ('dutiful') daughter made from her elderly parents' property or their estate through inheritance.

From a contemporary care perspective, the work of caring is translated into a property claim, albeit with lesser value than that of a son who is not required to provide care labour in this way. The relational basis of care is juxtaposed against an abstract right and valued differently. Whilst rights campaigners see the inequity of this position, others argue that recognition of a daughter's customary entitlement to land and livestock in their natal area provides some security without which she would be 'at the mercy of arbitrary acts of male kin depriving them of access to resources crucial to their livelihood' (Nyamu Musembi, 2013: 212). The problem remains that such a claim must be negotiated and justified, reflecting differentials in status.

Kalabamu's 'duty-beneficiary principle' resonates with Bernheim et al.'s (1985) formulation, based on data sets on inheritance decisions in the US, of a 'strategic bequest motive'. The authors argue that our understanding of 'bequest motives' remains incomplete and that what is needed is a fuller understanding of the ways in which testators are 'conditioning the division of bequests on the beneficiaries' actions' (Bernheim et al., 1985: 1046). Based on econometric research, the authors show how bequests are often used as compensation for services rendered by beneficiaries. Rather than an altruistic or ad hoc model of bequest decisions, Bernheim and colleagues argue that there is a strategic use of property to reward a child for care in old age which is more flexible and effective if used post-mortem in a will than inter-vivos as gifts. They cite Sussman et al.'s (1970) research based on a close study of the records of Cleveland Probate Court:

> They document the use of bequests as a means of payment by finding a significant effect of intra-family exchange on deviations from equal divisions of bequests. In case after case, 'reciprocity was expressed through the distribution to particular children for services rendered to parents [so that] children who took care of their elders … received the largest share of the parent's property or the only share if the property was small'.
>
> (Bernheim et al., 1985: 1072, citing Sussman et al., 1970: 290)

In more recent work carried out in the United Kingdom, Sloan (2013) has investigated how private law has responded to the provision of informal care. He is particularly concerned with the position of those who provide unpaid day-to-day caring for (propertied) others. The basis upon which they undertake this care is not spelt out in a formal agreement or reflected in a will. In colloquial terms the arrangement translates into a promise that 'I will leave my property to you' or 'you will inherit my farm' or that the unpaid caring gives rise to such an expectation. In legal terms the expectation translates into the equitable principle of proprietary estoppel. The dispute when it reaches the court revolves around the recognition and value of such a claim. It involves the 'rightful' but 'uncaring' inheritors, that is, family members of the intestate caree disputing the claim of the carer who may or may not be a family member. As Sloan reveals it is not clear what the basis for these claims is. Is it remuneration for unpaid labour, thereby valuing the labour of the carer in the realm of (public) work? Is it a reward for altruism, doing something beyond what is 'normally' expected of this individual – good citizenship? This altruism is easier to 'see' if it is not a family member but difficult to value. Or is it compensation for life chances foregone and/or constrained future possibilities? In this last instance, the assessment tends to be aligned with that of social welfare discourse (Stewart, 2017). While these cases may seem somewhat abstruse and relate to how responsibility for caring for and about the growing elderly population is distributed in 21st century welfare states, they expose the relative values attached to relationships of care. Does caring for someone with a bequeathable asset, to use Bernheim and colleagues' formulation, such as a 'family' home (the use value of which as shelter and site for social reproduction is transformed in the market into an inheritable asset) produce a quantifiable value? To what extent do the propertied seek to value on death those who have cared for them as well as or instead of those who have traditionally been assumed to inherit? To what extent will developmental states continue to expect the propertied to pay for such care from bequeathable assets (asset-based welfare (Hopkins & Laurie, 2015)) rather than develop inclusive social protection measures along the line advocated by the 3Rs agenda discussed above?

A Historical Perspective on Care Work and Inheritance

Malaya women through their accumulation strategies found themselves with significant bequeathable assets. McClintock (1992: 84) understands prostitution in colonial Kenya, as documented by White, as being founded on the conscious decision of women not 'to pass the property back through the male system, disinheriting fathers and brothers and keeping their money and their bodies for themselves'.

We go beyond this to explore what happened next. Women used their property to purchase or at least to secure care. Having provided care to men in the colonial city and thus taken men's wages as their earnings, women converted care labour into capital, buying houses and becoming landlords, generating value with their bodies. White captures their determination not to pass this asset back along patrilineal lines (they were not 'working for their families' as *Wazi Wazi* and *Watembezi* women were). But White does not explore what happened next to the value thus generated. Property-owning *malaya* women designated their own heirs not just in order to bypass or disinherit their male kin, but in order to purchase on the market that which they might not get as ageing women in a patriarchal context. They pay for care by promising it as a bequest to a younger woman. They transmitted property to a woman they had befriended or brought from their own rural home; they brought the chief and told him that the younger women were their wives (Bujra, 1975). Many years later it is their friendships with other women that they emphasised when speaking to White. White found no evidence that a woman who had worked in the *malaya* form and accumulated property independently then transmitted her property to a man. 'This was literal class formation: the creation of bonds of place and property between two women who were seemingly kinless' (White, 1990: 64).

This is a very different perspective to the way in which 'woman to woman marriage' (WTW) has been understood in the historical literature to which we now turn.

'Woman to Woman' Marriages: Bolstering Patriarchy?

Tracing the history of scholarship on this institution is itself a study in the evolution of the discourse of development and the influence of feminism. The early anthropological studies saw it as a straightforward means of tackling infertility and securing patriarchal property transfer. It was cast purely as a socio-economic process. A 'barren' older woman, to use the terminology of the time, has no sons, thereby making her vulnerable in a society which passes property down through male descendants and where her access to resources is dependent on her relationship with male kin. She therefore negotiates a marriage with a younger woman who is expected to bear sons. The younger woman tends to be conventionally less 'marriageable' often because she has borne a child early in life. The male provider of sperm was, traditionally chosen by the older woman from her husband's lineage or less often from her own. (It has become clear subsequently that in some communities/contexts the younger woman can decide (Greene, 1998; Cadigan, 1998; Njambi and O'Brien, 2000).) The male donor role gives rise to no claims over the children although the sexual relationship can continue. Explanations of the practice assert that there can be no sexual relationship between the women.

The same processes associated with 'normal' marriages within any community are required, particularly the 'exchange of gifts' – that is the provision of bride price which tends to be higher than that required for a heteronormative arrangement. The children of the marriage and indeed the younger woman's existing children belong as a result to the lineage of the older woman's husband or her lineage of birth depending on the context and custom.

In some communities, wealthy (propertied) women whether married or not have used this arrangement more freely. Early anthropologists tended to see these as 'royal' women. However, it became clear that such marriages were used more widely by women, particularly in the trading communities of West Africa (Nwoko, 2012). Thus, independently wealthy women could exercise relative autonomy in deciding on their heirs; establish their own lineage; and pass on their social status. While we can see that the *malaya* women in Nairobi were pursuing similar objectives, this 'trade related' form is not documented in relation to East Africa.[2]

2 It is interesting to note but outside the scope of this chapter that WTW are not recognised in the formal legal systems of West Africa, particularly in Nigeria. They are considered to be, in colonial discourse, 'repugnant to public morals' (Akpamgbo, 1977). However, one might speculate that their lack of recognition relates to the relative autonomy of the women themselves.

The continued prevalence of WTW practices suggests that it cannot be reduced to a pre-modern means of tackling 'barrenness' or, explained purely through functional analyses of family formation, although the importance of securing lineage through children, particularly sons, remains, as subsequent research and writing demonstrate. Reflecting the feminist sociological interest in the 'sex/gender' issue, scholars became preoccupied with understanding the roles undertaken by the parties, particularly that of the 'female husband'. They explored the extent to which the older woman assumes the role of the 'husband' including, to a large extent, the public persona, while the younger woman continues to undertake the 'wifely' productive and socially reproductive role. They recognised that the institutional patriarchy that the form embodies remains and reinforces gendered assumptions relating to the value of sons who are assumed necessary to secure the continuance of the male lineage. However, as we have seen, evidence suggests that there is variation in practice here.

Or Securing Care?

However, we also see the emergence of studies reflecting a shift described earlier to value women's voices and agency, which reveal far more nuanced understandings of this institutional arrangement. Once women's voices are heard, they describe the intimacy and affection that the relationship provides including the joy of children as well as the wider sense of social security and community inclusion that these children, particularly sons, produce.

Within a contemporary care perspective, these marriages are not 'forced': women exercise relative autonomy in their organisation and then in their practice. They provide an interesting example of bequest strategies based upon care. The older wealthier woman is cared for on a day-to-day basis as she grows older and more vulnerable due to reducing capacity to sustain herself. She gains the companionship and labour of the other woman and the children to whom she can pass on her inheritance. The younger woman, who is almost always a single mother, a young widow or otherwise socially disadvantaged and thus deemed 'less marriageable', is provided for in exchange for her productive and reproductive labour. She secures a home and a future for herself and her children including a valuable entitlement to inherit from the older woman based upon her SR labour. Women, both older and younger, report their satisfaction with the arrangement, including their ability to distance men in some instances.

Such 'traditional' practices have been critiqued through the lens of women's human rights discourse. Although as Nyamu Musembi (2013: 207) points out, WTW has not been labelled as a 'harmful cultural practice', it sits uneasily within rights-based scholarship and activism. Such marriages can still be seen to embody sexual, intergenerational and class-based subordination, demonstrating the contribution that feminist intersectional analysis offers (Nyamu Musembi, 2013), but they also lend themselves to a rereading informed by contemporary feminist debates on the way in which social reproductive labour is organised, its effects on those involved in its provision and how it is valued.

A Contemporary Perspective on Care Work and Inheritance

Disputes over WTW appear in the Kenyan courts and raise similar issues to those identified in relation to property claims by informal carers in the UK discussed earlier, although the socio-economic contexts are different. WTW practices are rooted in landed property and inheritance contexts. The disputes involve the younger woman widow (or widows if there is more than one WTW in this polygamous society) and/or the children resulting from the marriage and other family members from the older woman's husband's lineage. The latter argue that they are entitled to the property because the marriage did not take place or was in some way not valid. The former are seeking recognition and intervention to secure their inheritance. While the evidentiary discussion in the UK revolves around the form and extent of the unpaid caring undertaken, here it focuses on whether the marriage formalities have been followed and whether the marriage has been recognised in the particular community. The requirements for recognition in any particular community were documented in Kenya in Eugene Cotran's (1995) casebook on customary law. His statement of the practices (Cotran, 1968) is still used as an authoritative source in Kenyan case law to establish whether such a marriage is recognised and valid despite the evidence that practices may be evolving to meet contemporary contexts.[3] Once it is established that the customary marriage exists, the claims of a carer wife (and her descendants) are upheld because these entitlements flow from recognition of the marriage.

The Law of Succession Act (cap 160 Laws of Kenya) section 29 determines the issue: it is based on dependency. A wife or wives and the children of the deceased are defined as dependants, and the participants in WTW are included. The court then establishes whether the particular customary law recognises WTW. The evidentiary burden relating to SR work, in other words to quantify the value of the care, is much reduced within the institution of marriage. However, the carer must show that she cared within the framework of a recognised marriage: that she is not a carer/domestic worker/servant brought in to look after the older woman. If the latter, her documented and expended care labour has no evidentiary value and does not form the basis for an equitable property claim.

3 A point recognised by Koome J in Eliud Maina Mwangi v Margaret Wanjiru Gachangi [2013] eKLR Civil Appeal 281 (A) OF 2003 (a WTW case): 'Customary law is certainly not static. Like all other human inventions, it is dynamic and keeps evolving from generation to generation. Customary ceremonies cannot therefore be expected to be conducted in 2013 in exactly the same way that they were conducted in, say, 1930. To insist on rigid customary ceremonies at all times is the surest way of rendering customary law obsolete.'

While the Kenyan higher judiciary are mindful of the way in which such customary practices are to be understood in 'modern' courtrooms implementing constitutional rights to equality, they recognise them, unlike their Nigerian counterparts who are far more likely to see them as 'contrary to public morality'. In a recent case,[4] the judge pointed out that state law ensures equal inheritance rights and that daughters have equal rights to sons (and therefore such practices were no longer necessary). Judge Makhandia, nonetheless recognised the legitimacy of the WTW. Another recent case, decided after the implementation of the new 2010 constitution, illustrates the position. Katam v Chepkwony[5] involved a dispute over whether a WTW allegedly entered into by an 80-year-old propertied woman with no children and a younger woman with two sons existed within Nandi customary practices. Judge Ojwang argued that such 'ethnic culture bound family practices are likely to be replaced by more ecumenical public interest related practices [but] social change is only gradual'. He relied on Cotran's (1968) description and an article in *Ethnology* by Oboler (1980) to establish the practice. He reviewed the evidence offered as to whether the formalities for this customary marriage had occurred or whether the younger woman was a servant as alleged by the other parties. He upheld the marriage, allowing the younger woman and her two sons who had become children of the marriage to inherit.

Conclusion

These property claims revolving around inheritance emerge on the 'margins' in Kenyan contexts (although WTW is not an uncommon practice) and as such expose broader issues relating to SR and care. SR has been separated out from production in the development of capitalism, forcibly within the context of colonial labour relations, as illustrated by Luise White's work. It produced particular forms of commercialised SR work. Legal regulation constructed it as 'prostitution'. The law contributes to the way in which SR is valued. When undertaken by wives within the breadwinner/homemaker household model adopted by welfare states in the industrialised societies of the 20th century, it was provided through the male 'family wage' and a state 'social wage' (Federici, 2012). Claims for recognition were and still are channelled through familial property relationships. Within Kenya, customary laws in conjunction with state-based inheritance laws equally channel claims through a property relationship. Care labour provided by 'others' such as domestic workers in the household is sharply distinguished – as claims for remuneration in labour law – although it has proven exceptionally difficult to extend the boundaries of labour law beyond the gates of the factory and into the 'domestic' work place

4 Agnes Kwamboka Ombuna v Birisira Kerubo Ombuna [2014] eKLR Civil Appeal 106 of 2011.

5 Monica Jesang Katam v Jackson Chepwony & another [2011] eKLR.

(ILO, 2011; Stewart, 2015). Domestic workers find themselves on or beyond the margins of labour protection, their work attracting very little value in the labour market, despite the recent good intentions of ILO Convention 189 which seeks to ensure that such work is seen as 'work like any other' and entitled to the same legal protections.

From this perspective, the WTW form, albeit involving forms of subordination similar to those pertaining to 'ordinary' marriages, offers recognised if limited entitlements and intergenerational benefits in a context where the state presently offers little 'social infrastructure' for those who are in need of care and to those who undertake the care. Further research in relation to its contemporary form might reveal whether it is adaptable in a context of caring for older women in 'non welfare' states. It is however important to ensure that pressure is maintained on states to develop a social responsibility for care for its citizens.

Megan Vaughan (1991: 144) has argued that 'the problem of women' in the colonial period 'was shorthand for a number of related problems including changes in property rights, in rights in labour, and relations between generations'. Nowhere is this more clearly visible than in the struggles of *malaya* women in colonial Nairobi, as White has shown. This chapter has employed care labour as an interpretive lens by which to look again at the labour forms taken by prostitution and to connect these with contemporary issues of property, tenure, and inheritance. It has also shown the way in which women with access to some assets, produced by their own labour whether providing SR to men in colonial Nairobi or through their land-based activities in rural Kenya have used them to mitigate the effects of ageing. They use bequeathable assets to acquire care through an institutional form, which enables the women providing this labour to acquire some tangible assets which enable them in turn to mitigate the debilitating effects of unequal gender power relationships. While WTW can never be described as a progressive institution, it can nonetheless be seen as a means through which women resist injustice.

References

Akpamgbo, C., 1977. A 'Woman to Woman' Marriage and the Repugnancy Clause: A Case of Putting New Wine into Old Bottles. *Journal of Legal Pluralism and Unofficial Law* 9(14), 87–95.

Armstrong, A., 1992. *Struggling over Scarce Resources: Women and Maintenance in Southern Africa*. Harare: University of Zimbabwe Publications.

Bernheim, B., Shleifer A., and Summers. L., 1985. The Strategic Bequest Motive. *Journal of Political Economy* 93, 1045–1076.

Bibler, S. and Zuckerman, E., 2013. The Care Connection: The World Bank and Women's Unpaid Care Work in Select Sub-Saharan African Countries. WIDER Working Paper No. 2013/131. https://www.genderaction.org/carereport.pdf.

Bujra, J., 1975. Women 'Entrepreneurs' in Early Nairobi. *Canadian Journal of African Studies* 9 (2), 213–234.

Cadigan, R., 1998. Woman-to-woman Marriage: Practices and Benefits in Sub-Saharan Africa. *Journal of Comparative Family Studies* 29, 1–10.

Chanock, M., 1982. Making Customary Law: Men, Women and Courts in Colonial Northern Rhodesia. In Hay, M.J. and Wright, M. (eds), *African Women and the Law: Historical Perspectives*, pp. 11, 53–67. Boston University.

Conaghan, J., 2013. Feminism, Law and Materialism: Reclaiming the 'Tainted' Realm. In Davies, M., and Munro, V.E. (eds), *The Ashgate Research Companion to Feminist Legal Theory*, pp. 31–50. Ashgate Publishing Ltd.

Cotran, E., 1968. *Restatement of African Law* Vol. 1: *The Law of Marriage and Divorce*. Sweet and Maxwell.

Cotran, E. 1995. *Casebook on Kenya Customary Law*. Nairobi University Press.

Deininger, K., Goyal, A. and Nagarajan, H., 2010. Inheritance Law Reform and Women's Access to Capital: Evidence from India's Hindu Succession Act. Policy Research Working Paper 5338. The World Bank.

Elson, D., 2008. The Three R's of Unpaid Work: Recognition, Reduction and Redistribution, paper presented at the Expert Group Meeting on Unpaid Work, Economic Development and Human Well-Being. UNDP.

Falk Moore, S., 1978. *Law as Process: An Anthropological Approach*. Routledge.

Federici, S., 2012. *Revolution at Point Zero*. PM Press.

Fineman, M., 2008. The Vulnerable Subject: Anchoring Equality in the Human Condition. *Yale Journal of Law and Feminism* 20 (1), 1–25.

Fudge, J., 2013. From Women and Labour Law to Putting Gender and Law to Work. In Davies, M., and Munro, V. (eds), *The Ashgate Research Companion to Feminist Legal Theory*, pp. 321–340. Ashgate.

Greene, B., 1998. The Institution of Woman-Marriage in Africa: A Cross-Cultural Analysis. *Ethnology* 37 (4), 395–412.

Griffiths, A., 1997. *In the Shadow of Marriage: Gender and Justice in an African Community*. University of Chicago Press.

Hartog, H., 2012. *Some Day All This Will be Yours: A History of Inheritance and Old Age*. Harvard University Press.

Hellum, A., 1999. *Women's Human Rights and Legal Pluralism in Africa*. Tano Aschoug and Wond Books.

Hellum, A., Stewart, J., Sardar Ali, S., and Tsanga, A. 2007. *Human Rights, Legal Pluralities and Gendered Realities: Paths Are Made by Walking*. Weaver Press.

Hochschild, A., 1983. *The Managed Heart: Commercialization of Human Feeling*. University of California Press.

Hopkins, N. and Laurie, E., 2015. Social Citizenship, Housing Wealth and the Cost of Social Care: Is the Care Act 2014 'Fair'? *Modern Law Review* 78 (1), 112–139.

Hoskyns, C. and Rai, S., 2007. Recasting the Global Political Economy: Counting Women's Unpaid Work. *New Political Economy* 12 (3), 297–317.

International Labour Office (ILO)2011. *Domestic Work Convention no 189*. International Labour Office.

Kalabamu, F., 2014. Divergent Paths: Customary Land Tenure Changes in Greater Gaborone, Botswana. *Habitat International* 44, 474–481.

Manji, A., 1999. Imagining Women's 'Legal World': Towards a Feminist Theory of Legal Pluralism in Africa. *Social and Legal Studies* 8 (4), 435–455.

Manji, A., 2000. 'Her Name Is Kamundage': Rethinking Women and Property among the Haya of Tanzania. *Africa: Journal of the International African Institute* 70 (3), 482–500.

Mbilinyi, M., 1988. Runaway Wives in Colonial Tanganyika: Forced Labour and Forced Marriage in Rungwe District 1919–1961. *International Journal of Sociology of Law* 16, 1–29.

McClintock, A., 1992. Screwing the System: Sexwork, Race, and the Law. *Boundary* 2 19 (2), 70–95.

Merry, S., 2006. *Human Rights and Gender Violence*. University of Chicago Press.

Njambi, W., and O'Brien, W., 2000. Revisiting Woman to Woman Marriage: Notes on Gikuyu Women. *NWSA Journal* 12 (1), 1–23.

Nwoko, K., 2012. Female Husbands in Igbo Land: Southeast Nigeria. *The Journal of Pan African Studies* 5 (1), 69–82.

Nyamu Musembi, C., 2002. Are Local Norms and Practices Fences or Pathways? The Example of Women's Property Rights. In An-Na'im, A., and Hammond, J. (eds), *Cultural Transformation and Human Rights in Africa*, pp. 126–150. Zed Books.

Nyamu Musembi, C., 2013. Pulling Apart? Treatment of Pluralism in the CEDAW and the Maputo Protocol. In Hellum, Anne, and Sinding Aasen, Henriette (eds), *Women's Human Rights: CEDAW in International, Regional and National Laws*, pp. 183–214. Cambridge University Press.

Oboler, R., 1980. Is the Female Husband a Man? Woman/Woman Marriage among the Nandi of Kenya. *Ethnology* 19 (1), 69–88.

Odgaard, R., and Bentzen, A., 2007. Rural Women's Access to Landed Property: Unearthing the Realities within an East African Setting. In Hellum, A., Stewart, J., Ali, S., and Tsanga, A. (eds), *Human Rights, Legal Pluralities and Gendered Realities: Paths Are Made by Walking*. Weaver Press.

Oxfam, 2016. WE-Care (Women's Economic Empowerment and Care) [online]. Available at: <http://policy-practice.oxfam.org.uk/our-work/gender-justice/womens-economic-empowerment/we-care > [accessed 5 May 2017].

Parpart, J. and Staudt, K., 1989. *Women and the State in Africa*. Lynne Reiner.

Pearson, R., 2014. Gender, Globalisation and the Reproduction of Labour: Bringing the State Back In. In Rai, S., and Waylen, G. (eds), *New Frontiers in Feminist Political Economy*. pp. 19–38. Routledge.

Rai, S., Hoskyns, C. and Thomas, D., 2014. Depletion. *International Feminist Journal of Politics* 16 (1), 86–105.

Rittich, K., 2002. *Recharacterizing Restructuring: Law, Distribution and Gender in Market Reform*. Kluwer Law International.

Sepulveda Carmona, M., 2013. *Unpaid Care Work and Women's Human Rights: Report of the Special Rapporteur on Extreme Poverty and Human Rights*. United Nations.

Shrage, L. 1994. Comment on Overall's 'What's wrong with prostitution? Evaluating sex work'. *Signs: Journal of Women in Culture and Society* 19 (2), 564–570.

Sloan, B., 2013. *Informal Carers and Private Law*. Hart Publishing.

Stewart, A., 1996. Should Women Give Up on the State: An African Perspective? In Rai, S., and Lievesley, G. (eds), *Women and the International State*, pp. 23–44. Taylor & Francis.

Stewart, A., 2011. *Gender, Law and Justice in a Global Market*. Cambridge University Press.

Stewart, A., 2015. Care or Work: The Tyranny of Categories. In Mullally, Siobhán (ed.), *Care, Migration and Human Rights: Law and Practice*, pp. 11–26. Routledge.

Stewart, A. 2017. Carers as legal subjects. In Harding, R., Fletcher, R., and Beasley, C. (eds), *ReValuing Care in Theory, Law and Policy: Cycles and Connections*. pp. 148–164. Routledge.

Stewart, J., and Tsanga, A., 2007. The Widow's and Female Child's Portion: The Twisted Path to Partial Equality for Widows and Daughters under Customary Law. In Hellum, A., Stewart, J., Ali, S., and Tsanga, A. (eds), *Human Rights, Legal Pluralities and Gendered Realities: paths are made by walking*, pp. 407–436. Weaver Press.

Stichter, S. and Parpart, J., 1988. *Patriarchy and Class: African Women in the Home and the Workforce*. Westview Press.

Sussman, M., Cates, J., and Smith, D., 1970. *The Family and Inheritance and the Family Russell*. Sage Foundation.

Vaughan, M., 1991. *Curing their Ills: Colonial Power and African Illness*. Stanford University Press.

White, L., 1990. *The Comforts of Home: Prostitution in Colonial Nairobi*. University of Chicago Press.

World Bank, 2011. *World Development Report 2012: Gender Equality and Development*. World Bank.

Chapter 6

Resisting Apathy and Antipathy for Community in Human-Rights and Development Discourse

Locality, Human Interdependence and Participation

Oche Onazi

Introduction

Poverty remains a symptom of social injustice despite recent celebratory declarations that one billion people have escaped the deprivations and clutches of extreme poverty (defined in terms of people with incomes below US$1.90 a day (World Bank, 2017: 1)). Calls for a radical shift in approach away from liberal market income-related poverty measures, growth-led development and individualistic and consumerist behaviour towards a humane, ethical or compassionate response to the injustice of poverty in the global South continue to be ignored (Smith and Lamble, 2011; Ncube and Lufumpa, 2014: 1–9).

This chapter argues that human rights-based approaches to development have failed to provide a counter-narrative for development, and especially failed to nurture, through legal and political institutions, the concept of community, including community values as a way of achieving a more ethical and compassionate development approach. Unawareness of the significance of community is reflected in contemporary theories of law and development, as well as in legal and political theory more generally. Law and development scholarship (Trubek, 1972; Trubek and Galanter, 1974; Trubek and Santos, 2006; Davis and Trebilcock, 2008) generally neglects the socially constituted individual, whose well-being is dependent upon sharing and experiencing community life.

Many references are made to 'rural and urban local communities' (Ziai, 2009: 8) in the post-development literature that offers alternatives to development (Sachs, 1992: 1). These emphasise the ingenuity or agency of local communities whose struggles for better lives and resistance to exclusion demonstrate compassionate and socially just approaches that elude mainstream human rights and development discourse. Nevertheless, the critical literature lacks a sustained analysis of what the community concept entails, or how it constitutes (or should constitute) a viable alternative (Latouche, 1993; Escobar, 1995; Rahnema and Bawtree, 1997; Esteva and Prakash, 1997; Esteva and Prakash, 1998; Nandy, 1989).

DOI: 10.4324/9780203745298-8

This chapter proposes a novel and overarching ethic of community that not only prioritises and seeks to promote values of locality, human interdependence and participation as its constitutive elements, but also yields an alternative to state- and market-based approaches to human rights and development. Although the term community conjures up a variety of meanings that distinguish between rural, urban, national, global, political, occupational, religious, ethnic or virtual group affiliations, the chapter proposes an ethical concept that is derived from value-laden, close, warm, compassionate and harmonious social relationships between people in local, small, demarcated geographic territories with roles and responsibilities which support each other (Turner, 2014). An obvious implication of this is that people, even in the most homogeneous local communities, will have diverse experiences which intersect between common residency, interests, attachments, values, identity, culture, religion and nationhood among many other things. This is perhaps why some writers, most notably Philip Selznick, have defined the concept of community as 'a variable aspect of group experience' (Selznick, 1994: 359), which advantageously allows it to embody different structural forms and enables community members to transition between different affiliations. My aim is not to elevate or provide an empirical analysis of a particular 'local community' as an archetype, but to demonstrate the concept's potential in terms of the abstract moral principles which reveal its attractiveness as an ethical and applied concept. The chapter therefore sketches a vision of an ethic of community without describing in detail alternative forms of action for achieving social justice.

The chapter turns to philosophy, particularly African philosophy, to underscore the ethical significance accorded to human interdependence and, to some extent, to the interdependence between human beings and their immediate environment. The interest shown by communitarian literature in the Western legal and political philosophical tradition in the concept of community as a locality (Frazer, 1999: 143–147) has generally overlooked the need to elaborate on an ethical understanding of the concept (Ladd, 1998a; 1998b). In contrast African philosophy, insights of which have largely been marginalised in the discipline of philosophy (Janz, 2009: 1–4; Flikschuh, 2014) and drowned out in debates about development (Ake, 1996; Keita, 2011; Metz, 2017), has not been constrained by this predisposition. The chapter shows that a certain version of African philosophical communitarianism is better disposed to ground the proposed ethic of community, since it treats the concept of community as a type of ethical ideal constituted by concrete interdependent human relationships. The following sections demonstrate the failure to take the concept of community seriously in human rights and development discourse. I begin by showing that there is an apathy towards community, which is evidenced by marginal and insignificant references in human-rights texts and by the restriction of the concept to temporary, rural projects and consultation exercises in development policy and practice. In the next section, I argue that the antipathy towards community can be demonstrated by the absence of a comprehensive or overarching approach in human-rights and development thought and practice from a community ideal. Consequently, I outline an ethic of community that prioritises values of locality, human interdependence and participation extrapolated from the struggles and aspirations of the Makoko squatter community in Lagos, Nigeria, who are excluded from state- and market-based housing. I conclude by providing some suggestions on how to consider the concept of community more broadly as an alternative approach to human rights- and social justice-based alternatives to development.

Between Apathy and Antipathy

Several human-rights texts and development policy approaches can be used to illustrate the apathy and antipathy towards the concept of community. Articles 18, 27 and 29 of the Universal Declaration of Human Rights (UDHR) 1948 make three passing references to community. The drafters of the document never intended to establish any human rights other than individual rights. Despite warnings against doing so (American Anthropological Association, 1947), the list of human rights in the UDHR exclusively mirrored the concept of the individual then prevalent in Western Europe and North America. The UDHR was founded on and influenced by a notion of individual rights derived from an undifferentiated human nature (Martin, 2013: 61–64). The universality of human rights is derived from their natural character in that they exist prior to and independently of any type of social recognition, whether by community, society or nationality (Little, 2014: 585). Human beings have human rights independent of social practices, culture, morality or domestic laws. Such theories tend to ascribe to the rights-bearer certain fixed or essentialist physical features or properties (Donnelly, 1990: 40). The bearer of a human right is wholly autonomous (Freeman, 1995: 25) and discovers or is knowledgeable of his or her nature through reason (Ghai, 2000: 1096). Individual autonomy is amplified to the highest value, and human rights are the primary vehicle for realising and protecting that autonomy (Ghai, 2000: 1096).

Human-rights Instruments

Many human-rights instruments inspired by the UDHR, even those influenced by global south representatives, suggest antipathy for community, even though it may be argued that the right to self-determination, right to development and collective rights, suggest a transition from antipathy to apathy. It can be argued that the human right to self-determination in the UDHR, Articles 1 of the International Covenant on Civil and Political Rights (ICCPR) and the International Covenant of Economic, Social and Cultural Rights (ICESCR) imply a group, collective or 'community's' right to statehood and to economic, social and cultural development. Although the aspiration for self-determination may imply an ethnic community's right to seek statehood and self-government, it could also refer to a claim that falls short of statehood, such as economic, social and cultural treatment within a nation-state. Nevertheless, statehood suggests a discourse of states and not of local or place-based communities.

In contrast, religious and linguistic rights in Article 27 of the ICCPR may refer to the rights of a collective entity, that is not necessarily a state-like community. So also do the Declaration on the Rights of Persons Belonging to National or Ethnic, Religious and Linguistic Minorities (1992), the Declaration on the Rights of Indigenous Persons (2006), the UN Convention on the Elimination of All Forms of Discrimination against Women (1979), the UN Convention on the Rights of the Child (1989), and the UN Convention on the Rights of Persons with Disabilities (2009). In addition to group rights,[1] regional instruments, particularly the African Charter on Human and Peoples Rights (1981), seek to ground human rights in a duty-based communitarian framework, whether in terms of peoples or national, ethnic, religious or linguistic communities. On this basis, it may be argued that human rights are not hostile to the idea of community (Newman, 2011). However, these rights lack a comprehensive approach and suggest apathy to the concept of community. The emphasis on the concept of community has not been sufficiently significant in the above human-rights instruments (Howard, 1995; Gerwith, 1996; Ife, 2009; Nandorfy and Fischlin, 2011; Onazi, 2013) to ground human rights approaches to development in a community ideal. Another problem is that on the rare occasions that the concept of community has featured in the literature, it has been characterised as a group. As much as a community can be defined as a type of group, it is however not the most attractive version of the concept. As discussed in more detail in the present chapter in the section 'Resisting the Culture of Individualism', group-based conceptions of community – unlike relational versions – tend to imply an external, corporatist, homogeneous, transcendental or metaphysical entity, or refer to some type of the common good, which is detached from and determines the relationships between members of a community (Ladd, 1998b: 21). Group-based conceptions of community tend to distract attention from the concrete, complex and direct relationships which are fundamental to what it means to share community with others.

Human Rights-based Approaches to Development

Apathy towards the concept of community can also be observed in the convergence of the discourses of human rights and development through the Declaration on the Right to Development (United Nations Commission on

1 Most scholars hold the view that group rights are rights of individuals rather than the rights of the group itself (Donnelly, 1985: 1–21; Freeman, 1995; Casals, 2006: 7; Griffin, 2008: 256–275; Newman, 2011; Jones, 2013: 103). In other words, individual human rights matter insofar as they are supportive of group membership, and can be enjoyed independently of group membership. Group rights are thus not too dissimilar to civil and political rights such as the freedoms of association, expression, thought, conscience, religion and political participation.

Human Rights, 1986). The Declaration on the Right to Development Article 11 recognises 'peoples', which implies a community that may be the legitimate bearer of this right, however it is not clear what constitutes a 'people' (De Feyter, 2013: 20–21). Even if, as Rajagopal (2003: 221) argues, the right to development was the first instrument to introduce the right of communities, it remains unclear whether it refers to a right of all types of communities or to a specific type of ethnic, indigenous, linguistic or local community (De Feyter, 2013: 21). A competing interpretation questions its progressive potential; it remains a right of states and not local communities (Donnelly, 1985: 498–501; Shivji, 1989: 20; Ibhawoh, 2011: 78–79).

Nevertheless, the right to development does provide a legal framework for various policies and interventions by international development organisations such as the UN Development Programme. Principles of the Declaration on the Right to Development have inspired rights-based approaches to development, which provide a legal and conceptual framework to operationalise, plan and programme development through norms, standards and principles of human rights. However, this has not involved the integration of human rights into community development initiatives, which still appear to be carried out independently of any meaningful reference to human-rights principles. Clearly absent is the concept of community as an independent or overarching ethic for rights-based approaches to development and other international development initiatives.

Beyond rights-based approaches to development, the concept of community is conspicuous by its absence. Where the concept of community has been recognised, it has not been used as an independent or overarching ethic, but restricted to temporary rural projects and consultation exercises. The World Bank's Community-Driven Development (CDD) programme is the most obvious illustration of this point. With 219 projects in 79 countries in the global south, the CDD is arguably the largest internationally inspired community development initiative today.[2] The CDD programme focuses on specific types of (often rural) projects limited in scope and timescale in low middle-income and conflict affected countries. Nevertheless, the nature of the CDD project actually determines its time-frame. For instance, Indonesia's Kecamatan Development Programme, which was established in 1997, is still on-going, while Mongolia's Sustainable

2 For more details about the World Bank's Community-Driven Development (CDD) programme, see Community-Driven Development <https://www.worldbank.org/en/topic/communitydrivendevelopment> (aceessed 26 March 2020). Although the CDD is expressed in the language of participation and empowerment, which resonates with rights-based approaches to development, it operates outside the human rights monitoring and reporting framework (Onazi, 2013: 28); the World Bank has generally developed an ambivalent attitude towards human rights (Horta, 2002; World Bank, 2006). The World Bank's interest in the concept of community emerges under the auspices of its Comprehensive Development Framework (CDF), which is its attempt to bring decision- making processes closer to the poor through participation (Onazi, 2013: 28).

Livelihoods Project (2002–2007), Nigeria's Second National Fadama Development Project (2004–2009), Yemen's Social Fund for Development (1997–2009) and Honduras's Social Investment Fund Project (2001–2006) have all operated within specific time-frames (World Bank, 2009). I am not suggesting that the benefits of the CDD projects (such as water, sanitation, housing, electricity and school projects) cannot exceed their time-frame, although this will depend on the ability of the relevant communities to sustain them in the long term (Mansuri and Rao, 2004: 18). Rather, my point is merely to illustrate that the concept of community is defined quite restrictively 'by the parameters of a project, by project facilitators, or by the nature of administrative or identity boundaries' (Mansuri and Rao, 2004: 8). The concept of community is not used as an independent or overarching ethic that shapes theories and practices of development. The focus has been on how to improve the lives of certain (often rural) communities (Binswanger-Mkhize et al., 2009), but not more broadly on the concept of community as an ideal and a source of principles, values and practices that can shape the conduct of development on a holistic scale. A similar observation can be made about the World Bank's Poverty Reduction Strategy Papers (PRSPs), which influences community participation in relation to consultation exercises. Apart from the well-known criticism of PRSPs for the poor quality of participation in its consultation exercises (Kamruzzaman, 2009: 62–63; Lazarus, 2008: 1207; McGee et al., 2002; Fraser, 2005), it appears to have disrupted or failed to recognise and strengthen existing community institutions and initiatives. Where community institutions and initiatives have been recognised, they are adapted to suit pre-defined consultation or project objectives, which implies that participation ends up having a negative effect on the community concerned. (Udo-Udoma, 2014: 62).

Furthermore, the concept of community is valued only in so far as it is compatible with the dictates of the neoliberal market and economic growth (Fukuyama, 1996). The idea of reconciling community with the neoliberal market is incompatible with the idea of redistributive justice that inspired the adoption of the right to development (Bedjaoui, 1979: 63) and militates against the ethical dimension of human rights intended to mitigate market injustices (Cornwall and Nyamu-Musembi, 2004: 1418–1419; Rittich, 2004: 221; Uvin, 2007: 597–606). Antecedents of the apathy for the concept of community can be traced to theories of modernisation, structuralism, basic needs, dependency or even development ethics (Gasper, 2004: 205–212), which have taken the concept for granted. Even the capabilities approach (Nussbaum, 2006; Nussbaum, 2011; Sen, 2001) takes for granted the significance of community, although some notion of it may be implicit in Nussbaum's Aristotelian notion of personhood and importance of affiliation (Nussbaum, 2006: 159–160). Nevertheless, these elements are difficult to reconcile with Nussbaum's defence of political liberalism, independence, separateness and choice. Furthermore, she does not appear to view community and community values and relationships as central to the human condition or to her concept of human flourishing.

Resisting the Culture of Individualism

This section proposes an ethic that prioritises and seeks to promote values of locality, human interdependence and participation as an alternative to state- and market-based approaches to human rights and development. As an ethical concept, community according to John Ladd may be regarded as a social framework to facilitate 'the palpable dependence of human beings on one another, practically, socially and emotionally' (Ladd, 1998a: 15). It facilitates 'direct moral connections, mutual moral bonds, between members of a particular group of people' (Ladd, 1998a: 15). This conception of community is underpinned by a type of 'ethical mutualism', which is 'a particularized ethic of caring for others and being cared for by others in concrete sorts of ways' (ibid.). Ethical mutualism in turn points to a direct, complex, varied, egalitarian, vague and open-ended ethic of co-membership, which exists as the criterion for and ethical consequence of membership. Co-membership creates an ethic of 'giving and receiving, responsibilities and entitlements' (Ladd, 1998b: 163). Giving and receiving is differentiated by the needs and abilities of individuals in a particular community. The ethic of co-membership makes it obligatory for those with the ability to help or care for those in need 'as a function of his or her own needs, legitimate interests and personal requirements … and not the good will or interests of the giver' (Ladd, 1998b: 165). Those in need are entitled to request help from the well-off members of the community regardless of their capacity to reciprocate.

As attractive and comprehensive as Ladd's argument appears to be, it is difficult to find references to it or similar ethical conceptions of community in the communitarian tradition in mainstream Western legal and political philosophy.[3] This is not at all surprising because Ladd's approach is formulated in direct response to the ethical inadequacies of leading accounts of political community. His approach is more consonant with a certain strand of African philosophical communitarianism (Tutu, 1999; Gyekye, 2004; Mokgoro, 2007; Masolo, 2010; Metz, 2007, 2012b, 2013, 2016), which conceives the concept of community in terms of an ethic of caring, being cared for, and of giving and receiving involving the ability to interact with and support others. Here the term community is not designated to or attributed to a group, but instead refers to an ethical and relational ideal founded upon intrinsic and horizontal obligations between people. It is defined by a combination of the recognition of, the responsibility to, and the connection with others as if they were extensions of oneself, through normatively endorsed altruistic forms of conduct, such as benevolence, generosity, compassion, caring, helping, sharing and solidarity among other things (Gyekye, 1997: 70; Masolo,

3 A notable exception is the feminist ethic of care, which has significant resonances with the relational communitarian ethic described here (Fineman, 2008; Manji and Stewart, this volume). See Onazi (2020: 78–81) for a recent comparison between African relational communitarianism and relational feminism in Western legal, moral and political philosophy.

2010: 109; Bell, 2012: 66; Metz, 2013: 13). The normativity of the African relational conception of community has been appreciated as a voyage of discovering personhood, which is intrinsically connected to and determined by horizontal ethical obligations owed to others in a community (Cornell, 2014: 134) and typified by the Southern African concept of Ubuntu with its maxim, 'a person is a person through other persons' (Tutu, 1999: 34–35; Metz, 2007: 331).

Although the emphasis on altruistic relationships is common to most strands of African philosophical communitarianism (Masolo, 2004: 488–496; Bell, 2012: 66), it is arguably more typical to find teleological (Bujo, 1998), corporatist (Ake, 1987: 9) and metaphysical (Gyekye, 1997; Menkiti, 2004: 324–331) accounts of community in the literature, thus making it similar to Western legal and political philosophical communitarianism. However, unlike the Western legal and political philosophical communitarian tradition (Sandel, 1982; McIntyre, 1984; Miller, 1988; Etzioni, 1998), the African approach makes a significant contribution to the concept of community as a relational ethical phenomenon whereby harmonious dispositions of 'love, compassion, caring, friendship, and genuine concern for others characterize social relationships' (Bell, 2012: 66).

An Ethic of Community

I now turn to how a concept of community that prioritises and seeks to promote values of locality, human interdependence and participation as its constitutive elements might provide an alternative to state- and market-based approaches to human rights and development. Since there is often disagreement on what the concept and ethical values of community entail, the aim in this section is not to be prescriptive, but to provide a vision of such a community ideal. I take orthodox sociological definitions of community (i.e., social units in geographically small localities, neighbourhoods in towns and villages) as a starting point for two reasons. First, the idea of community as a locality, perhaps more than other conceptions of community, gives priority to the social constitution of the individual and draws attention to what it means to experience community ethically and empirically, and recognises that individuals are irreducibly communal beings (Crow and Allan, 1994: 1). Individuals are born into a family, and their immediate environment, including their local community, is responsible for their socialisation and ethical literacy (Appadurai, 1996: 179; Clarke et al., 2007: 94). Crucial in this respect is the significance of common residency, which can be appreciated 'as the most congenial condition for forming and sustaining community life' (Selznick, 1994: 359), even though it is not a definitive or conclusive characteristic of community. Second, local communities provide a sense of solidarity to many residents of villages and metropolitan cities in the global South resulting either from their exclusion from formal state and market institutions (Kushner and Maclean, 2015) or from urbanisation (Simone, 2001; 2004; 2009). Informal organisational affiliations are deployed to compensate individuals for the absence of the state or their inability to survive the depredations of capitalist market relations. These informal organisations include neighbourhood groups, community-based groups, kinship groups, women's groups, widows' groups, cooperatives, informal thrift or credit associations, work-based, religious and ethnic-based groups. Although the prevalence of groups or group-based organisations may be an indication of the underlying communal or group-based ethos in many African villages and cities, it is not the most plausible explanation of the importance of community to the lives of contemporary Africans. Moreover, as mentioned in the second section, a group is not the most attractive conception of community as it often implies an external, corporatist, homogeneous, transcendental or metaphysical entity, or some type of the common good, which is detached from and determines the relationships between members of a community (Ladd, 1998a: 21).

Locality

For purposes of alternative imaginaries of human rights and development, an ethic of community builds on sociological notions of community as locality and draws attention to the congeniality of dwelling in the community to the process of socialising the individual. Although the concept of community is conceived in physical, material and tangible terms – that is, a geographical location such as a neighbourhood, town or village – it is a material form loaded with meanings, values and sentiments that are imagined, experienced and understood in varying degrees by residents and often by non-residents. African philosophical communitarianism provides means of illustrating the value that may be attached to a locality. Although African philosophical communitarianism is generally anthropocentric and attaches an instrumental value to the physical environment, some writers have relied on the relational conception of community not only to attach an intrinsic value to the environment, but also to underscore the interdependence between human beings and their environment (Bujo, 2001: 22–23; Tangwa, 2004: 387–395; Behrens, 2010: 470–480; Behrens, 2013: 55–72). African relational environmentalism is comparable to the literature on the Andean concept of *buen vivir*, which has no universally agreed definition, but conceives the concept of community as a form of coexistence between human beings and the natural environment (Villalba, 2013: 1430; Merino, 2016: 272; Gudynas, 2016: 728).

Thinking of community in terms of locality may imply that the concept is nostalgic, rigid, static and unchanging (Crow and Allan, 1994; Putman, 1995; Little, 2002; Dench et al., 2006). However, a local geographical community is far more complex than it appears, because it comprises members who draw their sense of identity from a complex interaction of past, present and future. Apart from local communities exclusively constituted by ethnic, racial or religious groups, there is no reason to think of a community in strictly homogenous terms. Homogeneity implies a type of uniformity between people in terms of 'quality, ability, need, age or gender' (Ladd, 1998a: 16) that simply does not exist when one takes the differences among members of a local community into account.

Homogeneity would not only be at odds with the internal composition of a community, but also with the kind of asymmetries that make altruism and supportive relationships an indispensable aspect of community life. A better understanding of the ethical relations and obligations anticipated by the relational concept of community in African philosophical communitarianism aids understanding on this point. Although each person is ethically connected to the other from the start of life, this is not definitively constitutive of identity (Cornell, 2014: 134). Instead, each person embarks upon a journey to discover her or his 'singularity as a unique person' (ibid.), which in turn defines their ethical responsibilities to others and their overall place in the community. The support a person receives during this journey to personhood makes it incumbent on them to improve the community 'through a form of participation to strive for fidelity to difference and singularity' (Cornell, 2014: 135). The different journeys of each person produce a community that is internally diverse, but with different members ethically bound to support each other.

Human Interdependence

What sort of ethical values can be abstracted from a locality, and furthermore, how can these values promote alternatives to human rights and development? If the congeniality and ethical nature of dwelling is taken into account, then a variety of values ought to be prioritised ranging from reciprocity, mutual respect, cooperation, friendship, hospitality, solidarity and compassion to love. There may be advantages in highlighting the plurality of values that can be found in local communities but such a perspective may lack a single overarching sense of community which can mediate the differences between members and between communities. Human interdependence is arguably the best way of supplying the proposed ethic of community with overarching ethical and moral coherence. In African philosophical communitarianism human interdependence is far more prominent than mere interdependence between human beings and their immediate or physical environment. Human interdependence enriches the concept of community. The ethic of community is not thus an inelegant and unconditional imposition of the values of the collective entity on individuals; it is rather defined by the interdependent relationships of its members.

One implication of thinking about community as a sort of locality that serves as a framework for a variety of activities ranging from social relationships, practices and exchanges to the formation of multiple communities within that locality is that it draws attention to the significance of the value of human interdependence, that the ethic of community seeks to nurture, promote and protect. Human interdependence is also advantageous because it leads to other values, particularly solidarity, compassion, love and care for the human condition of others as the well-being of an individual is tied to the well-being of others, and to the well-being and survival of the community. Human interdependence entails that individuals are incomplete without other individuals; they are nurtured by relationships with other individuals for security and nourishment. Human interdependence is distinctly relational, which should not be mistaken for instrumental mutually reciprocal or beneficial relationships, but rather the vulnerabilities and asymmetries that make it incumbent on human beings to need each other as well as the human predisposition to connect with and enter relationships with other human beings.

Participation

Human interdependence encourages participation, and a disposition to be involved in activities with others in a given community or across a range of communities. Participation refers to processes which socialise individuals and are contingent upon opportunities for participation, whether within a family or through kinship ties, friendships and interaction with others. It entails a form of solidarity, a collaborative and caring attitude, empathy for the human condition, a willingness to work with others and share in their fortunes and misfortunes, and preparedness to act in their best interests (Metz, 2012a: 26).

Participation in the ethic proposed in this chapter is used in the Aristotelian sense, as a way to define the development of virtue and character (Aristotle, 2009: 5–10). Political participation nurtures good citizens and makes civic obligations incumbent on each citizen. In comparison with African philosophical communitarianism, the ability to be virtuous and exhibit good character is contingent on the ability to perform ethical duties to others (Metz, 2012b: 391). While the importance of virtue and character implies that African philosophical communitarianism and Aristotelianism are perfectionist in orientation (Hoffman and Metz, 2017: 157), the former differs from the latter because it considers ethical duties or obligations and not politics as preconditional to the attainment of virtue and character. In spite of this, the Aristotelian concept of politics can be reconciled with duties in African philosophical communitarianism to yield an approach that not only underscores the importance of pre-political interpersonal relationships in nurturing virtue and character, but also enriches political participation by infusing it with asymmetrical relational exchanges involved in community.

Participation is valuable in itself but also has an important instrumental dimension when members of a particular community come together to resolve common problems. Even in the instrumental sense, because it involves the pursuit of goals or resolution of problems – especially the desire of members of a community to improve the quality and dignity of their lives – participation attains an ethical and moral dimension contingent on the nature of the goals pursued. The ethic of community demonstrates an awareness of the complex interaction between the intrinsic and instrumental dimensions of participation. Local communities not only take ownership and control over matters that affect them the most; by taking part in decisions that affect individuals' communal lives they become better people through empathy for the human condition of others. In this respect, participation is more than an important mechanism for aggregating information and preferences or for affecting policy choices. This way of thinking can have a transformative effect on human rights and development, by making it less individualistic, and more oriented to compassionate ends. A focus on dwelling, particularly interdependence, encourages a disposition to participate and cooperate to resolve common problems, or simply to help each other in difficult situations. In what follows below, I turn to the literature on Makoko, a squatter community in Lagos, Nigeria, as the best way to illustrate the attractiveness of the ethic of community as well as to provide it with some empirical content.

Makoko

With approximately 300,000 residents,[4] Makoko in Lagos, Nigeria, is the world's largest squatter community located on water,[5] a feature that distinguishes it from most squatter communities across the globe today (UN-Habitat, 2010; UN, 2015; Mohabir et al., 2016: 400). Without state-provided housing and unable to afford private market housing, residents of Makoko – like most squatter communities across the world – have had to build their own homes and provide their clean water, sanitation, electricity, healthcare and education to live dignified lives. A profound sense and spirit of community continues to sustain the residents, whose lives are characterised by a heightened sense of inventiveness, cooperation, collaboration, resistance and resilience in the face of the hardship and deprivation resulting from exclusion from state and market institutions. Residents of the Makoko squatter community – with the support of the Social and Economic Rights Center (SERAC) – resisted an eviction attempt by the Lagos state government in 2012, which rendered thousands of people homeless (Funsho et al., 2013; Hoelzel and Akinsete, 2015; Ogunlesi, 2016). The eviction attempt appeared to be carried out in relation to the Lagos state government/World Bank's slum upgrading project – the Lagos Metropolitan Development and Governance Project (LMDGP), which came to a premature demise shortly after the incident (Udo-Udoma, 2014: 47).[6]

4 Makoko's population is a controversial subject, since no official census has been conducted till date (Ogunlesi, 2016). Depending on the source, the population of Makoko could range from 40,000 to 300,000 people.

5 Makoko is partially located on land. However, the chapter mainly refers to parts of the community located on Lagos Lagoon, since it has been the target of several eviction attempts by the Lagos state government for being an illegal settlement (Udo-Udoma, 2014: 6).

6 Other accounts suggest that the demolition exercise was carried out in connection with plans to transform Lagos into a mega-city (Hoelzel and Akinsete, 2015: 31). This version of events seems to be verified by the World Bank, which clearly distanced itself and the project from the actions of the Lagos state government (World Bank, 2014: 13).

A protest was staged by Makoko community, which generated media attention after a community leader was shot dead by the police. With public opinion on the side of Makoko community, the Lagos state government were persuaded to accept an alternative regeneration plan by the community. Makoko developed a community-led sustainable regeneration plan with support from International Non-Governmental Organisations (NGOs) and academics. The plan was presented to and accepted by the Lagos state government in 2014. In a separate but related development, the community constructed the Makoko floating school designed by Dutch architects NLÉ and supported by the UN Development programme/ Federal Ministry of Environment, Heinrich Böll Foundation and Tafeta and Partners. The structure was proposed not only as a school, but as a community centre, which is 'scalable and adaptable for other purposes' (Okoroafor, 2016). Although the school has received global accolades (Okoroafor, 2016) and was regarded as a model for flexible, responsive and locally sensitive community engagement, citizenship participation and urban governance (Hoelzel and Akinsete, 2015), it was destroyed by heavy rainfall in 2016 (Okoroafor, 2016), thereby raising doubts about the future of the Makoko squatter community.

Apart from an uncertain future, residents of Makoko have many pressing problems to overcome. Indeed, the stability required to improve the community and implement the regeneration plan is contingent on legal recognition and state support (Neuwirth, 2007: 77–78; Neuwirth, 2013: 515). Unfortunately, the struggles of Makoko squatter community are invisible to dominant approaches to human rights and development, which only offer a binary choice of state or market housing. What Makoko requires is an approach that supports their aspirations to create better lives for themselves and their loved ones inspired by their lived experiences and in recognition of their ingenuity and collective agency. Makoko squatter community's struggles are very close to the elements of the ethic of community outlined above, especially because their experiences direct attention to values of locality, human interdependence and participation.

Congeniality of Dwelling

I have suggested that dwelling is congenial to both individual and communal flourishing. Furthermore, that the contingent nature of dwelling influences the production and definition of values, experiences and relationships. Thinking of community in such terms captures the moral and ethical dimension revealed by the complex set of relationships among those who dwell in it, including the meanings they ascribe to their common existence, and how this is built into the fabric of the environment. This is one possible feature that distinguishes the concept of community proposed in this chapter from how it has been used in, for example, the World Bank's community-driven development approaches. There, community is simply used as an instrumental concept, which says little about why the concept is valuable.

Furthermore, local communities provide a sense of solidarity to many residents of villages and metropolitan cities in the global South resulting either from their exclusion from formal state and market institutions or from urbanisation. Thus, Makoko as a local community highlights not only the importance of dwelling, but also the forms of collaboration that many individuals within it have developed to create better lives for themselves and their loved ones, as a direct result of state and market exclusion. As a consequence, Makoko has become a thriving environment for practices, associations, networks and other forms of cooperation to improve their lives. Without state or market provisioning of public goods and services, residents of Makoko have developed forms of collaboration to respond to their essential needs (Ogunlesi, 2016). Residents of Makoko stand out for their impressive ability to organise and participate effectively in decision-making processes that affect their lives. Therefore, there is an important link between the activities in a given locality and the third element of the ethic discussed below.

Interdependence in the Face of Adversity

The multiple connections between individuals in various local communities, including their multiple communal affiliations, imply that the ethic of community must take the facts and implications of human interdependence seriously. Human interdependence advantageously leads to other values, particularly the solidarity, compassion, love and care for the human condition of others. Human interdependence entails that the well-being of an individual is tied to the well-being of others. Not only does the ethic of community seek to protect and promote values of human interdependence to provide a supportive environment in which a variety of individuals and communities can realise their potential, it also seeks to nurture a better understanding of the ways in which individuals owe their survival or well-being to other individuals. Human interdependence is clearly a value present in Makoko, which is expressed through social relationships, practices and exchanges. Recurrent threats of eviction or failed eviction attempts by the Lagos state government have reinforced the sense of human interdependence in Makoko. Indeed, the resistance to eviction has been a great source of solidarity, care, friendship and togetherness in the community. Threats of and the fear of impending eviction have amplified connections between individuals in Makoko. Most residents of Makoko have a heightened sense of awareness that each individual's well-being is tied to the well-being of others in the community, who are ultimately enmeshed in the well-being and survival of the community.

Spirit of Participation

Participation has been described as the processes of socialising individuals through a complex range of activities. It implies a collaborative attitude, empathy for the human condition of others and a willingness to work with others and to share in their fortunes and misfortunes. Furthermore, participation is irreducibly political, particularly in the Aristotelean sense, as a way to define the development of virtue and character. Participation is valued for its own sake, even though it often has an irreducible instrumental dimension when members of a community come together to resolve common problems that threaten their collective existence. Although it has an instrumental dimension, participation is fundamentally ethical and moral in nature because it is driven by the desire of members of a community to improve the quality of their lives and to live dignified lives.

These forms of participation are exemplified daily in the Makoko community, including the complex interaction between intrinsic and instrumental dimensions of it. Participation to collectively provide water, healthcare and education is not simply an instrumental value, but also an intrinsic one. This is an obvious implication of the survival mechanisms and forms of collaboration generated by residents of Makoko to respond to or compensate for the years of exclusion or inadequacies of formal state and market institutions. The Makoko community is a microcosm of the spirit of participation in excluded local communities across Africa (Simone, 2001; Simone, 2010; Neuwirth, 2007; Neuwirth, 2011). Participation is symptomatic of the great degree of creativity and inventiveness, apart from sociality, reciprocity and cooperation among those excluded from state and market institutions. The very existence of Makoko, a community made up of wooden housing units built on water, provides the most compelling illustration of this creativity, inventiveness and collaboration. However, the most recent and notable example of the community's participatory prowess is the emergence of Makoko's Floating School. Unlike the discredited participatory process evident in the Lagos state government/World Bank's slum regeneration project (Udo-Udoma, 2014: 62), residents of Makoko were fully involved in developing the Floating school (Okoroafor, 2016). Although the school project is celebrated as a success story of community engagement and participation, it should be praised for 'the powerful sense of ownership' (Okoroafor, 2016) it has conferred on residents of Makoko.

Conclusion

Although a comprehensive analysis of what the ethic of community would look like in concrete terms is beyond the scope of this chapter, my broad argument is that the ethic of community provides a criterion for developing new laws, institutions, approaches and practices to different social problems that have traditionally been dealt with through the dominant human-rights and development approaches. For instance, the ethic can provide an evaluative criterion for measuring, criticising and redesigning new and existing laws, institutions and practices according to the degree to which they encourage interdependence and participation among its members. A duty can be imposed on states to devise laws and policies that inculcate rather than discourage such values in citizens. For example, to what extent would forced evictions or the adoption of a policy of privatisation of public goods and services or the construction of new roads, railway networks or dams etc. enhance or disrupt values of locality, human interdependence and participation? Thus, the ethic can provide opportunity to address and critically evaluate different societal issues, for example, the design of institutions and the distribution of resources or the adjudication of competing claims.

The ultimate test for an ethic of community, however, is how it addresses difference, and overcomes rigid articulation of communal bonds that exclude strangers and outsiders. Since the consequence of defining the concept of community in terms of a single source of communal identity or in metaphysical or corporatist terms often rigidifies inclusion, this may be attenuated by emphasising the value of direct, relational, multiple, complex and interlocking sources of communal attachments. Taking human interdependence as the overarching value of an ethic of community can have a moderating effect on questions of exclusion by serving as a binding thread within and between communities. Problems of exclusion can be minimised not by appealing to an external metaphysical entity, but by cultivating the value of human interdependence. In a related sense, it provides an ideal to aspire to, and evaluate, criticise and modify the ethic of community when it falls short of the values it seeks to promote.

This chapter has assessed the lack of attention paid to the concept of community in human rights and development discourses and the legal and political arrangements characterised by liberal autonomous individualism. The alternative begins with an appreciation of the social nature of all individuals and their identities. An ethic of community represents a basic human instinct, highlighting the interdependent nature of community life, and entails other values such as compassion, love, friendship, cooperation, solidarity, mutual respect and recognition. Importantly, the interdependent nature of dwelling encourages those who reside in a particular community to participate and cooperate to achieve collective ends. Participation has intrinsic and instrumental dimensions linked by the desire of members of a community to improve the quality of their lives. An ethic of community can ultimately provide a means to resist and escape the harshness and exclusions of dominant and formal human rights and development initiatives.

An ethic of community raises a number of questions, including whether it is sufficiently comprehensive to dislodge the individualism inherent in mainstream market-based development approaches. The next task, beyond the scope of this chapter, is to demonstrate how this can be achieved in practice. An ethic of community is not merely an attempt to address the limitations of existing approaches to human rights and development, but an attempt to transcend and ground alternative community ideals. As contended in this chapter, an ethic that selects and builds on certain attributes of local communities, is one such alternative that is best understood as an idealised vision of what can be achieved in practice, particularly in communities excluded from meaningful participation in state and market institutions. The decisive test is the extent to which it can be deployed to address a variety of social problems, the opportunities for critical evaluation it provides, and the values and principles it articulates.

References

Ake, C., 1987. The African context of human rights. *Africa Today*, 34, 5–12.

Ake, C., 1996. *Democracy and development in Africa*. The Brookings Institute.

Alvarez, C., 1992. *Science, development and violence: the revolt against modernity*. Routledge, Taylor & Francis Group.

American Anthropological Association (Executive Board), 1947. Statement on human rights. *American Anthropologist*, 49 (4), 539–543.

Amit, V., 2000. Reconceptualising community. In: Amit, V., ed., *Realising community*. Routledge, Taylor & Francis Group.

Appadurai, A., 1996. *Modernity at large: cultural dimensions of globalisation*. University of Minneapolis Press.

Aristotle., 2009. *Nicomachean ethics*. Translated by Thomas Sinclair. Penguin Books.

Bedjaoui, M., 1979. *Towards a new international economic order*. Holmes & Meier.

Behrens. K.,2010. Exploring African holism with respect to the environment. *Environmental Values*, 19, 465–484.

Behrens, K., 2013. Towards an African relational environmentalism. In: Imafiadon, E. and Bewaji, I., eds., *Ontologized ethics: new essays in African meta-ethics*. pp. 55–77. Lexington Books.

Bell, R., 2012. *Understanding African philosophy: a cross-cultural approach to classical and contemporary issues*. Routledge, Taylor & Francis Group.

Binswanger-Mkhize, H.P., de Regt, J.P. and Spector, S., eds., 2009. *Scaling up local and community driven development: A real world guide to its theory and practice*. World Bank.

Bujo, B., 1998. *The ethical dimension of community: the African model and the dialogue between north and south*. Paulines Publications Africa.

Bujo, B., 2001. *Foundations of an African ethic: beyond the universal claims of western morality*. The Crossroad Publishing Company.

Casals, T., 2006. *Group rights as human rights*. Springer.

Clarke, S., Gimour, R. and Garner, S., 2007. Home, identity and community cohesion. In: Wetherell, M., Lafleche, M. and Berkeley, R., eds., *Identity, ethnic diversity and community cohesion*. pp. 87–100. Sage Books.

Cornell, D., 2014. *Law and revolution in South Africa: Ubuntu, dignity and the struggle for constitutional transformation*. Fordham University Press.

Cornwall, A. and Nyamu-Musembi, C., 2004. Putting the rights-based approach to development into perspective. *Third World Quarterly*, 25 (8), 1415–1437.

Crow, G. and Allan, G., 1994. *Community life: an introduction to local social relations*. Routledge, Taylor & Francis Group.

Davis, K. and Trebilcock, M., 2008. The relationship between law and development: optimists versus sceptics. *American Journal of Comparative Law*, 56, 895–946.

De Feyter, K., 2013. The declaration on the right to development revisited. *Journal of National Law University*, 1 (1), 15–32.

Dench, G., Gavron, K. and Young, M., 2006. *The new east: kinship, race and place*. Profile Books.

Donnelly, J., 1985. In search for a unicorn: the jurisprudence and the politics of the right to development. *California Western International Law Journal*, 15 (1), 473–509.

Donnelly, J., 1990. Human rights, individual rights and collective rights. In: Berting, J. et al., eds., *Human rights in a pluralistic world: individuals and collectives*. Meckler.

Donnelly, J., 2003. *Universal human rights in theory and practice*. Cornell University Press.

Douzinas, C., 2013. The paradoxes of human rights. *Constellations*, 20 (1), 51–57.
Escobar, A., 1995. *Encountering development: the making and unmaking of the third world*. University of Princeton Press.
Esteva, G., 1998. *Grassroots post-modernism: remaking the soil of cultures*. Zed Books.
Esteva, G. and Prakash, M., 1997. From global thinking to local thinking. In: Rahnema, M. and Bawtree, V., eds., *The post-development reader*. Zed Books.
Esteva, G. and Prakash, M., 1998. Beyond development, what? *Development in Practice. 8 (3)*, 280-296.
Etzioni, A., 1998. The responsive communitarian platform. In: Etzioni, A., ed., *The essential communitarian reader*. Rowman & Littlefield Publishers Inc.
Felice, W., 1996. *Taking suffering seriously: the importance of collective human rights*. State University of New York Press.
Fineman, M., 2008. The vulnerable subject: anchoring equality in the human condition. *Yale Journal of Law and Feminism*, 20 (1), 1–25.
Flikschuh, K., 2014. The idea of philosophical fieldwork: global justice, moral ignorance and intellectual attitudes. *The Journal of Political Philosophy*, 22 (1), 1–26.
Fraser, A., 2005. Poverty reduction strategy papers: now who calls the shots. *Review of African Political Economy*, 104 (5), 317–340.
Frazer, E., 1999. *The problem of communitarian politics: unity and conflict*. Oxford University Press.
Freeman, M., 1995. Are there collective human rights? *Political Studies*, 43, 25–40.
Fukuyama, F., 1996. *Trust: the social virtues and the creation of prosperity*. Free Press.
Funsho, S., Adegoke, A. and Alewale, B., 2013. Slum settlements regeneration in Lagos Mega-city: an overview of a waterfront Makoko community. *International Journal of Education and Research*, 1 (3), 1–16.
Gasper, D., 2004. *The ethics of development*. Edinburgh University Press.
Gerwith, A., 1996. *The community of rights*. University of Chicago Press.
Ghai, Y., 2000. Universalism and relativism: Human rights as a framework for negotiating interethnic claims. *Cardozo Law Review*, 21, 1095–1140.
Griffin, J., 2008. *On human rights*. Oxford University Press.
Gudynas, E., 2016. Beyond varieties of development: disputes and alternatives. *Third World Quarterly*, 37 (4), 721–732.
Gyekye, K., 1997. *Tradition and modernity: philosophical reflections on the African person*. Oxford University Press.
Gyekye, K., 2004. *Beyond cultures: Ghanaian philosophical studies*, Volume III. Council for Research in Values and Philosophy.
Hoelzel, F. and Akinsete, E., 2015. Towards a new community-led governance approach, integrating the global into the mundane – and why design matters. *The Public Sphere Journal*, 3, 26–45.
Hoffman, N. and Metz, T., 2017. What can the capabilities approach learn from an Ubuntu ethic? A relational approach to development theory. *World Development*, 97, 153–164.
Horta, K., 2002. Rhetoric and reality: human rights and the World Bank. *Harvard Human Rights Journal*, 15, 227–243.
Howard, R., 1995. *Human rights and the search for community*. West View Press.
Ibhawoh, B., 2011. The right to development: the politics and polemics of power and resistance. *Human Rights Quarterly*, 33, 76–104.

Ife, J., 2009. *Human rights from below: achieving human rights through community development.* Cambridge University Press.

Janz, B., 2009. *Philosophy in an African place.* Rowman & Littlefield Publishers, Inc.

Jones, P., 2013. Groups and human rights. In: Holder, C. and Reidy, D., eds., *Human rights: the hard questions.* pp. 100–114. Cambridge University Press.

Kamruzzaman, P., 2009. Poverty reduction strategy papers and the rhetoric of participation. *Development in practice*, 19 (1), 61–71.

Keita, L., 2011. *Philosophy and African development: theory and practice.* CODESRIA.

Kushner, D. and Maclean, L., 2015. Introduction to the special issue: the politics of the nonstate provision of public goods in Africa. *Africa Today*, 62 (1), vii–xvii.

Ladd, J., 1998a. The idea of community, an ethical exploration, part I: the search for an elusive concept. *The Journal of Value Inquiry*, 32, 5–24.

Ladd, J., 1998b. The idea of community, an ethical exploration, part II: community as a system of social and moral interrelationships. *The Journal of Value Inquiry*, 32, 153–174.

Latouche, S., 1993. *In the wake of the affluent society: explorations in post-development.* Zed Books.

Lazarus, J., 2008. Participation in poverty reduction strategy papers: reviewing the past, assessing the present and predicting the future. *Third World Quarterly*, 29 (6), 1205–1221.

Little, A., 2002. *The politics of community: theory and practice.* Edinburgh University Press.

Little, D., 2014. The justification of human rights. *Brigham Young University Law Review*, 3, 585–604.

Mansuri, G. and Rao, V., 2004. *Community-based and driven development: a critical review.* World Bank.

Martin, R., 2013. Are human rights universal? In: Holder, C. and Reidy, D., eds., *Human rights: the hard questions.* pp. 59–76. Cambridge University Press.

Masolo, D., 2004. Western and African communitarianism: a comparison. In: Wiredu, K., ed., *A companion to African philosophy.* Blackwell Publishing Limited.

Masolo, D., 2010. *Self and community in a changing world.* University of Indiana Press.

McGee, R., Levene, J. and Hughes, A., 2002. *Assessing participation in the poverty reduction strategy papers: a desk-based synthesis of experience in sub-Saharan Africa.* Institute of Development Studies.

McIntyre, A., 1984. *After virtue.* University of Notre Dame Press.

Menkiti, I., 2004. On the normative conception of a person. In: Wiredu, K., ed., *A companion of African philosophy.* pp. 324–331. Blackwell Publishing Limited.

Merino, R., 2016. An alternative to 'alternative development'? Buen vivir and human development in the Andean countries. *Oxford Development Studies*, 44 (3), 271–286.

Metz, T., 2007. Toward an African moral theory. *The Journal of Political Philosophy*, 15 (3), 321–341.

Metz, T., 2012a. African conceptions of human dignity: vitality and community as the ground of human rights. *Human Rights Review*, 13, 19–37.

Metz, T., 2012b. An African theory of moral status: a relational alternative to individualism and holism. *Ethical Theory Moral Practice*, 15, 387–402.

Metz, T., 2013. The western ethic of care or an Afro-communitarian ethic? Specifying the relational morality. *Journal of Global Ethics*, 9 (1), 77–92.

Metz, T., 2016. An African theory of social justice. In: Boison, C. and Murray, M., eds., *Distributive justice in debates in political and social thought: perspectives on finding a fair share.* pp. 171–190. Routledge, Taylor & Francis Group.

Metz, T., 2017. Replacing development: an Afro-communal approach to global justice. *Philosophical Papers*, 46 (1), 111–137.
Miller, D., 1988. The ethical significance of nationality. *Ethics*, 98 (4), 647–662.
Mohabir, R., Crooks, A., Croitoru, A. and Agouris, P., 2016. The study of slums as social and physical constructs: challenges and emerging research opportunities. *Regional Studies, Regional Science*, 3 (1), 399–419.
Mokgoro, G., 2007. Ubuntu and the law in South Africa. *Potchefstroom Electronic Journal*, 1, 15–26.
Nandy, A., 1989. *Science, hegemony and violence: a requiem for modernity*. Oxford University Press.
Nandorfy, M. and Fischlin, D., 2011. *Community of rights – rights of community*. Black Rose Books.
Neuwirth, R., 2006. *Shadow cities*. Routledge, Taylor & Francis Group.
Neuwirth, R., 2007. Squatters and the cities of tomorrow. *City*, 11 (1), 71–80.
Neuwirth, R., 2011. Global bazaar: shantytowns, favelas and *jhopadpattis* turn out to be places of surprising innovation. *Scientific American*, 305 (3), 56–60.
Neuwirth, R., 2013. More telescopic urbanism, please. *City*, 17 (4), 510–516.
Newman, D., 2011. *Community and collective rights*. Hart Publishing.
Nussbaum, M., 2006. *Frontiers of justice: disability, nationality and species membership*. Harvard University Press.
Nussbaum, M., 2011. *Creating capabilities: the human development approach*. Harvard University Press.
Ncube, M. and Lufumpa, C., (eds.), 2014. *The emerging middle-class in Africa*. Routledge, Taylor & Francis Group.
Ogunlesi, T., 2016. Inside Makoko: danger and ingenuity in the world's largest floating slum. *The Guardian*. Available online at: https://www.theguardian.com/cities/2016/feb/23/makoko-lagos-danger-ingenuity-floating-slum (accessed 20 January 2020).
Okoroafor, C., 2016. Does Makoko floating school's collapse threaten the whole slum's future? *The Guardian*. Available online at: https://www.theguardian.com/cities/2016/jun/10/makoko-floating-school-collapse-lagos-nigeria-slum-water (accessed 20 January 2020)
Onazi, O., 2013. *Human rights from community: a rights-based approach to development*. Edinburgh University Press.
Onazi, O., 2020. *An African path to disability justice: community, relationships and obligations*. Springer Nature.
Putman, R., 1995. Bowling alone: America's declining social capital. *Journal of Democracy*, 6 (1), 65–78.
Rahnema, M. and Bawtree, V. (eds.), 1997. *The post-development reader*. Zed Books.
Rajagopal, B., 2003. *International law from below: development, social movements and third world resistance*. Cambridge University Press.
Rittich, K., 2004. The future of law and development: second generation reforms and the incorporation of the social. *Michigan Journal of International Law*, 26, 199–243.
Sachs, W. ed., 1992. *The development dictionary: a guide to knowledge as power*. Zed Books.
Sandel, M., 1982. *Liberalism and the limits of justice*. Cambridge University Press.
Selznick, P., 1994. *The moral commonwealth: social theory and the promise of community*. University of California Press.
Sen, A., 2001. *Development as freedom*. Oxford University Press.
Shivji, I., 1989. *The concept of human rights in Africa*. CODESRIA Book Series.

Simon, F., Adegoke, A. and Adewale, A., 2013. Slum settlements regeneration in Lagos mega city: an overview of a waterfront Makoko community. *International Journal of Education and Research*, 1 (3), 1–16.

Simone, A., 2001. Straddling the divides: remaking associational life in the informal African city. *International Journal of Urban and Regional Research*, 25, 102–117.

Simone, A., 2004. *For the city yet to come: urban life in four African cities*. Duke University Press.

Simone, A., 2009. *City life from Jakarta to Dakar: movements at the crossroads*. Routledge.

Simone, A., 2010. The social infrastructures of city life in contemporary Africa. The Nordic Africa Institute, Discussion Paper 51, 8–17.

Smith, D. and Lamble, L., 2011. Africa's burgeoning middle class brings hope to a continent. *The Guardian*. Available online at: http://www.theguardian.com/world/2011/dec/25/africas-middle-class-hope-continent (accessed 20 January 2020).

Stewart, F. and Wang, M., 2003. Do PRSPs empower poor countries and disempower the World Bank, or is it the other way round. Working Paper Series 108. Queen Elizabeth House.

Tangwa, G., 2004. Some African reflections on biomedical and environmental ethics, In: Wiredu, K., ed., *A companion to African philosophy*. pp. 387–395. Blackwell Publishing Limited.

Taylor, C., 1995. *Philosophical arguments*. Harvard University Press.

Trubek, D., 1972. Towards a social theory of law: an essay on the study of law and development. *Yale Law Journal*, 82 (1), 1–50.

Trubek, D. and Galanter, M., 1974. Scholars in self-estrangement: some reflections on the crisis in law and development studies in the United States. *Wisconsin Law Review*, 1974 (4), 1062–1103.

Trubek, D. and Santos, A. eds., 2006. *The new law and economic development: a critical appraisal*. Cambridge University Press.

Turner, B., 2014. Robert Nisbet and the problem of community. *The American Sociologist*, 45 (1), 68–83.

Tutu, D., 1999. *No future without forgiveness*. Random House.

Udo-Udoma, O., 2014. World Bank public participation policies and processes in relation to the lives of beneficiaries in Slum upgrading projects. Case study: Makoko, Lagos, Nigeria. Master thesis in urban infrastructure, design and management, University of Cape Town.

UN-Habitat, 2010. *State of the cities 2010–11 - cities for all: bridging the urban divide*. UN-Habitat.

United Nations, 2015. *The millennium development goals report 2015*. United Nations.

United Nations Commission on Human Rights (UNCHR), 1986. *The declaration on the right to development (DRD)*. Adopted 4 Dec. 1986, G.A. Res. 41/128 U.N. GAOR, 41st Sess., at 3, Annex, U.N. Doc. A/Res/41/128 Annex (1987).

United Nations Development Programme, 2016. *Human development for everyone*. United Nations Development Programme.

Uvin, P., 2007. From the right to development to the rights-based approach: how 'human rights' entered development. *Development in Practice*, 17 (4–5), 597–606.

Villalba, V., 2013. Buen vivir versus development: a paradigm shift in the Andes. *Third World Quarterly*, 34 (8), 1427–1442.

World Bank, 2006. *World development report: equity and development*. World Bank Group.

World Bank, 2009. *Community-driven development: delivering the results people need.* World Bank Group.

World Bank, 2014. *Implementation completion and results report (IDA-42190). Report No: ICR00002968, on a credit in the amount of SDR 138.10 million (USD 200.00 million equivalent) to the Federal Republic of Nigeria for the Lagos metropolitan development and governance project.* World Bank Group.

World Bank, 2017. *Monitoring global poverty: report of the commission on global poverty.* World Bank Group.

Ziai, A., 2009. Development discourse and its critics. In Ziai, A., ed., *Exploring post-development.* pp. 3–17. Routledge, Taylor & Francis Group.

Part II

Rights and Injustices

Chapter 7

Transnational human rights obligations as vehicles for global justice

Wouter Vandenhole

Introduction

The current orthodoxy of human rights law is firmly rooted in a territorial state-centric model: in principle, the primary and only duty-bearer is the territorial state.[1] This myopic understanding of the duty-bearer side of human rights law is increasingly under strain. In many real-life contexts, human rights enjoyment is impacted upon by several states, and often also by so-called non-state actors (NSAs), such as companies, armed groups, and international organizations. Examples include the exploitation of natural resources, the imposition of austerity measures, peace operations, and responses to migration flows.

If we envisage any role for human rights law in resisting injustices, we need to go beyond the territorial state as the only or primary duty-bearer in human rights law. A new imaginary that invites us to look beyond the *territorial* state, and beyond the state *tout court* in resisting injustices is the notion of transnational human rights obligations. Transnational human rights obligations encapsulate both extra-territorial obligations of states and direct obligations of non-state actors.

Expanding the range of duty-bearers in human rights law beyond the territorial state may make human rights law more likely to resist injustices, but it also creates tensions and challenges. For one, it challenges the public international law fiction of the sovereign equality of states, and the very notion of state sovereignty. Other questions include whether the notion of transnational human rights obligations does not let the territorial state too lightly off the hook; and whether it may be used as an excuse for imperialist ambitions (political interference, regime change, military invasion). Therefore, the ultimate question may be whether one should seek rather to reinforce the territorial state so that it is in control of what is happening (and therefore also fully responsible under human rights law), than to expand the range of duty-bearers. The debate on the range of duty-bearers under human rights law is not just relevant to the global South, although it may have a

1 I use the term 'territorial state' as the state which currently is primarily responsible under international law. The extra-territorial state is the converse of the territorial state.

DOI: 10.4324/9780203745298-10

particular relevance there, in light of extreme power inequalities and the injustices these power inequalities produce in the past, present and in all likelihood also in the future.

In what follows, I will first explore whether the notion of global justice constitutes a good alternative to the notion of development to identify, analyse and discuss injustices, and resistance to those. In my opinion, injustices can only be identified against some notion of 'the good' and the 'just'. I suggest that global justice may be used as a complement to, rather than as a substitute for, development. Global justice is not a panacea that cures all the ills that development produces, but it may be useful in that it allows us to raise the right questions; it may signify as much inequality within the global South and within countries as between countries in the North and South; and it may remind human rights law of its role in resisting injustice regardless of citizenship.[2] In the next section, I introduce transnational human rights obligations as a concept that may help to resist injustices through human rights law. The third and final section outlines the conditions under which transnational human rights obligations may in effect contribute to resisting injustice. This chapter is a critical self-reflection about my academic work on transnational human rights obligations over the last decade. It is therefore somewhat over self-referential. The discussion on development and global justice is only meant to set the stage, and therefore cursory.

Development *and* global justice

The general arguments as to why we may need to re-imagine development or may have to move beyond the notion itself, are well rehearsed. The world has changed. Globalization has intensified (Anghie, 2013: 119): it has accelerated and deepened. The group of developing countries is no longer monolithic. The South is fragmenting[3] with 'emerging' donors such as China and the Arab countries (and soon India and Brazil).[4] Given the significant differences among developing countries, economically and otherwise, developing countries no longer share the same agenda (Anghie, 2013: 110, 122), and there is an increasing convergence of interests and agendas between some states on both sides of the divide.[5] New alliances of privileged classes across the territorial

2 Sen (2009) speaks about 'resistance to injustice' too. However, the commonality in vocabulary on this point does not suggest that I share Sen's analysis of justice. See also below.

3 The same could be said to some extent about 'the North', with some countries that both give Overseas Development Assistance (ODA) and receive loans from the IMF and other institutions.

4 As Woods has pointed out, these are in fact not new donors, rather their recent *increases* in aid have caught the attention (Woods, 2008).

5 These may vary depending on the states and issues at stake, e.g. nuclear energy for non-military purposes, trade or security.

boundaries in the North and South have emerged (Chimni, 2013). Similarly, it should not be assumed that the majority of the poor live in the poorest countries (the so-called Low-Income Countries or Least Developed Countries (LDC)) (Sumner, 2010). Moreover, discussions on development may be relegated to claims for development assistance at the expense of claims for structural change. For example, the Committee on the Rights of the Child tends to reduce questions of international assistance and cooperation to the 0.7% norm for official development assistance (Vandenhole, 2009: 61). Southern states too have argued along these lines, for example in treaty negotiations (Vandenbogaerde and Vandenhole, 2010: 227). The notion of development is deeply neo-colonial in the first place, as Rajagopal (1999: 22) has convincingly argued. Rajagopal (2000) consistently refers to the 'violence of development'.

Clearly, notions of development and a North-South divide are empirically under pressure.[6] Nevertheless, the notion of a North-South dichotomy remains relevant analytically[7] and politically, particularly in human rights fora. In recent debates on the right to development and corporate human rights obligations, North and South took diametrically opposite positions (on the right to development, see De Feyter (2013: 2–5); on corporate human rights obligations, see the debate on whether or not a treaty is needed to complement the United Nations Guiding Principles on Business and Human Rights (McBrearty, 2016: 11–12; Bilchitz, 2016: 220)).

Is global justice epistemologically a more appealing notion than development? Does it offer a suitable substitute for development? By *global* justice, I refer to justice beyond rather than within the *territorial* state, and beyond *social* justice to include also an ecological dimension. Global justice has been defined as including 'a concern for matters of justice that extend beyond the borders of one state' (Brock, 2013: 1). It therefore speaks directly to the notion of transnational human rights obligations,[8] and *may* be able to address global power disparities,

6 See inter alia, OECD, 2010, *Perspectives on Global Development 2010 – Shifting Wealth*, which adopts the concept of a 'four-speed' world. At the same time, it refers to South-South trade, investment and cooperation, and thus maintains the North-South divide as an overall framework. Kloke-Lesch and Gleichmann (2010: 13) have argued that the G20 is now the primary forum for international economic cooperation, and 'proved the traditional North-South paradigm outdated'. While North-South has never been a geographically accurate representation (think of New Zealand and Australia), further inroads have been made as more countries in the South have become emerging economies. North and South live cheek by jowl in Mumbai, Johannesburg and New Orleans. However, a majority of emerging economies are still recipients of ODA (Kloke-Lesch and Gleichmann, 2010: 15).

7 The underlying scheme 'hierarchy of wealth' of North-South has not necessarily been questioned or threatened, so that emerging economies may represent examples of upward mobility rather than the end of the North-South divide (Arrighi, Silver and Brewer, 2003: 3, 26–27).

8 In particular the extraterritorial obligations dimension, i.e., the human rights obligations incumbent on states other than the territorial state.

social inequalities and environmental degradation. But it does not necessarily do so, as global justice debates bear out. Some of these debates include questions as to whether global justice should pursue justice among states, or rather for all individuals; whether it is about global poverty alleviation or about global inequality; and whether global justice requires global government.

Addressing the first question, whether justice should be pursued among states or rather for all individuals, Brock (2013: 3) pits statists against cosmopolitans, but remains firmly within a Western perspective. Rawls, as a major proponent of the statist school, has been criticized for the premise that poverty is endogenous and therefore the responsibility of the state concerned, since it 'glosses over both historical injustices and the structure of the international economy' (Langford and Darrow, 2013: 429; Brock, 2013: 10–12; Chimni, 2008: 10–11). The statist school fails to acknowledge the historical and structural causes of global injustice. In contrast, institutional cosmopolitans such as Pogge acknowledge 'historical domination and neo-colonial exploitation of many poorer countries and persistent inequities in the global economic order and international trade' (Langford and Darrow, 2013: 433) as well as the role of foreign governments, companies and financial institutions (Brock, 2013: 11). Pogge (2005) argues that given the global economic order's role in global poverty, negative duties to not harm apply. Violation of these duties leads to an obligation to compensate for the avoidable human rights deficit. Compensation is not meant in monetary terms; rather, it is an obligation 'to make compensating *protection and reform efforts* for those whose human rights remain unfulfilled under this order' (Pogge, 2005: 68, emphasis in original). In *The Idea of Justice*, Sen (2009: 402–409), identifies obligations to recognize the interests of all, given the profound global interdependence: 'public reasoning about justice should go beyond the boundaries of a state or a region [...]'.

This leads us to the second question: whether global justice is primarily about poverty alleviation or about challenging inequality (Brock, 2013: 3). What is the substance of 'global justice'? Does it go beyond claims for international development assistance? Does it insist on alternative measures of cooperation that need to be taken seriously, such as addressing tax evasion, avoidance and exemption?[9] Is global justice fundamentally concerned with egalitarian justice? Here too, there are competing schools of thought, with some arguing in favour of egalitarian justice regardless of state membership, and others privileging 'equality among compatriots' only (Brock, 2013: 14–16). In other words, whereas 'global justice' potentially makes an attractive substitute for 'development', it does not even necessarily challenge global radical (Pogge, 2005: 55) or extreme inequality and is therefore deeply problematic.

Third, the more technical question as to whether global justice requires global government can quite easily be answered by pointing out that global *governance*, rather than global government is needed (Brock, 2013: 2, 6–7, 16–18). However, current forms of global governance do not show an inclination towards global

9 Beitz as discussed in Langford and Darrow (2013: 436–437), Brock (2013: 19–20).

justice. To the contrary, they tend to 'inflict economic violence of structural adjustment and the debt crisis' (Rajagopal, 1999: 20) Can they be made 'more responsive to the goals of global justice' (Brock, 2013: 17), and what should be the role, if any, of human rights law?

In sum, empirically, development and the North-South divide have become contestable and contested notions. Like development, global justice can be imbued with many different and opposing meanings. It is therefore not *per se* a more powerful narrative than development. Nonetheless, the notion of global justice may allow us to raise important questions, such as: whether an environmental dimension is also included; whether the historical and structural inequalities are to be taken into account; whether equality rather than poverty alleviation should be the primary goal; and what kind of governance is required to realize global justice. Moreover, since global justice is less directly entangled in the North-South binary, it may be able to capture as much about inequality within the global South and within individual countries as between them. Finally, it may remind human rights law of its fundamental role in resisting injustice regardless of citizenship. Therefore, I use the notion of global justice as a complement to, rather than as a substitute for, the notion of development.

I do not suggest that together, global justice and development offer a fully comprehensive and ideal vision of the good life or a just society. Both are also problematic concepts in some readings, as illustrated above. My point is rather that together, they help to identify the injustices that human rights law must assist in resisting.

Let us now turn to the imaginary of transnational human rights obligations, which seeks to broaden the circle of human rights duty-bearers beyond the territorial state.

Transnational human rights obligations

In 2015, we wrote:

> Traditionally, human rights law has a strong territorial bias. Human rights obligations are in principle incumbent on the territorial State, i.e. the State on the territory of which a human rights violation takes place. The duties of States are confined to the residents on their territory. Obligations beyond this 'territorial space' have been viewed as either being non-existent or minimalistic at best. This territorial paradigm has achieved particular prominence in the interpretation of international human rights treaties.
>
> (Vandenhole and van Genugten, 2015: 1)

However, the territorial paradigm has been increasingly challenged (Gibney, 2013; Baxi, 2016). In practice, the ability of states and other actors to impact human rights far from home has never been clearer. The 'intensification of globalisation' in the 1990s (Anghie, 2013: 119) has exacerbated socio-economic disparities across the world. The consequences of eco-destruction and climate change do not stop at the borders (Greenpeace and CIEL, 2015). The decentred position of the territorial state and the increased power and impact of corporations, international organizations and other NSAs, pose major challenges to human rights law. In practice, human rights law has become less and less relevant in the struggle for global justice, since it has failed by and large to adapt to changing realities in which states are no longer the only leading actor (Vandenhole, Türkelli, and Hammonds, 2013: 1031–1032). Moreover, human rights have become 'fused' with neo-liberal economic policy (Anghie, 2013: 120), in what Baxi has termed 'the trade-related, market-friendly paradigm of human rights' (Baxi 2002: 144–152).

Terminologically, I use the notion of obligations to refer to substantive human rights obligations (which in public international law are referred to as primary norms); and responsibility to talk about responsibility for human rights violations (referred to as secondary norms) (Vandenhole and van Genugten, 2015: 5). Within the obligations category, human rights obligations of foreign states are called extraterritorial obligations. Transnational human rights obligations is an umbrella term that includes extraterritorial human rights obligations as well as *direct* human rights obligations of other actors than states (NSAs) (Vandenhole and van Genugten, 2015: 5).

The extraterritorial dimension of human rights has not been absent in the efforts of global South countries to use human rights law to further their political projects, e.g. in the right to development (Anghie, 2013: 117), but it never gained much traction and seemed largely limited to questions of development assistance and cooperation (Vandenhole and Benedek, 2013: 332–333). In recent years, peoples in both the North and South have challenged trade and investment regimes, agricultural subsidies, resource exploitation and environmental degradation, among other things, by relying on transnational human rights obligations.[10]

Elsewhere, I have suggested a legal blueprint for transnational human rights obligations and responsibility (Vandenhole, 2015a). In order to assign human rights *obligations*, prior to and outside the realm of alleged violations, an abstract touchstone (degree of control; influence)[11] is to be preferred. In other words, whenever for example a company exercises a degree of control or influence on the work floor, but also in the marketplace or the community, it has human rights obligations.

10 See in particular the work of the ETO Consortium available online at <http://www.etoconsortium.org/> and the Centre for International Environmental Law available online at < http://www.ciel.org> [accessed 18 January 2020].

11 Proximity is not relevant in moral theory for negative obligations though, only for positive (Langford and Darrow, 2013: 441), and this line of thinking could be extended to human rights law.

The scope of transnational obligations can also be defined in the abstract. That scope is bound to be variable. One factor that will impact on the scope is the nature of the obligation. I use the now broadly accepted tripartite typology of obligations that has been developed in the area of economic, social and cultural rights, that is the obligations to respect, protect and fulfil. The obligation to respect is a negative obligation, the obligations to protect against third parties and to fulfil that are positive obligations (Committee on Economic, Social and Cultural Rights, 2017: paras. 10–24). The scope of the obligation to fulfil is incumbent on extra-territorial states and NSAs will for example vary *inter alia* commensurate with capacities, resources and influence. The scope of the obligation to protect will be defined commensurate with varying degrees of positions to regulate or influence. Arguably, more generally the degree of control or influence exercised – which I suggested as a criterion for assigning obligations – will also impact on the scope of transnational obligations.

The distribution of human rights obligations among duty-bearers is very un-developed. Whereas it may be open to challenge, the primary obligation of the domestic State still seems to be the logical point of departure. Other states and NSAs have complementary obligations. Complementary obligations may apply simultaneously (e.g., the obligation to respect) and therefore amount to parallel obligations. When obligations are only triggered due to the inability or unwillingness of the primary duty-bearer, they are secondary or subsidiary (Vandenhole, 2015a: 118–129). As to the distributive allocation of obligations to fulfil among other actors than the domestic state, we have proposed a *differentiated* human rights obligations regime based on an abstract system of allocation. Extraterritorial obligations to fulfil are primarily incumbent on those states traditionally belonging to the donor community. A *prima facie* assessment of the availability of *financial* resources to an extra-territorial state may be based primarily on the allocations actually made in the national budget for development assistance and cooperation. Political or legal commitments made in internal development policies, domestic legislation or bilateral agreements can equally be relied on to identify particular states as duty-bearers under the extraterritorial obligation to fulfil (Vandenhole and Benedek, 2013: 341–346).

The second core question is how to assign *responsibility* for human rights violations in case of a *plurality* and a *diversity* of violators (state and non-state). I find the international law responsibility regime unsatisfactory (Vandenhole, 2015b: 65–68), and have suggested three building blocks for a human rights responsibility regime that is more suitable and appropriate to address instances of plural and diverse human rights violators. Such a regime is based on the principle of shared responsibility, rather than on independent responsibility of each actor. It allows for differentiation of responsibility along a continuum, rather than employing strict categories such as aiding and abetting, direction and control, coercion and circumvention. Liability for monetary compensation is commensurate with the degree of responsibility (nonetheless, in line with a people-centred perspective the entire compensation can be sought by the victims from any of the violators involved). The latter draws on the international civil liability regime rather than on the public international responsibility law regime. (Vandenhole, 2015a: 130–134).

Extraterritorial human rights obligations, in particular in the area of economic, social and cultural rights, have benefited from unofficial codification in the *Maastricht Principles on Extraterritorial Obligations of States in the area of Economic, Social and Cultural Rights* (hereafter: Maastricht Principles).[12] This set of principles was adopted in September 2011 by a group of experts in international law and human rights, representing all regions of the world and included current and former members of human rights treaty bodies, regional human rights bodies and Special Rapporteurs. The Maastricht Principles also refer to 'obligations of a global character' (Principle 8), which are grounded in arguments that human rights are universal ('all people have human rights and […] all States have the responsibility to protect those rights – for all people' (Gibney, 2013: 47)). The Commentary to the Maastricht Principles explains these obligations of international cooperation to include: the development of international rules to establish an enabling environment for the realization of human rights and the provision of financial or technical assistance, 'the obligation to refrain from nullifying or impairing human rights in other countries'; and the obligation 'to ensure that non-state actors whose conduct the state is in a position to influence are prohibited from impairing the enjoyment of such rights' (De Schutter et al., 2012: 1104).

The obligations of a global character do away with the distinction between primary and complementary obligations. In human rights law, one of the most prominent proponents of this line of thinking is Salomon (2007). Direct human rights obligations of NSAs are more contested (Vandenhole and Gibney, 2014: 8), and have not yet been the subject of comprehensive attempts at codification.[13]

In sum, transnational human rights obligations seek to move beyond the (territorial) state as the sole duty-bearer under human rights law; this is in order to better address the realities of injustices. Does this transnational human rights obligations (THROs) imaginary serve (better) resistance to injustice and claims for development and global justice?

12 Maastricht Principles on Extraterritorial Obligations of States in the area of Economic, Social and Cultural Rights, 2011. Available online at <http://www.etoconsortium.org/nc/en/main-navigation/library/maastricht-principles/?tx_drblob_pi1%5BdownloadUid%5D=23> [accessed 18 January 2020].

13 Piecemeal attempts can be found in the 2003 *Norms on the Responsibilities of Transnational Corporations and Other Business Enterprises with regard to Human Rights* (UN Norms) and the 2002 *Tilburg Guiding Principles on the World Bank, IMF and Human Rights* (Tilburg Principles) as updated in 2015 (van Genugten, 2015).

Transnational human rights obligations, development and global justice

Historically, but arguably also 'intrinsically', the modern[14] human rights project originated in the liberal tradition (Vandenhole, 2009: 364–372), and 'was significantly shaped during the inter-war transition from colonialism to development, as well as by the apparatuses that were developed to manage anti-colonial resistance movements' (Rajagopal, 2003: 292).[15] Does the THROs imaginary have the ability to fundamentally alter this ideological propensity? Can it be instrumental in resisting injustice, or even in fostering development and global justice? Can THROs contribute to resistance against injustices on the ground and become really people-centred? – for this is indeed the yardstick against which to measure the strengths and limits of human rights law to deliver on the promise of global justice.

Earlier in this chapter, I argued that the threefold added value of global justice as a complement to development is that it allows us to raise questions such as whether an environmental dimension is also included; whether the historical and structural inequalities are taken into account; whether resisting radical inequality rather than poverty alleviation is the primary aim; and what kind of governance is required to realize global justice. Thus, global justice may be able to capture not only inequality between North and South, but also within and between countries of the global South, and it may further remind human rights law of its fundamental calling to contribute to justice regardless of citizenship. In what follows, I submit that the THROs imaginary quite forcefully draws attention to structural inequalities between states and between states and non-state actors, and hence suggests that global governance should be bound by human rights regardless of statehood and territoriality considerations, and that it does de-emphasize citizenship as a condition for human rights enjoyment. Admittedly, it delivers less on drawing attention to the environmental dimension of global justice. Human rights law has failed so far to seriously engage with ecological sustainability. That does not mean that it could not potentially do so. However, given human rights' anthropocentric inclinations of focusing on *human* interests only, the THROs imaginary is bound to remain of marginal relevance to questions of environmental justice beyond human interests. It has little if anything to add on exposing and addressing inequality within states. In what follows, I look in somewhat more detail into the added value of the THROs imaginary, and engage with some counterarguments.

Anghie questions the usefulness of a human rights vocabulary to address questions of justice because of its statist bias:

14 Baxi distinguishes between modern and contemporary human rights (Baxi, 2002: 24–41), and argues that in contemporary human rights, 'the originary authors of human rights are people in struggle and communities of resistance' (Baxi, 2002: vi). I am grateful to professor Abdul Paliwala for pointing out this important nuance.

15 Rajagopal, too, brings social movements and their struggles to the centre, in his history and theory 'from below' (Rajagopal, 2003: 295).

> [c]omplex issues remain as to whether 'human rights' should be the principal vocabulary by which to discuss questions of international justice; especially as they remain focused, by and large, on relations between the state and its citizens, a framework that inhibits discussions of international justice and redistribution, fields that are now dominated by private law regimes dealing with international trade and investment.
>
> (Anghie, 2013: 123)

It is precisely this statist bias that THROs seek to overcome: THROs reconceptualize human rights law so as to include a range of duty-bearers beyond the domestic state. THROs speak directly to the human rights threats that come from external states and dominant forces of economic globalization, such as the international financial institutions and transnational corporations (TNCs). In other words, they seek to address the injustices peoples are exposed to:

> The peoples of developing countries face dangers from a number of different sources: from a hostile international system that often reproduces neo-colonial structures, on the one hand, and on the other from authoritarian rulers who commit massive violence in the name of sovereignty and nationalism, even while often effectively acting on behalf of the foreign agents and instrumentalities they condemn.
>
> (Anghie, 2013: 125)

Similarly, THROs also seek to impose direct human rights obligations on TNCs, and hence rectify the failure of the UN system to address human rights violations by TNCs (Baxi, 2013: 612).

Therefore, THROs potentially bring to the fore questions of structural inequality, power and exploitation by addressing human rights obligations and responsibility for violations by extra-territorial states and non-state actors. Admittedly, there is a marked tendency to reduce the issue of extraterritorial human rights obligations in a North-South setting to a simple obligation of providing development assistance, but that is not an approach that I share (see above, section 2). With Benedek, I have argued that extraterritorial human rights obligations to co-operate internationally for development should not be drawn so narrowly (Vandenhole and Benedek, 2013). Development assistance may be one feature of the obligation to cooperate internationally for development, but it does not provide an exclusive definition.[16] A similar approach was taken in the Maastricht Principles, which also clearly distinguish between international cooperation and international assistance (Principle 33).[17] Extraterritorial human rights obligations

16 It is also only one source of development finance. See Clunies-Ross (2004).

17 The Maastricht Principles have nevertheless been criticized on this point as building on 'a model that takes the existing structures of the global economy as a given, grafting onto them relatively minor modifications which do not in any significant

do not only comprise the obligation to fulfil (provide) but all types of obligations covered by the well-established tripartite typology of obligations relating to economic, social and cultural rights. Moreover, they do not only apply to development co-operation in the strict sense, but to all policy areas such as development cooperation, agricultural and other trade policies, and sanctions.[18]

But THROs may also create tensions and challenges. Some fear that challenging the role of the domestic State as the sole human rights duty bearer may provide a welcome argument for recalcitrant states to abnegate their obligations – which I call escapism. However, seeking to extend the scope of duty-bearers does not imply a complete shift in obligations and responsibility from the territorial state to other actors, but rather a framework for attribution and distribution of human rights obligations and responsibility to a plurality of actors. In other words, THROs complement but do not substitute the current human rights legal framework with the territorial state as duty-bearer. As pointed out elsewhere, 'in recent standard-setting exercises distributive allocation of human rights obligations among duty-bearers is the dimension that is least developed. All take the primary obligation of the territorial state as the natural point of departure' (Vandenhole, 2015a: 127). Whereas this may be reassuring for those who fear that the territorial state will be able to escape its obligations, it limits THROs' potential to fully engage with structural inequalities and the domination of international financial institutions, companies or foreign states over the territorial state.

Another argument against the THROs imaginary, and particularly the idea of extraterritorial obligations, may be that they will be used as a justification for imperialist ambitions (political interference, military invasion). Third World Approaches to International Law (TWAIL) scholars have raised doubts about whether human rights law can promote Sen's (1999) notion of 'Development as Freedom':

> international human rights law … is also a double-edged instrument. International human rights law is also used to legitimize an international legal system that advances the interests of private actors at the expense of the global common good, and provides cover for the use of force against developing countries, among other things, to protect their economic and commercial interests.
>
> (Chimni, 2013: 271)

These concerns may become all the more real when it is claimed that states have extraterritorial obligations to protect and fulfil human rights. As extraterritorial obligations to protect may be invoked, for example, to justify foreign

way challenge things to bring about a significant change in levels of poverty and economic equality across borders' (Wilde, 2016: 167).

18 See also Vandenhole (2007: 85–86, 106). Compare Salomon (2007: 98–99).

intervention, a fear of 'human rights imperialism' is legitimate (Modirzadeh, 2010: 384–389, 386). In an attempt to prevent this kind of human rights imperialism, Principle 10 of the Maastricht Principles stipulates that '[t]he State's obligation to respect, protect and fulfil economic, social and cultural rights extraterritorially does not authorize a State to act in violation of the UN Charter and general international law.' It is questionable however whether this Principle counters the risk satisfactorily, since many instances of foreign intervention or human rights imperialism may not be in contravention of the Charter or public international law.

Conceptually, by questioning the centrality of the (domestic) state, THROs challenge the international law fiction of the sovereign equality of states, and even the whole notion of state sovereignty (Jacobsen, Sampford and Thakur, 2013: 5–7; Vandenhole, 2009: 368–369). While this may open up interesting avenues for re-imagining international law, it has met with resistance from states in the North and in the South alike, which may in turn cast serious doubts on the political viability of the THROs imaginary. In both development and human rights negotiations and declarations, the North keeps emphasizing the primary responsibility of the territorial state, whereas the South fears undue interference from the North. For example, in the 2015 UN General Assembly Resolution *Transforming our world: the 2030 Agenda for Sustainable Development* (paras 41 and 63), each country's 'primary responsibility for its own economic and social development' is invoked. That works as a two-edged sword: it allows the North to avoid responsibility, and it helps the South to claim respect for its sovereignty. The way European states have responded to the migration crisis following the war in Syria provides another example of 'states' lethal sovereignties' (Baxi, 2016: 19).

Should we conclude that '[i]instead of abandoning the state as a focus for human rights activism, we may need to refocus on the existing obligations of the State' (Clapham, 2006: 5)? I do not think we should. Notwithstanding the risks and challenges of escapism (by the territorial state) and imperialism (by external actors) by allocating human rights obligations to other actors apart from the territorial state, it is in my view no longer tenable to focus exclusively on the human rights obligations incumbent on the territorial state if human rights are to hold out any promise of resisting injustice and bringing global justice. What these risks and challenges show is that whatever potential THROs may have to address global injustices, they will not automatically and self-evidently realize that potential. Leveraging THROs towards addressing structural inequality, power and exploitation will continue to face conceptual and strategic challenges. In other words, THROs are not a magic new formula that will automatically produce development and global justice.

Conclusion

Notwithstanding the fact that modern human rights are Western in origin and have been part and parcel of an imperialist project, developing countries have tried to use human rights to further their political projects, and people living in developing countries have couched their resistance to injustices in human rights language, as Baxi and Rajagopal amongst others have amply illustrated. In this chapter, I have argued that human rights law can contribute to development and global justice if it creates new duty-bearers, such as extra-territorial states and non-state actors. This is not to say that I pursue a 'transformed global order with human rights at the centre' (Langford and Darrow, 2013: 432), nor that I believe that reconceptualization alone can sharpen human rights' global justice edge. My point is rather that in order for human rights law to claim potential relevance for development and global justice, it is necessary to incorporate transnational human rights obligations within it. Key to transnational human rights obligations' *real* relevance for resistance to injustices is how they will map onto struggles of social movements and peoples, and hence on the law from below as a law of resistance rather than one of domination (Rajagopal, 2003: 295).

References

Anghie, A., 2013. International human rights law and a developing world perspective. In: S. Sheeran and N. S. Rodley, eds., *Routledge Handbook of International Human Rights Law*. pp. 109–125. Routledge.

Arrighi, G., Silver, B. J. and Brewer, B. D., 2003. Industrial Convergence, Globalization, and the Persistence of the North-South Divide. *Studies in Comparative International Development*, 38 (1), 3–31.

Baxi, U., 2002. *The Future of Human Rights*. Oxford University Press.

Baxi, U., 2013. International development, global impoverishment, and human rights. In: S. Sheeran and N. S. Rodley, eds., *Routledge Handbook of International Human Rights Law*. pp. 597–634. Routledge.

Baxi, U., 2016. Some Newly Emergent Geographies of Injustice: Boundaries and Borders in International Law. *Indiana Journal of Global Legal Studies*, 23 (1), 15–38.

Bilchitz, D., 2016. The Necessity for a Business and Human Treaty. *Business and Human Right Journal*, 1(2), 203–227.

Brock, G., 2013. Theories of global justice. In: J. Linarelli, ed., *Research Handbook on Global Justice and International Economic Law*. pp. 1–25. Edward Elgar.

Brown, C., 2010. On Amartya Sen and "The Idea of Justice". *Ethics & International Affairs*, 24 (3), 309–318.

Chimni, B., 2008. The Sen Conception of Development and Contemporary International Law Discourse: Some Parallels. *The Law and Development Review*, 1 (1), Article 2.

Chimni, B., 2013. Critical theory and international economic law: a third world approach to international law (TWAIL) perspective. In: J. Linarelli, ed., *Research Handbook on Global Justice and International Economic Law*. pp. 251–273. Edward Elgar.

Clapham, A., 2006. *Human Rights Obligations of Non-State Actors*. Oxford University Press.

Clunies-Ross, A., 2004. Development Finance: Beyond Budgetary Official Development Assistance. *Michigan Journal of International* Law, 26, 389–410.

Committee on Economic, Social and Cultural Rights, 2017. General Comment No. 24 on State Obligations under the International Covenant on Economic, Social and Cultural Rights in the Context of Business Activities, UN Doc E/C.12/GC/24.

De Feyter, K., 2013. *Towards a Framework Convention on the Right to Development* [pdf]. Friedrich Ebert Stiftung. Available online at <http://library.fes.de/pdf-files/bueros/genf/09892.pdf> [Accessed on 14 July 2017].

De Schutter, O. et al., 2012. Commentary to the Maastricht Principles on Extraterritorial Obligations of States in the Area of Economic, Social and Cultural Rights. *Human Rights Quarterly*, 34 (4), 1084–1169.

Gibney, M., 2013. On terminology: Extraterritorial obligations. In: M. Langford, W. Vandenhole, M. Scheinin and W. van Genugten, eds., *Global Justice, State Duties: The Extraterritorial Scope of Economic, Social and Cultural Rights in International Law*. pp. 32–50. Cambridge University Press.

Greenpeace and CIEL, 2015. Extraterritorial Obligations in the Context of Eco-destruction and Climate Change [pdf]. Available online at: < http://www.ciel.org/wp-content/uploads/2015/06/ETOs_CC_16Jan15.pdf > [Accessed 13 July 2017].

Jacobsen, T., Sampford, C., and Thakur, R., 2013. *Re-envisioning Sovereignty: The End of Westphalia?* Ashgate.

Kloke-Lesch, A. and Gleichmann, C., 2010. Global development beyond the North-South paradigm. In: T. Fues and P. Wolff, eds., *G20 and Global Development. How Can the New Summit Architecture Promote Pro-Poor Growth and Sustainability*. German Development Institute.

Langford, M. and Darrow, M., 2013. Moral theory, international law and global justice. In: M. Langford, W. Vandenhole, M. Scheinin and W. van Genugten, eds., *Global Justice, State Duties: The Extraterritorial Scope of Economic, Social and Cultural Rights in International Law*. pp. 419–444. Cambridge University Press.

Maastricht Principles on Extraterritorial Obligations of States in the area of Economic, Social and Cultural Rights, 2011. *Netherlands Quarterly of Human Rights*, 29 (4), 578–590.

McBrearty, S., 2016. The Proposed Business and Human Rights Treaty: Four Challenges and an Opportunity. *Harvard International Law Journal*, 57, 11–14.

Modirzadeh, N. K., 2010. The Dark Sides of Convergence: A Pro-Civilian Critique of the Extraterritorial Application of Human Rights Law in Armed Conflict. *US Naval War College International Law Studies (Blue Book) Series*, 86, 349–410.

OECD, 2010. *Perspectives on Global Development 2010. Shifting Wealth*. OECD.

Pogge, T., 2005. Severe Poverty as a Violation of Negative Duties. *Ethics & International Affairs*, 19 (1), 55–83.

Rajagopal, B., 1999. International Law and the Development Encounter: Violence and Resistance at the Margins. *American Society of International Law Proceedings*, 93, 16–27.

Rajagopal, B., 2000. Postdevelopment as a Vision for a Third World Approach to International Law. *American Society of International Law Proceedings*, 94, 306.

Rajagopal, B., 2003. *International Law from Below: Development, Social Movements and Third World Resistance*. Cambridge University Press.

Salomon, M. E., 2007. *Global Responsibility for Human Rights*. Oxford University Press.

Sen, A., 1999. *Development as Freedom*. Oxford University Press.

Sen, A., 2009. *The idea of Justice*. Belknap Press/Harvard University Press.

Sumner, A., 2010. Global Poverty and the New Bottom Billion: What if Three-quarters of the World's Poor Live in Middle-income Countries? *IDS Working Papers*, 349, 1–43.

Vandenbogaerde, A. and Vandenhole, W., 2010. The Optional Protocol to the International Covenant on Economic, Social and Cultural Rights: An Ex Ante Assessment of its Effectiveness in Light of the Drafting Process. *Human Rights Law Review*, 10 (2), 207–237.

Vandenhole, W., 2007. EU and development: Extraterritorial obligations under the International Covenant on Economic, Social and Cultural Rights. In: M. Salomon, A. Tostensen and W. Vandenhole, eds., *Casting the Net Wider: Human Rights, Development and New Duty-Bearers*. pp. 85–106. Intersentia.

Vandenhole, W., 2009. The limits of human rights law in human development. In: E. Claes, W. Devroe and B. Keirsbilck, eds., *Facing the Limits of the Law*. pp. 355–374. Springer.

Vandenhole, W., 2015a. Obligations and responsibility in a plural and diverse duty-bearer human rights regime. In: W. Vandenhole, ed., *Challenging Territoriality in Human Rights Law: Building Blocks for a Plural and Diverse Duty-Bearer Regime*. pp. 115–135. Routledge.

Vandenhole, W., 2015b. Shared responsibility of non-state actors: a human rights perspective. In: N. Gal-Or, C. Ryngaert and M. Noortmann, eds., *Responsibilities of the Non-State Actor in Armed Conflict: Theoretical Considerations and Empirical Findings*. pp. 55–78. Brill.

Vandenhole, W. and Benedek, W., 2013. Extraterritorial human rights obligations and the North-South divide. In: M. Langford, W. Vandenhole, M. Scheinin and W. van Genugten, eds., *Global Justice, State Duties: The Extraterritorial Scope of Economic, Social and Cultural Rights in International Law*. pp. 332–366. Cambridge University Press.

Vandenhole, W. and Gibney, M., 2014. Introduction. Transnational human rights obligations. In: M. Gibney and W. Vandenhole, eds., *Litigating Transnational Human Rights Obligations: Alternative Judgments*. pp. 1–9. Routledge.

Vandenhole, W., Erdem Türkelli, G. and Hammonds, R., 2013. New human rights duty-bearers: Towards a re-conceptualisation of the human rights duty-bearer dimension. In: A. Mihr and M. Gibney, eds., *Handbook of Human Rights*. pp. 1031–1046. Sage.

Vandenhole, W. and van Genugten, W., 2015. Introduction: an emerging multi-duty-bearer human rights regime? In: W. Vandenhole, ed., *Challenging Territoriality in Human Rights Law: Building Blocks for a Plural and Diverse Duty-Bearer Regime*. pp. 1–11. Routledge.

Van Genugten, W., 2015. *The World Bank Group, the IMF and Human Rights. A Contextualised Way Forward*. Intersentia.

Wilde, R., 2016. Dilemmas in promoting global economic justice through human rights law. In: N. Bhuta, ed., *The Frontiers of Human Rights: Extraterritoriality and its Challenges*. pp. 127–176. Oxford University Press.

Woods, N., 2008. Whose Aid? Whose Influence? China, Emerging Donors and the Silent Revolution in Development Assistance. *International Affairs*, 84 (6), 1205–1221.

Chapter 8

Human Rights, Suffering and Responsibility

Andrew T. Williams

The truth
Has to be melted out of our stubborn lives
By suffering.
Nothing speaks the truth
Nothing tells us how things really are
Nothing forces us to know
What we do not want to know
Except pain.
And this is how the gods declare their love.
Truth comes with pain.
(Ted Hughes, *The Oresteia*)

Introduction

Many think today that we are failing human rights or human rights are failing: either way, injustices, inequalities, sufferings are perpetrated on a massive scale without any seemingly effective response in the name of human rights. Why then bother with them at all? If they are incapable of preventing abuse and provoking true change, if they have reinforced abusive conditions, or they are simply confusing, what value is served by giving the subject further attention and, like some modern-day Sisyphus, endlessly trying to prop up (as some would see it) an inadequate concept?

My answer is based on a series of linked propositions, which together sketch a justification for maintaining adherence to *a* specific notion of human rights within or across borders in order to counter fundamental *injustices*. First, strong, persistent and contemporary critiques (in particular those associated with neo-colonialist and imperialist epistemologies and practices) have created an ambient culture of doubt about human rights, a doubt provoked and amplified when those in the global North examine the record of states in the South in the context of 'development'.

Second, despite the doubt, many assume that human rights language still has significant cohering universal value and are reluctant to jettison the discourse

DOI: 10.4324/9780203745298-11

altogether. But instead of trying to resolve the critiques and find some convincing foundation for human rights, a practical and institutionalised conception has been preferred – one which sees the necessity of channelling action for human rights, as listed in international conventions, through existing national and inter-state institutions.[1] These institutions are ascribed with a first-level responsibility for protecting and realising human rights. I reject this approach for a number of reasons, the most significant of which is that it reinforces the philosophical incoherence of human rights by placing primary responsibility for their realisation on existing (dysfunctional) institutions which it would be naïve to believe will act justly and for the fulfilment of human rights; they too easily avoid or ignore, deflect or postpone human rights responsibilities often on self-serving grounds (if only for the preservation of the institution itself). The critique that human rights are the creatures and tools of the powerful (whether or not they might benefit the powerless from time to time) is then easily levelled, further undermining human rights aims. Ironically, the subjects of human rights are distanced from those institutions invested with the responsibility for their protection.

Third, whilst still recognising the value and need for collective action to obtain justice (for human rights), I argue that it is the *personal* commitment to respond to, and accept first-level responsibility for, known human suffering that must provide the essential counterweight to the institutional domination of development and human rights. I do not claim that this is *the* solution to human rights failure or failings. I simply argue that the combination of *personal* ethos and *institutional* ethos (instead of the latter standing as proxy for the former) is necessary to ensure that the value of human rights is not negated by real and convincing critiques ranged against them. In particular, I see this as essential when combatting the social collapse that will and already does accompany global disasters (war, environmental destruction, violence and poverty being the most prominent) that are the concern of development and global injustice discourses. I justify this by showing how the very language of human rights imputes such a personal and collective commitment before demonstrating how sources of political philosophy support my contention. In this way, human rights as a means for responding to suffering may be reimagined.

These propositions need amplifying. I do so below.

First Proposition

It would be absurd to ignore the benefits for some people's lives that have been won in the name of human rights. I do not need to rehearse them other than to point to the lists of achievements produced annually by the human rights industry that speak to positive differences made in various locations. Few seriously doubt the powerful effect human rights have had, their ability to challenge the actions and behaviour of governments, states and corporations, and to

1 This approach is exemplified in the work of Charles Beitz (2009).

provide something of a guide for the betterment of some people's lives. Though this may not have been transformative on every occasion, human rights optimists (some would say evangelists) can always and reasonably point to successful changes and reforms brought about internationally and nationally through the medium of human rights. This belief underscores much of the human rights-based approach to development that has been promoted by a number of international institutions.[2]

None of this has prevented the parallel evolution of a host of critiques against the whole discourse of international human rights. These take at least three forms: the first is the functionalist critique reflected in the work of David Kennedy. The second is more impassioned and resistant, recognising the neo-colonial preferences inherent in human rights that still mirror the David Livingstone-type ideology of transplanting and making universal the doctrines of Christianity, commerce and (western) civilisation. The third is philosophical and revolves around resistance to any kind of foundationalism, which seeks to identify an immutable core to human rights applicable everywhere to everyone.

Kennedy's argument is the least sophisticated and most avowedly pragmatic of the three and is prompted by a number of questions: do international human rights work; do they do what they promise; are the unintended consequences of their promotion too high a price to pay? Kennedy's (2012) critical responses are more than a decade old now, but he has revisited them recently and found no reason to recant. He argues that 'Human rights is no longer the way forward – it focuses too longingly on the perfection of a politics already past its prime' (Kennedy, 2012: 34). He worries that the 'human rights revolution may have been a delay and diversion: a status quo project of legitimation and an establishment career option for those who might otherwise have contributed to a new global politics' (Kennedy, 2012: 33). Several years on, his checklist of concerns has only grown, but his original formulation remains relevant and powerful for the most part. He still contends that human rights may be too dominant in the field of emancipatory politics and cut off oxygen for other vocabularies. If articulations of justice are not framed in human rights norms they do not acquire the purchase they should. He sees human rights as too narrow, as failing to encompass the wider contexts where the problems and injustices of the world really exist, and preferring labels for individuals at the expense of more refined understanding about identities and relationships. Human rights are also tainted by their adherence to the western liberal tradition. They promise much which cannot be delivered, treat symptoms not causes, and enable bureaucracies of human rights to flourish that have turned ideals into checklists and protocols that pay lip service to justice rather than enhance it. In each case, Kennedy's arguments are persuasive.

2 See for instance UNOHCHR, 2006, 'FAQs on a Human Rights Based Approach to Development Cooperation', available online at https://www.ohchr.org/Documents/Publications/FAQen.pdf (accessed 4 March 2020).

The second key form of critique is more political than pragmatic but not unrelated. Many authors have seen in human rights language *and* practice the exposition and continuation of colonialism and the arrogant belief that the West is at the pinnacle of human society and that its norms and methods of governance and social justice are naturally superior (Douzinas, 2000). There are some overlaps with Kennedy's analysis, if only in the *uses* to which human rights have been put rather than their underlying values. In other words, the actions of western or northern governments or corporations distort human rights for their own, usually economic, interests. Even if Christian ethics are not present in the skeleton of human rights, the civilising mission of colonialism and the identification of commercialism or capitalism as the natural environment for human rights to flourish mean that it is not possible to escape the persistent colonial mind-set in the worlds of human rights (Mutua, 2008: 10).

Upendra Baxi (2002) provides the most focused example of this critique. His formulation of human rights as premised on a trade-related market-friendly paradigm adds to the appreciation of others that the discourse of human rights owes its origins, its articulations and its operation to a capitalist mentality rooted in a Eurocentric sense of rightness. Costas Douzinas (2000) and others unpick these foundations and applications of international human rights norms which, they argue, too easily place faith in human rights as a concept untainted by the interests of capital and states (e.g., Shivji, 1989).

The third main challenge is philosophical: though there are good accounts justifying the language and application of human rights articulated in national and international instruments, there are equally strong (and, some would suggest, stronger) arguments that dispute their claims to usefulness or naturalness for all societies and for all times. Though *some* human rights might be deemed appropriate for all societies irrespective of era, they can never be specific enough to be immutable and without caveats. The failure to resolve these philosophical questions has caused many who see the value in human rights to fall back upon their practical value. In other words, rather than dispense with human rights altogether, it is thought better to focus on what they can and might do.

These three critiques seem to me to be ultimately romantic and likely to prompt an enervating melancholia. Human rights are seen through a lens of some ideal that can never be achieved. Kennedy's critique is typical of much so-called pragmatic opposition to human rights in which any crack in the glass of human rights promises is seen as an illustration of their hopelessness. By failing to fulfil world peace, structural equality, the end of poverty, the fulfilment of participatory democracy, a better life for all, universal health care and education, and saving the environment, human rights are regarded as a disappointment. The hubris redolent within the human rights texts themselves encourage such romanticism; they do, after all, project mantras of virtue that allow for little dissent or nuance. The preamble to the European Convention of Human Rights, for instance, allows little negotiation about the meaning of justice or democracy in any location in its *re*-affirmation of a:

> profound belief in those fundamental freedoms which are the foundation of justice and peace in the world and are best maintained on the one hand by an effective political democracy and on the other by a common understanding and observance of the Human Rights upon which they depend.

Whatever my views may be of these critiques or responses to them, they challenge the solidity if not the value of human rights now and for the future. At the very least, they create potential fault lines in concerted action to respect, promote and realise human rights. In particular, those who see the universalisation of human rights as threats to national security, identity or wealth accumulation are able to exploit the uncertainties and questions they raise. It is much easier to oppose the rights of 'others' whether they be refugees, minorities, those in poverty, if those campaigning with and for them are consistently fighting off intellectual attacks from governments and other vested interests.

Second Proposition

The criticisms outlined above provide an ambient culture of doubt about human rights, particularly when those in the global North examine the record of states in the South. Despite this, many are reluctant to jettison the discourse altogether. There remains a widely-held assumption that there is significant value in the aims and language of human rights.

However, instead of trying to resolve such critiques and find coherent themes or foundations, the tendency has often been to re-focus on the practical. Michael Ignatieff, for instance, believes it is much better 'to seek to build support for human rights on the basis of what such rights actually *do* for human beings' rather than construct some all-encompassing foundational claim (Ignatieff, 2001: 54). He presupposes that either we already know what human rights are and what they are for or that this does not matter too much. This may have considerable practical merit, but it *is* exclusionary. It denies any differing development of human rights possibilities because it assumes the subject to be closed; human rights are what they *are* not what they might become.

Jack Donnelly (2002) goes one step further in suggesting that there is no point in looking for human rights justifications at all because the general international consensus evident in instruments such as the Universal Declaration of Human Rights is sufficient to enable us to look at the practice of human rights without having to rationalise theories that might underpin them.[3]

The attraction of this position is that it sidesteps questions as to what human rights are for. Consensus need only be sought on needs, abuses and injustices. For those who believe that these are obvious, at least in egregious violations, attention can then shift to the insistent call to *do* something as long as we are

3 Richard Rorty (1993) seems to agree with this although still looks for a foundational premise despite saying there is none.

busy about it. Charles Beitz, for instance, contends that a 'practical conception' of human rights is to be preferred. By taking the 'doctrine and practice of human rights as we find them in international political life as the source materials for constructing a conception of human rights' he ignores any search for an underlying meaning or a fundamental moral idea (Beitz, 2009: 102). Rather, the emphasis is on constructing a plausible doctrine whose content is historically contingent, determinable by global practice, and narrowed by a scheme of exclusions. These include, Beitz argues, interests that would not 'reasonably be seen as worthy of protection by most members of existing societies'; 'values for which a failure to secure or protect them in a society would not provide any intelligible reason for action to appropriately situated outside agents' and 'values for the deprivation of which no remedy is achievable through some permissible form of international action for which there is a reasonable expectation of success' (Beitz, 2009: 106). Beitz's position is a self-confessed modest account. His emphasis is on those concerned with getting on with addressing the plight of others. By avoiding messy ideas about foundations, meaning and morality, the call to arms provoked by evident wrongdoing will always tempt us to refrain from diverting attention to matters of philosophical consistency.

Invariably, the practical approach relies upon an institutionalisation of state action to work. This applies both within a state's borders and when states seek to act internationally to interfere in the affairs of a human rights abusing state, whether that abuse is deliberate or not. So, for Beitz human rights 'apply in the first instance to the political institutions of states'. Being of international concern, 'the international community may through its political institutions hold states accountable' for carrying out that first level responsibility (Beitz, 2009: 109). In this way Beitz justifies the existing architecture of human rights institutions operating at the global level scrutinising institutions at the national level.

There's no suggestion in Beitz's account that these national and international institutions monopolise action. But the inevitable tendency is to see all responsibility accruing to, and being channelled through, them. That's understandable: if state institutions fail to protect (or themselves breach) articulated rights then it seems sensible for inter-state institutions to provide some oversight. And if *they* fail (as they do more often than not) then the fault is institutional and the remedy is institutional reform. This can be quite comforting: not only can responsibility for fulfilling the practical concerns of human rights be pushed entirely onto these institutions, but when things go wrong it is to these institutions we turn for a response. They become the avenue for human rights fulfilment *and* blame. Response and responsibility are both institutionalised in a circular process that can become insular and conservative for the institutions concerned and the interests they represent, a closed world which most people can never enter, let alone influence. The development of new human rights (or more carefully articulated existing rights) becomes more unlikely as a result *until* they are itemised and written down, accepted and listed officially, can be tracked with some degree of certainty, and are the subject of institutional agreement. The resulting human rights text or charter is reified as though it represents the real world, excluding any document or voices emerging other than from or through 'recognised' institutions and those allowed to speak within or to them.

Several other problems with the practical/institutional approach (absent a philosophical core) arise. The recognition of texts is susceptible to political manipulation by those ardently antagonistic to certain types of human rights. The debate about civil and political rights on the one hand and economic, social and cultural rights on the other is emblematic of such a politics of recognition. It assumes that even in texts that are institutionally embraced there is conceptual clarity on the nature and scope of particular human rights. But the notion of certainty in this context is another myth. Interpretation is at the whim of politics as well as jurisprudence. The familiar lists of rights (contained in the UN instruments in particular) do not lend themselves to simple reading. They *encourage* interpretation. But the only authorised version can be declared by existing institutions.

Equally, the institutional focus for action *without* clarity of philosophy can prompt arguments based on very simplistic and familiar utilitarian principles. This is a natural consequence of this way of thinking. Adopting an approach based on the medical concept of 'triage' can persuade us that short-term responses are inherently more valuable than long-term approaches, which otherwise seek to change systems, underlying conditions, and embedded power relations (Farmer, 2004: 230–231). Immediate humanitarian relief for particular victims, understandably deemed a priority, can be justified on the basis of numbers 'saved' or assisted in comparison to unquantifiable numbers who will predictably suffer when structural violence is allowed to go unchecked.

Institutionalising human rights may also provide the space for responsibility to be institutionalised as well. The institution and its ethos rather than the human rights in issue become the focus of attention. Stan Cohen's (2001) sociology of denial and the neo-institutionalism and organisation theories of international relations both warn us about the consequences, particularly the possibility of repression of responsibility in the interests of whatever pragmatic or political priority (national security or economy often being the most prominent) is identified from time to time. So-called rational choice seems to forgive all manner of wrongs and allows responsibility to be avoided or ignored. Such an approach can be a breeding ground for indifference, deflection and self-preservation, none of which lend themselves to the costly promotion or fulfilment of human rights interests and even less to holding institutions (and their members) and individuals to account for the violation of those rights or a failure to protect them.

For these reasons, the preference for the practical and institutional approach seems to me as much a challenge for human rights as a solution. But how do we avoid throwing out the benefits of the practical and institutional approach (such as they are) whilst addressing its underlying failings? How do we reinforce the value in *doing something* to address human wrongs through institutional cooperation and coordination without losing sight of the purpose of human rights?

Third Proposition

My tentative response to this dilemma is complicated and I only sketch out my proposition here. I begin with the appreciation that avoiding the search for an underlying philosophy for human rights is counter-productive. Some sense of foundation would help reach grounded judgements about the development and application of particular human rights articulations or claims and provide a basis for assessing the rightful action of any institutions (governmental or non-governmental) that purportedly work for human rights. I have argued elsewhere that the fundamental appeal of human rights is their promise to respond to human suffering (Williams, 2007). Just as we may look to a minimum core in some (economic) rights to provide a platform for action, so we may look to this promise to respond to human suffering as the minimum (or immanent) core that creates a commitment to do something.

But this is not enough. Rather than allow human rights practice to be defined and dominated by institutions and the ethos they develop, it is the *personal* commitment to respond to, and accept first-level responsibility for, known human suffering which I suggest provides a plausible basis to address the institutional domination of human rights and ultimately their failure or failings. In other words, it is the combination of *personal* ethos and *institutional* ethos (instead of the latter subsuming the former) that is necessary if the promise inherent in human rights discourse is to be fulfilled.

This dual proposition requires explanation.

First, the term 'human rights' necessarily implies a moral quality that invokes notions of personal *as well as* collective responsibility. To be human is to be moral, to be in association with others and thus to be conditioned by morality. Human rights must therefore be a moral concept or at least a concept affected by morality. It is then a matter of determining what the parameters of that morality are. Some work still needs to be done to reach that point rather than simply rely on an assertion of morality. To do so requires unpicking the terms 'human' and 'right' to see if 'human rights' are indeed inextricably a moral matter. Only then can a moral foundation be posited.

As far as the 'human' element is concerned, it is plausible to argue that the term 'human' connotes a certain transcendence. It allows us to think of the concept as unconfined by location or time. Patently, geography cannot determine who is considered 'human'. No one can argue seriously that 'human rights' are limited to those who reside in a particular country or continent. Although we might be talking about humans who were the subject of rights, the restriction of human rights only to those who can qualify by residence would be a denial of the universal 'human' descriptor. This would not preclude a corpus of rights described in some other fashion: citizens' rights or such like. Nor, by extension, would it preclude a national constitutional document such as a Bill of Rights. But if any state is to rely upon 'human' as an adjective of 'rights' then restricting their application to a group of people on the basis of limited criteria would be inherently self-contradictory.

The matter of time is a little more complicated. Certainly, the term 'human' could apply to all human life that has existed, does exist, and will come into existence. To be human is not reasonably confined by time, unless we argue that a necessary condition of being human is to be alive. Although such a condition may have practical value (limiting the number of those who qualify for anything associated with being a living human) it is absurd to suggest that *in theory* those who have died or are to be born are disqualified from being defined as 'human'. Indeed, in classic dilemmas such as abortion, human embryo experimentation and the treatment of those clinically dead, the determination of when a person becomes or ceases to be a 'human being' may be debatable, but the argument that it is *not human* is less palatable. From a general perspective, it would therefore be wrong to bar such entities who are no longer alive (or who are yet to be born) from human rights language altogether.

Such an expansive possibility need not imply an undue self-defeating indeterminateness. Although we might in practice apply limits to our acknowledgment of all possible members there is, for instance, ample precedent for accepting that both past and future lives might benefit from the application of human rights norms. The environmental movement is premised on this understanding. Thus, from identifiable dead individuals to those in gestation but considered 'not yet alive' and beyond to future generations, there are many occasions when it has been acknowledged that 'human' extends beyond the here and now. This does not feel particularly contentious philosophically although the law might grapple with jurisdictional issues of distance in space and time (backwards or forwards) as a restriction on those who might be the subject of a legal claim.[4]

None of this is to say that the term 'human' is not without its practical definitional problems particularly with the advent of biotechnology, artificial intelligence and genetic engineering. What it is to be human (outside time issues) throws up a number of significant ethical questions, particularly at the margins of life from conception to 'death'.[5] But these matters should not disguise the vast set of subjects who can be identified with relative ease as 'human'. Indeed, such general recognition is vital if we are to refute claims (which it is hardly controversial to say we must) restricting any definition of humanity made on the basis of some deep-seated racism, nationalism, or psychology of 'pseudospeciation' as Erik Erikson was purported to have called

4 There are many instances where human rights have been used to relate to past victims or potential future victims. The abuses visited on the victims of the Holocaust, war, colonialism, slavery, have all been the subject of accepted human rights-based claims, although admittedly it has never been easy to bring them to fruition.

5 When a foetus becomes a 'human' or when a person ceases to be such as a result of brain-death, for instance are critical questions for all societies. But this does not detract from the general identification of 'humans'.

it.[6] Provided we reject the spurious arguments of those who deny humanity for those who are 'different', who inject hate into their belief that those not of their 'group' are less than human and worthy of destruction or 'rule', the word 'human' is still apt. It clearly is not to be restricted to 'citizens' or members of any particular state or community or geographical territory.

The term 'rights' on the other hand suggests some sense of demand or claim and some sense of response (either recognised or denied). It connotes a connection between people, perhaps even between 'peoples'. Whatever categories we might otherwise care to ascribe (which Wesley Hohfeld (1964) provided, with rights appearing as claims, liberties, immunities, and powers), this connectivity is a central characteristic. John Finnis (1980: 199) described it as 'a three-term relation between one person, one act-description, and one other person'. Tom Campbell defined rights more narrowly as 'claims to entitlements that individuals (and perhaps groups) can justifiably make on other people and organisations' (Campbell, 2006: xi). What the nature of that demand or claim and what the response might be remains open. Both could depend on the link made between 'rights' on the one hand and the identity of those who make the demand on the other. So, for 'citizens' rights' for instance, or 'the rights of corporations' the key element is the *relationship* the rights mentioned conjure. Their assertion or articulation entails a *beneficiary* (who doesn't have to be a claimant – others can claim for them), a *benefit* (requiring someone to cease doing or prevent something, or to do or give something) and a *benefactor* (who could be the state, another person, or some agency, institution, or organisation) who it is claimed should provide the benefit sought.[7] This tripartite equation situates the topic of rights in the moral domain, acknowledging *relationship* as the central quality of human rights.

Linking 'human' with 'rights', therefore, creates a crucial relationship-in-being, a connection between those who demand and those required to respond that is unlimited in theory by geography or some other means of separation.[8] The core aspect of humanity is the bond between *all* human beings. As James Griffin (2008: 2) put it, a human right is 'a right that we have simply in virtue of being human'. Whatever content we give 'rights' they have to apply to *all* 'human' subjects. And by attaching rights to all human subjects, we invest in

6 According to Laurence J. Friedman, Erik Erikson coined the term to describe the process of denying a person's designation as a 'human' on the grounds that they did not belong to a particular ethnic or other group. In other words, what amounted to the 'human species' was always contingent on the determination by particular groups that all who were not members were not a member of that species. For more on this idea see Friedman (2008) and Kai Erikson (1996).

7 Using these terms is *not* intended to impute that an element of gift is involved in this relationship. The transfer of a benefit, a 'good', may still be the subject of obligation. The point of the terminology is to emphasise the sense of connection rather than a determination of whether this is charitable or not.

8 Which might amount to a 'jural correlative' in Hohfeld's terms (Hohfeld, 1964: 65).

them power to persuade or force other subjects and institutions to realise those rights for themselves or others. No matter what rights we are talking about and wherever we are looking to have them enforced, they have to apply without discrimination, at least as a primary position. In the first instance, it would be antithetical to suggest that certain human beings are not entitled to certain 'human rights' (as opposed to any other types of rights) on the basis of their membership of a particular group. Otherwise, we would revert back to the discrimination and denial inherent in pseudospeciation.

As I have already said, this is not to assert that some rights might not be denied in certain circumstances or some greater rights are granted to some people on certain grounds. But these would have to be morally justifiable *exceptions* that would not undermine the basic understanding I have outlined.[9] And it would not necessarily follow that we would be repudiating the premise of 'human rights' by doing so.

There is support for this within traditional western scholarship. David Luban wrote: 'A human right … will be a right whose beneficiaries are all humans and whose obligors are all humans in a position to effect the right' (Luban, 1980: 174). His limited notion of obligor is, however, unsatisfactory because it leaves the third element of my equation (the benefactor) open to unstated empirical evaluation. 'Being in a position' to do something about a right suggests there must be an assessment about whether a person or institution (the obligor) *can* in practice act effectively. That seems to me unnecessarily indeterminate at an early definitional stage.

This is an underlying problem experienced by many theorists. Amartya Sen, for instance, although acknowledging the distinction between a 'reason' to do something to prevent a violation of a human right and a *duty* to do something, is still trapped by the need for 'one to be in a position' to do that something (Sen, 2009: 372). My concern, however, is with the plausible parameters of the relationship between beneficiary and benefactor before we turn to what may provoke that relationship and demand the transfer of 'benefit', the imposition of responsibility.

Knowing that all human beings *should be* affected by 'human rights', both as beneficiaries and benefactors (in theory) is nonetheless a useful first step. It adds to the appreciation that human rights apply to all human beings wherever they are and arguably *whenever* they might live or might have lived.[10] Whether or how we realise those rights is another matter.[11]

9 For instance, in the punishment of offenders where certain liberties are restricted.

10 The seemingly irrelevant inclusion of those who are not alive but were once or will come to be is important for a number of reasons in relation to issues such as compensation of past human-rights violations or the protection of human rights (such as might be linked to the quality of the environment) in the future.

11 The possibility of owing a duty to persons from the past has been the subject of specific questions of justice. Debates on these cases, such as the historical crime of slavery in the USA, the harm done by reason of colonialism etc., have provoked considerable argument without any resolution. Nonetheless, the point is that there is the possibility that human rights can attach to people who have passed away and

It is true that some of my analysis sits uneasily with Hannah Arendt's (2017) (and others') critiques of human rights. Her identification of the most crucial right being the 'right to have rights' underpins a view that without recognition as a member of a community, human rights do not have real purchase (Arendt, 2017). The stateless can call for their rights to be respected, but without citizenship attaching to them and some authority accepting responsibility vis-à-vis those rights, the likelihood is any claim will not be 'heard' and no respondent will emerge. All they have left is their humanity without any practical content to their 'rights'. To be human then means little in rights terms, as Jean-Francois Lyotard (1996) made clear. This is a powerful argument, the impact of which is regularly apparent nowadays on the stateless and those who cross borders. In effect, it is based on a political realist account of human rights that suggests the only rights we have are those given to us as citizens or residents of a particular state. Though possibly true in practice, this doesn't mean we should give up on human rights as a moral (rather than legal) concept. There is still value in arguing for change. As Etienne Balibar suggests:

> the recognition and institution of citizens' rights, which practically command the development of human rights, have to be organized beyond the *exclusive* membership to one community; they should be located, so to speak, 'on the borders,' where so many of our contemporaries actually live.
> (Balibar, 2001: 28)

He concludes that 'the important question is permanent *access to* rather than simply *entitlement to* citizenship, and therefore humanity' (ibid.). The matter, he writes, is one of process rather than principle. The humanity that is implied in human rights requires a means to be found for their realisation and *not* a surrender to the practical barriers put in their way by legal jurisdiction and political partiality. This is part of the promise of 'human rights': to transcend the political and the geographical (as well as the legal), at least at the level of their conceptual recognition and to apply to all humans at all times. In doing so, it also accepts the possibility, if not necessity, of a moral foundation to enable human rights to appeal across borders.

For my part, if I am right about the theoretical all-inclusive nature of both beneficiary and benefactor founded on relationship and responsibility, the key issue for human rights becomes the nature of the benefit claimed and/or provided. This is where the bulk of work in the field takes place. Establishing who is entitled to make a claim and who can and should respond will still be significant questions requiring philosophical justification but determining *what* the claim can and should be *for* and what can and should be responded *to* (and to what extent) will be of prior importance.

people yet to be born. In law, this might be troublesome, but an argument for the application of such rights from a global or restorative justice perspective can be made.

The reasoning above underpins my final proposition that collective and personal responses to suffering are the most plausible immanent theme of human rights, and the core subject matter of the benefit to be provided. Although I recognise other claims to moral foundation resting, for instance, on concepts of equality (all persons should be treated equally in the organisation of society), of freedom (all persons should be enabled to live their lives without unreasonable interference by individuals or institutions), of democracy (all persons in a particular society should be engaged in collective decisions that affect their lives), and of fairness (all people should be treated fairly in the distribution of benefits and burdens associated with living in society with others), none of these seem to me to offer sufficient cause for the ubiquitous transcultural and often emotional attachment to, and advocacy for, human rights in the modern era.[12] Nor do any of these deny the fundamental appreciation that whatever human rights might be for, they *should* be about relieving manifest suffering.

Thomas Scanlon (2017), for one, substantiates this in relation to the search for equality. The relief of suffering is one of four basic and important moral values which provide strong reasons for the elimination of various inequalities. Even the others he mentions (prevention of stigmatising differences in status; avoiding unacceptable forms of power or domination; preserving the equality of starting places which is required by procedural fairness) can be interpreted as responding to human suffering. It is not difficult to appreciate each as capable of inducing physical or psychological suffering: it is this which gives them moral value. In all cases, wrongdoing that emanates from causing or failing to alleviate suffering is morally objectionable because someone is made to suffer unnecessarily or relief of their suffering is unnecessarily or unreasonably refused or delayed.

To substantiate this further I look to some aspects of political philosophy which are concerned with the margins of obligation for people beyond one's own borders. Whether that falls within the discipline of 'development' is really unimportant. Being enraptured by 'development' as somehow defining or limiting or influencing the nature of human rights and their associated obligations in the global South or elsewhere would be a mistake if my initial propositions hold good. If all humans are in relationship with each other and from this flows the idea of human rights, then any idea of development is unnecessarily restrictive if it is tied to geography. This is not to assert that the deep inequities of colonialism are not crucial in identifying past and present injustices and past and present human rights violations. But development as a subject or discipline does nothing to remedy these injustices. Indeed, by perpetuating difference it reinforces the institution of (neo-)colonialism through the

12 The work of Abdullahi An-Na'im (2010), Enrique Dussel (2013) and others have shown how the western liberal concept of human rights should not mean that other traditions cannot lay claim to appreciation of the objectives and principles of human rights *tout court*.

dichotomy of 'developing' and 'developed'. The former remains the colonised, the latter the colonisers. That fundamentally contradicts the interpretation of human rights I have been advocating above.

So, looking beyond development, its idea and logic, for human rights foundations is a necessary step in my formulation. When we examine various positions within contemporary political philosophy, which attempt to define duties owed beyond a bordered community, what do we see? Here, the response to human suffering is ubiquitous whether within a developing, developed or under-developed economy, community or discourse.

Although there is undoubtedly resistance to acknowledging a duty to protect human rights beyond state boundaries (in the realist tradition of international relations theory), if my articulation of the originality of human rights in this third proposition holds good, such approaches may be dismissed. By definition, they do not accord with the implications of using the descriptor 'human' in association with 'rights'. Commentators who deny the existence of significant obligations beyond political communities are not discussing a logical construction of the concept of human rights. They may claim that all just societies should protect certain rights for their citizens, but in maintaining the pre-eminence of sovereign states to determine their own affairs they preclude external review and even judgement beyond circumstances of the most egregious violence.

Consequently, we should consider accounts of global justice which at least implicitly acknowledge the rightfulness, if not the duty, of external scrutiny of and intervention in a state's internal affairs in certain circumstances (the breach of specific universal rights). In this territory of political philosophy, there is no such thing as a timeless understanding of what is 'good' for all people in all locations. Presupposing a list of rights which impose or reflect some vision of the 'good' should therefore be treated with circumspection. Otherwise, the critique that such a list is the imposition of Western ideological imperialism would undermine the claim to universality (and thus undermine the whole idea of 'human' rights). But a justification of what is 'good' that is integral to *all* human beings regardless of nationality or any other characteristic still lies at the heart of judging when intervention is deemed justified. This inevitably leads to considerable disagreement about the scope of the principle. How far can one go in expressing a universal 'good' without falling foul of the original critique?

Perhaps the unstated point of departure is provoked by the question: are we prepared to deny judgement of another society on *all and any* grounds? In other words, is there not a point where the suffering of people demands action? It is at this level (which might be termed the debate concerning minimalism) that I suggest political philosophy provides an appreciation of the *undeniable* or *intolerable* upon which we can then construct 'human' rights.

Accounts of human rights within notions of cosmopolitan justice may not be the best place to begin unpicking this undeniable (or intolerable) core. The notion of well-being as something which demands universal recognition is likely to be at the thicker end of a conception of the universal 'good'. In other words, the basic moral position of cosmopolitanism makes little if any distinction between human beings wherever they may reside. A tendency ensues to ascribe to everyone a wide range of universal rights the realisation of which is believed to be necessary regardless of culture or citizenship.

A consensus may still be unachievable, however. We might find adherence to the Universal Declaration of Human Rights (UDHR) to be a common position, but this rarely encourages cosmopolitans to argue that direct examination of and intervention in the affairs of states is justified for *any* breach of *any* UDHR article. Rather, the grounds for intervention are severely limited either in the understanding of the breach of rights that justifies intervention or the rules governing the timing and scale of some otherwise legitimate intrusion. Simon Caney, for one, points to the first requirement for intervention as 'just cause'. To be legitimate, intervention must only be against a political regime which has violated 'people's human rights (where this includes rights to a decent standard of living as well as rights against torture, murder, unjust imprisonment, or enslavement)' (Caney, 2005: 248). He argues that all human rights may in theory be covered by such a provision. He acknowledges that some people claim that intervention can only be legitimate if the breach is of *fundamental* human rights. However, his other requirements (proportionality, preference for less 'awful measures', 'likelihood of success', and 'legitimate authority') would most likely prevent intervention other than for the violation of 'fundamental rights' (Caney, 2005: 248). Relying on this kind of practical consequence rather than principled foundation does not hide the fact that it is significant human suffering which provokes the necessity for a response.

David Miller takes a different view but nonetheless accepts the moral imperative for intervention resulting from the violation of 'basic human rights'. He says that when 'basic rights are threatened or violated, this triggers a responsibility on the part of outsiders to come to the aid of those whose rights are imperilled' (Miller, 2007: 197). Those basic rights are decided on the basis of two main criteria: an explanation of their 'moral urgency' and a justification based on non-sectarian foundations – everyone must have reason to accept them. Miller then states that a long list of such rights is therefore unlikely. The violation of many specific rights simply does not conjure up a sense of moral urgency to do something about them. Instead, he suggests, a humanitarian strategy 'which appeals to basic human *needs*' is preferable (Miller, 2007: 179). The application of the descriptor 'human' takes us back to the universal. In that sense is there anything different between 'human needs' used to define 'human rights'? Whether or not there is a distinction, the intrinsic notion of needs is defined by Miller as 'those items or conditions it is necessary for a person to have if she is to avoid being harmed' (179). In this context harm 'can be identified in physical or biological terms', but Miller argues that it should also extend to denying individuals the possibility of living a 'minimally decent life' (181). He acknowledges that what is decent can vary from place to place although the need attached should not. In determining whether a particular society is violating basic human rights in order to justify intervention, he returns to the 'moral urgency' requirement of explaining why particular violations (rather than particular rights) 'can impose relatively demanding obligations on third parties who are not themselves responsible for the violations' (197). On a practical level it seems difficult to escape 'physical-cum-biological' harm only as capable of satisfying this condition: in essence, human suffering, which it is reasonable to expect everyone, everywhere would not wish others to experience.

Miller's account does not distinguish him greatly from John Rawls, at least not in practical consequences. Rawls argues that a limited conception of human rights 'cannot be rejected as peculiarly liberal or special to the Western tradition' (Rawls, 1993: 65). For him a 'special class of urgent rights' represents 'a necessary, though not sufficient, standard for the decency of domestic political and social institutions' (79–80).

Michael Walzer, is even more restrictive, yet paradoxically more expansive at the same time. He justifies intervention in general on the grounds of assisting 'secessionist movements (once they have demonstrated their representative character), to balance the prior interventions of other powers, and to rescue peoples threatened with massacre' (Walzer, 2015: 108). The latter he interprets as 'acts "that shock the moral conscience of mankind"' (107), although just intervention as a whole he interprets as reflecting 'deep and valuable … commitments to human rights' (108). It seems that the human rights he has in mind are associated more with intentional harm directed at a population than failures to fulfil the whole corpus of human rights in the various international instruments. Thus, egregious human rights abuses such as 'enslavement' and 'massacre' trigger consideration of the exception to the principle of non-interference in the affairs of other states.[13]

For others, the case for intervention is more limited still. Jack Donnelly (2002) looks for overlapping consensus and finds this to exist only in the case of genocide. Here alone, he argues, there is no convincing case for avoiding a response. But violations of other human rights have not acquired similar status. Why the special legalistic definition of genocide should privilege it above 'common massacre' or 'gross and systematic' torture, killings, arbitrary deprivation of liberty, enslavement etc. is difficult to judge. Either way, the wrong that is deemed intolerable cannot be disassociated from human suffering.

With some justification, therefore, the relief of mass human suffering is the one factor that has universal appeal. Even the most restrictive mainstream accounts are founded on a humanitarian understanding that it is right that suffering should elicit a response. More expansive accounts merely seek to broaden our interpretation of suffering. Most accept that this has limits because it is wrong to impose a notion of the good life upon another society. Human suffering remains integral to all accounts of human rights and the moral obligation to do something in response to violations.

13 Walzer (2015) – enslavement is mentioned on p. 90.

The only significant area of contention at this minimal level seems to focus on causation. Some accounts of international human rights and justice restrict themselves to the deliberate infliction of suffering on people by states. Even then, more restrictive interpretations draw little practical distinction between suffering resulting from human agency and that resulting from natural crises. The exact nature of the response may differ (for instance, holding states or individuals to account through prosecution may be an alternative to prevention or redress), but the necessity of doing something in response to human suffering is integral to all accounts. The humanitarian appeal, indubitably concerned with human suffering, is one that is difficult to resist regardless of questions of responsibility.[14]

Even in mainstream western traditions, therefore, the moral imperative focuses on responding to human suffering wherever it occurs. This I suggest is the immanent core of human rights. Whatever other notions and motivations are added, this remains the basis upon which more developed theories are constructed. If that is the strong moral position, then it becomes a matter of practice how responsibility to respond to human suffering is distributed.

Conclusion

If I am right about the immanent core and its justification, then my concluding thought holds that only through the admission of personal responsibility associated with the collective can that foundational purpose of human rights be fulfilled. Without a personal commitment to do something in response to known suffering, institutions will be left as the only responsible entities. For all the problems that institutions represent, that is likely to lead to an enduring failing of the immanent core.

The concept of accountability is fundamental here. Accountability is not discretionary and cannot be viewed only as an imperfect duty. At the very least it requires holding institutions (wherever they are located) to *account* for their (lack of) response to known suffering. It also necessitates an account of such suffering to be heard. The structuring of what might be termed 'adjudicative justice' must thus first be based on the necessity for society and individuals directly affected to bear witness to their suffering and for responsible individuals or authorities to account for whether, how and to what extent they have responded to known suffering.

This opens several subsidiary questions that need to be resolved: who or what is responsible and encompassed by this injunction? How is the requirement of double-accounting to be achieved? And who can invoke such processes? My sense is that a threefold notion of accountability could underpin the promise of response by individual and collective alike.

14 Thomas Nagel (2005) provides a clear commitment to respond to the humanitarian appeal even though he may deny the broader obligations suggested by cosmopolitanism.

First, the principle should incorporate the possibility for suffering to be narrated, what might be described as *témoignage* for those observing *and* for those experiencing suffering where so ever and how so ever it may occur.[15] Susan Sontag wrote, 'it seems a good in itself to acknowledge, to have enlarged, one's sense of how much suffering caused by human wickedness there is in the world', ignorance of which is a form of 'moral defectiveness' (Sontag, 2003: 102). The immediate individual obligation is to call out suffering whenever it is observed. It is easy to decry this obligation as 'noise' without action, easily produced to alleviate guilt rather than a true commitment to respond. That would be an error. We should know by now the importance of recounting the suffering of others (and ourselves) in bringing systemic violence in particular to light. Without personal observation the wrongs of institutions and states can be hidden and become normalised. To underestimate its value in the entire process of responsibility for suffering is to underestimate the need for personal acknowledgement of the other and their condition.

But it is insufficient to publicise suffering personally simply to satisfy our individual moral health. There must also be a collective and institutionalised commitment to hear and respond. Upendra Baxi has long pointed to the necessity of incorporating the voices of suffering within the adjudicative practice of law and politics. For him 'human rights enunciations matter, if at all, only if they provide shields against torture and tyranny, deprivation and destitution, pauperization and powerlessness, desexualisation and degradation' (Baxi, 2003: 102). Those who suffer must be given resources and opportunities to express the nature of their suffering so as to invoke the moral responsibility to do something in response. This has direct relevance to the anticipation and realisation of suffering. Individuals and institutions who can respond must have the capacity to hear what is feared and fully examine what has been experienced. The proper practice of human rights impact assessments, for instance, could provide some scrutiny. Public inquiries, people's tribunals or civil society campaigns provide some degree of accountability, as do ever-expanding multiform media.

From this minimal responsibility, which lies ultimately in access to stories and storytelling and to duties to investigate, a deeper personal obligation can develop. Calling on everybody to respond to suffering through hearing and relaying stories of people's experiences alone may be necessary but it is not sufficient; a commitment to act is also required, and this is inherently political. As our ability to see suffering that is increasingly distant from us (in time as well as location) is enhanced by technology, so our responsibility to do something is increased. Some philosophers advocating personal responsibility suggest a

15 This is one of the principles adopted by Medecins sans Frontieres to justify their role in bearing witness to suffering that they encounter in their operations. However, this does not exclude the possibility of self-witnessing in my definition of the term.

financial or political commitment.[16] Giving money and providing resources seems appropriate, but bearing witness is the first necessary step (which would include time to listen to and recount stories). Without that communication, personal and institutional responsibility to respond may lack sufficient direction.

Second, accountability should also incorporate calling to account (individually or in association with others) those public authorities and institutions *and* both corporate and individual persons to reason and explain how their responsibility for suffering (or their failure to respond where they can) has arisen. The legal process is incapable of fulfilling this particular demand effectively. With access to law severely restricted (by jurisdiction and procedure), other bodies are needed with power to bring or hear such proceedings. This would be more commensurate with the so called 'Paris Principles' related to the status of national human rights institutions promoted by the United Nations but with powers of adjudication and enforcement rather than simply recommendation.[17] Parliamentary processes may also serve a purpose here but mistrust in modern politics suggests caution in ascribing exclusive control.

Third, accountability should also be construed as the reckoning of responsibility. This again is familiar territory for modern legal orthodoxy. But that does not mean that its characteristics adequately fulfil this role when tribunals and courts are involved. Though criminal justice systems retain significant monopolies over formal adjudication, other means for determining responsibility have developed through truth commissions, public inquiries and people's tribunals.

By developing this threefold notion of accountability, the immanent core I propose has a significantly greater chance of being realised. As usual, though, the devil is in the detail when designing and implementing practical processes. But doing something for a reason lies at the base of my series of propositions. That doesn't mean we have to be ruled by pragmatism. This often shunts responsibility to representative institutions on the grounds that we cannot individually achieve what's needed. But the accountability I propose above, *requires* constant individual vigilance and participation, willingness to listen and to speak. It means that we should engage with all institutions to develop their ethos so as to make imperative their response to the immanent core of human rights, but we should simultaneously realise our individual responsibility to act too. That may be an inherently dangerous obligation. It may also challenge us to question the extent of our individual complicity in systems of injustice. But if the climate crisis today tells us anything, it is that relying on institutions to save us will never be sufficient. Taking individual responsibility where we have resources and capacity to do something is an absolute necessity. We shouldn't need an existential emergency to tell us this if the obligation to respond to human suffering lies at the centre of the commitment to human rights.

16 See, for instance, Peter Singer (2009), though there are many other examples of demands for political engagement, protest, etc.

17 See UNGA (1994) Resolution 48/134 4 March 1994 on National Institutions for the Promotion and Protection of Human Rights.

If international human rights are not to become consumed by irony (everyone knowing that they are no more than a romantic notion to be pronounced even though we know them to be flawed), starting with the imperative of a personal and collective response to suffering should provoke thought and action. That takes us far beyond sustainable (or any other form of) development as currently conceived and operated. Indeed, development itself might be a concept that encourages the prospect of suffering. If that is right, a coherent understanding of human rights may be a far better discourse to shape the interaction between peoples.

References

An-Na'im, A., 2010. *Human Rights in Cross-Cultural Perspectives: A Quest for Consensus*. University of Pennsylvania Press.

Arendt, H., 2017. *The Origins of Totalitarianism*. Penguin.

Balibar, E., 2001. Outline for a Topography of Cruelty: Citizenship and Civility in the Era of Global Violence. In *We the People of Europe? Reflections on Transnational Citizenship*. Princeton University Press.

Baxi, U., 2002. *The Future of Human Rights*. Oxford University Press.

Baxi, U., 2003. Voices of Suffering, Fragmented Universality, and the Future of Human Rights. In Robert McCorquodale (ed.), *Human Rights*. Routledge.

Beitz, C., 2009. *The Idea of Human Rights*. Oxford University Press.

Campbell, T., 2006. *Rights: A Critical Introduction*. Routledge.

Caney, S., 2005. *Justice Beyond Borders: A Global Political Theory*. Oxford University Press.

Carrodetti, C. 2017. *Relativism and Universalism of Human Rights and Regional Protection*. Online Bibliography. Oxford University Press.

Cohen, C., 2001. *States of Denial: Knowing about Atrocities and Suffering*. Polity.

Donnelly, J., 2002. *Universal Human Rights in Theory and Practice*. Cornell University Press.

Douzinas, C., 2000. *The End of Human Rights*. Hart Publishing.

Dussel, E., 2013. *Ethics of Liberation: In the Age of Globalization and Exclusion*. Duke University Press.

Erikson, K., 1996. On Pseudospeciation and Social Speciation. In Charles B.Strozier and Michael Flynn (eds.), *Genocide, War and Human Survival*. Rowman and Littlefield Publishers, pp. 51–57.

Farmer, P., 2004. *Pathologies of Power: Health, Human Rights and the New War on the Poor*. University of California Press.

Finnis, J., 1980. *Natural Law and Natural Rights*. Clarendon Press.

Friedman, L., 2008. Erik Erikson on Identity, Generativity, and Pseudospeciation: A Biographer's Perspective. *Psychoanalysis and History*, 3 (2), 179–192.

Griffin, J., 2008. *On Human Rights*. Oxford University Press.

Hohfeld, W., 1964. *Fundamental Legal Conceptions as Applied in Judicial Reasoning*. Yale University Press.

Ignatieff, M., 2001. *Human Rights as Politics and Idolatry*. Princeton University Press.

Kennedy, D., 2012. The International Human Rights Regime: Still Part of the Problem? In R. Dickinson, E. Katselli, C. Murray and O. Pedersen (eds.), *Examining Critical Perspectives on Human Rights*. Cambridge University Press, pp. 19–34.

Luban, D., 1980. Just War and Human Rights. *Philosophy and Public Affairs*, 9 (2), 160–181.
Lyotard, J., 1996. *The Other's Rights*. Begradski-Krug.
Miller, D., 2007. *National Responsibility and Global Justice*. Oxford University Press.
Mutua, M., 2008. *Human Rights: A Political and Cultural Critique*. University of Pennsylvania Press.
Nagel, T., 2005. The Problem of Global Justice. *Philosophy and Public Affairs*, 33 (2), 113–147.
Rawls, J., 1993. The Law of Peoples. *Critical Inquiry*, 20 (1), 65.
Redfield, P., 2008. Sacrifice, Triage, and Global Humanitarianism. In M. Barnett and Thomas G.Weiss (eds.), *Humanitarianism in Question: Politics, Power, Ethics*. Cornell University Press.
Rorty, R., 1993. Human Rights, Rationality, and Sentimentality. In Stephen Shute and Susan Hurley (eds.), *On Human Rights*. Basic Books.
Scanlon, T., 2017. *Why Does Inequality Matter?*Oxford University Press.
Sen, A., 2009. *The Idea of Justice*. Harvard University Press.
Shivji, I., 1989. *The Concept of Human Rights in Africa*. African Books Collective.
Singer, P., 2009. *The Life you Can Save*. Picador.
Sontag, S., 2003. *Regarding the Pain of Others*. Penguin.
UNGA, 1994. Resolution 48/134 4 March 1994 on National Institutions for the Promotion and Protection of Human Rights.
UNOHCHR, 2006. FAQs on a Human Rights Based Approach to Development Cooperation, available online at https://www.ohchr.org/Documents/Publications/FAQen.pdf (accessed 4 March 2020).
Walzer, M., 2015. *Just and Unjust Wars*. Basic Books.
Williams, A., 2007. Human Rights and Law: between sufferance and insufferability. *The Law Quarterly Review*, 123, 133–138.

Chapter 9

The human right to water and beyond

Some reflections on water justice and water reform in Zimbabwe

Bill Derman and Anne Hellum

Introduction

Water is a fascinating substance to explore competing visions of how this essential material should be regarded, understood, and governed. Should it be through the market with water primarily regarded as a commodity? Alternatively, is water so essential that it should be viewed as a common property of all humankind and all species (Linton, 2010; Bakker, 2003)? Is water a property of nature or an active participant whose 'materiality and geo-ecological properties shape social relations, even as those social relations act on and transform water's materiality' (Perrault, 2014: 235)? The Dublin Principles (1992) and their expression in Integrated Water Resources Management (IWRM), which are the current dominant paradigms of international and national water governance, assume that market principles, recognizing water's economic value, will ensure the most efficient way of managing water resources for the common good (International Conference on Water and the Environment, 1992).[1] The human right to water was seen as a historical watershed in slowing down the march toward the fictitious commodification[2] linked with the wave of privatization of water that went hand in hand with the implementation of IWRM (Bakker, 2010). Its recognition of water as key for the realization of other human rights, including life, health and food and its importance for gender equity and the environment, brought promises of greater social and environmental justice (Derman, et al., 2007). Furthermore, Sustainable Development Goal 6 on water reinforces the international attention to water in its various dimensions and cites IWRM as important for ensuring the availability and sustainable management of water and sanitation for all (United Nations Development Program, 2015).

1 Dublin Statement on Water and Sustainable Development (adopted 31 January 1992), International Conference on Water and the Environment (ICWE), Dublin, Ireland 26–31 January 1992. For IWRM see Integrated Water Resources Management (IWRM), International Decade for Action 'Water for Life' 2005–2015 (un.org) (accessed 25 March 2021).

2 The term is Karl Polanyi's as discussed by Nancy Fraser (2013: 119).

DOI: 10.4324/9780203745298-12

This chapter addresses the complex and changing relationships among theories of justice and the existing international and national law and policy frameworks guiding water governance. Our water justice perspective combines feminist social justice and environmental justice approaches to consider different but overlapping water policy frameworks, namely Integrated Water Resource Management (IWRM) and the human right to water.

We find Nancy Fraser's (2003; 2008; 2013) feminist social justice theory, that combines three interdependent dimensions of justice – redistribution, recognition and representation – a fruitful starting point to explore the options and limits of these different but overlapping international water governance frameworks, especially considering their potential to transform unequal social, economic and political relations. This multi-scalar approach is applied at different levels of governance (from the local to the international) and to spatial scales (from a well to a river basin) (Schlosberg, 2007; Walker, 2012).

A justice framework leads us to ask who benefits and who is burdened by current laws, policies and practices. From a feminist social justice perspective, analysis of the redistributive implications of IWRM and the human right to water requires a focus on women's equal right to water and participation in water governance for all categories of users, including class, ethnicity, race, disability and political affiliation at family, household, neighbourhood, village, town and catchment levels.

Fraser's theory limits itself to human relationships and does not extend to the non-human world. Nevertheless, water is not just subject to the human requirements of justice but to its own materiality. Focusing on water's importance for sustainability leads to considerations of environmental justice. For example, privileging water for mining industries and large-scale agriculture can threaten the livelihoods of downstream animals and human communities which rely on those waters for survival. To ensure livelihood security for both current and future generations, proponents of environmental justice, such as Schlosberg (2004: 521–528) have shown how considerations of distribution, recognition and representation may be broadened to include socio-ecological dimensions that address the life-securing and life-threatening dimensions of water. It is possible to think about water justice in a way that incorporates what is similar from a human and nonhuman perspective including common needs, sentience, interests, agency, physical integrity and the unfolding of potential (Schlosberg, 2007: 133). Schlosberg does not require equality but a sustainable existence based on 'a simultaneous recognition of, and bond with, the rest of the natural world' (Schlosberg, 2004: 142). We therefore give some consideration to integrating social justice with environmental justice in the different sections of this chapter.

We have selected Zimbabwe as a case to explore the complex intersections between different frameworks of water governance and theories of justice in light of twenty years of research experience tracing water policies and laws at international, national and local levels and in rural and urban contexts (Hellum, Kameri-Mbote and van Koppen, 2015; Mehta et al., 2016). In the early 1990s

Zimbabwe, like many other African nations, engaged in water reform to provide good governance on the basis of national priorities and international frameworks in a process initially led by the World Bank. The Water Act (1998) and the Zimbabwe National Water Authority Act (ZINWA) (1998) were passed which were consonant with what became known as Integrated Water Resources Management (IWRM).[3] Shortly thereafter, Zimbabwe carried out a radical land reform and resettlement programme under its ruling party the Zimbabwe African National Union-Patriotic Front (ZANU-PF). Following the contested and violent elections of 2008, the Government of National Unity (GNU) was formed which lasted for four years, 2009–2013. The economic and political crisis, which accompanied the radical land reform, led to the breakdown of public provision of electricity, water services and public health services followed by extensive cholera outbreaks. In 2013 a new Constitution was adopted, under the GNU, which included rights to gender equality, health, environment and clean water. The GNU also introduced a new water policy, which included both IWRM and the human right to water (Government of Zimbabwe, 2013).

This chapter examines the impact of Zimbabwe's water reforms on social and environmental justice, especially considering race, class and gender-based patterns of water distribution and use, and users' participation in water governance. The following section explores international law and policy frameworks for water governance in the context of theories of social and environmental justice. The three following sections respectively consider Fraser's (2003, 2008, 2013) principles of redistribution, recognition and representation in the context of Zimbabwe, especially in relation to the adoption of IWRM and the human right to water. This is followed by the conclusion.

Water justice within and beyond international law and policy frameworks

The quest for social and environmental justice has gradually, if only partially, made its mark on international and national water laws and policies. The Brundtland Commission (1987) coined the term sustainable development as a response to environmental degradation on the one hand, and global poverty on the other. A follow-up meeting of experts in Dublin in 1992 resulted in the 1992 Dublin Statement on Water and Sustainable Development (the Dublin Principles) which laid the discursive foundations for the Integrated Water Resource Management (IWRM) approach that has been the dominant paradigm for water governance since the late 1990s. The Dublin Principles sought to balance the prevailing neoliberal economic discourse, voiced by the World Bank, with the growing movement for participatory natural resource management and the importance of water for the environment. Thus, Principle No. 4 states that 'water has an economic value in all its competing uses, and should be

3 For an account of how IWRM spread to Africa, see Allouche (2016).

recognized as an economic good' but, to strike a balance, it continues, 'within this principle, it is vital to recognize the basic right of all human beings to have access to clean water and sanitation at an affordable price'. The Dublin Principles also took cognisance of the close relationship between water, gender and development. The gender dimension of sustainable water management was anchored in Principle No. 3: 'Women play a central part in the provision, management, and safeguarding of water'. Demand management, along with decentralization, and privatization, became the catchwords and modalities for water reform across the globe in the late 1990s.

In light of water's centrality for all life, the Committee on Economic, Social and Cultural Rights (CESCR) in 2002 addressed the human right to water under the right to an adequate standard of living of the International Covenant on Economic, Social and Cultural Rights (ICESCR) (ICESCR Committee, 2002, General Comment No 15 (GC 15) 2002). The Committee concluded that a human right to water is embedded in Article 11 on the right to an adequate living standard. It interpreted Article 11 in the context of existing treaties, such as the Convention on the Elimination of All Forms of Discrimination against Women (CEDAW) and the Child Rights Convention (CRC), and the indivisibility of the rights to water, food, health and life. GC 15 is generally sensitive to the needs of poor and vulnerable groups and women in the articulation of the normative content of the right. Whereas the right to water applies to everyone, it states that: 'States Parties should give special attention to those individuals and groups who have traditionally faced difficulties in exercising this right, including women, children, minority groups, indigenous peoples, refugees, asylum seekers, internally displaced people, migrant workers, prisoners and detainees' (ICESCR, 2002, GC 15: para 6).

The human right to water was seen as a legal tool with the potential to ensure redistribution of water, by recognizing the water needs of vulnerable groups and participation in decision-making processes concerning water resources and entitlements (Hellum, Ikdahl and Kameri-Mbote, 2015). What uses are included in the definition of the human right to water is contested. In light of water's centrality to other human rights such as the right to life, the right to health and the right to food, GC 15 (para 6) concluded that the human right to water included water for personal and domestic use but also recognized that priority should be given to water resources required to prevent malnutrition, starvation and disease. However, UN General Assembly Resolution 64/292 on the Human Right to Water and Sanitation remains silent on water for broader livelihood needs. In contrast, General Recommendation No. 34 on the rights of rural women of the CEDAW Committee calls upon States to ensure that 'rural women have access to essential services and public goods, including: (a) Sufficient, safe, acceptable and physically accessible and affordable water for personal and domestic uses, as well as for agriculture/irrigation' (CEDAW Committee, 2016, General Recommendation 34).

Despite the increasing international and national recognition, large groups of people have yet to enjoy the human right to water. Southern and eastern African countries fell short of meeting the United Nations water-related Millennium Development Goals (MDGs) with just 61% water coverage.[4] African women still carry the burden of drinking water collection. The state's failures to ensure water provision service and to reduce intra-household division of labour interact to reinforce deep gender inequalities in relation to health, education, participation and work (UN Development Programme, 2006: 47, 48). Africa continues to fare worst in meeting water and sanitation goals (World Health Organization, 2017).

The poor socio-economic record calls for a shift to thinking of 'justice *beyond* and *outside* the law from justice *before* and *according* to the law' (Baxi, 2016: 10). For Baxi global laws and policies are based on unexamined assumptions that, unless addressed, will perpetuate existing injustices.

Fraser contends that the Westphalian nation-state paradigm no longer suffices to deal with justice issues because of the profound inequalities among nation-states and the power of transnational actors. She finds that this division of political space may block the poor and the un- or mis-recognized from challenging the forces that oppress them (Fraser, 2008; 2013). Fraser (2003: 218), in her earlier work, observes that our new globalized society contains 'two analytically distinct orders of subordination: class stratification, rooted primarily in economic system mechanisms and status hierarchy, based largely in institutionalized patterns of cultural value'. Status in this formulation leads to misrecognition while class leads to maldistribution. In both cases, it leads to lack of representation or the absence of 'parity participation' (Fraser, 2013: 164). While these are all interconnected, they cannot be reduced to each other. Within these generalizations, the sense or feelings of social injustice are shaped by pre-existing normative principles and public discourses (Honneth, 2003: 250).

An overall challenge is to link social and environmental justice. The link between the resource (environmental communities of water) and human communities can be found in the idea of sustainability. Accordingly, the management of water has to consider needs of future generations. Human produced water shortage, pollution and climate change is not just an injustice against human communities but also non-human nature (Schlosberg and Collins, 2014). Like Schlosberg (2007; Schlosberg and Collins, 2014) and Walker (2012), we seek to integrate broader socio-ecological concerns in the three essential components of justice: redistribution, recognition and representation, enunciated by Fraser.

Inclusion of intergenerational justice is often lacking in water governance due to lack of emphasis upon the elements of justice in water policies and laws. Intergenerational justice is an implicit and explicit central concern in the emerging literature on environmental rights (Walker, 2012; Schlosberg, 2007; Sikor et al., 2014; Caney, 2006; Hiskes, 2009). Succeeding generations should

4 http://www.un.org/waterforlifedecade/africa.shtml (accessed 15 December 2019).

be able to have access to clean water, to fish in and irrigate from non-polluted waters, and to have access to rivers not damaged by bad mining practices. To the concern of those focusing on food and energy, we should add water (Agyeman et al., 2016). The plurality of environmental injustice experiences calls for broad and pluralistic conceptions of justice (Schlosberg, 2014: 40). Therefore, this requires consideration of which prevailing systems of injustice are being challenged with reference to maldistribution, misrecognition and misrepresentation. The following sections indicate how this perspective facilitates analysis of water justice beyond the parameters of international law and policy frameworks in Zimbabwe.

Redistributive challenges of water laws and policies in Zimbabwe

In contrast to social theories that merely emphasise identity, Fraser points to an approach to justice that comprehends the present crisis as a 'social process that is mediated by history, culture, geography, politics, ecology and law' (Fraser, 2013: 227). The question of water justice calls for analysis of the relationship between international and national laws, policies and practices that affect the distribution of water for past, present and future generations and for other species.

Historical injustices

A major challenge for former colonies like Zimbabwe is the unmaking of the racialised, class-based and gendered patterns of distribution of land and water carried over from the colonial era. When Zimbabwe achieved independence in 1980, approximately 50% of the land and its related water sources were owned by the white minority. Most of the black population lived in what today is termed communal areas with no formal land or water rights. In 1998, 85% of agricultural water (which was two-thirds of all surface water) was used by 4,500 mostly white large-scale commercial farmers (Manzungu, 2001: 101).

Rhodesian water laws emphasized the use of water for commercial agriculture, industries and provision of water services to the settler population. The laws largely ignored the black majority population's need for water for domestic and productive purposes. The unjust land distribution in which the black population was forced out of the best land meant that they lost access to wetlands and rivers. Colonial land and water laws barred most black Zimbabweans from owning land or applying for water rights. Yet, Rhodesian legislation required the colonial authorities to respect the primary-use rights of Tribal Trust Land inhabitants. In these areas the inhabitants utilized existing water resources without asking permission from colonial authorities. Nevertheless, colonial water law did not see these local uses as having customary law rights (Derman and Hellum, 2002).

With independence, the black majority government of Zimbabwe had to address the structures of racial and colonial rule while maintaining its economy. We focus on how this applied to the water sector.

IWRM and distributive justice

Zimbabwe, like other nations in southern and eastern Africa, embarked on water reforms in the 1990s aimed at democratization, integration, decentralization and sustainable water management. Though informed by the global focus on the perceived strengths of IWRM, these reforms were also partially informed by national needs (Mtisi and Nicol, 2003; Derman and Manzungu, 2016).

Redistribution was set out as a major goal in the national policy paper, *Water Resources Management* (Government of Zimbabwe, 2000) and the earlier Rukuni (1994) *Land Tenure Commission Report.* The proposals included dam building to provide water to communal lands and ending of the priority date system for access to water. Catchment Councils were established as the new decentralized management entities, and there were proposals to set aside water for 'new users' (meaning black farmers). However, the need for revenues to support the new water management system resulted in issues of redistribution taking second place (Derman and Manzungu, 2016).

Water can be difficult and expensive to re-allocate. Nonetheless, a central goal of the Water Act of 1998 and the 2000 Water Policy was to improve equity in access to water for all Zimbabweans. The 1998 Act created a permit system, which replaced water rights in perpetuity. According to the Act, 'all water is vested in the President' (s 3) which means it is state owned. However, the fundamental division between commercial and primary water was retained. Commercial use of water requires a permit and payment. The use of primary water – water for household needs, cattle and growing food in and around the house – does not require a paid permit. Like the Rhodesian Water Acts, the Water Act of 1998 does not consider primary water as an enforceable water right. Local community-based water governance regimes, which have co-existed with the Rhodesian Water Acts, were not integrated and protected by the laws and policies that since 2000 have framed the national water governance systems (Hellum et al., 2015; van Koppen and Schreiner, 2019).

Permits to use water for commercial agriculture are often granted by national water governance institutions without sufficient consideration of existing small-scale users who lack the resources to fulfil the formal requirements for obtaining a water permit (van Koppen and Schreiner, 2019). The aim of the permit model, the backbone of IWRM, is to ensure that water is allocated for the highest economic returns to cities, industry and commercial agriculture (van Koppen and Schreiner, 2014). Water for livelihood is given minimal attention within the permit model that was adopted in Zimbabwe. It constitutes a distributive model that upholds the colonial dispossession of subsistence and small-scale farmers.

The human right to water and distributive justice

The human right to water obliges states parties to ensure that water is made available and affordable for all. 'Water, and water facilities and services must be affordable for all. The direct and indirect costs and changes associated with securing water must be affordable and must not compromise or threaten the realization of other covenant rights' (ICESCR Committee, 2002, GC 15: para 26). By putting an obligation on states to prioritize water services for socially and economically disadvantaged groups, the human right to water constitutes a potential tool for redistribution. How did Zimbabwe respond? In the aftermath of the economic and political crisis, which led to the breakdown of water service provision, the Zimbabwe Government of National Unity (GNU) voted in 2010 for the UNGA Resolution 64/292 on the right to water and sanitation. Section 77 of the new Constitution, adopted by Parliament in 2013, includes the right to water. In turn, the Water Policy of 2013 recognizes the right to clean drinking and primary water, and the right to equal gender participation at all levels of governance. The state thus has a duty to ensure that clean water is made accessible to all citizens for an affordable price. In principle, this represents a shift to a rights-based approach that has a transformative potential. Citizens, as individual rights holders, can in principle, hold local and national authorities accountable for breach of the duty to provide water although in practice this has been difficult.[5]

However, the human right to water as a tool of distributive justice, must be understood in the context of political and social relations that enable or constrain action (Young, 1990: 25). As Perrault (2014: 239) points out, it makes little sense to deal with justice apart from the social relations of production and reproduction that shape individual and collective lives, and thus necessitates consideration of the political economy of water law.

In spite of the language of the 2013 Constitution and Water Policy, the investment in infrastructure to distribute water to all rural and urban citizens has remained subject to the economic constraints and political priorities of the national government (Human Rights Watch 2013). These priorities were the completion of the Tokwe-Mukosi Dam whose waters are mainly to be used for large-scale production of sugar for biofuels, and the possible rebuilding of water supply infrastructure for Harare, the capital city. The government, relying on the World Bank, African Development Bank, the Australian and Chinese governments for the rehabilitation of its urban water supply and sewage treatment, agreed that public water service provision should be based on cost-recovery (Hellum, Derman, Sithole and Rutsate, 2015). To accomplish this, city authorities and the ruling party have installed some pre-paid water meters while disconnecting homes from the water system if residents do not pay their water bills. The attempts to

5 The Harare Residents Trust has been in the forefront of holding water and municipal authorities accountable.

privatize water service provision and install water meters have been met with fierce resistance by civil society and women's organizations who invoke the human right to water (Hellum, Sithole, Derman et al., 2015).

Non-human nature

In Zimbabwe there was initially an effort to reserve waters for the environment and to reduce river pollution through a 'polluters pay' policy. Currently, there is little evidence that Zimbabwe's water managers are taking into account longer-term environmental concerns and their consequences for future generations. The management of water quality was transferred from ZINWA to the new Environmental Management Agency (EMA) in 2002. However, EMA are understaffed, under-funded and susceptible to political and economic interests (Government of Zimbabwe, 2016). Mining (both large and small-scale) has taken precedence over other economic activities at a very high cost to water quality and the environment more generally. For example, there are multiple conflicts around alluvial gold mining in rivers and the continued use of cyanide and mercury, with an extreme example being the pollution of the Odzi River by diamond miners (Mambondiyani, 2012; Saunders and Nyamunda, 2016).

Concluding remarks

The emphasis on redistribution which accompanied the early post-independence period water reforms has been lost (Manzungu, 2001; Derman and Manzungu 2017). The human right to water coexists with a neo-liberal policy based on cost recovery. Those who have suffered most from the breakdown of public water and sanitation services are the poor; especially, poor mothers, children, the disabled, the sick, and the chronically ill. Rural peasant women have suffered disproportionately from the decline in sources of clean drinking water and lack of investment in water for small-scale agriculture (Hellum, Derman, Sithole et al., 2015). In Harare, Zimbabwe's largest city, the lack of water service provision has led to an unprecedented exploitation of groundwater, not only by the poor, but also by private companies who extract and sell water from private boreholes thus further lowering the water table, especially during the dry season. Because of the collapse of the sewage system, many of Harare's boreholes are polluted, leading to threats of typhoid and cholera epidemics.

Recognition

For Nancy Fraser, redistribution and recognition are two mutually constitutive dimensions of justice, whereas recognition is primary for Axel Honneth (Fraser, 2003; Honneth, 2003). Fraser, who regards appropriate recognition as essential for distribution, names three forms of status misrecognition; these are cultural domination, non-recognition, and disrespect (Fraser, 2008: 7). Water justice, as a more just socio-ecological distribution of water resources, requires recognition and rebalancing of the multiple norms and institutions and the national and international power/knowledge that govern the management and distribution of water within any society (Zwarteveen and Boelens, 2014).

The next sub-section addresses community-based water management norms and institutions generated by communal area residents in Zimbabwe, focusing particularly on issues raised by recognition and non-recognition on water distribution.

Community-based water norms and practices

The residents of rural and peri-urban areas, from the colonial period up to now, have been left to manage water with little, if any, state assistance. Water governance is thus strongly influenced by the norms and practices developed by the local communities themselves. The Shona proverb 'water is life' insists that to deny water is to deny life, forming part of a broad right to water for livelihood, for humans, animals and nature (Derman and Hellum, 2002). 'Water is life' underlies community-based water management and water sharing practices in many southern and eastern African countries (van Koppen, Giordano and Butterworth, 2007). These norms and practices form the basis for rural and peri-urban women's multiple water uses, not only for domestic uses and sanitation, but also for growing, preparing and selling food and other products that are vital for family welfare and food security. Making no strict division between water for domestic and productive uses, these local norms respond to women's needs as providers of care and food.

These norms and practices have not been recognized and thus are rendered invisible under colonial or post-colonial water laws, and undermined by the dominant preference for large-scale land and water deals between international and national companies and national governments.[6] In rural areas, permits to use water for agriculture are often granted by national water governance institutions without consideration of small-scale users who lack the resources to fulfil the formal requirements for obtaining a water permit. These small-scale users, most of them women producing food and other items for livelihood, are easy victims for 'water grabbing' in a situation where governments tend to side with large-scale users who are powerfully connected and will pay for water (Mutopo and Chiweshe, 2014). Yet, the recognition by the state of communal norms and practices could provide an alternative framing for water rights which would protect small-scale users.

6 For example, the Marange diamond mines, the Tokwe-Mukosi Dam and Green Fuel ethanol production.

Domestic and productive water

The above described cultural and legal forms of misrecognition also calls for analysis of the framing of the human right to water, especially whether it recognizes the economic and social practices of poor water users and managers, most of them rural women. A key concern is where the line between water for domestic and for productive uses should be drawn. International water rights discourses are, as mentioned earlier, inconsistent and ambiguous. The scope and extent of the human right to water, as defined in GC 15, para C, is based on its link to the right to life, the right to food, and the right to health. In contrast, the UN General Assembly's Resolution 64/ 292 is limited to water for personal and domestic use and reinforces the domestic/productive dichotomy, thus preventing the international right to water discourse from expanding beyond the narrow confines of gender and class biased economic and legal paradigms.

The CEDAW Committee's understanding of water rights in GC34 (Hellum, 2017) has the potential to redress the misrecognition and marginalization of women's work. Nevertheless, water laws and policies in Tanzania, Mozambique and Zimbabwe do not utilize human rights instruments such as CEDAW to broaden their interpretations of water use, but instead restrict themselves to either the IWRM or a narrow interpretation of the UNGA resolution (Derman and Prabhakaran, 2016).

Non-human nature

The issue of recognition of non-human nature is complicated and discussion has focused mainly on pollution, degradation of water quality and loss or contamination of fish. A long-standing issue in former colonies such as Zimbabwe is whether, and to what extent, the criminalization of riverine and wetland cultivation can be reconciled with the State's duty to respect and protect people's access to water sources in rural areas. Assuming that these practices disturbed river flow and caused erosion, the colonial governments enacted legislation that prohibited wetland and stream bank farming within 100 feet of the stream or river. Newer hydrological and agricultural research shows that sustainable wetland farming under proper management by communal farmers is possible and economically viable; yet these laws are still in force in Zimbabwe. Since independence they have, however, been only randomly enforced (Derman, 1997). In many instances, these customary practices have been tolerated, because they provide a lifeline for poor communities (Sithole, 2000) especially during the current social and economic crisis (Rutsate et al., 2015). Existing national regulation of riverbank and wetland cultivation in former colonies in Africa epitomizes the tense relationship between the duty to protect poor women's and families' right to livelihood and the duty to protect the environment. How uses of riverbanks and wetlands under proper management by poor farmers can be made ecologically viable is an issue that calls for innovative, interdisciplinary and holistic approaches.

Concluding remarks

These examples illustrate a key concern regarding gender justice – namely the close relationship between the skewed distribution of economic resources between women and men and the lack of recognition of women's work, justified on the spurious basis of economic/legal distinction between productive and domestic work. Fraser (2000), Young (1990) and Dahl (1986) argue that the concepts of equality and justice based on formal, apparently neutral, criteria are often poorly equipped to accommodate the experiences and claims of women within marginalized social communities. Thus, the standard for measuring international and national water laws and policies should be whether women's uses of water are placed on an equal footing with those of men. We have also seen how recognition of poor women's uses can come into conflict with the concerns of the environment and future generations – pointing to a gap between social justice and environmental justice theory.

Representation (participation)

Fraser (2008) argues that democratic representation at the international, national and local level is necessary to address the social and economic inequalities constituted and reproduced at the interface of economic maldistribution and socio-cultural misrecognition. For her, representation must be based on the equality or 'all-affected' principle which holds that all those affected by a given social structure have moral standing as subjects of justice in relation to it (Fraser, 2008: 38). Walker suggests in relation to environmental justice that at the core of recognition and misrecognition are cultural and institutional processes of disrespect (Walker, 2012: 50). The following sub-section addresses democratization in the different but overlapping paradigms of water governance in Zimbabwe, IWRM and the human right to water.

IWRM water governance as a practice of misrecognition

The IWRM was based on decentralization, stakeholder-participation and the principle of subsidiarity. Thus, the Water Act of 1998 divided Zimbabwe into seven catchment areas[7] each with a Catchment Council and, in turn, divided into Sub-catchment Councils. These new water governance institutions were to be made up of elected representatives from the different economic sectors

7 Save, Mazowe, Sanyati, Mzingwane, Manyame, Runde and Gwayi.

including communal farmers.[8] However, there was no inclusion of people with disabilities, women, farm workers, and minority communities. While there has been a continuous understanding that women are farmers, farm workers, traders, managers and in general essential to agriculture of all kinds, they were mis- and un-recognized. As farmers and as business people in a family enterprise they have not been regarded as co-owners, co-managers or business partners, but rather as wives (Katsande, 20164). In the formation of Catchment and Sub-catchment Councils, no efforts were made to ensure that women were part of the process. While women were formally eligible to be elected, the Water Resources Management Strategy (2000), the Water Act (1998) and the statutory instruments were all silent about the ways and means of enhancing women's participation and representation. An equal rights strategy involving quotas, in line with CEDAW, was at the point of implementation rejected by male water experts and ZANU-PF politicians, arguing that a rights-based approach was a western imposition and contrary to African consultative democracy (Hellum, 2001). In sum, the definition of stakeholders to be represented in the new water management system largely reproduced existing forms of cultural domination.

There was little effort to assess the access to water and governance participation needs of communal farmers. Communal area farmers in general and women farmers in particular were rendered invisible and their concerns, even if raised, were dismissed (Derman and Manzungu, 2016; Mtisi and Nicol, 2003; Mabiza, 2013). The concerns of most non-commercial water-users without water permits, who lived in the communal areas, and physically far from the meetings of the Catchment and Sub-catchment Councils were not taken seriously. Without funding for attending meetings, they were not able to participate in the development of the new legislation or in the operations of the councils. It remains to be seen whether the extensive land reform, which has meant the resettlement of most large-scale farms by small-scale farmers, will lead to any changes.[9]

The human right to water as a step to undo practices of misrecognition?

International human rights and development discourse assumes that women's participation in decision making may be one of the most successful mechanisms for meeting their needs and demands for water and sanitation at the international, national and local level. GC 15 para 16 on the human right to water emphasizes the need to ensure that 'Women are not excluded from decision-making processes concerning water resources and entitlements. The disproportionate burden women bear in the collection of water should be alleviated' (ICESCR Committee, 2002).

8 These included small-scale miners, large-scale miners, communal area farmers, resettlement farmers, large-scale farmers, cities, the catchment manager (an employee of ZINWA) and chiefs as ex-officio members.

9 There has been active resistance by resettled farmers to paying for water (Mtisi, 2011).

Article 14.2(a) of CEDAW obliges States Parties to ensure that rural women have the right to participate in the elaboration and implementation of development planning at all levels.

Defining gender balance as a national value, the 2013 Constitution calls for proactive measures to promote the full participation of women in all spheres of Zimbabwean society based on equality with men. The new Water Policy recognizes the disproportionate burden on women of the water crisis and calls for increased representation of women in water governance. It requires that 'At least 30% of the Catchment and Sub-Catchment Councils positions will be reserved for women and the youth. At least 3 board members in the ZINWA board will be women, youth or worker representatives.'[10] Currently five of the nine ZINWA Board Members are women.

In principle, these changes in law and policy are reflected in greater representation of women in water governance. Whether this is sufficient to address existing maldistribution, misrecognition and misrepresentation in the water sector is very doubtful. No concrete measures have been taken to promote rural and urban women's participation by alleviating their disproportionate burden of fetching water.

Non-human nature

In the contest between what is thought of as development and the environment, short-term 'development' has come first in recent years. Several civil society organizations have sought to speak for a range of environmental interests including wildlife, trees and water.[11] In addition, Article 73 of the new Zimbabwean Constitution provides for rights to a non-harmful environment and to maintain the environment for the current and future generations. In terms of the protection of water on the sub-Catchment councils, there were to be four representatives from the mining sector: two from the small-scale and two from the large-scale. The objective was for the management units to know about mining activities and how it was affecting water use and quality. Polluters were supposed to self-identify and notify the Catchment Manager what materials and chemicals they were putting into the water. They would be colour-coded for relative dangerousness. The companies or individuals would pay a fine and stop placing dangerous substances (coded red) into the river system. However only two years into the operationalization of the new institutions, water quality was placed in the newly created Environmental Management Agency and out of ZINWA and the Ministry of Water. Efforts to have the

10 There is no apparent rationale as to why women and youth are grouped together, or for the 30% quota.

11 Zimbabwe Environmental Law Association (ZELA), Harare Residents Trust for protection of wetlands, Zimbabwe Environmental Research Organisation (ZERO) among others.

decentralized institutions have the capacity to monitor water quality were not implemented.

The major state institution that should be securing these rights is EMA, now part of the Ministry of Environment, Climate Change, Tourism and Hospitality Industry, designed to be the voice for a broadly conceived environment (non-human nature).[12] The Zimbabwe Environmental Lawyers Association (ZELA) has been attempting to get EMA to do its job. While there is significant potential for greater recognition of environmental issues, this is unlikely to happen in the context of a predatory state and economic crises (Bavister-Gould, 2011). Civil society organizations are severely hampered by a violent and repressive State where ZANU-PF loyalists control national and local water and justice sector institutions.

Concluding remarks

In the contested political and economic terrain of Zimbabwe, the realization of the right to clean water and environmental protection for the benefit of present and future generations will not take place without the participation and empowerment of well-organized and represented urban and rural communities with appropriate balance of gender, class, disability, age and other significant social characteristics. Despite the new Constitution, the Public Order and Security Act (POSA) and the Access to Information and Protection of Privacy Act (AIPPA) remain in force, stifling the freedom of expression necessary to debate water and environment issues. There have been frequent arrests, kidnappings and beatings of peaceful members of civil society activist organizations.[13] While civil society and the women's organizations have, to a certain degree, appropriated space to defend the right to water and environment in urban settings, there appears to be no rural counterparts to protect current rural water users.

Conclusion

We have shown how the relationship between IWRM, the human right to water and Zimbabwe's water laws, policies and practices may be analysed from a water justice framework infusing Fraser's social justice theory with environmental justice to include both human and non-human users and uses within

12 The Department of Water is now in the Ministry of Lands, Agriculture, Water, Climate and Rural Settlements.

13 There is a substantial literature on the human rights violations carried out by the Zimbabwe government and its ruling party. Almost every human rights organization (for example, Amnesty International, Human Rights Watch, among others) has issued reports on Zimbabwe. The single best Zimbabwe source for documentation is the Zimbabwe Human Rights Forum, available online at: www.hrforumzim.com (accessed 16 February 2020).

the principles of distribution, recognition and representation. This integrated perspective calls the narrow definition of the human right to water and the assumption that the IWRM permit system is the most effective way of managing water for the common good into question. It leaves unresolved theoretical and practical challenges for consideration of justice in terms of redistribution, recognition and representation for both human and non-human uses and users.

The Zimbabwe case shows how changes in water laws and policies informed by IWRM and later the human right to water had a marginal impact on the unjust distribution of water between large- and small-scale users. In addition, women's disproportionate burden of water collection, storage, and distribution has not been systematically addressed. Understanding maldistribution in Fraser's terms is useful because it encompasses both the interpretation and implementation of formal laws and policies and how injustices derive from the relations of power that are exercised through international, national and local water governance. There remains an unresolved challenge about the obligations of this generation towards the next and future generations. The current predatory state and the extreme poverty that it has produced threaten nature itself and the environment for current and future generations.

The Zimbabwean study also demonstrates the close relationship between maldistribution and misrecognition. Recognition has favoured large water users who can pay, rather than the vast majority of Zimbabweans who struggle for access. In particular, the water governance system has rendered invisible small-scale water users, most of them women. This is linked to the mismatch between the narrow conception of the human right to water in the UNGA resolution and community-based water norms that include water for livelihood for humans, animals and nature. This reinforces Fraser's (2000) argument that concepts of equality and justice based on formal criteria that appear neutral are often poorly equipped to accommodate the experiences and claims of women within marginalized social communities. We suggest that assessing laws and policies with strong connections to water should rest on how they respond to the existing social and political hierarchy between different human and non-human uses and users. Towards this end, it is important to bear in mind that universal justice is not achieved through uniform governance systems but requires recognition of difference. The continued criminalization of streambank cultivation epitomizes the tense relationship between, on the one hand, the duty to protect poor women's and families' right to livelihood and, on the other, the duty to protect the environment. There is urgent need for an integrated approach to distribution and recognition of the concerns of the poor and the environment.

Schlosberg, as noted earlier, contends that given the plurality of environmental injustice experiences there should be broad and pluralistic conceptions of justice (Schlosberg, 2014: 40). This pluralism is evident in our description of how the redistribution, recognition and representation of different water users and uses were negatively affected by the adoption of the IWRM and later the human right to water into a single water governance system in Zimbabwe. We have also seen how justice concerns vary spatially and by the cause of harms. Examples include community efforts to stop water pollution by diamond mining companies in eastern Zimbabwe, and opposition by women to prepaid meters in urban areas (Mambondiyani, 2012; Maguwu, 2012; Hellum et al., 2015). How to conceptualize and achieve justice pluralism can only be achieved by exploring how participants in these struggles view and define their campaigns.

The Zimbabwe case shows that despite the rhetoric employed by the state around the reallocation or redistribution of power and resources, the colonial patterns of maldistribution, misrecognition and misrepresentation largely remain in place. Because of the ongoing economic difficulties, there is no expectation for change in Zimbabwe until there is a new government with different priorities. Until there is more secure employment, water justice for humans and non-humans will continue to be a distant goal. Despite the state rhetoric on sustainability, the pressures upon the current generations are too great to give adequate attention to the protection of the environment for future generations. Taking a broader view of justice illuminates the limitations of the current framing of the human right to clean drinking water and IWRM. However, the path to greater justice remains unclear until there is greater respect for human rights.

References

Agyeman, J., Schlosberg, D., Craven, L. and Matthews, C., 2016. Trends and directions in environmental justice: From inequity to everyday life, community, and just sustainabilities. *Annual Review of Environment and Resources*, 41, 321–340.

Allouche, J., 2016. The birth and spread of IWRM: A case study of global policy diffusion and translation. *Water Alternatives*, 9(3), 412–433.

Bakker, K. J., 2003. *An uncooperative commodity: privatizing water in England and Wales.* Oxford University Press.

Bakker, K. J., 2010. *Privatizing water: governance failure and the world's urban water crisis.* Cornell University Press.

Bavister-Gould, A., 2011. Predatory leaderships, predatory rule and predatory states, Concept Paper 021. Development Leadership Program. Available online at:https://www.dlprog.org/publications/research-papers/predatory-leaderships-predatory-rule-and-predatory-states: (accessed January 8, 2020).

Baxi, U., 2016. Towards a climate change justice theory? *Journal of Human Rights and the Environment*, 7, 7–31. Available online at DOI: https://doi.org/10.4337/jhre.2016.01.01 (accessed on January 8, 2020).

Caney, S., 2006. *Justice beyond borders: a global political theory.* Oxford University Press.

CEDAW Committee, 2016. General Recommendation 34 on the rights of rural women.

Dahl, T. S., 1986. *Feminist jurisprudence.* Norwegian University Press.

Derman, B., 1997. How green was my valley? Land use and economic development in the Zambezi Valley. In B. Isaacman (ed.), *Research in economic anthropology*. Greenwood, p. 331.
Derman, B. and Hellum, A., 2002. Neither tragedy nor enclosure: Are there inherent human rights in water management in Zimbabwe's communal lands? *European Journal of Development Studies*, 14(2), 31–50.
Derman, B., Hellum, A., Manzungu, E. et al., 2007. Intersections of law, human rights and water management in Zimbabwe: Implications for rural livelihoods. In B. van Koppen et al. (eds), *Community-based water law and water resource management reform in developing countries*. CABI, p. 248.
Derman, B. and Manzungu, E., 2016. The complex politics of water and power in Zimbabwe: IWRM in the Catchment Councils of Manyame, Mazowe and Sanyati (1993–2001). *Water Alternatives*, 9(3), 513–530.
Derman, B., and Manzungu, E., 2017. Reflections on the right to water from a political ecology perspective. In M. Langford and A. Russell (eds.), *The human right to water: Theory, practice and prospects*, Cambridge University Press, p. 624.
Derman, B. and Prabhakaran, P., 2016. Reflections on the formulation and implementation of IWRM in Southern Africa from a gender perspective. *Water Alternatives*, 9(3), 644–661.
Fraser, N, 1997. *Justice interruptus: critical reflections on the 'postsocialist' condition*. Routledge.
Fraser, N., 2000. Rethinking recognition. *New Left Review*, 3. Available online at: https://newleftreview.org/issues/II3/articles/nancy-fraser-rethinking-recognition (accessed January 8, 2020).
Fraser, N., 2003. Social justice in the age of identity politics: Redistribution, recognition, and participation. In N. Fraser and A. Honneth (eds.), *Redistribution or recognition?: a political-philosophical exchange*. Verso, p. 7.
Fraser, N., 2008. *Scales of justice: Reimagining political space in a globalizing world*. Columbia University Press.
Fraser, N., 2013. *Fortunes of feminism. From state managed capitalism to neoliberal crisis*. Verso.
Government of Zimbabwe, 2000. *Water resources management*. Harare: Ministry of Water Resources and Development.
Government of Zimbabwe, 2016. *Report of the Auditor-General on the environmental monitoring of mining operations by the Environmental Management Agency under the Ministry of Environment, Water and Climate*. Harare: Office of the Comptroller and Auditor-General of Zimbabwe.
Government of Zimbabwe, 2013. *National water policy*. Harare: Ministry of Water Resources and Development.
Hellum, A., 2001. Towards a human rights based development approach: The case of women in the water reform process in Zimbabwe. *Law, Social Justice and Global Development*, 2. Available online at: http://www2.warwick.ac.uk/fac/soc/law/elj/lgd/2001_1/hellum/ (accessed January 8, 2020).
Hellum, A., 2017. Engendering the right to water and sanitation: Integrating the lived experiences of women and girls. In M. Langford and A. Russell (eds.), *The human right to water: Theory, practice and prospects*. Cambridge University Press, p. 276.
Hellum, A., Derman, B., Sithole, E. and Rutsate, E., 2015. Governance, Gender Equality and the Right to Water and Sanitation in Zimbabwe: Contested Norms and Institutions in an Unstable Economic and Political Terrain. In A. Hellum, P. Kameri-Mbote, and B. van Koppen (eds.), *Water is Life*. Weaver Press.

Hellum, A., Ikdahl, I., and Kameri-Mbote, P., 2015. Turning the tide: Engendering the human right to water and sanitation. In A. Hellum, P. Kameri-Mbote, and B. van Koppen (eds.), *Water is life: Women's human rights in national and local water governance in southern and Eastern Africa*. Weaver Press.

Hellum, A., Kameri-Mbote, P. and van Koppen, B., 2015. The human right to water and sanitation in a legal pluralist landscape: Perspectives of Southern and Eastern African women. In A. Hellum, P. Kameri-Mbote, and B. van Koppen (eds.), *Water is life*. Weaver Press.

Hellum, A., Sithole, E., Derman, B., Mangwanya, L. and Rutsate, E., 2015. Zimbabwe's urban water crisis and its implications for different women: Emerging norms and practices in Harare's high density suburbs. In A. Hellum, P. Kameri-Mbote, and B. van Koppen (eds.), *Water is life*. Weaver Press.

Hiskes, R., 2009. *The human right to a green future: environmental rights and intergenerational justice*. Cambridge University Press.

Honneth, A., 2003. The point of recognition: A rejoinder to the rejoinder. In N. Fraser and A. Honneth, *Redistribution or recognition?: a political-philosophical exchange*. Verso.

Human Rights Watch, 2013. *Troubled Water: Burst Pipes, Contaminated Wells, and Open Defecation in Zimbabwe's Capital*, available online at: https://www.hrw.org/report/2013/11/19/troubled-water/burst-pipes-contaminated-wells-and-open-defecation-zimbabwes (accessed 3 December 2021).

ICESCR Committee, 2002. *General Comment No. 15, The right to water* (Twenty-ninth session), U.N. Doc. E/C.12/2002/11 (2003).

International Conference on Water and the Environment (IWCE), 1992. *The Dublin Statement on Water and Sustainable Development*. Available online at: http://www.wmo.int/pages/prog/hwrp/documents/english/icwedece.html (accessed May 24, 2017).

Katsande, R., 2016. Interrogating marriage as an organizing framework in land based businesses: A case study of women horticulture farmers in Mashonaland West Province of Zimbabwe. PhD Thesis. University of Zimbabwe.

Linton, J., 2010. *What is water? The history of a modern abstraction*. University of British Columbia Press.

Mabiza, C., 2013. IWRM, Institutions and livelihoods under stress: Bottom up perspectives from Zimbabwe. PhD thesis. Delft University.

Maguwu, F., 2012. The story of Zimbabwe's Marange diamonds: Pollution, politics, power. *The Africa Report*. Available online at: https://www.theafricareport.com/6292/the-story-of-zimbabwes-marange-diamonds-pollution-politics-power/: (accessed January 7, 2020).

Mambondiyani, A., 2012. The pollution fallout from Zimbabwe's blood diamonds. *Yale Environment*, 360. Available online at: https://e360.yale.edu/features/the_pollution_fallout_from_zimbabwes_blood_diamonds (accessed December 29, 2019).

Manzungu, E., 2001. A lost opportunity: The case of the water reform debate in the fourth parliament of Zimbabwe. *Zambezia* XXVIII (1), 97–120.

Mehta, L., Movik, S., Bolding, A., Derman, B., and Manzungu, E., 2016. Introduction to the Special Issue – Flows and practices: The politics of Integrated Water Resources Management (IWRM) in southern Africa. *Water Alternatives*, 9(3), 389–411.

Mtisi, S., 2011. Water reforms during the crisis and beyond: Understanding policy and political challenges of reforming the water sector in Zimbabwe. Working Paper 333 Overseas Development Institute (ODI).

Mtisi, S. and Nicol, A. 2003. Caught in the act: New stakeholders, decentralisation and water management processes in Zimbabwe. Sustainable livelihoods in Southern Africa, Research Paper Series No. 14. Available online at: http://www.ids.ac.uk/files/wRP14.pdf (accessed May 4, 2017).

Mutopo, P. and Chiweshe, M., 2014. Water resources and biofuel production after the fast-track land reform in Zimbabwe. *African Identities*, 12(1), 124–138.

Perrault, T., 2014. What kind of governance for what kind of equity? Towards a theorization of justice in water governance. *Water International*, 39(2), 233–245.

Rukuni, M., 1994. *Report of the Commission of Inquiry into Appropriate Agricultural Land Tenure Systems*. Harare: The Commission on Land Tenure.

Rutsate, E., Derman, B. and Hellum, A. 2015. A hidden presence: Women farm-workers right to water and sanitation in the aftermath of the fast track land reform. In A. Hellum, P. Kameri-Mbote, and B. van Koppen, eds., *Water is life*. Weaver Press.

Saunders, R., and Nyamunda, T., 2016. *Facets of power: Politics, profits and people in the making of Zimbabwe's blood diamonds*. Weaver Press.

Schlosberg, D. 2004. Reconceiving environmental justice: Global movements and political theories. *Environmental Politics*, 13(3), 517–540.

Schlosberg, D., 2007. *Defining environmental justice: theories, movements, and nature*. Oxford University Press.

Schlosberg, D. and Collins, L., 2014. From environmental to climate justice: climate change and the discourse of environmental justice. *Climate Change*, 5(3), 359–374.

Sikor, T., Martin, A., Fisher, J. and He, J., 2014. Toward an empirical analysis of justice in ecosystem governance. *Conservation Letters*, 7, 524–532. Available online at: https://conbio.onlinelibrary.wiley.com/doi/full/10.1111/conl.12142 (accessed January 8, 2020).

Sithole, B., 2000,. Use and Access to Dambos in Communal Lands in Zimbabwe. PhD Thesis. University of Zimbabwe.

United Nations Development Program, 2006. *Human Development Report beyond scarcity: Power, poverty and the global water crisis*. Available online at: http://hdr.undp.org/sites/default/files/reports/267/hdr06-complete.pdf (accessed January 8, 2020).

United Nations Development Program, 2015. United Nations Sustainable Development Goals. Available online at: https://www.undp.org/content/undp/en/home/sustainable-development-goals.html (accessed January 8, 2020).

van Koppen, B., 2017. Water allocation, customary practice and the right to water: Rethinking the regulatory model. In M. Langford and A. F. S. Russell (eds.), *The human right to water: theory, practice and prospects*. Cambridge University Press. p. 53.

van Koppen, B., Giordano, M. and Butterworth, J., 2007. Community based water law and water resource management reform in developing countries: rationale, contents and key messages. In B. van Koppen, M. Giordano, and J. Butterworth (eds.), *Community-based water law and water resources management reform in developing countries*. CABI. p. 1.

van Koppen, B, and Schreiner, B., 2014. Priority general authorisations in rights-based water use authorization in South Africa. *Water Policy*, 16(2), 59–77.

van Koppen, B. and Schreiner, B., 2019. A hybrid approach to statutory water law to support smallholder farmer-led irrigation development (FLID) in Sub-Saharan Africa. *Water Alternatives*, 12(1), 146–155.

Walker, G. P., 2012. *Environmental justice*. Routledge.

World Commission on Environment and Development, 1987. *Our common future*. Oxford University Press.

World Health Organization, 2017. Progress on drinking water, sanitation and hygiene: Update and SDG guidelines, available online at: https://apps.who.int/iris/bitstream/handle/10665/258617/9789241512893-eng.pdf;jsessionid=EF070E D5AA1394A8AE4171DE210DE62B?sequence=1 (accessed January 8, 2020).
Young, I. M., 1990. *Justice and the politics of difference*. Princeton University Press.
Zwarteveen, M. and Boelens, R., 2014. Defining, researching and struggling for water justice: some conceptual building blocks for research and action. *Water International*, 39(2), 143–158.

Chapter 10

Access to justice for refugees

Dallal Stevens

Introduction

Seldom in recent times has the movement of people and refugees received so much media and political attention.[1] And, one might think, for good reason. At 79.5 million forcibly displaced people, of whom 26 million are refugees (20.4 million under the mandate of the United Nations High Commission for Refugees (UNHCR) and 5.6 million Palestinians registered with the United Nations Relief and Works Agency (UNRWA)); 45.7 million are internally displaced peoples and 4.2 million are asylum seekers (UNHCR, 2019). But much of that attention in 2015 and 2016 was focused on European Union (EU) attempts to deter migrants and refugees from making the journey to Europe; on reasons why the EU should prevent arrivals; and on the problems caused by smuggling and trafficking networks. Few reports, with notable recent exceptions (Squire et al.,, 2017; MEDMIG, 2016), explained why so many people chose to take the hazardous route to Europe or described the situation of those who sought sanctuary in neighbouring countries and have languished for years or decades in terrible conditions because states are unwilling or unable to care for them or provide them with basic rights. Few reports have explored why the 70-year-old refugee protection framework has patently failed those for whom it was ostensibly designed, explained why state parties are unable to co-operate usefully to address refugee movements in a humane and effective manner (effective from the individual as opposed to state perspective), or examined what hope there is for the future.[2]

1 Refugees are broadly defined by the UNHCR to include 'individuals recognized under the 1951 Convention relating to the Status of Refugees; its 1967 Protocol; the 1969 OAU Convention Governing the Specific Aspects of Refugee Problems in Africa; those recognized in accordance with the UNHCR Statute; individuals granted complementary forms of protection; or, those enjoying "temporary protection."'

2 I say ostensibly because the system constructed in 1950/51 was established very much with state interests in mind.

DOI: 10.4324/9780203745298-13

In this chapter, I argue that refugee law and the refugee protection framework are at 'crisis point'– to use a much-overused term – and therefore ripe for a new imaginary. I am particularly interested in the concepts of asylum and protection and discussing why international cooperation and solidarity (as originally understood in the development of the refugee protection framework) appear to have little traction at present, when, in the words of the UNHCR, 'the international refugee regime is predicated on cooperation between States' (UNHCR, 2011a, para 1). I focus on the extent to which the current legal framework is failing refugees and whether recent initiatives, such as the Sustainable Development Goals, the World Humanitarian Summit, the interest of the World Bank in forced displacement, the New York Declaration for Refugees and Migrants of September 2016 and the Global Compact on Refugees 2018 constitute new 'paradigmatic shifts' as claimed, and thus provide a workable new model.

The chapter opens with an explanation of why I frame the issue as one of 'access to justice' before proceeding to explore three important elements of the current refugee framework: asylum and protection, international cooperation, and the problems with refugee law. The final part examines the shift away from law to alternative economic and political initiatives, particularly in light of the 2016 New York Declaration, in which the 193 UN Member States committed to improve the support and protection of all people on the move, including those migrating for humanitarian, developmental or human-rights-related reasons, or the adverse effects of climate-change. Member States agreed to develop a 'global compact for safe, orderly and regular migration' and a 'global compact on refugees' that builds upon the Comprehensive Refugee Response Framework outlined in the Declaration; the Compact was proposed by the UN High Commissioner for Refugees in his 2018 annual report to the UN General Assembly, agreed in a special conference in December 2018 and endorsed by the UN General Assembly in the same month.

Why access to justice?

Although I have entitled this chapter 'Access to justice for refugees', the meaning of justice and injustice is open to debate and critique. In addition, in the refugee context, talking about access to justice may be regarded as somewhat unusual. Refugee and asylum law and policy are primarily concerned with four issues: access to *asylum*, access to *refugee status*, access to *protection*, and the achievement of a *durable solution* (repatriation, resettlement or integration). Refugee law practitioners and academics rarely talk about access to justice, nor is the access to asylum necessarily viewed as an issue of justice, broadly speaking.[3] Where questions of access to justice are raised in asylum law, these generally relate to traditional

3 This contrasts with the climate displacement literature. See, for example, Buxton, 2019; Gonzalez, 2018–2019.

procedural understandings of justice, such as access to legal advice or due process and fairness, which are commonly treated as administrative law issues.[4] A different approach was taken in a 2017 collection I co-edited with Maria O'Sullivan entitled *States, the Law and Access to Refugee Protection: Fortresses and Fairness.* In this volume, we purposely introduced the idea of 'access to justice' in the asylum context, which we define as *physical* access to territory and access to a quality asylum *procedure* (O'Sullivan and Stevens, 2017: chapter 1).

For the purposes of this contribution, I want to extend the exploration of access to justice for refugees to access to social justice, by which I mean justice as fairness, access to equal liberties and equal opportunity, somewhat in the Rawlsian sense. There are three main reasons for doing so. First, there is arguably a problem with the meaning of core concepts of asylum and protection that form the basis of the refugee regime (Stevens, 2013; Storey, 2016). Second, there are substantial discrepancies surrounding the nature of any asylum or protection granted by party and non-party states to the 1951 UN Convention relating to the Status of Refugees ('the Refugee Convention'). Third, access to opportunities has emerged as a crucial requirement for refugees caught up in protracted refugee situations. This last problem is of particular concern. The UNHCR has estimated that, by the end of 2018, some 15.9 million refugees (78% of all refugees) were in a protracted situation (where 25,000 or more refugees from the same nationality have been in exile for five or more years) with 5.8 million having existed for more than 20 years (UNHCR, 2019: 22). There is nothing fair or just about languishing for years without hope. That the refugee system has failed them is indisputable.

Asylum and protection

A crucial aspect of the international refugee law regime is that primary responsibility for protecting and assisting refugees and returnees lies with host states (UNGA, 1998, para 13). That said, the first point to stress is that the concepts of asylum and protection are not as clear as might be expected from such crucial aspects of refugee law and policy. Several definitions of asylum and protection have emerged since the contemporary refugee regime was established in the early 1950s. There is a right to seek *and enjoy* asylum from persecution in Article 14(1) of the Universal Declaration of Human Rights. This has long been considered problematic as it does not denote a 'pure' right to asylum because there is no right *to be granted* asylum. Indeed, as Lauterpacht (1948: 374) has noted, the wording adopted was 'artificial to the point of flippancy'. This can be contrasted with the EU Charter of Fundamental Rights, which contains a simple right to asylum in Article 18 and has been interpreted by

4 See, for example, Refugee Action's report entitled *Tipping the Scales: Access to Justice in the Asylum System*: < www.refugee-action.org.uk/tipping-scales-access-justice-asylum-system/> (accessed 9 June 2020).

some as providing a greater obligation on Member States (Velluti, 2013: 28; Gil-Bazo, 2008).[5]

This raises the question as to what asylum means. Is it clear what obligations might be imposed on a hosting state or is 'the right to seek asylum' simply a right of the individual to cross a border and make a request to another state to admit her on exceptional humanitarian grounds? It is widely accepted that asylum is a broad term (O'Sullivan and Stevens, 2017: chapter 1). It could simply be viewed as referring to asylum as safety and sanctuary, which has a long history dating back to Greek and Roman times (Price, 2009); it could mean the whole range of rights and obligations provided by the Refugee Convention, or it could refer to little more than tolerated stay in the host state (Price, 2009). It is also possible to align asylum with protection where both terms are understood as reflecting the idea of safety, though the understanding of 'protection' has altered over time and can mean different things to different actors in the field, adding to its complexity (Stevens, 2013; Stevens and Dimitriadi, 2018). There are also temporal and geographical aspects to protection. Protection in the emergency phase of a movement of large numbers of people to a host country will differ from protection five or ten years into exile. Equally, places of protection often change as people move from camps to urban environments, or from countryside to cities.

My own work has examined the unsettling situation in which there has been an undue proliferation of protection-related concepts, such as international protection, temporary protection, subsidiary protection, complementary protection, humanitarian protection, internal protection and effective protection, without a thorough exploration of what protection *actually* means and in particular contexts, and the consequences for the individual of such wide usage (Stevens, 2013; Stevens, 2016). When recent developments in the responsibility to protect doctrine are added to the analysis, the position is even more confusing. This is perhaps best reflected in an on-going debate between leading refugee lawyers, both academic and judicial, in which there remains a significant difference of opinion as to what protection means in law regarding the definition of a refugee in the 1951 Convention and in what circumstances protection is provided (Storey, 2016). A straightforward view is that protection denotes the rights contained in the Convention – which broadly cover 'the need to escape, to be accepted and to be sheltered' (Hathaway, 2005: 94). There are guarantees of civil and political as well as socio-economic rights to help integrate refugees in the country of asylum; basic rights to work, to property, to social security; and obligations to guarantee protection against discrimination, religious freedom and access to courts. A recent contribution to the debate, by Aleinikoff and Zamore, posits that 'international protection' comprises:

5 Article 18 states: 'The right to asylum shall be guaranteed with due respect for the rules of the Geneva Convention of 28 July 1951 and the Protocol of 31 January 1967 relating to the status of refugees and in accordance with the Treaty establishing the European Community.'

> three core commitments: offering safe haven to forced migrants who have escaped violent and other atrocious conditions that make their lives at home intolerable; enabling forced migrants to rebuild their lives or providing for their welfare when they are unable to do so; and helping forced migrants exit from the category of the uprooted.
>
> (Aleinikoff and Zamore, 2019, p. 30)

They refer to these three commitments as 'safety, enjoyment of asylum, and solutions' (Aleinikoff and Zamore, 2019: chapter 2).

Obtaining the gold standard of refugee status by asylum seekers is no mean feat. The hope in 1951 was that all states would sign up to the Refugee Convention and agree to be bound by its obligations. This has not yet been fully achieved, though 148 countries are party to either the Convention or the later 1967 Protocol,[6] which removed the geographical (to Europe alone) and temporal (events pre-1 January 1951) limitations of the Convention. State parties to the Protocol undertake to apply Articles 2 to 34 of the Convention to refugees (Art 1(1)) and agree to no time or geographical limitation. This seems to suggest the willingness of states to provide refugees with minimal core standards of treatment, but not all is as it appears. First, many state parties are just that: signatories who have made minimal or no changes to their domestic arrangements for determining who is a refugee or ensuring that refugees are treated in accordance with the obligations in the Convention. As a consequence, there has been a shift of responsibility in such countries towards the UNHCR or NGOs (Kagan, 2011), which effectively take over the responsibilities of the state and often focus heavily on rights-based approaches or on needs, or combine both in a confusing way (Stevens, 2016). Forced displacement has generally been regarded primarily as a humanitarian issue by UN agencies and NGOs, and increasingly by states. Humanitarian actors initially viewed their role as providing material assistance, but since the 1990s and the development of what has been called the 'protection egg', the idea of a rights-based approach to humanitarian protection began to emerge (Stevens, 2013). The UNHCR has moved away from its original goal of legal protection towards material assistance and service provision. This has added to an increasingly complex situation in which the provision of needs and the advancement of rights are often combined into an overarching concept of 'protection', often with unintended consequences. One significant consequence is the adoption of a 'protection' role by organisations who do not have a protection mandate and are unfamiliar with the legal basis of protection under refugee law (Stevens, 2016).

6 States Parties to the 1951 Convention relating to the Status of Refugees and the 1967 Protocol <www.unhcr.org/uk/protection/basic/3b73b0d63/states-parties-1951-convention-its-1967-protocol.html> (accessed 7 February 2020).

A second issue is that a state can enter reservations against specific articles of the Convention leading to a significant watering down of its effectiveness.[7] Thus, all Convention rights other than those concerned with non-discrimination, freedom of religion, access to courts and protection against *refoulement* may be modified or excluded by a signatory state. In states that have not signed up to international refugee law the position is even more uncertain, with an unedifying political soup of 'internal aliens' legislation and policy combined with UNHCR and NGO practice on the ground. Many Middle Eastern countries, for example, are in this position. They rely on immigration laws for all categories of non-national entrants and have minimal legal provision for asylum claimants or refugees. There is often a Memorandum of Understanding between the state and the UNHCR, which takes responsibility for refugee status determination, resettlement and co-ordination of humanitarian action and service provision with other NGOs. Events during recent years in Europe and the United States have tragically revealed that state co-operation on refugees, whether motivated by legal obligation or a moral sense of duty, has become heavily distorted or driven by alternative interests such as securitisation, border control, and perceived political imperatives to control migration (O'Sullivan and Stevens, 2017; Squire et al., 2017; Fitzgerald, 2019). Few states pay heed to the views of migrants, many of whom articulate a notion of asylum and protection that is refreshingly clear and logical: a place of safety; shelter; access to employment; education for children; and the right to be joined by family. We have reached a crisis point in refugee protection, with state parties failing in their duties under Convention law and non-state parties providing minimal or uncertain rights to asylum seekers and refugees. In short, there is a lack of clarity as to what constitutes protection or how this should be achieved.

The movement of Syrians to the EU and to Lebanon from 2011 provides greater insight into the various asylum and protection issues associated with each region.

The EU (Member States are parties to the Refugee Convention and its Protocol and have a sophisticated regional asylum framework)

Despite the existence of a Common European Asylum System (CEAS) with common standards of asylum, there are numerous uncommon outcomes (Guild, 2016) and several uncommon standards. Not only do recognition rates for the same nationalities vary widely across the EU[8] but reception conditions,

7 *Per* Art. 42, reservations can be entered against all except Arts 1, 3, 4, 16(1), 33, 36–46, which are deemed core. For example, a State Party can limit its obligations to refugees regarding jobs and employment, housing, public education, public relief and assistance, labour legislation and social security, freedom of movement, the provision of identity and travel papers, and expulsion, *inter alia.*

8 A striking example is provided by first instance refugee recognition rates in 2015 for Eritreans in Sweden (95%), France (32%) and the UK (36%): UNHCR n.d.b, Statistics <popstats.unhcr.org/en/asylum_seekers> (accessed 3 June 2020).

approaches to unaccompanied minors and family reunification also differ considerably. Of course, the major issue has been gaining access to EU territory in the first place, with Member States erecting fences, passing criminalisation legislation and closing routes.[9] The double layering of protection through an international law framework and a regional system has failed to achieve fairness and humane treatment or alleviate suffering. Indeed, there are substantial grounds to argue that EU structures and protocols have contributed towards greater suffering and increased the vulnerability and precarity of many thousands of people. From a procedural justice perspective, access to equal and fair opportunities to claim and be granted asylum is patchy at best, notwithstanding a system ostensibly constructed to harmonise standards.[10]

Lebanon (is not a state party to Refugee Convention and controls entry with immigration and foreigner laws alongside the Arab concept of 'hospitality')[11]

In contrast, Lebanon had an open-door policy until 2015, at which point it felt it could no longer cope. Although Lebanon permitted greater access to its territory until 2015, there was widespread discrimination and its policies on the ground did not support access to important rights such as work and education for most Syrians. In 2015, the UNHCR declared that 'Given the limited possibilities to move to other countries, refugees continue living in a stressful context with no way out. Lebanon and the refugees it is hosting are in a very delicate state: the situation requires special and immediate measures.'[12] Arguably, such special and immediate measures were never forthcoming and the conditions for the majority of Syrians in Lebanon remain extremely precarious. Over 20 per cent of the country's population are refugees (892,310 Syrians were registered by UNHCR at 31 May 2020, and over 475,000 Palestinians with UNRWA at 1 January 2019).[13] In 2019, 55

9 Many Member States have engaged in such practices – see O'Sullivan & Stevens, 2017. Most notoriously, in September 2015, Hungary erected a fence on its southern border, changed its laws to allow for expedited removals to Serbia, and introduced a criminal offence of up to three years' imprisonment and/or expulsion for unauthorised entry through the border fence.

10 For detailed analysis of migration to the EU in 2015 and 2016, see Squire et al., 2017.

11 Lebanon is used as an example here but its circumstances are not unique. Both Jordan and Turkey are host to substantial numbers of Syrians and have adopted alternative and different mechanisms to refugee law to address their situations. Further, it should be noted that conflict, underdevelopment and social injustice are drivers of migration from other places such as Iraq, Afghanistan, the Horn of Africa and numerous other sub-Saharan countries.

12 UN News Centre, 'Conditions of Syrian refugees in Lebanon worsen considerably, UN reports', 23 December 2015: www.un.org/apps/news/story.asp?NewsID=52893#.WSvZBYWcFaR.

13 See UNHCR, n.d.a. Operational Portal Refugee Situations, Syria Regional Refugee Response: <https://data2.unhcr.org/en/situations/syria/location/71> (accessed

per cent of Syrians were living below the Survival Minimum Expenditure Basket (SMEB) of US$87 per person per month, and unable to meet their survival needs for food, health and shelter, while 73 per cent of Syrian refugee households were living below the Minimum Expenditure Basket (MEB) – or poverty line (UNICEF/UNHCR/WFP, 2020). Labour market restrictions were imposed at the end of 2014, creating increasing difficulty for migrants to cover their basic needs.[14] Food security has worsened since 2014, with 63 per cent of the Syrian refugee population now food insecure to some extent (UNICEF/UNHCR/WFP, 2020). Thirteen per cent of children between 3 and 5 years attend early education programmes, while 69 per cent of 6- to 14-year-olds attend school and 78 per cent of 15- to 17-year-olds do not go to school (UNICEF/UNHCR/WFP, 2020).

International cooperation, burden-sharing, international solidarity

Unfortunately, the problems facing refugees do not stop with the difficulty of defining the meaning of protection. For protection or access to justice to be realised, there is a need for inter-state support and collaboration to address the examples above which exemplify the serious consequences for individuals seeking asylum of the failures of mutual responsibility. If the events of the current crisis have proven anything, it is that states appear to have forgotten the underlying principle that inspired the drafting of the Refugee Convention: international cooperation. It 'reflects the reality that refugee challenges are inherently transnational and cannot be addressed by any one State alone' (UNHCR, 2011b, para 1). It is therefore worth reflecting briefly on the history of cooperation promoted by the Refugee Convention and EU treaties.

In 1950, France proposed Recital (4) for inclusion in the Preamble to the Refugee Convention to the ECOSOC Social Committee of 1950. It recognised that 'the right of asylum places undue burden on certain countries because of their geographical situation' and that the scope and nature of the refugee issue meant that a satisfactory solution 'cannot be achieved without international cooperation *to help distribute refugees throughout the world*' (emphasis added).

This was intended 'to point to the need for a collective effort to solve the problem of refugees' (Zimmermann, 2011: 237). The French delegation believed that because a few countries were hosting very large numbers of refugees it would probably be impossible to ensure that they would be adequately catered for and that the existence of an international convention would

21 June 2020); <https://www.unrwa.org/where-we-work/lebanon> (accessed 21 June 2020).

14 News Centre, 'Conditions of Syrian refugees in Lebanon worsen considerably, UN reports', 23 December 2015: <www.un.org/apps/news/story.asp?NewsID=52893#.WSvZBYWcFaR> (accessed 9 June 2020).

not, of itself, solve the problem. Alleweldt explains it thus: 'this Recital was designed to express the idea that high numbers of refugees make it very difficult for one State to respect all provisions of the 1951 Convention. In such exceptional situations, it would be advisable to solve the problem by international cooperation' (Alleweldt, 2011: 237). Not all countries were in favour of this proposal. Some saw within it 'an implicit obligation to admit refugees to their territories, which they were not willing to assume' and this early version was consequently rejected (Zimmermann, 2011: 237). France insisted that there could be no resolution to the refugee problem without cooperation. A revised version of the Recital was eventually adopted by ECOSOC and attempts by the United Kingdom during the Conference of Plenipotentiaries negotiating the Convention to delete the reference to the 'burden of receiving States' were not successful (Zimmermann, 2011: 237). The final version of Recital 4 of the Preamble to the Convention states:

> *Considering* that the grant of asylum may place unduly heavy burdens on certain countries, and that a satisfactory solution of a problem of which the United Nations has recognised the international scope and nature cannot be achieved without international cooperation [and expresses] the wish that all States, recognising the social and humanitarian nature of the problem of refugees, will do everything within their power to prevent this problem of becoming a cause of tension between States.

It acknowledges that the grant of asylum may lead to 'unduly heavy burdens' on some states and that while the responsibility is on the country of asylum to protect and assist refugees, it is accepted that sometimes this cannot be done alone.[15] However, the Recital makes no demands on states to assist one another in any meaningful or concrete manner despite proposals by the UN Secretary-General at that time, Trygve Halvdan Lie, who regarded it 'as crucial to an effective regime' to include a specific obligation on co-operation or burden-sharing (Goodwin-Gill, 2016).

Some might interpret Recital 4 as demanding that a balance be found between the rights of refugees and the burdens of receiving states, but this is perhaps an interpretive step too far. The Preamble merely acknowledges that refugee influxes can lead to 'unduly heavy burdens' for the receiving state and

15 It is important to note that regional instruments, such as the Dublin Regulation in the EU (Regulation (EU) No 604/2013 of the European Parliament and of the Council of 26 June 2013 establishing the criteria and mechanisms for determining the Member State responsible for examining an application for international protection lodged in one of the Member States by a third-country national or a stateless person), can include an obligation to examine an asylum application on the first country of irregular entry. This inevitably imposes a greater burden on those countries more easily accessed by people crossing the Mediterranean, such as Italy and Greece.

that 'international cooperation' is needed to solve the problem. The Convention does not tell us what form international cooperation should take and it certainly does not sanction a form of cooperation that limits the rights of refugees in any way, restricts entry or contains people in their regions of origin.

The dynamic nature of refugee law policy has led to significant discussion of what the international community should be doing in relation to asylum seekers and refugees, and various regional instruments also refer to the need for international cooperation. In the EU, Member States are not only party to the Refugee Convention and its Protocol and therefore should be conscious of the importance of cooperation to the sustainability of the refugee regime; they are also expected to apply EU principles such as solidarity to immigration and asylum policies. Article 80 of the Treaty on the Functioning of the EU (TFEU) states:

> The policies of the Union set out in this Chapter and their implementation shall be governed by the *principle of solidarity and fair sharing of responsibility,* including its financial implications, between the Member States. Whenever necessary, the Union acts adopted pursuant to this Chapter shall contain appropriate measures to give effect to this principle [emphasis added].

The addition of what has been described as a 'peremptory rule' to the TFEU can be regarded as a very significant moment. Yet, despite the inclusion of the key principle of solidarity, it is not clear how it is to be interpreted. Gregor Noll has argued that the word has its roots in Roman civil law and refers to 'the relationship between the creditor and a group of people responsible for the debt' (Noll, 2016: 3); 'If', he opines,

> we read Article 80 through the original Roman law meaning of solidarity, we see that this limited scope is very problematic indeed. In the Roman law of obligation, solidarity presupposes a contract between a creditor and a debtor. By letting 'the principle of solidarity' govern no more than relations 'between the Member States', the drafters of Article 80 TFEU distanced themselves from this concept of solidarity.
>
> (Noll, 2016: 3)

Even the development of what he terms 'French social solidarity' by nineteenth century positivists is unable to save the concept for the EU because, unlike the French Revolution, the EU is uncompromisingly top-down and *dirigiste*. For Noll, 'the label "solidarity" in the treaties is a meaningless appropriation of a historical experience particular to the French nation state' (Noll, 2016: 4). Moreno-Lax, by contrast, offers an alternative analysis of the meaning of solidarity from an EU perspective. She has explored solidarity as a soft-law and normative obligation and contrasted its procedural and substantive aspects. She argues that solidarity denotes more than international cooperation and includes shared responsibility towards third countries as well as to asylum seekers and refugees (Moreno-Lax, 2017). She regards fairness as an inherent criterion of solidarity.

Moreno-Lax's view of solidarity goes beyond the general approach long adopted by the EU in its relationships with countries of the global south. The EU tended to consider solidarity as an important value that is to be respected (as outlined in Article 80 TFEU) and encouraged in other parts of the world. For example, in *The Africa-EU Strategic Partnership – A Joint Africa-EU Strategy*, the text opened with the following:

> Africa and Europe are bound together by history, culture, geography, a common future, as well as by a community of values: the respect for human rights, freedom, equality, solidarity, justice, the rule of law and democracy as enshrined in the relevant international agreements and in the constitutive texts of our respective Unions.[16]

The partnership, one is told, will be governed by strengthened political dialogue, co-management and co-responsibility, burden-sharing and mutual accountability, and solidarity and mutual confidence, amongst other factors. The meaning of solidarity here is rather vague and there is no further explanation as to what it might entail. Recently the term 'solidarity' has been adopted by the EU in the context of migration: in July 2017, a meeting entitled 'A shared responsibility for a common goal: solidarity and security' was attended by eight African and eight EU countries.[17] Its focus was clearly on fighting human trafficking and smuggling and controlling irregular migration and borders. Though the EU now recognises that greater investment in – and support for – African countries is required, there is no doubt that the idea of solidarity for the EU *vis-à-vis* third countries means involving EU migration and mobility objectives in assisting them.

Reflection on notions of international cooperation and solidarity is, of course, not unique to the EU. At the UN level, much discussion has taken place in the Executive Committee of the UNHCR, which currently consists of 98 member states, including states that are not party to the Refugee Convention or Protocol but which host large numbers of refugees, such as Jordan and Lebanon. The result has been an interesting study in semantics, with various Conclusions exploring notions of 'burden-sharing', 'international solidarity' and, in 2011, 'international responsibility' alongside the traditional notion of

16 *The Africa-EU Strategic Partnership – A Joint Africa-EU Strategy*, 2007: www.africa-eu-partnership.org/sites/default/files/documents/eas2007_joint_strategy_en.pdf (accessed 5 February 2020).

17 The meeting was between the Ministers of Foreign Affairs and Development Cooperation and other representatives of Algeria, Austria, Chad, Egypt, Estonia, Ethiopia, France, Germany, Italy, Libya, Malta, The Netherlands, Niger, Spain, Sudan, Tunisia, and the Deputy High Commissioner of UNHCR and the Director General of IOM.

'international co-operation', each stressing their importance to refugee protection and asylum.[18]

For example, the 2009 Conclusion on Protracted Refugee Situations recognises that:

> protracted refugee situations also impose considerable burdens and generate significant problems and challenges in different sectors for host States and communities which are often developing, in transition, or with limited resources and facing other constraints.[19]

It calls upon states and other relevant actors to commit themselves to 'international solidarity and burden sharing' and to 'comprehensive, multilateral and multisectoral collaboration and action' in order to address the root causes of protracted refugee situations, to ensure that people are not compelled to flee their countries of origin to find safety elsewhere and to resolve such situations 'in full respect for the rights of the affected person'.[20]

What we are still not provided with is a clear global framework of the core elements of international cooperation and how to achieve it. Solutions suggested by the 2009 Conclusions include the provision of adequate development and humanitarian funding, support for hosting communities and countries of origin, and durable solutions such as voluntary repatriation, promoting local integration in the host country, and providing resettlement possibilities in third countries. There are repeated calls for states 'to respond in concert and wholeheartedly, in a spirit of true humanitarianism and international solidarity'.[21] In 2011, the UNHCR (2011a) sought to develop a Common Framework on International Cooperation to Share Burdens and Responsibilities by drawing on past lessons and provided examples of cooperative arrangements that might be adopted at different stages of the displacement cycle. As yet, such a common framework has not been forthcoming, though the 2016 New York Declaration anticipated change.

18 See *inter alia* UNHCR, Ex Com Conclusion of the Executive Committee on International Cooperation from a Protection and Solutions Perspective No. 112 (LXVII) 2016; Ex Com Conclusion on International Cooperation and Burden and Responsibility Sharing in Mass Influx Situations No. 100 (LV) 2004; Ex Com Conclusion on International Solidarity and Refugee Protection No. 52 (XXXIX) 1988; Protection of Asylum-Seekers in Situations of Large-Scale Influx No. 22 (XXXII) 1981.

19 UNHCR, Conclusion on Protracted Refugee Situations (accessed 20 December, 2020).

20 UNHCR, ExCom Conclusion on Protracted Refugee Situations No. 109 (LXI) 2009, para c.

21 UNHCR, ExCom Conclusion in International Solidarity and Refugee Protection No. 52 (XXXIX) 1988.

Present-day challenges to asylum and refugee law

One might assume that refugee law – as one of the rare normative frameworks designed to protect a specific category of persons – should be able to deliver a higher degree of justice for asylum seekers and refugees, but this is increasingly not so.

There is an interesting paradox at the heart of the international refugee protection regime. In the early 1950s, recourse was made to law to provide refugees with more assistance and greater protection; to reduce their vulnerability; provide them with a new territory of residence where necessary; and help with their integration by creating hope and opportunities for a flourishing future. With no oversight mechanism in the Refugee Convention, there is a presumption that states will implement the rights contained in it in good faith (Hathaway, 2005: 992). Of course, that is not what has transpired. The international legal framework, despite its emergence after the Second World War and the intention that it should focus on large-scale displacement, has not coped well with so-called mass influxes due to what has been termed the individualised nature of the refugee definition.[22]

Furthermore, the idea of international cooperation on asylum (where it leads to states admitting refugees and sharing responsibility for them) appears to be a historical detail in many parts of the world, or at best is *ad hoc*. With some notable exceptions, such as former Yugoslavia, the last 30 years have witnessed numerous attempts by states to limit or remove their legal obligations through various means: the imposition of visas, carriers' liability legislation,[23] border controls, fence building, readmission arrangements, privatisation of immigration control, criminalisation of asylum seekers and numerous deterrence methods (see for example, O'Sullivan and Stevens, 2017; Gammeltoft-Hansen, 2011). Cooperation has turned largely into: (i) agreed objectives to contain refugees and asylum seekers in their regions, close to the country of origin; (ii) the introduction of 'partnership agreements' with third (migrant-producing) countries that impose obligations for cash; and (iii) an economic exercise where financial – that is, development – aid is pumped into countries neighbouring the country of origin in the hope that they will be able to contain the movement of peoples on to countries in the global North. Many examples now exist. Australia utilises bilateral and multilateral agreements in the Asia-Pacific region to manage migration to its territory. In particular, it has provided

22 There is an expectation in the definition that each person seeking refugee status will have his or her case assessed on an individual basis. There is scope for group-based refugee determination to be undertaken but the ability to deal with large movements of peoples is limited. See Kneebone, Stevens and Baldassar (2014, Ch 1) for an extended discussion.

23 Carriers' liability legislation imposes financial sanctions on airline and shipping companies who carry passengers not in possession of the correct and valid identity and travel documentation. For example, in the United Kingdom, the penalty is £2000 per passenger.

significant financial and diplomatic inducements to Indonesia to prevent migration. Australia has also employed off-shore processing in the Pacific island states of Papua New Guinea and Nauru.[24] The EU (and individual Member States) has long sought to stop the flow of migrants from Africa through proposed off-shore processing centres[25] and agreements that link migration with development, such as the 2000 Cotonou Agreement between the EU and the African, Caribbean and Pacific Group of States. In 2016, in response to the 'migration crisis' of 2015–2016, the EU introduced a new Migration Partnership Framework that focuses on 'priority countries of origin and transit – Mali, Nigeria, Niger, Senegal and Ethiopia'.[26] The objective is 'to develop win-win relationships with the European Union's partners to tackle the shared challenges of migration and development'.[27] In addition, on 18 March 2016, the EU-Turkey Statement was announced in which the EU and Turkey agreed to a series of measures to address the movement of people across the eastern Mediterranean from Turkey to Greece. These included: the prevention of irregular migration from Turkey to the EU; the return of all new irregular arrivals in Greece after 20 March 2016; a 1+1 scheme, whereby for every Syrian returned to Turkey from the Greek islands, a selected Syrian would be resettled from Turkey to the EU; and an additional 3 billion Euro to be mobilised by the end of 2018, in addition to 3 billion already committed to Turkey in 2015.[28] In 2017, France's President Macron hinted at revisiting the idea of off-shore asylum processing centres in Libya ('hotspots'), despite that

24 This was done under Australian policies termed *the Pacific Solution* of 2001–2008 and *Operation Sovereign Borders* which have operated since 2013. The Papua New Guinean government claimed to have closed its detention/processing centre on Manus Island following a PNG Supreme Court ruling that the detention by Australia of asylums seekers and refugees on the island was illegal. However, hundreds of people continued to live at the centre even after the Australian government formally pronounced the centre closed on 31 October 2017. See generally Giannacopoulos and Loughnan (2020).

25 Off-shore processing was first proposed in 2003 by the United Kingdom's Prime Minister Tony Blair; the idea was taken up by the German Interior Minister, Otto Schily, in 2005 and put into effect on a bilateral basis by Italy when Prime Minister Silvio Berlusconi and Libya's Colonel Muammar Gaddafi signed an *Accordo di Amicizia e Cooperazione* (Treaty of Friendship and Cooperation) in 2008.

26 European Commission, 'Migration Partnership Framework: A New Approach to Better Manage Migration', 13 December 2016: <eeas.europa.eu/sites/eeas/files/factsheet_migration_partnership_framework_update13_12_2016.pdf> (accessed 9 June 2020).

27 See for further discussion, Report from the Commission to the European Parliament, the European Council and the Council, *Fourth Progress report on the Partnership Framework with third countries under the European Agenda on Migration*, COM(2017) 350 final, 13 June 2017.

28 EU Commission – Fact Sheet, Implementing the EU-Turkey Statement – Questions and Answers, 15 June 2016: https://ec.europa.eu/commission/presscorner/api/files/document/print/en/memo_16_963/MEMO_16_963_EN.pdf (accessed 5 February 2020).

country's current turmoil and recorded ill-treatment of asylum seekers and migrants, only to backtrack rapidly.[29] However, he did go on to host a mini-summit with the heads of state of Germany, Italy, Spain, Chad and Niger and the High Representative/Vice President of the Union for Foreign Affairs and Security Policy to address migration from Africa. An agreed joint plan focused on dismantling smuggling networks, increasing practical and financial support for Chad and Niger, recognising the need to resettle particularly vulnerable people requiring international protection and initiating protection missions in Niger and Chad for resettlement of refugees.[30]

Much state behaviour has seriously undermined the role of refugee law under the terms of the Refugee Convention. With so many refugees in parts of the world where there is an inability to provide the conventional and anticipated 'protection' of the Refugee Convention[31] and the remainder capable of meeting their responsibilities but plainly unwilling to do so, the options for the UNHCR and its partner NGOs have been few. Furthermore, unlike many human rights treaties, there is 'no free-standing mechanism to promote interstate accountability under the auspices of an independent expert supervisory body' and no facility for aggrieved refugees to petition the UNHCR (Hathaway, 2005: 994). Its role is very much 'standard-setting and private representations to states' (ibid.). This anomaly may be due to history in that the 1948 Genocide Convention shares the lack of an independent supervisory mechanism with the Refugee Convention (ibid.).

Hathaway claims that governments believe that 'there is a lack of balance in the mechanisms of the refugee regime which results in little account being taken of the legitimate interests of the states which refugees flee' (Hathaway, 2005: 999). Indeed, there appears to be little incentive for any government to admit refugees and uphold the duty of protection – in other words, to abide by refugee law. The behaviour of EU states in recent times has done little to encourage developing countries to fulfil their refugee or human rights obligations. Why should they when they see others behaving badly and getting away with it? Yet, paradoxically, many low- and middle-income countries continue to accept enormous numbers of displaced people, while the EU – notwithstanding Germany's generosity in 2015 and 2016 towards Syrians, Afghans and Iraqis – continues to seek ways to limit entry of asylum seekers and economic migrants and to regionalise protection.

29 C. Farand, 'Emmanuel Macron says France will set up refugee "hotspots" in Libya', *Independent*, 30 July 2017; 'Migrants: Macron prêt à agir sur le sol libyen', *Le Figaro*, 28 July 2017.

30 Joint Statement Addressing the Challenge of Migration and Asylum, Paris, 28 August 2017: www.bundesregierung.de/Content/DE/_Anlagen/2017/08/2017-08-28-statement-refugee-migration-english.pdf?__blob=publicationFile&v=1 (accessed 9 June 2020).

31 84% of the world's refugees were hosted in developing regions under the UNHCR's mandate, with the least developed countries providing asylum to 4.9 million refugees (28% of the global total): UNHCR, 2017.

Thus, the last three decades have borne witness to a move away from what might be described as the early conceptualisation of refugee law, arguably simple in its objective, in which governments are willing to accept refugees, take responsibility for those seeking asylum in their territories, provide refugees with the rights in the Convention, and assist other states when they are unable to cope. This ideal has been replaced by widely varying commitments to Refugee Convention obligations, numerous *non-entrée* policies, restrictive asylum policy and a complex architecture of long-term humanitarian aid and assistance that is now metamorphosing once more into a humanitarian plus development model, involving the World Bank and private enterprise.

A paradigmatic shift in responsibility for refugees?

Just as many academics and, presumably, practitioners are questioning the conceptual framework or discourse of development, international organisations, the World Bank, the UN and researchers are looking to development as a possible panacea to forced displacement. There have been remarkable changes in recent years in this regard, leading to a notable shift in direction. I suggest that there have been four key drivers influencing refugee protection: the Global Program on Forced Displacement (GPFD), adopted by the World Bank in 2009; the Sustainable Development Goals (SDGs), adopted in September 2015; the World Humanitarian Summit (WHS) in Istanbul in May 2016; and the Summit on Addressing Large Movements of Refugees and Migrants in September 2016, that led to the New York Declaration and Global Compact on Refugees.

Let us first consider the World Bank. Since the GPFD was established in 2009, it has been a considerable battle to persuade the World Bank that the forcibly displaced require its intervention. Only recently did it finally acknowledge forced displacement as a significant development challenge. Niels Harild, the former manager of the GPFD, explained that a paradigmatic shift was required in the Bank towards understanding that displacement was fundamentally a development issue with social, economic and fiscal implications. He put it thus:

> This [shift] requires a policy and mind-set change from short-term thinking to a long-term comprehensive approach. Life improvements for those living in protracted displacement and support for lasting solutions can only come about by addressing holistically: housing, livelihoods, service access, inclusion and governance.[32]

32 World Bank, 'The evolution of World Bank Group's role in forced displacement – Interview with Niels Harild, former manager of WBG's Global Program on Forced Displacement (GPFD)', 6 January 2016: <www.worldbank.org/en/news/feature/2016/01/06/the-evolution-of-world-bank-group-role-in-forced-displacement> (accessed 5 February 2020).

To achieve this shift, the World Bank accepted that middle income countries such as Jordan, Lebanon and Ethiopia must now be eligible for development aid. Following the London conference in February 2016, *Supporting Syria and the Region*, [33] the World Bank's Board of Directors offered Jordan US$100 million in financing at rates usually reserved for least developed countries. By September 2016, the US$300 million GPFD programme had been set up.[34] Together with other pledges made in London, the Jordan Compact hoped to create 200,000 job opportunities for Syrian refugees while they remained in Jordan.[35] This was to be achieved in the first instance through special economic zones (SEZs).[36]

Almost at the outset, the viability of the SEZ model in Jordan was questioned. In February 2017, the International Rescue Committee reported that there was 'limited and uneven progress'. While it acknowledged that the Jordan Compact included several interventions from the traditional humanitarian response to economic development initiatives, there was a concern that many interventions were aimed at generating economic growth rather than addressing Syrian refugees' specific needs and their barriers to finding legal employment (IRC, 2017, 12). The report continued:

> This may reflect the fact that refugees' voices went largely unheard at the start of the Compact negotiation process. In addition, solutions that have received the most attention over the last year – namely the EU trade concessions and special economic zones (SEZs) – are very thinly supported by rigorous evidence of what works to support refugees' livelihoods in protracted displacement settings. While important to test new and innovative solutions in these contexts, the Compact has arguably placed too much emphasis on interventions that are high-risk and expensive and has

33 On 4 February 2016, the UK, Germany, Kuwait, Norway and the UN co-hosted a conference on the Syria crisis in London. The conference raised over US$11 billion in pledges – $5.8 billion for 2016 and a further $5.4 billion for 2017–20: <www.supportingsyria2016.com/about/>.

34 World Bank, '$300 million to Improve Employment Opportunities for Jordanians and Syrian Refugees', 27 September 2016: www.worldbank.org/en/news/press-release/2016/09/27/300-million-to-improve-employment-opportunities-for-jordanians-and-syrian-refugees (accessed 5 February 2020).

35 *The Jordan Compact: A New Holistic Approach between the Hashemite Kingdom of Jordan and the International Community to deal with the Syrian Refugee Crisis*, 4 February 2016: <www.gov.uk/government/uploads/system/uploads/attachment_data/file/498021/Supporting_Syria__the_Region_London_2016_-_Jordan_Statement.pdf> (accessed 9 June 2020).

36 See for discussion of World Bank's role in Jordan: World Bank, *Jordan - Country partnership framework for the period FY17–22*: <documents.worldbank.org/curated/en/528081467900685594/Jordan-Country-partnership-framework-for-the-period-FY17–22> (accessed 9 June 2020).

> not invested enough in solutions that we know will meet the urgent needs of vulnerable populations.
>
> (IRC, 2017, 12)

Crawley and Pascucci were even more hard-hitting, with Crawley noting the surprising lack of 'serious discussion of human rights' and Pascucci the unsubstantiated belief in 'refugee-friendly capitalism' (Crawley, 2017: 27; Pascucci, 2017: 199). A recent study by Al-Mahaidi, exploring the Jordan Compact and the resort to SEZs, confirms that such scepticism was not misplaced. While it is claimed by the Jordanian Government that the numbers of work permits reached 176,920 by the end of December 2019, it is likely that the statistics are inaccurate for a variety of reasons and, apparently, less than half are active (Al-Mahaidi, 2020).

At the same time, the Global Concessional Financing Facility (GCFF) for the Middle Eastern and North African region (MENA) was announced during the 2016 World Bank Group-International Monetary Fund Spring Meetings. It aims to assist Jordan and Lebanon to address the impact of Syrian refugees. Initial pledges by seven countries and the European Commission reached over US$140 million, with an objective of raising US$1 billion in contributions over the next five years for Jordan and Lebanon.[37] In April 2017, the World Bank announced that the total concessional financing of US$1 billion had been unlocked by the GCFF[38] and in December 2019, at the first Global Refugee Forum,[39] the Bank announced that up to $2.2 billion would be available 'for a dedicated window for refugees and host communities over the next three years'.[40]

A few weeks after the London Conference, the first WHS took place. In the Report prepared for the Summit by the then UN Secretary-General, Ban Ki-moon, entitled *One Humanity: Shared Responsibility*, which took 3 years of consultation and 'reached over 23,000 people in 153 countries', five core

37 See GCFF website: <globalcff.org/about-us> (accessed 9 June 2020).

38 World Bank, 'New support for refugees and host communities in Jordan and Lebanon brings total concessional financing to US$1 billion', 21 April 2017 <www.worldbank.org/en/news/press-release/2017/04/21/new-support-for-refugees-and-host-communities-in-jordan-and-lebanon-brings-total-concessional-financing-to-us-1-billion> (accessed 9 June 2020).

39 The first Global Refugee Forum was a key part of the Global Compact on Refugees (see below), bringing together the international community 'to demonstrate solidarity with the world's refugees and the countries and communities that host them', and was regarded by the UNHCR as putting in place a new comprehensive refugee response model: <https://www.unhcr.org/uk/programme-and-practical-information.html> (accessed 9 June 2020).

40 The World Bank, 'World Bank announces $2.2 billion scale-up in support for refugees and host communities at first Global Refugee Forum', Press Release, 17 December 2019 <https://www.worldbank.org/en/news/press-release/2019/12/17/world-bank-announces-us22-billion-scale-up-in-support-for-refugees-and-host-communities-at-first-global-refugee-forum#:~:text=The%20%242.2%20billion%20complements%20efforts,July%202017%20to%20June%202020> (accessed 5 June 2020).

responsibilities that linked back to the Plan of Action for *Transforming Our World: the 2030 Agenda for Sustainable Development* (the SDGs) were proposed for discussion at the Summit. Their emphasis on the human is very evident:[41]

1 Political leadership to prevent and end conflicts
2 Uphold the norms that safeguard humanity
3 Leave no one behind
4 Change people's lives – from delivering aid to ending need
5 Invest in humanity.

Specifically on refugees, the Report placed the following issues squarely on the Agenda: (i) the sharing of responsibility for addressing large-scale movements of refugees; (ii) the development of a new international cooperation framework on predictable and equitable sharing of responsibility to respond to large-scale refugee movements; and (iii) reinforcement of the principle of *non-refoulement* and reemphasising the importance of the 1951 Convention relating to the Status of Refugees and the 1967 Protocol thereto (UNGA, 2016a: 24, 55).

The WHS had a mixed reception. While it was certainly unique in its attempt to consult widely amongst many stakeholders with no fixed agenda at the outset, the Secretary-General's Report was described as having unclear goals; as being weak on rights and protection insofar as displacement was concerned; having unclear outcomes; and a lack of certainty as to whether states would agree to undertake the suggested commitments. However, it did establish the context for the subsequent UN Summit for Refugees and Migrants on 19 September 2016 in New York, whose aim was 'to address large movements of refugees and migrants, with the aim of bringing countries together behind a more humane and coordinated approach'.[42]

This was an important moment in which state willingness to share responsibility for migrants, asylum seekers, refugees, internally displaced people and those fleeing natural, climate-induced or environmental disasters could be put to the test. Summarising the importance of the Summit, the view of the UN is upbeat:

> It was the first time the General Assembly had called for a summit at the Heads of State and Government level on large movements of refugees and

41 The SDGs themselves make specific mention of refugees and internally displaced persons (IDPs) as 'people who are vulnerable' and who need empowering (para 23): UNGA, Resolution adopted by the General Assembly on 25 September 2015, 70/1. Transforming Our World: the 2030 Agenda for Sustainable Development, A/RES/70/1, 21 October 2015 <sustainabledevelopment.un.org/post2015/transformingourworld> (accessed 9 June 2020).

42 UN Summit for Refugees and Migrants 2016 <refugeesmigrants.un.org/summit> (accessed 9 June 2020).

> migrants and was a historic opportunity to come up with a blueprint for a better international response. The Summit was a watershed moment to strengthen governance of international migration and a unique opportunity for creating a more responsible, predictable system for responding to large movements of refugees and migrants.[43]

Those attending the New York summit were under no illusions about the need to show international leadership and respond adequately and humanely to the many problems of global migration. In the resulting New York Declaration for Refugees and Migrants, it was clearly stated in paragraph 7 that: 'Large movements of refugees and migrants have political, economic, social, developmental, humanitarian and human rights ramifications, which cross all borders. These are global phenomena that call for global approaches and global solutions'. Many reaffirmations of the Refugee Convention and the 1967 Protocol were made as the foundation of this renewed international refugee protection regime, of the 'fundamental principle of *nonrefoulement*' and of the right to seek asylum. The 'centrality of international cooperation to the refugee protection regime' was underlined, as was commitment to 'a more equitable and predictable sharing of responsibility for hosting and supporting the world's refugees'. Delegates agreed that a comprehensive refugee response should be developed and initiated by the Office of the UNHCR (a new 'comprehensive refugee response framework' (CRRF)) involving states, relevant UN entities, national and local authorities, international organisations, international financial institutions, civil society partners, the private sector, the media and refugees themselves.[44] Its aim was:

> to guide enhanced international responses, and set in motion two processes for the development of two 'global compacts' – one on refugees and the other for the safe, orderly and regular migration – to strengthen further the ways in which the international community addresses human mobility.
>
> (UNHCR, 2018: 2)

Despite the inclusive language and ambitious intentions, the Declaration was met with some scepticism. Aleinikoff (2017: 26) succinctly summed up some of the concerns:

> [T]he summit yielded no new concrete undertakings, no new goals (compare the recently adopted Sustainable Development Goals and the outcome from the Paris Climate Change Agreement), no new sources of

43 Ibid.

44 The CRRF is contained in Annex 1 to the New York Declaration for Refugees and Migrants 2016.

> funding for international organizations, NGOs, and hosting states, and no plans for transformation of international organizations and structures that have been unable to adequately respond to large-scale flows of human beings across borders.

Between 2016 and 2018, however, the CRRF was rolled out across various locations and, in 2018, the Global Compact on Refugees was agreed. Volker Türk, then UNHCR Assistant High Commissioner for Protection promoted the Compact in the following terms:

> The Compact aims to ease the pressures on host countries by strengthening the resilience of refugees and their host communities, particularly through greater development cooperation. It further promotes responsibility sharing with host countries by focusing on solutions, both in expanding opportunities for resettlement and other solutions in third countries, and in fostering the necessary conditions for refugees to return to their home countries in safety and dignity.
>
> (Türk, 2018: 577)

Türk sees the complementarity between humanitarian and development actors, and the roles of the World Bank and private sector, as crucial to achieving the Compact's objectives. Nonetheless, as with the Declaration, the Compact has been heavily critiqued with numerous articles and commentaries describing its failings and the opportunities missed. Hathaway, for one, does not mince his words when he describes it as:

> a shameful sop that doesn't eliminate barriers to access; doesn't dependably get refugees to a place of protection; doesn't ensure dignified and empowering protection for the duration of risk; doesn't require meaningful burden and responsibility sharing; and doesn't guarantee solutions either for refugees or for their host communities.
>
> (Hathaway, 2018: 603–4)

Concluding thoughts

Large-scale refugee movements have once again thrown states into confusion. The careful construction of a refugee law regime, based upon the commitment of states to basic principles of protection and international cooperation, seems unable to withstand the winds of self-interest, fear and xenophobia. Those states capable of accepting many more refugees, such as in the EU, the USA and Australia, are largely unwilling, due mainly to anti-immigration policies and rhetoric that have been prevalent since the 1980s, the exploitation of migration for political ends, increasing association of asylum and migration with terrorism – particularly in the wake of 9/11 – rising populism and nationalism, and a current backlash against neoliberal globalisation.[45] Those already host to thousands, if not millions, are becoming weary and disgruntled. Few are willing to offer a durable solution that involves long-term residency. The term 'refugee' has become tainted by association with powerlessness and victimhood.

In a recent contribution, Chimni argues:

> There is an urgent need to deal with real-world issues that are central to shaping a just response to the global refugee problem. These include the crises in global capitalism, hyper-nationalism, xenophobia, the antagonistic relations of capitalism with nature, the growing reserve army of labour, internal conflicts (both developmental and non-developmental), hegemonic interventions, competitive diplomacy, a cynical approach to international legal obligations, and Islamophobia. The Refugee Compact clearly bears the stamp of a text to which scholars and researchers of the global South appear to have contributed little.
>
> (Chimni, 2018: 633–4)

This intervention goes to the heart of many of the current problems. For the majority of the forcibly displaced, there is a move away from protection through law and rights towards humanitarianism and a concept of development that is increasingly promoted by the World Bank. The Bank argues that the best course of action is for humanitarian and development actors to work together, with the humanitarian response first, followed by a development effort (World Bank Group, 2017: 2). It defines the development approach as 'centred on such concepts as economic opportunity, medium-term sustainability, and cost-effectiveness', with the forcibly displaced and their hosts acting as economic agents 'who make choices and respond to incentives' (ibid.). The approach is focused on institutions and policies and is reliant upon partnerships with and between governments, the private sector and civil society (ibid.).

This shift is seen by many as positive by largely removing 'the damaging humanitarian-development divide' and perceiving forced displacement crises as 'uniquely humanitarian emergencies' (Zetter, 2015: 16). While a rights-based approach is still regarded as important in institutional circles, in many parts of the world, such as the MENA region, this has not proven particularly successful in improving the lives of the displaced. Faith placed in economic development with SEZs and job creation, lauded by some well-respected academics (Betts and Collier, 2017), has not yet proved the panacea.

If these new initiatives can improve life opportunities – particularly education and work – there may be some hope, but the resort to a neoliberal model of capital finance, loans, product development and improved state access to key markets, as advocated by the EU, is worrying. There is limited evidence that such initiatives will succeed or that the person-centred, ground-up approach

45 With the clear exception of Germany.

advocated at the summits in Istanbul and New York is much more than rhetoric. Chimni notes the silence of scholars of the global south in the development of the Compact; yet, there is arguably a greater silence: the voices of those affected, who are rarely considered despite growing evidence of their role in achieving real change for the individual.[46] Until they are, there will be no meaningful access to justice for refugees and no meaningful solutions for those forced to flee their homes and countries. It is therefore time, at this crucial juncture, that this is adequately acknowledged and addressed by all institutional stakeholders – global, regional and national – and that the major stakeholders, the refugees themselves, are empowered to reshape their own futures.

References

Aleinikoff, T.A., 2017. Toward a global system of human mobility: Three thoughts. Symposium on Framing Global Migration Law (2017). *American Journal of International Law* 111, 24–28.

Aleinikoff, T.A. and Zamore, L., 2019. *The Arc of Protection: Towards a New International Refugee Regime*. Stanford Briefs.

Alleweldt, R., 2011. Preamble to the 1951 Convention. In Zimmermann, A. ed. *The 1951 Convention relating to the Status of Refugees and its 1967 Protocol–A Commentary*. Oxford University Press.

Al-Mahaidi, A., 2020. Securing economic livelihoods for Syrian refugees: the case for a human rights-based approach to the Jordan Compact. *The International Journal of Human Rights*, 1–20: <https://www.tandfonline.com/doi/full/10.1080/13642987.2020.1763314> (accessed 21 June 2020).

Betts, A. and Collier, P., 2017. *Refuge – Transforming a Broken Refugee System*. Penguin Books, Allen Lane.

Buxton, R., 2019. Reparative justice for climate refugees. *Philosophy* 94 (2), 193.

Chimni, B.S., 2018. Global Compact on Refugees: One step forward, two steps back. *International Journal of Refugee Law* 30 (4), 630–634.

Crawley, H., 2017. Refugee Economics. *Nature* 544, 26–27.

Easton-Calabria, E., 2016. Refugee-run organisations as partners in development. *Forced Migration Review*, 52, 72–74.

Fitzgerald, D.S., 2019. *Refuge Beyond Reach: How Rich Democracies Repel Asylum Seekers*. Oxford University Press.

Gammeltoft-Hansen, T., 2011. *Access to Asylum: International Refugee Law and the Globalisation of Migration Control*. CUP.

Giannacopoulos, M. and Loughnan, C., 2020. 'Closure' at Manus Island and carceral expansion in the open air prison. *Globalizations* 17 (7), 1118–1135.

Gil-Bazo, M., 2008. The Charter of Fundamental Rights of the European Union and the right to be granted asylum in the Union's law. *Refugee Survey Quarterly* 27 (3), 33–52.

46 See for example, Easton-Calabria, 2016. See also the work of the Refugee Studies Centre, based at the University of Oxford, in its Humanitarian Innovation Project and especially 'bottom-up innovation': <https://www.oxhip.org/2015/7/refugeeinnovation/> accessed 7 February 2020.

Gonzalez, C.G., 2018–19. Climate justice and climate displacement: Evaluating the emerging legal and policy responses. *Wisconsin International Law Journal* 36, 366.

Goodwin-Gill, G.S., 2016. *The Challenges to International Refugee Law in the Current Crisis.* The Single Protection Procedure: Meeting International Obligations. Conference, 3 March 2016. Dublin.

Guild, E., 2016. Does the EU Need a European Migration and Protection Agency? *International Journal of Refugee Law* 28 (4), 585.

Hathaway, J.C., 2005. *The Rights of Refugees under International Law.* Cambridge University Press.

Hathaway, J.C., 2018. The global cop-out on refugees. *International Journal of Refugee Law* 30 (4), 591–604.

IRC. 2017. *In search of work – Creating jobs for Syrian Refugees: A Case study of the Jordan Compact.* February. https://www.rescue.org/report/search-work-creating-jobs-syrian-refugees.

Kagan, M., 2011. 'We live in a country of UNHCR' – The UN surrogate state and refugee policy in the Middle East. UNHCR New Issues in Refugee Research, Research paper No 201.

Kneebone, S., Stevens, D. and Baldassar, L. eds. 2014. *Refugee Protection and the Role of Law: Conflicting Identities.* Routledge.

Lauterpacht, H., 1948. The Universal Declaration of Human Rights. *British Yearbook of International LaMEDMIGw* 25, 354–381.

MEDMIG. 2016. November. Report. Destination Europe – Understanding the dynamics and drivers of Mediterranean migration in 2015: www.medmig.info/wp-content/uploads/2016/12/research-brief-destination-europe.pdf (accessed 9 June 2020).

Moreno-Lax, V., 2017. *Solidarity as a legal obligation and its role in international refugee law.* Beyond Crisis: Rethinking Refugee Studies, RSC ConferenceMarch. Oxford.

Noll, G., 2016. Failure by design? On the constitution of EU solidarity. In *Searching for solidarity in EY asylum and border policies, A Collection of Short Papers following the Odysseus Network's First Annual Policy Conference, Université libre de Bruxelles*, Brussels: <odysseus-network.eu/wp-content/uploads/2015/09/Searching-for-Solidarity-Short-Papers.pdf> (accessed 9 June 2020).

O'Sullivan, M. and Stevens, D. 2017. Access to refugee protection: Key concepts and contemporary challenges. In O'Sullivan, M. and Stevens, D., eds., *States, the Law and Access to Refugee Protection: Fortress and Fairness.* Hart.

Pascucci, E., 2017. Refuge: Transforming a broken refugee system. *Fennia* 195 (2), 197–201.

Price, M., 2009. *Rethinking Asylum – History, Purpose and Limits.* Cambridge University Press.

Squire, V., Dimitriadi, A., Perkowski, N., Pisani, M., Stevens, D. and Vaughan-Williams, N. 2017. *Crossing the Mediterranean Sea by Boat: Mapping and Documenting Migratory Journeys and Experiences*, Final Project Report: <www2.warwick.ac.uk/fac/soc/pais/research/researchcentres/irs/crossingthemed/ctm_final_report_4may2017.pdf> (accessed 9 June 2020).

Stevens, D., 2013. What do we mean by "protection"? Special Issue: Critical Issues in Refugee Law. *International Journal of Minority and Group Rights* 20(1), 233–262.

Stevens, D., 2016. Rights, needs or assistance? The role of the UNHCR in refugee protection in the Middle East. Special Issue: The strengths and weaknesses of regional protection frameworks for refugees. *International Journal of Human Rights* 20(2), 264–283.

Stevens, D. and Dimitriadi, A., 2018. Crossing the Eastern Mediterranean Sea in search of protection. *Journal of Immigrant and Refugee Studies*, 1–18.

Storey, H., 2016. The meaning of "protection" within the refugee definition. *Refugee Survey Quarterly* 35(3), 1–34.

Türk, V., 2018. The promise and the potential of the Global Compact on Refugees. *International Journal of Refugee Law* 30(4), 575–583.

UNGA. 1998. Executive Committee of the High Commissioner's Programme, Forty-Ninth Session, Annual Theme International Solidarity and Burden-Sharing in All Its Aspects: National, Regional and International Responsibilities for Refugees, A/AC.96/904. 7 September.

UNGA. 2015. Resolution adopted by the GA on 25 September 2015, 70/1. Transforming Our World: the 2030 Agenda for Sustainable Development, A/RES/70/1. 21 October.

UNGA. 2016a. *One Humanity: Shared Responsibility*, Report of the Secretary-General for the World Humanitarian Summit, A/70/709. 2 February.

UNGA. 2016b. Resolution adopted by the GA on 19 September 2016, 71/1. New York Declaration for Refugees and Migrants, A/RES/71/1. 3 October.

UNGA. 2018. *Report of the United Nations High Commissioner for Refugee*, Part II, Global Compact on Refugees, A/73/121 (Part 2), New York. 17 December.

UNHCR. 1981. ExCom Conclusion on Protection of Asylum-Seekers in Situations of Large-Scale No. 22 (XXXII). October.

UNHCR. 2011a. Discussion Paper: International Cooperation to Share Burden and Responsibilities. Expert Meeting, Amman, Jordan. 27 and 28 June.

UNHCR. 2011b. Concept Note: Expert Meeting on International Cooperation to Share Burden and Responsibilities. 27 and 28 June. <www.unhcr.org/4df871013c.pdf> (accessed 9 June 2020).

UNHCR. 2017. Global Trends: Forced Displacement in 2016. 19 June.

UNHCR. 2018. From Commitment to Action: Highlights of Progress towards Comprehensive Refugee Responses since the Adoption of the New York Declaration. August < www.unhcr.org/5ba109ca2d> (accessed 9 June 2020).

UNHCR. 2019. Global Trends: Forced Displacement in 2018. 20 June.

UNHCR. n.d.a. Syria Regional Refugee Response, Inter-agency Information Sharing Portal. <data.unhcr.org/syrianrefugees/country.php?id=122≥ (accessed 9 June 2020).

UNHCR. n.d.b. Statistics <popstats.unhcr.org/en/asylum_seekers≥ (accessed 9 June 2020).

UNICEF/UNHCR/WFP. 2020. Vulnerability Assessment of Syria Refugees in Lebanon, 2019. 17 March <https://data2.unhcr.org/en/documents/download/73118> (accessed 21 June 2020).

Velluti, S., 2013. *Reforming the Common European Asylum System – Legislative developments and Judicial Activism of the European Courts*. Springer.

World Bank Group. 2017. *Forcibly Displaced: Toward a Development Approach Supporting Refugees, the Internally Displaced, and their Hosts*. <openknowledge.worldbank.org/bitstream/handle/10986/25016/9781464809385.pdf?sequence=11&isAllowed=y> (accessed 9 June 2020). World Bank.

Zetter, R., 2015. *Protection in Crisis: Forced Migration and Protection in a Global Era*. Migration Policy Institute.

Zimmermann, A. ed. 2011. *The 1951 Convention Relating to the Status of Refugees and its 1967 Protocol – A Commentary*. Oxford University Press.

Chapter 11

Islamic Law, Social Justice and Injustices

The Case for Islamic Welfare Systems

Shaheen Sardar Ali and Faqir Asfundyar Yousaf

> And those in whose wealth is a recognized right for (the needy) who asks and him who is prevented (for some reason) from asking.
>
> (The Qur'an, Verse 70:24–25)[1]

Introduction

This chapter investigates new and evolving elements of Islamic legal traditions as discursive and contested spaces focusing on the social justice and welfare arm of Islamic finance. Drawing upon Frederic Charles Schaffer's (2016) process of 'elucidation', we adopt a three-stage analysis, of some key concepts within Islamic legal traditions that have a bearing on law and social justice. These include Islamic law, Islamic state, Islamic finance, *riba, zakat, sadaqa,* and *qard hasan.* [2] Beginning with a process of 'grounding' – i.e., how people create and understand concepts, we proceed to 'locate' them in their specific historical and linguistic contexts. Finally, we propose to 'expose' these concepts in order to understand how these shifts are employed as tools of power through individual, state and societal interventions.

This enquiry has wider implications beyond an exploration of how we understand the evolution of historic and new concepts in Islamic law and their relationship to social justice and injustices. It attempts to include voices from various Muslim constituencies, other than those traditionally holding the reins of knowledge, to highlight how these heretofore passive voices are changing the way in which Islamic socio-legal knowledge is developing. 'New intellectuals' as Carool Kersten (2011) describes them, have changed the landscape of Islamic knowledge since the twentieth century. The mosque and state as

1 Translations of the Holy Qur'an are, unless otherwise stated, from Yousuf Ali (1990).

2 It is important to bear in mind that 'Islamic law', 'Islamic state' and 'Islamic finance' are 'new' and emerging concepts in the twentieth century whereas *riba, zakat, sadaqa* and *qard hasan* are terms that have existed for fourteen centuries and some even prior to Islam.

DOI: 10.4324/9780203745298-14

repositories of authentic and legitimate ('Islamic') knowledge are being consistently challenged and an increasingly literate, lay Muslim population is appropriating this space. Peter Mandaville suggests that there is:

> [A] trend in the Muslim world towards a greater critical awareness of religion. Muslims are increasingly willing to take Islam into their own hands, relying on their own readings and interpretations of the classical sources or following 'reformist' intellectuals who question traditional dogmas and challenge the claims of the ulama to be privileged sources of religious knowledge.
>
> (Mandaville, 2001: 178)

This chapter therefore attempts to shed light on how contemporary Muslim communities in all their plural articulations 'live' these concepts – in resisting both western and colonial hegemonic articulations of Islamic knowledge as well as the religious and secular 'establishment' (elites and government) within Muslim jurisdictions. It raises a number of questions: What was/is the perception and impact of Qur'anic verses on social and distributive justice (through *zakat, sadaqa* and *qard hasan*) in Muslim communities and the formal legal systems of the Muslim world? Are religious 'rights' of the needy and vulnerable limited to ethical responses in state and society? To what extent do new and evolving Islamic concepts provide alternative conceptualization of social justice by formalizing the rights of the vulnerable and needy for example through state-enforced *zakat* and fund raising by non-governmental organizations? Do they constitute new 'synthetic' constructs of time, place and socio-political exigencies of post-colonial Muslim polities on the one hand and globalized, transnational 'travelling' Islam on the other? Finally, how do the 'lived' Islamic practices of Muslim individuals and communities impact on their academic and theoretical meanings and *vice versa*?

We advance the argument that new and evolving Islamic concepts are part of plural reactive (and to some extent, proactive), socio-economic, political and historical processes. Therefore, on the one hand, protagonists of Islamic law, Islamic state, Islamic economics, and Islamic finance, some Muslim scholars, activists and laity as well as a few (Muslim) governmental constituencies aspire to reinstate an idealized Muslim world order through this vocabulary. Simultaneously, and in keeping with a pluralist Islamic tradition, others resort to new perspectives on long-established concepts including *riba, zakat, sadaqa* and *qard hasan* through increased formalization of these concepts. Through a process of 'elucidation' we try to reflect how people 'live' Islam and its concepts by generating new iterations of an established tradition which are lending new meanings to existing terms and concepts.

New and Evolving Islamic Concepts: 'Islamic' Law, 'Islamic' State, 'Islamic' Economics, 'Islamic' Finance

A discourse on social justice and welfare in Islam is framed by key concepts including Islamic law, Islamic state, Islamic economics, and Islamic finance. In spite of the speed with which these twentieth century concepts and terms have gained currency, an impression is put out that these are long established, monolithic, uncontested categories within Muslim communities, states and governments. A close investigation discloses a more complex reality, that is, a rich and varied tapestry of concepts, past and present, draped in old and new meanings including those forming the subject matter of the present enquiry. It is equally important to bear in mind that just as new concepts evolve, old ones may fade away from popular consciousness to be 'revived' at particular historical moments (Hamidullah, 1975; Walker, 2014).[3] Histories of colonization and globalization demonstrate how hegemonic powers appropriated and continue to appropriate these conceptual frameworks, established as well as new, wrapped in meanings beyond the understandings of Muslim communities.[4]

Contemporary English language scholarship inserts the adjective 'Islamic' before 'law', 'state', 'finance' in order to ascribe it to Muslims and Islam.[5] Seeking to 'ground' these terms to ascertain their meanings is linked to locating them in their historical context. This is a challenging enquiry due to lack of exact translations and equivalents in non-western languages understood by the majority of the world's Muslim population. Equally challenging is the question of what 'Islamic' law, state, finance and so on, mean to the English-speaking Muslim and non-Muslim person.

'Islamic' law, state and finance are post-colonial, modern twentieth century phenomena and locating them in their historical meanings would be difficult as the descriptor – 'Islamic' – did not exist in pre-colonial times. To most Muslims, the closest relative of 'Islamic' law would be '*fiqh*' – jurisprudence, as the science of law based upon the Qur'an and *sunna*, and secondary and subsidiary sources of law including *ijma, qiyas, ijtihad* and others. Quite erroneously and in a reductive mode, *Shari'a* and Islamic law have also been understood by some to be synonymous and used inter-changeably – mostly in western discourse on Islam – an unduly limited and limiting synonymity. This may well be due to lack of an exact translation of Sharia into English and other European

3 One such example is that of the Medina Charter or the Constitution of Medina as described by some scholars (Hamidullah, 1975; Walker, 2014). See Wikipedia, *The Constitution of Medina.*https://en.wikipedia.org/wiki/Constitution_of_Medina (accessed 20 August 2020). An important foundational document of state and government and inter-faith peaceful existence, social justice and solidarity, this document, twice as old as the Magna Carta, has faded from Muslim consciousness.

4 For instance, the term 'Anglo-Muhammadan law' is entirely a colonial construct invented to explain a body of 'Anglicised' rules governing family law of Muslims.

5 Even 'terrorism' is 'Islamic' or 'Muslim' and we have heard Muslims described as 'Islamic' persons!

languages. As Ali has elsewhere stated, '*Shari'a* is an all-encompassing framework of life transcending legally enforceable rules and covering moral, ethical, social, political and economic aspects of life' (Ali, 2016: 4). It is more than law as understood in English language literature and an example of how meanings and scope of words become blurred and often lost in translation. Modern day usage of *Shari'a* as Islamic law has implications: since *Shari'a* is informed by the religious text in Islam and believed to be of divine origin by Muslims, therefore by *conflating the two, its English equivalent of Islamic law is elevated to the position of the divine and immutable law*. Furthermore, by accepting Islamic law as akin to statute law, *Shari'a* is stripped of its ethical and moral dimensions; hence the 'front-loading' of the commercial arm of Islamic finance in ignorance of its social justice components.

For anything akin to a state-enforced law, Muslim communities would employ different terminology such as *qanun, farmaan, siyasa shari'a* as laws/regulations prescribed by the ruler – in other words, these descriptions of 'law' are all linked to political power and authority of the ruler and may also be described as state law. In South Asian languages, for instance, when people refer to rules and principles of the religious text in Islam, they are more likely to use the term *sharia't* (Arab-speaking persons would use the term *Shari'a). Islamee qanun* (Urdu) or *qanun al-Islamiya* (Arabic), the exact translation of the English term 'Islamic law', is a misnomer for these persons and communities. *Islamee qanun* for the Muslim layperson means the 'law of Allah and His Prophet' and the 'way of Allah and His Prophet'. The terms employed are *Shari'a, Qur'an* and *Sunna*, and *not* 'Islamic law' as understood in colonial and post-colonial *Shari'a* inspired law adopted by Muslim states (see e.g. Fyzee, 1949).[6] The outcome of this distinction is that moral/ethical injunctions of the Qur'an and Sunna (for instance relating to social justice) fall under *Shari'a* but not under 'Islamic' law – i.e., state enforced laws in Muslim jurisdictions.

Thus 'grounding' and locating of 'Islamic' law highlights the disconnect between what the term denotes in English and how Muslim communities in the non-western world understand it. Islamic law in its colonial and post-colonial variants is a modern phenomenon – at best a hybrid of its classical form and substance. The inevitable outcome of historical, socio-economic and political processes, Islamic law as generally experienced today exemplifies continuities, discontinuities and ruptures. Modernity, globalization and the nation state increasingly interact with religion, diverse cultures and official and unofficial legal orders, resulting in synthetic phenomena such as modern Islamic finance, banking and welfare systems.

Equally 'new' is the twentieth century modern concept described by both Muslim and non-Muslim scholars as an 'Islamic' state within which, so its

6 During the colonial period, other terms for describing 'Islamic law', also gained currency but have since been assigned to the archives of history. 'Muhammadan' law is an example.

proponents argue, Islamic finance and systems of social welfare and justice can reside and flourish (Noori and Amin, 1986). The model informing a so-called 'Islamic' state harks back to the first Muslim state established by the Prophet Muhammad through a foundational document, known as the Medina Charter or the Constitution of Medina (Hamidullah, 1975; Walker, 2014). Despite its reference in some scholarly writings, the Medina Charter is hardly mentioned in state and governmental discourse or among grassroots communities. Nevertheless, Muslim proponents of an 'Islamic' state refer to this document as the ideal to aspire to for implementing social justice and welfare (Tobroni, 2020). Poor economic and political performance of post-colonial Muslim states led to what critical Muslim scholars described as corrupt, western-inspired rulers in the Muslim world; hence the slogan of 'political Islam' to dismantle post-colonial structures and replace them with an 'Islamic state'. Weiss's observation is apt: 'Thus the articulation of present day Islamist writers of the ideal of an Islamic state is used as an analytical tool to study past events as well as providing the means to interpret the present' (Weiss, 2002: 11).

Abul A'la Maududi linked enforcement of *sharia* and social justice to the need for an Islamic state and 'Islamic' democracy wherein ethical injunctions would be translated into legally enforceable rules. In *The Islamic Law and Constitution*, he states that the Qur'an 'not only gives guidance in the political, social and economic fields; it prescribes punishments for certain crimes and enunciates principles of monetary and fiscal policy. These cannot be translated into practice unless there is a State to enforce them' (Maududi, 1969: 158). What Maududi therefore appears to be proposing is the formalization of 'rights' such as *zakat* payment to the poor and needy as categorized in the Qur'an. But is this understanding of *zakat* and rights proposed by Maududi and other Islamists also followed by Muslim populations? If *zakat* is a legally enforced right (as defined in contemporary times), then against whom does it arise and who has the power to enforce it?

Is the establishment of an 'Islamic state' as defined by her proponents a pre-requisite for Islamic finance, *zakat* and social justice? Linked to this is the question whether it is the task of the state (including an Islamic state) to collect *zakat*, in view of the fact that *zakat* is an act of personal worship. In Pakistan, Sudan and other Muslim majority jurisdictions, *Zakat* took centre stage in this discourse and argumentation for ushering in a world 'Islamic' order, albeit with equally robust detractors.

Islamic finance law consists of rules (and institutions) that base their objectives and operations on Islamic law and *sharia*. A variant of Islamic commercial law, Islamic finance law 'is based on certain parts of classical Islamic law concerning commercial transactions' (Foster and Archer, 2012). In popular Muslim consciousness, though, Islamic finance is simply and perhaps only equated with 'interest-free' banking and the prohibition of (i) *riba* (exorbitant or excessive interest, or usury); (ii) *gharar* (uncertainty, risk or speculation); and (iii) *maysir* (gambling and games of chance). In theory, engaging in religiously permissible, non-exploitative, equitable and ethical financial activities forms the cornerstone of Islamic finance; in practice, for many centuries the reality has been otherwise, and the vast majority of the Muslim world has engaged with conventional (interest-based) financial regimes in one form or another.

The grounded experience of various Muslim communities of *riba, gharar* and *maysir* is that whilst all three practices are strictly prohibited in Islamic legal traditions, prohibition of *riba* alone is considered by most Muslims as *the* basis for an Islamic financial regime. It is equally a fact that despite this clear understanding of the prohibition, *riba* has been practised in one form or another throughout the Muslim world.

In attempting to ground and locate *riba* and how Muslim traditions deal with it, we made some enquiries into how this term was understood in various Muslim communities and its links with social justice in Islam.[7] In South Asia and the Middle East, an Islamic financial regime is linked to the absolute, unequivocal prohibition of *riba* whereas in Malaysia and other Southeast Asian countries, emphasis is placed on risk sharing.[8] Both however support social justice by minimizing human exploitation through prohibition of exorbitant interest and high risk ventures. In an increasingly monetized economy where debt is an intrinsic element of most business ventures, contemporary application of the seventh century Arabian notion of *riba* is unrealistic. Consequently, these 'old' concepts appear to have assumed 'new' meanings. A legal professional in Kuwait (interview, May 2017) described the difference between *riba* and interest (in conventional financial and banking regimes):

> One of the main objectives of Islam was to reduce inequalities among people and genders; hence the laws of inheritance and *zakat*. Simultaneously, Islam tried to bring about social justice by enjoining solidarity, one example of which is the *qard hasan* – benevolent loan. A deep reading of the Qur'an and the Sunna make it adequately clear that advancing a loan to a person in financial crisis is considered a charitable act in itself but even more so if the debtor is unable to return the money at the stipulated time and the creditor 'gifts' the debt. *Qard hasan*'s ultimate 'goodness' therefore, would be to 'donate' it to the debtor; that is a way of expressing solidarity with those in need. *Riba* is that compound interest which a creditor demands of a debtor when they are unable to repay at the agreed time due to inability to pay. Taking undue advantage of the vulnerability of the debtor is prohibited in Islam.

7 The research involved a series of interviews and focus group discussions with a variety of participants especially in Kuwait and Pakistan.

8 I am grateful to Dr Lena Rethal for alerting me to this.

Another legal professional in Kuwait reported that:

> In contemporary times, the [prohibition of *riba*] is extended to commercial loans taken from banks or other sources to raise capital for business. Prohibition of *riba* is then equated with interest charged on [commercial] loans ... But it is also understandable why interest on commercial loans is classed as *riba*. After all, the entire risk is taken by the borrower and the bank simply earns idle money as interest. This is where the social justice aspect of Islamic finance ought to play a proactive part in resolving this dilemma.
>
> (interview, May 2017)

The paradox of prohibition of interest on loans as clear and unequivocal and its simultaneous practice in Muslim communities is one that we tried to 'ground' and 'locate'. For example, in Pakistan, an interviewee explained:

> Yes, interest on loans is completely prohibited in Islam – who does not know that? But, *sood* (interest) was always a part of the economy in Muslim communities. Not necessarily by choice but by force of circumstances. Most people had no running regular income; neither did they have bank accounts or access to means of funding. So, in the community there were people with money who lent money on interest and others who desperately needed liquid cash. It was and is simply a matter of supply and demand. Unfortunately, people in their greed or in their need forgot about the ethics of borrowing and lending. I can understand people wanting profit on money lent for business and profit-making ventures. But if a person is desperate for some cash due to a medical emergency or such matter, then as Muslims, we ought to extend money to them without expecting a return ... however ... this is the ideal and not the reality.[9]

Alternative Regimes for Social Justice? *Zakat, Sadaqa* and *Qard Hasan*

Classical Islamic finance has two arms: first, there is the 'profit-and-loss-sharing' paradigm, where lender *and* borrower share the risk of making or losing money, rather than the lender alone being guaranteed a fixed, pre-determined return. Islamic finance, being equity-based, treats the financier and entrepreneur as joint partners, co-joined in risk-taking and profit-sharing. Capital is unsecured, unguaranteed, not entitled to predetermined or fixed interest, and may appreciate or depreciate depending on the market. This understanding of Islamic finance is all but erased by Muslims who have been using the

9 Comment during discussions with Muslim community members in Pakistan in spring 2016.

conventional, capitalist, exploitative regime for centuries. Those in positions of economic strength are able to *not* take risks when lending and to dictate terms that include exorbitant interest rates. Those who have no choice, play along with this regime, leading to the underdevelopment of social justice-based Islamic finance.

Second, there is the entrenched requirement of promoting social justice through mandatory almsgiving (*zakat*), voluntary almsgiving (*sadaqa*), and 'benevolent loans' (*qard hasan*). In a debt-based contemporary economy, how are new and changing epistemologies emerging to displace previous/existing ones and what is their impact on how Muslims, individually and collectively, understand and apply them to their lives and work? For example, how did the term *riba* come to acquire the meaning/s it has over centuries and how is it side-stepped in the modern economic and financial circles of Islamic finance? Of the two arms of Islamic finance, the commercial and profitable has attracted closer attention than the charitable. This section looks at the main concepts and institutions of this charitable arm and its potential as a vehicle for social justice.[10]

Classical Islamic finance theoretically extends equal credence to its profitable and charitable arms and thus to a human-friendly response in comparison with capitalist financial regimes. In practice, however, contemporary Islamic finance has prioritized the profitable over its charitable arm, largely ignoring the moral economy that was an integral component of its classical antecedent. Furthermore, contemporary Islamic finance law is a law operating without a fully supporting legal system, transposed as it is, on the western financial regime. The emergent picture is one that combines Islamic *form* with Western *substance*, and appears to mimic it.

Zakat as Obligatory Payments to the Needy

Almsgiving (in the form of *zakat*), one of the five pillars of the Islamic faith, is a fundamental principle of Islam and Islamic finance. A core principle of Islam is to achieve purification, and this is embedded within the core meaning of *zakat* which originates from its literal meaning: to 'grow' (in goodness) and become 'pure'.[11] By giving *zakat*, Muslims shed impurities of their wealth by sharing it with those who are unable to sustain themselves and their families. In addition to its other benefits, it has as objectives the circulation of resources, monetary and otherwise, and the lessening of the gap between rich and poor for 'social

10 *Wakf* is another institution for advancing social justice: it is the '[permanent] transfer of a corpus of valuable property to ownership of God with declaration of dedicating its usufruct perpetually for religious, charitable or pious purposes as recognized by Shariah' (Mannan, 1995: 270). Discussion of *wakf* is not included due to limitations of space.

11 See Institute of Islamic Banking and Insurance Website: 'What is Islamic Banking?' (https://islamic-banking.com/explore/islamic-finance/islamic-banking#What%20is%20Islamic%20Banking?) (accessed 23 March 2021).

benefit' or 'public welfare' (*al-maslaha al-ijtima'yya* and *al-maslaha al-'amma*). It has been called 'a key component of the moral economy' (Latief, 2012: 310). Every Muslim is obliged to pay two types of *zakat. Zakat al-fitr* is given to the poor during Ramadan. Under *zakat al-amwal*, Muslims whose wealth reaches a minimum level are generally obliged to pay a small percentage, the rate varying depending upon the type of wealth.[12]

Zakat (and/or its equivalent and similar concepts, *sadaqa*, charity) is mentioned at least fifty-seven times in the Qur'an. Of this, in thirty-two instances, it is coupled with the injunction to offer *salat* (prayer). In verse 73:20 of the Qur'an, the word *zakat* appears thus:

> So recite what is easy from it and establish prayer and give *zakat* and loan Allah a goodly loan. And whatever good you put forward for yourselves – you will find it with Allah. It is better and greater in reward. And seek forgiveness of Allah. Indeed, Allah is Forgiving and Merciful.[13]

In some verses of the Qur'an, *zakat* and *sadaqa* are used interchangeably to refer to a general charitable obligation. and this limited guidance leaves it open to varying interpretation (Asad, 1981). Categories of beneficiaries set out in Verse 9:60 can be interpreted differently:

> Alms are for the poor and the needy, and those employed to administer the (funds); for those whose hearts have been (recently) reconciled (to Truth); for those in bondage and in debt; in the cause of Allah; and for the wayfarer: (thus is it) ordained by Allah and Allah is full of knowledge and wisdom.

Another translation of verse 9:60 runs thus:

> *Zakat* is only for the poor and needy, and those employed to administer it, and those whose hearts are made to incline to truth, and to free captives, and those in debt, and in the way of Allah and for the wayfarer – an ordinance from Allah. And Allah is knowing, wise.[14]

The Qur'an does not elaborate on how *zakat* ought to be administered, leaving it to Muslim communities to develop parameters for collection and disbursement. Issues arose quite early as a result of this ambiguity, including whether *zakat* ought to be institutionalized or remain personal; and whether the state

12 Generally, 2.5 per cent. Farmers may be levied 5–10 per cent of their harvest depending on the type of irrigation. Wealth originating from buried treasure too, can be taxed, at up to 20 per cent.

13 Translation by Yousuf Ali (1990).

14 Translation by Muhammad Ali (2013).

ought to collect *zakat* and, if so, centrally or otherwise. But most important is the question whether Muslims are obliged to pay it voluntarily or as an obligatory and legally enforceable tax to a state agency (Salim, 2008a: 116; Latief, 2012: ch. 5).

Timur Kuran, recalling the Golden Age of Islam (the era of the four Rightly Guided Caliphs), observes that during the time of the Prophet Muhammad as well as for some of the period of the Golden Age, 'the state did indeed enforce the collection of *zakat*, and a substantial portion of the proceeds must have accrued to various disadvantaged groups. We possess no reliable evidence, however, on whether this redistribution brought about a major reduction in inequality' (Kuran, 2004: 4). However, in discussions on the subject in various Muslim jurisdictions, the oft-repeated anecdote of the Golden Age was brought to my attention thus: 'In the era of the Rightly-Guided Caliphs, a time came when the *bait-ul-maal* (state treasury) had ample resources as Muslims paid in *zakat* into it but there was no one to receive it.' This statement was cited as an indicator of well-being and lack of impoverishment among the early Muslim communities of Makkah and Medina. In a similar vein, a Saudi newspaper claimed that if rich citizens paid their *zakat* regularly, 'there would not be a single poor family in the kingdom.'[15] Thus the meaning and connotation of *zakat* carries an idealistic imaginary of a world free from want and inequality.

The practice of *zakat* in Muslim jurisdictions is far from uniform, most likely a result of the multifaceted functions – spiritual, political and economic – that *zakat* is meant to perform: it is a personal act of worship to purify one's soul and one's wealth, a means of state revenue-raising, and a way of reducing poverty and inequality (Salim, 2008a: 116). *Zakat*, in addition to its spiritual value, acted as support for 'certain socioeconomic and sociopolitical structures necessary in early Islam' (ibid.). As in other areas of the Islamic legal traditions, the four main juristic schools are not always in agreement in determining the type of wealth subject to *zakat*, who should pay and receive *zakat*, and the types of mechanism for *zakat* distribution. Brought up as a Hanafi Sunni in the South Asian understanding of *zakat*, the first-named author was surprised to learn that there was more than one interpretation relating to this act of worship: a Sudanese student explained how only that part of her jewelry which was not worn throughout the year for which *zakat* was due was subject to *zakat*. My South Asian version dictated that every item of jewelry must be subject to *zakat*, whether worn or not. The varied interpretations of *zakat* highlight the importance of appreciating the impact of location and context on how these concepts are susceptible to evolution and change.

Today, *zakat* ranges from complete state incorporation as a regular tax (Saudi Arabia, Libya, Yemen, Malaysia, Pakistan, Sudan),[16] to institutions receiving

15 'The Rich Fail to Pay Zakat, Scholars Claim', Global Islamic Finance (www.global-islamic-finance.com) (accessed 15 March 2021).

16 Sudan, Yemen and Pakistan include implementation of *zakat* as a state function in their constitutions.

voluntary payments (Jordan, Egypt, Bahrain, Kuwait), to an act of private conscience and personal piety (Morocco, Oman) (Salim, 2008a: 117). Indonesia, the country with the largest Muslim population in the world today, has also joined the ranks of Muslim states where *zakat* has been incorporated as a regular tax. The various regional and provincial governments have enacted regulations where mandatory *zakat* of 2.5 per cent is deducted from the salary of civil servants (Buehler, 2008: 260–2).

Of state-led *zakat*, Pakistan's example has attracted the closest attention, not least due to the ambitious Islamization agenda of General Zia. In 1980, the first Zakat and Ushr Ordinance set out structure, collection and disbursement mechanisms for *zakat*. The Ministries and Departments of Religious Affairs undertaking this task are now called Department of Religious Affairs, Zakat and Ushr. While Pakistan was perceived as a pioneer in instituting Islamic finance, including a structured system of implementing *zakat*, it cannot be described as a success story for others to emulate. Pitfalls of the system were many, leading one to agree with An-Na'im and others who argue that religion cannot be 'enforced' by state institutions and must remain within the private domain (see generally An-Na'im, 2008; Ali, 2016). While the state may, and ought to, facilitate respectful and tolerant practice of religion and belief, it is not her function to impose and Islamize people's personal practice. There is no evidence that state-implemented *zakat* collection has had any salutary effect on improving the economic situation of millions of Pakistanis living below the poverty line.[17]

A number of social, religious, economic and political problems emerged in the wake of state involvement in *zakat* administration (Salim, 2008a: 118–19). By incorporating *zakat* into state structures, an 'official' Islam was established, privileging a particular understanding advanced by one juristic school to the exclusion of others. After fierce opposition from Shi'a Pakistanis, whose understanding of *zakat* did not allow for state intervention, in 1981 the Zakat and Ushr Ordinance was amended, granting Shi'a Muslims exemption from state-collected *zakat*. In an atmosphere of contestation, conservative Sunni *ulema* were indignant that Sunni would convert to Shi'a to avoid paying *zakat*. Also, the formalization of *zakat* led to many people taking advantage of exemption clauses. After much ambivalence, the government of Pakistan took a step back by declaring that any Muslim account holder could seek exemption by filing a declaration to the effect that they would pay *zakat* directly to beneficiaries.

The institutionalization of *zakat* in Pakistan has led to a resistance to paying it into government hands. Practices on the ground are disparate and far from homogeneous. From decades of personal experience, the first-named author would say that most *zakat* payers prefer to give directly to the beneficiaries. Yet

17 In fact, it is feared that the number of those living below the poverty line has increased over the past decades (UNDP, 2017).

even here there is great variation depending upon individual preferences and ideas as to what *zakat* is meant to achieve. A few striking examples from the Swat Valley will make the point. Mr. A believed in converting *zakat* beneficiaries to *zakat* payers, and each year would hand one or two families a significant capital sum to set up a business or similar venture. A year later he would assess the situation and, if required, again give *zakat*. By year three most would be breaking even or in profit and in no further need of charity. Mr. B, by contrast, announced his '*zakat* payment day' in mosques and in the community, and people would line up to receive one rupee's *zakat* each. This was barely enough to buy a family a meal, yet Mr B felt he was doing good work by handing out *zakat* to hundreds of people rather than just a few. Mr. C however believed that by using his *zakat* to pay for the education of children who could not afford it (fee, books, clothes etc.), long-term benefits would result with more persons becoming capable of earning their keep and perhaps even becoming *zakat* givers rather than receivers.

There is thus a variety of narratives regarding *zakat* payments. For instance, some of our personal friends and family believe in supporting projects of *zakat*-deserving individuals and families such as repairing their dilapidated roof or paying school/college fees for their children. A reality underlying these modes of dispensing *zakat* is the personal relationship or link between the *zakat* giver and *zakat* receiver.

Such variation, of course, continues, but new practices have set in too. Trusted organizations such as the Eidhi Foundation, Muslim Aid, Islamic Relief and Muslim Hands are now recipients of *zakat* from professionals and communities in Pakistan and overseas; development and humanitarian agencies are now receiving *zakat*, lending some formality to what has historically been considered personal worship and private piety (see Latief, 2012; Salim, 2008b: 1–5).[18] Scholars, activists, Muslim charitable institutions as well as states and governments have joined in the discourse of *zakat* and social justice in Islam. Muslim societies are reshaping the institutions of *zakat* to make it a more effective tool for social justice and development in the modern world. Its aim is to explore the use of *zakat* to fund development programmes that have a lasting impact on poverty and social inequality, as opposed to short-term consumption. Bremer advances the view that *zakat*, an important tool for social justice in Islam, is 'undergoing a period of innovation and critical examination … It is an attempt to make the transition from idealized religious and historical models into operational institutions that can meet the very real challenges of the present' (Bremer, 2013).

18 A similar trend is reported from Indonesia. See Latief (2012). Salim (2008a) depicts a clear shift in *zakat* practice among Indonesians, from merely 'a [form of] financial worship' representing religious piety to becoming part of the Indonesian socio-political/economic system. The efforts of *zakat* agencies to incorporate the state's role in optimizing *zakat* collection, for example, by issuing *zakat* laws and urging Muslims to channel their *zakat* funds to officially recognized *zakat* agencies, have characterized this structural shift.

Zakat as a pillar of the Islamic faith and one of the five mandatory forms of *ibadat* (worship) does not appear to have changed in any significant way over the centuries. It was and remains an act of personal worship with some evidence that it has been at times collected by state officials as mandatory payments to the national exchequer. However, this was the exception and not the norm and Muslim communities have resisted moves towards formalization of this act of personal worship. It is also a fact that in maintaining informal dispensation of *zakat* monies, Muslims have mostly paid out to persons who they personally believe qualify for these funds. It is also not unknown that wealthy, *zakat* paying individuals employ these funds for personal social and political enhancement.[19]

Qard Hasan: The Charitable Loan

> If the debtor is in a difficulty, grant him time until it is easy for him to repay. But if ye remit it by way of charity, that is best for you if ye only knew.
>
> (Qur'an 2:280)

The basic proposition of verse 2:280 is that if the debtor finds it difficult to return the loan amount to the creditor, then the latter should either afford him further time to repay, or forego the loan amount in favour of the debtor as charity (*sadaqa*). This verse shows the tilt of the Qur'an towards a financial system that is primarily equity-based rather than debt-based. The verse prohibiting *riba* also indicates that whereas trade is permitted and encouraged, *riba* is prohibited. It is an exhortation to the creditor to let go of his or her legal rights to the capital lent if the debtor finds it difficult to return the capital amount. It is also instructive that the discussion on interest finds itself 'sandwiched' between discussions on charity and discussions on loans in the Qur'an. Verse 2:276 of the Qur'an is an instance:

> Allah will deprive usury of all blessing, but will give increase for all deeds of charity: for He loveth not creatures ungrateful and wicked.

It also indicates that achieving the tilt towards a debt-free society would slowly but perhaps surely pave the way towards a society based on charitable or equitable modes of financing. Thus, interest, which sprouts from a debt-based mode of financing, ceases to be a discursive focus. This charitable perspective is also part of Islam's commitment to social justice: 'the attitude of Islamic financial institutions is that they should forsake some of their profits by, for instance, extending a *qard hasan* to help the distressed borrower' (Professor Rodney Wilson, as cited by Warde, 2010: 148). Despite its express affirmation in the Qur'an and the potential for empowering entire communities, this element of

19 It is not unknown for political families to utilize their *zakat* funds to cement their vote bank by publicly distributing it within their constituencies.

Islamic finance is practised only to a very limited extent in Muslim countries (Abdul Gafoor, 1995; Wright, 1995); its implementation by Islamic banks, too, is not uniform, with some, for example, requiring service charges to be paid and others not.[20]

In classical jurisprudence, the only 'acceptable' loan is the *qard hasan*, [21] as it does not involve interest on the principal. A *qard* should be repaid with goods of an identical description rather than with the very same goods originally borrowed. There is, as we might expect, contestation: Hanafis take the view that, where identical goods cannot be repaid, then their value at the time they were loaned is to be repaid; Hanbalis adopt the position that the value of the goods as of the date they became unavailable is to be repaid.

Although *qard hasan* forms an important nominal pillar of Islamic finance, its impact on the lives of needy individuals and communities is minimal. To begin with, the capital available to Islamic financial institutions is a very small fraction of the entire sector's capital, both nationally and internationally. From this small fraction, that dedicated to *qard hasan* is even smaller. Second, lacking stringent mechanisms for identifying and monitoring deserving cases (for example, a student needing a college registration fee, a farmer needing farm implements, or a villager needing to repair a damaged roof), projects aimed at empowering the poor have been misused. Pakistan's government-sponsored Yellow Cab Scheme of the 1990s, which provided *qard hasan* loans to the unemployed to buy cars to use as taxis, is a case in point.[22] A great many undeserving persons had used their connections to obtain these *qard hasan* loans and few borrowers returned the loan. Thus, repaid capital was not available to re-loan, consequently the scheme was discontinued.

Concluding Observations

This chapter attempted to investigate new and emerging Islamic concepts through an interpretivist lens by employing a three-stage process. First, grounding a concept; second, locating it in its historical context, and finally 'exposing' the politics behind changing meanings of concepts, especially where 'official' and 'legitimate' meanings are assigned to serve elitist interests. Equally important is the challenge mounted against such hegemonic approaches by an increasingly literate and interested lay Muslim population who express their own understandings of these concepts.

20 *Qard hasan* is the basis for a few Islamic microfinance schemes, such as Amanah Ikhtiar Malaysia (which charges a service fee for training, advice, etc.). Islamic Relief has also extended some *qard hasan* loans.

21 The term is spelt variously in different jurisdictions with different languages and dialects. In Iran, it is known as *qard al-hasanah*, in Malaysia *al-qardhul hasan*, in Pakistan *qarz-e-hasana*, Bangladesh *qard-e-hasan* and in Jordan *al-qird-al-hasan* (Timm, 1995).

22 Anwer Sumra, Yellow Cab Scheme: Delivery of only 400 of 5,000 taxis finalised. *The Express Tribune*, 11 December 2011 (tribune.com.pk).

In answering the question posed in this chapter – have new Islamic concepts provided an alternative vocabulary reflecting both the ethical norms of Islamic traditions as well as the Muslim populations? – some observations come to mind. Foremost in these reflections is the reality that various Muslim constituencies are appropriating these to stake claims to a 'pure', 'pristine' and 'authentic' Islamic tradition. Whereas previously rulers and scholars laid claim to religious knowledge and its implementation, the lay population today presents a robust and vocal claim to Islamic knowledge and its application. The lay population define *zakat* as a tool for social justice, but through neither state institutions nor non-governmental organizations which advance a more formalized impersonal application of *zakat* and *sadaqa*. The adherents of each perspective ground and locate their assertions in Muslim histories.

Similarly, 'new' concepts such as Islamic law, Islamic state, Islamic finance have been appropriated and assigned new meanings to reflect socio-economic and political projects of Muslim communities, states and governments. Scholars including Maududi have ascribed their own specific meanings to these concepts, as have their political followers. The government of Iran uses 'Islamic' liberally to describe every aspect of her state and government including finance. Saudi Arabia, on the other hand, desists from using the term 'Islamic law' as, in their view, this denotes secular law, and therefore uses the term '*nizam*' to distinguish it from *Shari'a* (religiously inspired law). Similarly, they do not use 'Islamic' finance to describe financial regimes informed by the Islamic legal traditions. Both states describe themselves as bastions of Islam – one of Shi'a and the other of Sunni Islam with little common ground regarding what constitutes 'Islamic'!

A further and not a very pleasing observation has to be made here: Has the Islamic finance market demonstrated that by ignoring the welfare arm of Islamic finance, it is only doing what some Muslims are thinking and doing – i.e., paying lip service to Islamic financial ethics and not walking the talk? Have *sood (riba), zakat, sadaqa* and other principles, become part of new 'Islamic' paradigms where financiers and the Muslim 'street' speak the same language?

What is the role of scholars and writers of Islamic law in recording these evolving shifts in concepts and meanings? In writing this chapter we observed a paradox in the proliferating work on the subject: At one end of the spectrum is the mushrooming descriptive and at times apologetic literature on an ideal and idealistic Islamic financial regime propounded as the panacea for all (economic) ills in the Muslim world. At the other end is emerging literature (on mostly unsuccessful) case studies of Muslim countries that have applied various models of Islamic finance while operating western financial regimes. This duality and experimental application of principles of Islamic finance is not lost on a handful of critical scholars who highlight the gaps between the rhetoric and reality of Islamic financial regimes. There have been few studies on the social justice and welfare aspects of these financial regimes and especially of the grounding within Muslim communities of the understanding and practices of *zakat, sadaqa* and *qard hasan*.

Equally ambivalent is the policy and practice of these concepts in governmental institutions and political statements within Muslim jurisdictions, although an increasingly interventionist role of some Muslim states is discernible. Malaysia is an example of a Muslim country where the discourse on *zakat, sadaqa* and *qard hasan* is most proactive and appropriated by the political arena. Monthly deduction of *zakat* on salaries of government officials is an example where *zakat* is linked to tax payments. Bearing in mind the fact that Qur'anic verses on *zakat* present it as an act of worship, is this policy in keeping with the ethics of *zakat* and social justice? In particular, how would the state justify bringing only a small fraction of potential *zakat* payers within its net, that is salaried persons – to the exclusion of business persons and others whose wealth is not so easily susceptible to calculation?

In conclusion, the underlying issue remains not one of whose right it is to pay *zakat* and to whom. It is that of the relationships between *zakat* paying individuals on the one hand and *zakat* recipients on the other. The challenge is how best to achieve effective channelling of welfare obligations to remove injustices and enhance the social justice aspect of Islamic finance.

References

Abdul Gafoor, A., 1995. *Interest-Free Commercial Banking*. APPTEC.

Ali, S., 2016. *Modern Challenges to Islamic Law*. Cambridge University Press.

An-Na'im, A., 2008. *Islam and the Secular State*. Oxford University Press.

Asad, M., 1981. *The Message of the Qur'an*. Dar al-Andalus.

Bremer, J., 2013. *Zakat and Economic Justice: Emerging International Models and Their Relevance for Egypt*. Takaful 2013 Third Annual Conference on Arab Philanthropy and Civic Engagement, 4–6 June 2013 p. 52. http://dar.aucegypt.edu/bitstream/handle/10526/4297/Zakat%20and%20Economic%20Justice%2052-76.pdf?sequence=1 (accessed on 7 March 2017).

Buehler, M., 2008. The Rise of Shari'a By-laws in Indonesian Districts: An Indication of Changing Patterns of Power Accumulation and Political Corruption. *South-East Asia Research*, 16 (2), 260–262.

Foster, N. and Archer, S., 2012. *Islamic Financial Law: Law without a Legal System*. Conference paper, Business Inbetween Cultures: The Development of Islamic Finance. European Association for Banking and Financial History e.V., Sarjevo, 15–16 November 2012, p. 1. http://www.eabh.info/fileadmin/pdf/conferences/2012/foster_paper.pdf (accessed 20 August 2020).

Fyzee, A.A.A., 1949. *Outlines of Muhammadan Law*. 4th edn. Oxford University Press.

Haikal, M.H., 2015. *Hadrat Abu Bakr Siddiq*. Islam International Publications.

Hamidullah, M., 1975. *The First Written Constitution in the World: An Important Document of the Time of the Holy Prophet*, 3rd. edn. Lahore: Ashraf Press.

Kersten, C., 2011. *Cosmopolitans and Heretics: New Muslim Intellectuals and the Study of Islam*. Hurst & Company.

Kuran, T., 2004. *Islam and Mammon: The Economic Predicaments of Islamism*. Princeton University Press.

Latief, H., 2012. Islamic Charities and Social Activism: Welfare, Dakwah and Politics in Indonesia. PhD Thesis, Utrecht University.

Mandaville, P., 2001. *Transnational Muslim Politics. Reimagining the Umma.* Routledge.

Mannan, M.A., ed., 1995. *D.F. Mulla's Principles of Muhammadan Law.* Lahore: PLD Publishers,.

Maududi, A.A., 1969. *The Islamic Law and Constitution.* 4th edn. Lahore: Islamic Publications.

Muhammad Ali, M., 2013. *Translation of the Holy Quran in English.* Createspace Independent Publishing Platform.

Noori, Y. and Amin, S., 1986. *Legal and Political Structure of an Islamic State: Implications for Iran and Pakistan.* Royston.

Salim, A., 2008a. *Challenging the Secular State: The Islamization of Law in Modern Indonesia.* University of Hawaii Press.

Salim, A., 2008b. *The Shift in Zakat Practice in Indonesia: From Piety to an Islamic Socio-Political-Economic System.* Asian Muslim Action Network and Silkworm Books.

Schaffer, F., 2016. *Elucidating Social Science Concepts. An Interpretivist Guide.* Routledge.

Timm, H. 1995. The Cultural and Demographic Aspects of the Islamic Financial System and the Potential for Islamic Products in the German Market. PhD Thesis, Stralsand University. https://grin.com./document/34464 (accessed 5 December 2021).

Tobroni, F., 2020. The Similarity of the Medina Charter and the Indonesian Constitution in Human Rights Protection. *Journal of Islamic Law,* 4 (2), 836.

UNDP (United Nations Development Programme), 2017. *The National Human Development Report for Pakistan.* UNDP. Available online at: https://www.pk.undp.org/content/pakistan/en/home/library/human-development-reports/PKNHDR.html (accessed 20 June 2019).

Walker, A., 2014. Constitution of Medina. In Fitzpatrick, C. and Walker, A. eds. *Muhammad in History, Thought, and Culture: An Encyclopedia of the Prophet of God* (2 vols.) Vol I, ABC-CLIO, pp. 113–115.

Warde, I., 2010. *Islamic Finance in the Global Economy.* 2nd ed. Edinburgh University Press.

Weiss, H., 2002. *Zakat and the Question of Social Welfare: An Introductory Essay on Islamic Economics and its Implications for Social Welfare.* Nordiska Afrikainstitutt.

Wright, W., 1995. Islamic Banking in Practice: Problems in Jordan and Saudi Arabia. Occasional Paper No. 48, Centre for Middle Eastern and Islamic Studies, University of Durham.

Yousuf Ali, A., 1990. *The Holy Qur'an: Text, Translation and Commentary.* Sheikh Muhammad Ashraf.

Chapter 12

Countering Corruption to Promote Social Justice in the Global Fund to Fight AIDS, Tuberculosis and Malaria

The Case of Uganda

Monica Twesiime Kirya and Sharifah Sekalala

The Global Fund: Saving Lives and Promoting Social Justice?

Founded in 2002, the Global Fund to Fight AIDS, Tuberculosis and Malaria raises and invests more than US$4 billion a year to support vital health programmes run by local experts in countries and communities most in need.[1] It has been described as part of a revolution in global health that 'is fundamentally altering the way the haves of the world assist the have-nots' (Cohen, 2006: 162). The Global Fund is revolutionary in two senses: first, in the large amount of money involved, with nearly $44 billion disbursed by early 2020,[2] and second, in constituting an unprecedented global partnership between governments, private companies, private philanthropic foundations, civil society organisations, and people affected by the target diseases (Rushton and Williams, 2011).

In the early 2000s, the global HIV pandemic was at its height, particularly in Sub-Saharan Africa. It was fuelled in part by massive reductions in public spending on health and other social services under structural adjustment policies imposed by the World Bank and the International Monetary Fund in the 1980s and 1990s. In Uganda, for example, structural adjustment led to the privatisation of some health care, introduction of user fees in public health facilities, and other changes that narrowed access to treatment and prevention. While it remains difficult to prove a direct causal link between these policies and the spread of specific diseases, there is no doubt that structural inequalities contributed to the burgeoning HIV epidemic, especially in countries whose economies had been subjected to structural adjustment (Sanders and Sambo, 1991; Lugalla, 1995; Parker, 2002; Cheru, 2002; Abouharb and Cingranelli, 2006).

1 See 'Global Fund Overview' on the Global Fund website, https://www.theglobalfund.org/en/overview/ (accessed 20 February 2021). All dollar amounts in this chapter are US dollars.

2 See Global Fund Data Explorer: Investments, https://data.theglobalfund.org/investments/home (accessed 2 February 2020).

DOI: 10.4324/9780203745298-15

The Global Fund was formed in response to this situation, addressing HIV and two other widespread and lethal diseases, tuberculosis and malaria, that often occur as co-infections with HIV. All three diseases are both preventable and treatable. All three are also considered 'diseases of poverty' (Stevens, 2004), and the Global Fund specifically aims to improve the health of the poorest and most vulnerable members of society in countries of the global South. Since 2002, health programmes supported by the Global Fund have saved 32 million lives, and the number of deaths caused by AIDS, tuberculosis (TB), and malaria each year has been reduced by 40% overall in countries where the Fund invests (Global Fund, 2019a: 8). However, these impressive figures mask the day-to-day challenges of poverty and exclusion faced by those who are being kept alive on the Fund's charity, many of whom live under corrupt governments controlled by elites who continue to enrich themselves at the expense of the poor.

In addition to saving lives, the Global Fund's work is guided by a commitment to social justice. A board member, Peter Piot, describes the Fund's essential elements as 'a laser focus on measurable outcomes; prioritizing people-centered services, human rights and a commitment to social justice; and preserving a passion for saving lives'.[3] The Fund seeks to ensure that its investments provide lifesaving services to marginalised groups such as women, lesbians, gays, and transsexuals, as well as persons living with HIV/AIDS. Its internal management principles call for promoting good governance, representation, and oversight through Global Fund-supported bodies such as the Country Coordinating Mechanisms (Global Fund, 2017a). As a relatively new organisation, the Fund has continuously sought to improve its practices and methods of work.

However, there are aspects of the Global Fund's approach that undermine its social justice goals. For instance, some commentators have argued that the Fund's cooperation with pharmaceutical and other medical supply industries serves a capitalist agenda that is inconsistent with the stated social justice principles (Baker, 2014). The Fund receives huge financial endowments from multinational corporations, including through associated partnerships and foundations, leading to a problematic association between the pursuit of health and development goals and the pursuit of profit (Faubion, Paige, and Pearson, 2011).

Furthermore, since its inception in 2002, the Fund has been plagued by intermittent corruption scandals. This is perhaps unsurprising, as many of the countries where it operates – such as Uganda – are characterised as highly corrupt.[4] These scandals prompted us to ask how the Global Fund deals with

3 Global Fund Board Steps Up Efforts to Expand Impact Against HIV, TB and Malaria – News & Stories – The Global Fund to Fight AIDS, Tuberculosis and Malaria. News Release (accessed 20 February 2021).

4 See Transparency International's Corruptions Perceptions Index 2019, https://www.transparency.org/cpi2019 (accessed 20 February 2020).

the threat that corruption poses to its social justice goals. Our starting point is that corruption is a form of social injustice, and following from that, we discuss how the Fund could improve its efforts to mitigate corruption to better achieve its goals of saving lives and promoting social change. Our study was based on a desk review of scholarly literature, news reports, and the Global Fund's official statements and documents.

We chose Uganda as a case study because the corruption scandals surrounding Global Fund operations in that country illustrate some of the shortcomings of the Fund's mechanisms for transparency, accountability, and participation. In shedding light on these issues, we also hope to illustrate the limitations of philanthropy and aid in bringing about the transformation necessary for the attainment of social justice in developing countries such as Uganda.

Corruption as Social Injustice

For purposes of our discussion, we adopt Rawls's (1971) basic ideas of social justice as fairness: each person has the right to the most extensive basic liberty that is compatible with similar liberty for everyone else, and social and economic inequalities should enable the least advantaged to make improvements to their lives. In addition, we find compelling Sen's (1993, 2001) and Nussbaum's (2003) ideas that capabilities are essential to the achievement of social justice. Accordingly, a public health system should aim to enable the people in a society, especially the most vulnerable, to lead healthier lives, not just in terms of being disease-free, but also in terms of social and psychological well-being. This is in line with the World Health Organization's definition of health as 'a state of complete physical, mental, and social well-being and not merely the absence of disease or infirmity'.[5]

While the term 'corruption' has multiple meanings, we follow Transparency International in considering corruption as 'the abuse of entrusted power for private gain'.[6] We further consider corruption to be a form of social injustice, an interpretation that is not universal in the scholarly community. 'Most people will probably say that they hate corruption because it is unjust. Most of the academic literature on corruption, however, has seen it as a problem of development rather than as a problem of social justice' (You, 2006).

Rothstein proposes a specific normative criterion for assessing the exercise of government power: impartiality. Misuse of public power can take the form of biased, partial, or particularist governance that favours some and excludes others in a competition for scarce resources, which the winner then shares with allies and kin (Rothstein, 2011; Mungiu-Pippidi et al., 2011). Such governance is an

5 From the Constitution of the World Health Organization, which entered into force in 1948.

6 See 'What Is Corruption?' on the Transparency International website, https://www.transparency.org/what-is-corruption (accessed 20 February 2020).

aspect of neopatrimonial regimes (Bratton and Van de Walle, 1997; Erdmann and Engel, 2007; Bach and Gazibo, 2012; Mkandawire, 2015). Particularism contrasts with ethical universalism, considered the ideal regime-type, where every citizen is treated equally by the state and there is equitable access to public resources (Mungiu-Pippidi et al., 2011).

Sumpf (2016: 3) suggests that corruption impedes justice by compromising the government's ability to deliver health, educational, and welfare services, which are essential for the realisation of economic, social, and cultural rights. In corrupt settings, service delivery favours those able to influence the authorities and excludes the disadvantaged and those without friendship and kinship connections. This unfair distribution of public goods weakens the capability of individuals, especially the poorest, to achieve an appropriate quality of life (Sen, 2001; Nussbaum, 2003). For example, in a survey by Afrobarometer (2015), 12% of respondents had paid bribes to access public health care, but poor people were twice as likely as better-off people to have paid such bribes.

Social justice, including a focus on the most disadvantaged, should be the moral foundation of public health (Powers and Faden, 2008; Gostin and Powers, 2006). While the Global Fund has made significant advances in improving the health and well-being of the poorest people, corruption continues to hobble its efforts. Intermittent corruption scandals in the Fund do not merely smear its reputation but endanger the lives and well-being of those it purports to help. Frequent reports of corruption can lead to apathy, resentment, and erosion of social trust among the populations that the Fund assists (Burbidge, 2015: 8).

Corruption in the Global Fund in Uganda

In its Policy to Combat Fraud and Corruption, the Global Fund 'recognizes that fraud and corruption, in all their forms, are a threat to the fight to end the epidemics.' It states that fraud and corruption corrode public health systems, facilitate human rights abuses, and divert funds, medicines, and other resources away from countries and communities in need. The effect is to limit the Fund's impact and reduce the trust that is essential to its partnership model (Global Fund, 2017b).

Uganda's Global Fund grants have indeed been plagued by corruption. In 2005, the Fund suspended all grant making in Uganda after an audit discovered that money was being stolen with impunity (Africa Confidential, 2007). After the 2005 scandal, a judicial inquiry was set up. It found that the Permanent Secretary of the Ministry of Health authorised expenditure from the Fund for activities that did not fall under the project's docket. Many 'immunisation campaigns' or 'supervision visits' were undertaken by ministers for the purpose of winning favour with specific constituencies, and the Office of the First Lady also received money from the Fund.[7] Although hundreds of instances of misuse

7 The Commission of Inquiry into the Mismanagement of the Global Fund to Fight AIDS, Tuberculosis and Malaria in Uganda was headed by Justice James Ogoola, a

were documented, only a few people, mainly low-level staff – and no high-ranking government officials – were convicted (Human Rights Watch, 2013).

The 2005 suspension was followed by another in 2007, when two Uganda grants were terminated because of unsatisfactory performance. This was followed by a 2008/2009 audit and review undertaken by the Global Fund's Office of the Inspector General (OIG) to assess the Ugandan government's progress in investigating irregularities and recovering mismanaged funds. The OIG sought assurance that its investments in Uganda would be safeguarded. It examined the Fund's established structures, systems, and processes and concluded that 'the controls in place were not adequate to safeguard Global Fund investments' (Global Fund, 2009: 2).

An audit conducted in November 2015 revealed that drugs had been stolen, health workers were using expired kits to test for HIV, and condoms that were supposed to be distributed free of charge were being sold (Global Fund, 2016). Acute shortages of key drugs and discrepancies between inventory figures and actual stocks were also found. Seventy per cent of the 50 health facilities visited during the audit reported stock-outs of at least one critical medicine, with HIV drugs being the most affected, and 54% of the health facilities had accumulated expired medicines. Anti-malarial medicines that were distributed under the private sector co-payment mechanism were being sold in pharmacies at prices 42% higher than recommended, for 5,000 instead of 3,500 Ugandan shillings.[8] The OIG noted that only 46% of funds disbursed to the Ministry of Finance between January 2013 and June 2015 had been spent by the time of the audit. A programme to procure food packs for patients with multidrug-resistant TB, started in 2012, had neither bought nor distributed any packs as of November 2015. The auditors found that an apathetic attitude prevailed at the Ministry of Health, with poor grant management and implementation and irregular attendance at meetings.

In 2017, the OIG issued a clarification that the variance between expected and actual stocks at the National Medical Stores (NMS) was due to the omission of data from the warehouse management system provided by NMS to the OIG audit team. In addition, power disruptions, systems crashes, and incomplete data back-up restoration had affected the reliability of data in 2014. The OIG said they had found no evidence that internal control failures identified by the audit had been exploited for fraudulent gain, and the Office therefore closed the investigation without a formal report. The OIG nonetheless reiterated its finding of persistent and significant internal control deficiencies (Global Fund, 2017c).

respected Ugandan jurist; its final report was issued in May 2006 and is on file with the authors. See also 'The Global Fund Welcomes Ugandan Corruption Inquiry Report', *Global Fund News Release* 15 November 2019, https://www.theglobalfund.org/en/news/2006-06-02-the-global-fund-welcomes-ugandan-corruption-inquiry-report/ (accessed 20 February 2020).

8 At the time (2015), one US dollar was equivalent to 3,200 Ugandan shillings (UGX).

The 2017 update from the OIG did not necessarily absolve Ugandan institutions of fraud and corruption in connection with Global Fund grants. While the statement pointed to inadequate data management, previous research found inefficiency in other areas as well, along with problems in the organisational culture of the health ministry. For instance, Maniple (2011) points out the absence of an efficient system for delivering medical supplies to health units, resulting in failure to keep up with delivery schedules. Baez-Camargo (2012) highlights the power relations between the central government and decentralised health units that dispense medicines. She found that local health workers were so frightened of unannounced monitoring visits by the Medicines and Health Service Delivery Monitoring Unit (MHSDMU) under the Office of the President that they maintained a 'safety stock' of drugs in reserve, refusing to dispense them to patients in need.

Drug stock-outs are caused not only by inefficient delivery systems, but also by pilferage. Baez-Camargo (2012) notes that the decentralisation of health services facilitates the extraction of rents, especially in a context where civil servants are poorly salaried, sometimes not paid, and have few prospects for career progression. In such circumstances, 'the profit margins resulting from selling drugs at inflated prices in the private sector constitute an incentive for persistent drug leakages from the public to the private sector' (Baez-Camargo, 2012: 3).

Moreover, corruption in Uganda has been described as systemic and endemic – a 'way of life' – and rent seeking is a key motivation for holding public office. Many Ugandan public servants consider corruption as inevitable and refraining from corruption as futile (Ssemujju, 2009; Persson, Rothstein, and Teorell, 2013; Scharbatke-Church and Chigas, 2016). This makes it unlikely that discrepancies identified by the OIG were due merely to incorrect data entry and inefficiency. Corruption is, by its nature, hidden and difficult to prove with direct evidence, and proof of corruption is often based on circumstantial evidence (Scherer, 2003).

The persistence of corruption in Uganda has been attributed to its central role in regime consolidation under neopatrimonial rule (Mwenda and Tangri, 2005; Tangri and Mwenda, 2006; Tangri and Mwenda, 2013). Public office is seen as a reward for political support, with expectation that such office will be used for rent seeking amid a general lack of opprobrium for corruption. Reform initiatives such as civil service restructuring, public expenditure management, decentralisation, innovations in service delivery, and legal and institutional measures to curb corruption are personalised as a commitment of the President (Robinson and Friedman, 2005). However, whatever reform momentum once existed has been lost, and any early gains reversed, as political motivations and the proliferation of informal institutions have taken precedence over good governance. The chief goal of the country's rulers is to preserve the institutional foundations of neopatrimonial politics, where patronage relations based on kinship, family, and community ties hold sway. As a result, central and local public institutions have been captured by political constituencies within the ruling party (Robinson and Friedman, 2005; Tangri and Mwenda,

2013). Copious amounts of development aid, including from the Global Fund, have been a source of patronage that has enabled the regime to consolidate its power (Mwenda and Tangri, 2005).

This has several implications for the way Global Fund resources are managed and accounted for. Baez-Camargo (2012) examined how informal power networks and relationships affect the management of the Ugandan drug supply chain. She found that formal Ministry of Health structures were eclipsed by the power of the General Manager of the National Medical Stores, whose personal relationship with the President gave the Manager wide scope for discretionary action. Even attempts at reform become personalised in the President. For instance, the MHSDMU was created under the Office of the President and its officials report directly to him; this has resulted in a harsh authoritarian regime of impromptu visits and summary sackings but has done little to improve service delivery (Maniple, 2011).

Thus, the Global Fund faces an uphill task in trying to counter corruption in its operations in Uganda. In a context of personalised rule, where formal structures are often a façade, the power to influence health outcomes is embedded in informal networks dedicated to self-enrichment. Tighter financial and administrative controls address only the symptom and not the cause. The question is, therefore, whether and how the Fund can navigate the prevailing informal institutions in Uganda and other countries to achieve its objective of saving lives while also helping to improve social justice and living conditions for the most vulnerable citizens. A question is the ability of the Global Fund to reinfuse social justice ideals into public health delivery systems that have, unfortunately, been warped by market-oriented values of self-enrichment in a predatory state.

Global Fund Structures: Enabling or Hindering Accountable Health Service Delivery?

The Global Fund has put in place several mechanisms to promote transparency, accountability, and participation and to minimise corruption. We consider the role of Country Coordinating Mechanisms, Public-Private Partnerships, Local Fund Agents, and the Office of the Inspector General.

Country Coordinating Mechanisms

Country Coordinating Mechanisms (CCMs) are the country-level pillars of the Global Fund. They develop and submit grant proposals to the Fund's headquarters. Ideally, CCMs also provide oversight of grant implementation. In each country, the CCM consists of representatives from government agencies, the health professions, academia, donors, civil society organisations, and key affected populations (people living with HIV/AIDS, tuberculosis, and/or malaria).[9]

9 See the website of the Uganda Country Coordinating Mechanism (UCCM) for the Global Fund, https://www.globalfundccm.org.ug/uccm-membership/.

The Fund's efforts to ensure wider representation in CCMs are commendable but may be insufficient to guard against elite capture and neopatrimonialist tendencies in the Fund's governance at country level. The CCM's participatory model may not effectively check the personalised governance and authoritarian accountability measures, such as the MHSDMU in Uganda, that undercut public health goals. Furthermore, since corruption in Uganda is endemic, the CCM itself may be vulnerable to corruption. Sekalala's research on the Uganda CCM for example, found that the CCM election process contained irregularities and had not been transparent, which led to the election of a brother and sister from the same organisation, Most At Risk Populations (MARPS) Network (2017). This instance was justified as necessary and merit-based because they needed people with the skills to navigate the Global Fund bureaucracy. Nonetheless, such practices create the appearance of bias and nepotism and could reduce public trust in the Global Fund.

The involvement of civil society and affected populations with the CCM is meant to promote participation and ensure that voices of the Fund's beneficiaries are heard. However, the attempt to involve as many people as possible in Uganda made it practically impossible for all the representatives to participate meaningfully, with some elected representatives subsequently relegated to 'reserve status'. Having many people also made it difficult to achieve consensus during meetings (Sekalala, 2017).

Civil society in developing countries is often top-down and elitist, and having those groups at the table does not necessarily ensure effective participation of the poorest and most vulnerable. Moreover, civil society organisations are often conflated with non-governmental organisations (NGOs), yet many NGOs lack constituencies and are more accountable to the donors who fund them than to the public whose interests they supposedly serve (Barr, Fafchamps, and Owens, 2005). Furthermore, NGOs tend to adopt 'safe' approaches to their work and avoid criticising rulers, who can clamp down using licensing and other regulatory frameworks to neutralise perceived threats (Dupuy, Ron, and Prakash, 2016). For these reasons, civil society involvement in the CCM may not do much to check governmental excess and promote social justice.

Furthermore, including members of affected populations in a CCM does not necessarily ensure effective representation of these constituencies. In Uganda, where groups such as homosexuals are systematically marginalised, oppressed, and stigmatised, their involvement with the CCM has been problematic (Sekalala, 2017). According to Gaventa (2006: 23), 'simply creating new institutional arrangements will not necessarily result in greater inclusion or pro-poor policy change. Rather, much depends on the nature of the power relations which surround and imbue these new, potentially more democratic, spaces.' In spaces such as the CCM, participation is often nominal and based on mere physical presence. Power relations dictate 'who may enter, with which identities, discourses and interests,' with implications for the transformative potential of such spaces and their ability to check the abuse of power (Gaventa, 2006: 26).

Redressing the power imbalances that limit accountability and participation is a complex task that may be beyond the Global Fund's remit. Nonetheless, the Fund should guard against merely symbolic participation in the CCMs in order to realise its public health and social justice goals.

Public-Private Partnerships

The Global Fund promotes private service delivery as part of its efforts to fight disease. As of July 2019, private sector partners have contributed over $2.7 billion to the Fund. Private sector companies also serve on the ground as principal recipients and sub-recipients of grants, implementing programmes. The private sector is represented in CCMs and on the Global Fund Board, which provides high-level oversight.[10]

The Fund takes advantage of private sector expertise to improve grant implementation and promotes country-level collaboration with private sector partners, using business processes to maximise efficiency and value for money. This includes support for improving supply chain management, use of technologies such as mobile phones, as well as training, marketing, and other advisory services. It encourages private sector partners to share their skills, expertise, resources, and networks.

Scholars have cast doubts on the perceived benefits of public-private partnerships (PPPs). Nickel and Eikenberry (2009) criticise 'marketized philanthropy', pointing out that it ignores the market's negative impacts on human well-being. The market's incompatibility with and insensitivity to social justice has been discussed by several authors (Plant, 2002; Lister, 2013). Therefore, philanthropic partnerships with the private sector must be carefully managed, lest profit motives interfere with philanthropic goals.

Other scholars question the long-term impact of PPPs on health systems with respect to equity, accessibility, and the quality of care (Kanya et al., 2014; Nachtnebel et al., 2015; Gideon and Unterhalter, 2017). The private sector is not necessarily more efficient, accountable, or effective than the public sector when it comes to provision of health services (Basu et al., 2012). Concerns have also been raised about accountability in PPPs (Buse and Harmer, 2007; Bruen et al., 2014), since private companies answer to their shareholders and not to the public.

In Uganda, PPP schemes encouraged private entities to deliver and sell anti-malaria medicines and to create differential pricing policies that resulted in these medicines being sold at twice the recommended price. This phenomenon highlights the problem of monetising public resources and of treating health care not as a need or a right but as an entrepreneurial activity from which individuals and organisations can profit.

10 See 'Private and Non-government Partners' on the Global Fund website, https://www.theglobalfund.org/en/private-ngo-partners/ (accessed 20 February 2020).

It has been suggested that the private sector can play a role in advancing transparency and accountability, as corruption can increase the cost of doing business (Taylor and Benderson, 2017). However, this view does not consider the fact that corruption can also help businesses access markets, eliminate competition, or manipulate prices (Leff, 1964; Bayley, 1966; Scott, 1969). In countries such as Uganda, corruption may not significantly increase the cost of doing business if firms can find other means to increase profit or reduce costs.

In Uganda, there is often little or no distinction between the private and public sectors, as many politicians and bureaucrats use public resources to access business opportunities that would otherwise have been unavailable to them. This was fostered by the privatisation process of the early 1990s, which allowed politicians and bureaucrats to enrich themselves (Booth et al., 2014: 56). In such a situation, PPPs can reinforce, rather than mitigate, unequal power relations that give rise to corruption. It is unclear what safeguards the Global Fund has put in place to minimise the potential conflicts of interest posed by private sector involvement in its efforts towards public health and social justice goals.

Local Fund Agents

The Global Fund also promotes accountability through Local Fund Agents (LFAs), described as the Fund's 'eyes and ears on the ground'. The LFA – there is usually one per country – 'works closely with the country team to evaluate and monitor activities before, during and after the implementation of a grant'.[11] LFAs are also charged with reporting grant-related risks to the Office of the Inspector General. They have been criticised, however, for having insufficient health sector knowledge and programme management experience as well as a fixation on indicators, problems compounded by high staff turnover in some LFAs (Wafula and Mugenyi, 2014).

Most LFAs are international audit firms selected through a competitive bidding process for their financial management skills. In Uganda, PricewaterhouseCoopers (PwC) and Deloitte & Touche have been involved in overseeing and auditing Global Fund grants. Both are among the 'big four' global accounting firms. Such firms have been criticised for protecting the profitable health market, often at the expense of the public interest (Sikka, Willmott, and Lowe, 1989; Huber, 2015).

LFAs may be the eyes and ears of the Global Fund, but they are not part of the Fund. This hands-off approach to oversight highlights the Fund's distance from its beneficiaries. Even though LFAs participate in CCM processes by attending meetings, they are not involved in programme design, implementation, technical assistance, or audit, leading to lack of clarity about their role (Wafula and Mugenyi, 2014).

11 See 'Local Fund Agent' on the Global Fund website, https://www.theglobalfund.org/en/lfa/ (accessed 20 February 2020).

International audit firms such as PwC are frequently staffed by expatriates in the countries where they work. In such cases, Solthis (2014: 18) observes, 'being "local" is little more than a geographical indication of the placement of the LFA's office, and not a guarantee of a good knowledge of the context, the actors, or the practices of the country'. And yet LFAs need such knowledge, because corruption surrounding the Fund's operations is typically embedded in a specific local context.

Moreover, firms such as PwC are often professional enablers of 'anti-social financial practices' such as money laundering and corruption (Sikka, 2008; Khair, Lauwo, and Otusanya, 2017: 3). Sikka (2008: 15–16) observes that accounting firms are capitalist organisations that seek to maximise profit, and they may be willing to bend the rules in order to do so. He quotes Hanlon (1994: 150), who says that these firms' 'emphasis is very firmly on being commercial and on performing a service for the customer rather than on being public spirited on behalf of either the public or the state'.

The reliance on firms such as PwC to be the Fund's local agents may therefore be problematic, since the goals and values of the firms do not necessarily align with social justice but are based on self-interest and profit maximisation.

Office of the Inspector General

The Office of the Inspector General is the arm of the Global Fund responsible for safeguarding its assets, investments, reputation, and sustainability. 'Through audits, investigations, and consultancy work, the OIG promotes good practice, reduces risk and reports on abuse.'[12] When wrongdoing is suspected, the Fund leaves the prosecution and punishment of culprits to partner governments. However, the Fund may choose not to work with the culprits, or it may insist on return of misappropriated funds and/or deduct unrecovered monies from future grants. It may also seek to reorganise its staff, structures, and processes in a country to mitigate the risk of corruption. This approach is pragmatic, given the Fund's limited leverage in domestic politics and the fact that its investigations are administrative and not criminal.

The Fund's anti-corruption strategy relies heavily on whistleblowing to denounce fraud and human rights violations. Through its 'I Speak Out Now' platform, the Fund encourages members of the public to report fraud and abuse online or by telephone.[13] Its whistle-blowing policy emphasises that 'the Global Fund is committed to safeguard whistle-blowers, and provides the opportunity to treat all whistle-blowing reports as either confidential or

12 See 'Office of the Inspector General' on the Global Fund website, https://www.theglobalfund.org/en/oig/ (accessed 20 February 2020).

13 See 'About I Speak Out Now' on the Global Fund website, http://www.ispeakoutnow.org/ (accessed 20 February 2020).

anonymous. The choice between confidential or anonymous whistle-blowing is that of the whistle-blower alone' (Global Fund, 2019b).

Despite the Fund's commitment to ensuring confidentiality and anonymity, the efficacy of whistleblowing in contexts such as Uganda is questionable. De Maria (2005) warns of the dangers of exporting Western whistle-blower concepts to the developing world, where corruption is often socially constructed, legitimised, and accepted, the rule of law is routinely flouted, and the notions of a public domain and a public service ethic are underdeveloped. De Maria also notes that whistleblowing works better in anonymous urban spaces, where workers can make disclosures about colleagues with some expectation of confidentiality. He cautions that in close-knit communities where there are strong work–family connections, whistle-blowers risk potential retaliation through social shunning, physical harm, or even death. In Uganda, whistle-blowers have lost their jobs, been arrested without charge, and in some cases allegedly murdered (Allio, 2003; Kasasira, 2009; New Vision, 2017).

Uganda's 2010 Whistleblowers Protection Act allows for anonymous disclosures under section 3(2), but it goes on to render this useless by providing that a person who makes an anonymous disclosure is not entitled to protection under the Act. Moreover, the protection offered to whistle-blowers is inadequate, as it does not include identity change or relocation (Kagaba, 2010). The Global Fund has provided an anonymous online channel for whistleblowing, but it should nonetheless leverage its power with partner governments to promote robust whistle-blower protection laws and systems at national level.

Conclusion: Towards a Philanthropy that Promotes Social Justice

There is no doubt that the Global Fund has achieved substantial results in reducing AIDS, tuberculosis, and malaria. In addition, the Fund has made significant efforts to ensure participation in its governance structures and has put in place several mechanisms to minimise corruption so that its grants can achieve their intended purpose of reducing deaths from the three diseases.

However, as described above, there are several limitations in the Fund's approach to participation, transparency, accountability, and corruption. These include a participation model that is vulnerable to elite capture and symbolic participation; a reliance on public-private partnerships that may not serve social justice goals; the use of local agents that might have limited contextual knowledge and are prone to act in their own, rather than the public's, interest; and a reliance on whistle-blowing to sniff out corruption in contexts where protection is weak and whistle-blowers are frequently in danger.

The Global Fund's goal of saving lives is important but saving people from disease is just a start towards promoting social justice: people should also be able to enjoy good health along with mental and social well-being in just societies. As Nickel and Eikenberry (2009: 985) argue:

> Poverty [and] disease … should inspire philanthropic action. However, when philanthropic action sustains rather than eliminates these conditions, we must ask ourselves if it is philanthropic action at all. … transformative philanthropic action would recognize and declare the irrationality of the system itself.

As a multi-partner venture involving an array of public and private entities, the Global Fund has some leverage to influence the complex political realities that enable corruption in the countries where it works. Unless some of the contradictions that give rise to corruption are resolved, the Fund's vision – to be a global philanthropic actor with strong humanitarian, social justice, and moral objectives – is diminished. Accordingly, the Fund should take steps to ensure that participation by civil society and affected populations in CCMs is not simply tokenistic. It should strive to ensure that the profit maximisation goals of private sector actors involved in its public-private partnerships do not contravene its public health and social justice ideals, and that accounting firms serving as LFAs protect the public interest and not their own. Finally, the Fund should promote whistle-blower protection on the ground in recipient countries, even in the most difficult settings. In this manner, the Fund will continue not only to save lives, but also to promote social justice across the globe in accordance with its stated aims.

References

Abouharb, M. and Cingranelli, D., 2006. The Human Rights Effects of World Bank Structural Adjustment, 1981–2000. *International Studies Quarterly*, 50 (2), 233–262.

Africa Confidential, 2007. Doctor, Doctor: How Healthcare Funds Went Astray Just before an Election – And How the President's Allies Are under Investigation Again. *Africa Confidential*, 48 (20).

Afrobarometer, 2015. *People and Corruption: Africa Survey 2015: Global Corruption Barometer.* Transparency International.

Allio, E., 2003. National Drug Authority Bosses in Row over Laboratory Chief. *New Vision*, 30 May.

Bach, D. and Gazibo, M., 2012. *Neopatrimonialism in Africa and Beyond.* Routledge.

Baez-Camargo, C., 2012. Using Power and Influence Analysis to Address Corruption Risks: The Case of the Ugandan Drug Supply Chain. U4 Brief 2012:6. U4 Anti-Corruption Resource Centre, Chr. Michelsen Institute.

Baker, B., 2014. Industry-Led Tiered-Pricing or Country-Led, Real Equitable Access: The Global Fund's Task Force Proposal Gets Worse Instead of Better. Infojustice.org (blog), 28 March. Available online at: <http://infojustice.org/archives/32565> (accessed 20 February 2020).

Barr, A., Fafchamps, M. and Owens, T., 2005. The Governance of Non-governmental Organizations in Uganda. *World Development*, 33 (4), 657–679.

Basu, S., Andrews, J., Kishore, S., Panjabi, R. and Stuckler, D., 2012. Comparative Performance of Private and Public Healthcare Systems in Low- and Middle-Income Countries: A Systematic Review. *PLoS Medicine*, 9 (6), e1001244.

Bayley, D., 1966. The Effects of Corruption in a Developing Nation. *Western Political Quarterly*, 19 (4), 719–732.

Booth, D., Cooksey, B., Golooba-Mutebi, F. and Kanyinga, K., 2014. *East African Prospects: An Update on the Political Economy of Kenya, Rwanda, Tanzania and Uganda.* Overseas Development Institute.

Bratton, M. and Van de Walle, N., 1997. *Democratic Experiments in Africa: Regime Transitions in Comparative Perspective.* Cambridge University Press.

Bruen, C., Brugha, R., Kageni, A. and Wafula, F., 2014. A Concept in Flux: Questioning Accountability in the Context of Global Health Cooperation. *Globalization and Health*, 10 (1), 73.

Burbidge, D., 2015. *In the Shadow of Kenyan Democracy: Widespread Expectations of Widespread Corruption.* Routledge.

Buse, K. and Harmer, A., 2007. Seven Habits of Highly Effective Global Public-Private Health Partnerships: Practice and Potential. *Social Science & Medicine*, 64 (2), 259–271.

Cheru, F., 2002. Debt, Adjustment and the Politics of Effective Response to HIV/AIDS in Africa. *Third World Quarterly*, 23 (2), 299–312.

Cohen, J., 2006. The New World of Global Health. *Science*, 311 (5758), 162–167.

De Maria, W., 2005. Whistleblower Protection: Is Africa Ready? *Public Administration and Development*, 25 (3), 217–256.

Dupuy, K., Ron, J. and Prakash, A., 2016. Hands Off My Regime! Governments' Restrictions on Foreign Aid to Non-governmental Organizations in Poor and Middle-Income Countries. *World Development*, 84, 299–311.

Erdmann, G. and Engel, U., 2007. Neopatrimonialism Reconsidered: Critical Review and Elaboration of an Elusive Concept. *Commonwealth and Comparative Politics*, 45 (1), 95–119.

Faubion, T., Paige, S. and Pearson, A., 2011. Co-opting the Global Health Agenda: The Problematic Role of Partnerships and Foundations in Developing Priorities. In S. Rushton and O. Williams, eds., *Foundations in Global Health Governance*, pp. 209–227. Palgrave Macmillan.

Gaventa, J., 2006. Finding the Spaces for Change: A Power Analysis. *IDS Bulletin*, 37 (6), 23–34.

Gideon, J. and Unterhalter, E., 2017. Exploring Public Private Partnerships in Health and Education: A Critique. *Journal of International and Comparative Social Policy*, 33 (2), 136–141.

Global Fund, 2009. Follow Up Review of the Global Fund Grants to Uganda. Office of the Inspector General. Audit Report TGF-OIG-09-005. Available online at: <https://www.theglobalfund.org/media/2595/oig_ugandafollowuprevieofglobalfund grants_report_en.pdf?u=637166001420000000> (accessed 14 February 2020).

Global Fund, 2016. Global Fund Grants to the Republic of Uganda. Office of the Inspector General. Audit Report GF-OIG-16-005. Available online at: <https://www.thegloba lfund.org/media/2646/oig_gf-oig-16-005_report_en.pdf?u=637166002560000000> (accessed 14 February 2020).

Global Fund, 2017a. The Global Fund Strategy 2017–2022: Investing to End Epidemics. Available online at: <https://www.theglobalfund.org/media/2531/core_ globalfundstrategy2017-2022_strategy_en.pdf?u=637066531950000000> (accessed 14 February 2020).

Global Fund, 2017b. The Global Fund Policy to Combat Fraud and Corruption. Available online at: <https://www.theglobalfund.org/media/6960/core_combatfraudcorruption_policy_en.pdf> (accessed 14 February 2020).

Global Fund, 2017c. Update from the Office of the Inspector General: Uganda. Available online at: <https://www.theglobalfund.org/en/oig/updates/2017-05-15-update-from-the-office-of-the-inspector-general-uganda/> (accessed 14 February 2020).

Global Fund, 2019a. Results Report 2019. Available online at: <https://www.theglobalfund.org/media/8752/corporate_2019resultsreport_report_en.pdf> (accessed 14 February 2020).

Global Fund, 2019b. Whistle-blowing Policy and Procedures for the Global Fund to Fight AIDS, Tuberculosis and Malaria. Available online at: <https://www.theglobalfund.org/media/2942/core_whistleblowing_policy_en.pdf?u=637001818240000000> (accessed 14 February 2020).

Gostin, L. and Powers, M., 2006. What Does Social Justice Require for the Public's Health? Public Health Ethics and Policy Imperatives. *Health Affairs*, 25 (4), 1053–1060.

Hanlon, G., 1994. *The Commercialisation of Accountancy: Flexible Accumulation and the Transformation of the Service Class*. St. Martin's Press.

Huber, W., 2015. The Structure of the Public Accounting Industry: Why Existing Market Models Fail. *Journal of Theoretical Accounting Research*, 10 (2), 43–67.

Human Rights Watch, 2013. 'Letting the Big Fish Swim': Failures to Prosecute High-Level Corruption in Uganda. Available online at: https://www.hrw.org/report/2013/10/21/letting-big-fish-swim/failures-prosecute-high-level-corruption-uganda.

Kagaba, C., 2010. The Whistleblower Deserves Deeper State Protection. *Daily Monitor*, 7 March. Available online:https://allafrica.com/stories/201003080810.html (accessed 20 February 2021).

Kanya, L., Obare, F., Warren, C., Abuya, T., Askew, I. and Bellows, B., 2014. Safe Motherhood Voucher Programme Coverage of Health Facility Deliveries among Poor Women in South-western Uganda. *Health Policy and Planning*, 29 (suppl. 1), i4–i11.

Kasasira, R., 2009. Fotogenix Faces Shs 8 Billion Tax Fraud Inquiry. *Daily Monitor*, 10 August.https://allafrica.com/stories/200908101168.html (accessed 20 February 2021).

Khair, A., Lauwo, S. and Otusanya, O. J., 2017. The Culpability of Accounting Practice in Promoting Bribery and Corruption in Developing Countries. *International Journal of Economics and Accounting*, 8 (2), 1–32.

Leff, N., 1964. Economic Development through Bureaucratic Corruption. *Behavioral Scientist*, 8 (13), 8–14.

Lister, A., 2013. The "Mirage" of Social Justice: Hayek against (and for) Rawls. *Critical Review*, 25(3/4), 409–444.

Lugalla, J.L., 1995. The Impact of Structural Adjustment Policies on Women's and Children's Health in Tanzania. *Review of African Political Economy*, 22 (63), 43–53.

Maniple, E., 2011. Fighting Health Sector Corruption in Uganda: The Deliverables Must Change. Editorial. *Health Policy and Development*, 9 (1), iii–vi.

Mkandawire, T., 2015. Neopatrimonialism and the Political Economy of Economic Performance in Africa: Critical Reflections. *World Politics*, 67 (3), 563–612.

Mungiu-Pippidi, A. et al., 2011. *Contextual Choices in Fighting Corruption: Lessons Learned*. Report 4/2011. Norwegian Agency for Development Cooperation (NORAD).

Mwenda, A. and Tangri, R., 2005. Patronage Politics, Donor Reforms, and Regime Consolidation in Uganda. *African Affairs*, 104 (416), 449–467.

Nachtnebel, M., O'Mahony, A., Pillai, N. and Hort, K., 2015. Effectively Engaging the Private Sector through Vouchers and Contracting: A Case for Analysing Health Governance and Context. *Social Science & Medicine*, 145, 193–200.

New Vision, 2017. Former UNBS Spokesperson Ssebunya Dies. *New Vision*, 18 April. Available online at: https://www.newvision.co.ug/new_vision/news/1451309/unbs-spokesperson-ssebunya-dies (accessed 20 February 2021).

Nickel, P.M. and Eikenberry, A.M., 2009. A Critique of the Discourse of Marketized Philanthropy. *American Behavioral Scientist*, 52 (7), 974–989.

Nussbaum, M., 2003. Capabilities as Fundamental Entitlements: Sen and Social Justice. *Feminist Economics*, 9(2/3), 33–59.

Parker, R., 2002. The Global HIV/AIDS Pandemic, Structural Inequalities, and the Politics of International Health. *American Journal of Public Health*, 92 (3), 343–347.

Persson, A., Rothstein, B. and Teorell, J., 2013. Why Anticorruption Reforms Fail: Systemic Corruption as a Collective Action Problem. *Governance*, 26 (3), 449–471.

Plant, R., 2002. Hayek on Social Justice: A Critique. In J. Birner and R. van Zijp, eds., *Hayek, Co-ordination and Evolution: His Legacy in Philosophy, Politics, Economics and the History of Ideas*, pp. 164–177. Routledge.

Powers, M. and Faden, R., 2008. *Social Justice: The Moral Foundations of Public Health and Health Policy*. Oxford University Press.

Rawls, J., 1971. *A Theory of Justice*. Harvard University Press.

Robinson, M. and Friedman, S., 2005. Civil Society, Democratisation and Foreign Aid in Africa. Discussion Paper 383. Institute of Development Studies.

Rothstein, B., 2011. *The Quality of Government: Corruption, Social Trust and Inequality in International Perspective*. University of Chicago Press.

Rushton, S. and Williams, O., 2011. *Partnerships and Foundations in Global Health Governance*. Palgrave Macmillan.

Sanders, D. and Sambo, A., 1991. AIDS in Africa: The Implications of Economic Recession and Structural Adjustment. *Health Policy and Planning*, 6 (2), 157–165.

Scharbatke-Church, C. and Chigas, D., 2016. Facilitation in the Criminal Justice System: A Systems Analysis of Corruption in Police and Courts in Northern Uganda. Occasional Paper. Institute for Human Security, Fletcher School of Law and Diplomacy, Tufts University.

Scherer, M., 2003. Circumstantial Evidence in Corruption Cases before International Arbitral Tribunals. *Oil, Gas & Energy Law Journal (OGEL)*, 5.

Scott, J., 1969. Corruption, Machine Politics and Political Change. *American Political Science Review*, 63 (4), 1142–1158.

Sekalala, S.R., 2017. Who Gets to Sit at the Table? Interrogating the Failure of Participatory Approaches within a Right to Health Framework. *International Journal of Human Rights*, 21 (7), 976–1001.

Sen, A., 1993. Capability and Well-Being. In A. Sen and M. Nussbaum, eds., *The Quality of Life*, pp. 30–53. Clarendon Press.

Sen, A., 2001. *Development as Freedom*. Oxford University Press.

Sikka, P., 2008. Enterprise Culture and Accountancy Firms: New Masters of the Universe. *Accounting, Auditing & Accountability Journal*, 21 (2), 268–295.

Sikka, P., Willmott, H. and Lowe, T., 1989. Guardians of Knowledge and Public Interest: Evidence and Issues of Accountability in the UK Accountancy Profession. *Accounting, Auditing & Accountability Journal*, 2 (2).

Solthis, 2014. *Managing Risk in Fragile States: Putting Health First! Optimising the Efficiency of the Global Fund's Grants*. Solthis.

Ssemujju, I.N., 2009. Corruption Endemic in Uganda. *Guardian*, 13 March. Available online at: https://www.theguardian.com/katine/2009/mar/13/corruption-endemic-in-uganda (accessed 20 February 2021).

Stevens, P., 2004. *Diseases of Poverty and the 10/90 Gap*. International Policy Network.

Sumpf, D., 2016. *A Review of the Relationship between Corruption and Social Justice*. United Nations Economic and Social Commission for Western Asia (UNESCWA).

Tangri, R. and Mwenda, A., 2006. Politics, Donors and the Ineffectiveness of Anti-corruption Institutions in Uganda. *Journal of Modern African Studies*, 44 (1), 101–124.

Tangri, R. and Mwenda, A., 2013. *The Politics of Elite Corruption in Africa: Uganda in Comparative African Perspective*. Routledge.

Taylor, A. and Benderson, M., 2017. *The Maritime Anti-Corruption Network: A Model for Public-Private Cooperation against Graft*. Center for the Advancement of Public Integrity, Columbia Law School.

Wafula, F. and Mugenyi, C., 2014. *The Local Fund Agents: A Review of Changing Roles, Functions, and Performance from 2002 to Date*. Aidspan.

You, J.S., 2006. *Corruption as Injustice*. Paper prepared for the 2006 Annual Meeting of Midwest Political Science Association, Chicago, 20–23 April. Available online at: <https://docplayer.net/136651430-corruption-as-injustice.html> (accessed 12 February 2020).

Chapter 13

'In My Own Village'

Chronotopes, Governmentality and the Changing Regulation of Traditional Medicine in Kenya

John Harrington

Introduction

Traditional medicine in Kenya has been the focus of increasing official attention over the past decade. Legislation has been proposed, and in some cases passed, to regulate the practice of traditional healers, to control the supply of medical materials and to protect the interests of local communities in their medical knowledge. Long neglected, marginalized and disparaged, it is now targeted by diverse national bodies and international agencies with influence in Kenya. The 'quest for governance', identified by Kibet Ng'etich (2008), is at last making progress. This chapter explores the discourses through which these initiatives have been framed and (partly) achieved. After briefly sketching the most important developments, I draw on governmentality theory to suggest that each proceeds on the basis of 'problematizing' aspects of traditional medical knowledge and practice. Such problematizations are inherently discursive and have an important rhetorical dimension. They are effective in law and policy to the extent that they are considered natural or plausible. In considering the plausibility of problematizations, I suggest that we need to attend to style and form in addition to substantive content, arguing in particular that vivid spatio-temporal images (or 'chronotopes') have encapsulated the diverse threats to and promise of traditional medicine in contemporary Kenya. In the rest of the chapter, I seek to show the purchase of this framework by reviewing in more detail campaign materials, legislative debates, national and international policy literature, and academic interventions. These sources are supplemented by a series of interviews which I conducted with government officials and researchers, the leaders of healers' associations, and activists. On the basis of this material, I identify a number of key, and in some cases rival, chronotopes which anchor different doctrinal and policy positions. Figures such as the village, the community, the nation and the globe, familiar from debates on traditional medicine elsewhere in Africa, are given a distinct inflection with reference to Kenyan history and contemporary contexts.

DOI: 10.4324/9780203745298-16

Traditional Medicine in Kenya: Practice and Reform

It is estimated that over 70% of the Kenyan population relies on traditional medicine as its primary source of health care, while more than 90% have used medicinal plants at one time or another (IEA, 2011: 11). Although the great bulk of state health care resources is allocated to the delivery of biomedical services, traditional healers are considerably more accessible to ordinary Kenyans. While the doctor-patient ratio is approximately 1:33,000, that for traditional healers is 1:950.[1] Most are herbalists, though that is often combined with work as traditional birth attendants, bone setters and spiritualists or faith healers (Lambert and Leonard, 2011: 20). Their patients tend to have lower incomes and be less educated than the average Kenyan (ibid.: 19). In rural areas and the poorer city districts healers partly make good persistent deficits in access to health care, owing to lack of physical facilities and hospital stock outs for example.[2] They are known by reputation, collecting and processing raw materials themselves (Prince and Geissler, 2001). In more affluent urban areas, by contrast, healers supplement biomedicine, operating commercial clinics with their own staff, production systems and internet presence (Ng'etich, 2008: 28). Formal training in traditional medicine is not available in Kenya and the subject is largely absent from medical school curricula. Becoming a healer often involves acknowledging a special vocation and carrying on family traditions after a period of apprenticeship (Prince and Geissler, 2001). It is important to note that traditional medicine is not monopolized by practitioners: self-care with well-known plants is widespread (TICAH, 2010: 7).

Recent reform initiatives have focussed on regulating the practice of traditional medicine (by legal and non-legal means), and the expansion of intellectual property law to protect traditional medical knowledge. Practice has been the target of measures such as the Kenya Medicinal and Aromatic Plants project supported by the Japanese Development Agency to train healers in record keeping and hygiene, the selective mapping of healers and their practices by World Bank-funded consultants, and the revision of regulations for the production and storage of herbal medicines laid down by the Pharmacy and Poisons Board.[3] A series of legislative proposals have attempted to create a system of licensing and discipline, though none of these has been passed due to considerable resistance from within the medical profession and endemic divisions between healers themselves.[4] A Traditional Medicine Practitioners Bill introduced in 2014, which failed to pass both houses of parliament, would have made some form of educational qualification a

1 Africa Health Workforce Observatory – Human Resources for Health Country Profile: Kenya – March 2009, quoted in Lambert and Leonard (2011: 29).

2 Traditional Healer, Kakamega County, Interview 31 June 2013.

3 See respectively KWG-MAPS (2011); Lambert and Leonard (2011); and Pharmacy and Poisons Board (2010).

4 Senior Pharmacist, Ministry of Health, Interview 19 February 2013; Former Patent Inspector, Kenya Industrial Property Institute, Interview 11 July 2013.

prerequisite for the inclusion of a healer on a comprehensive national register, itself a requirement of lawful practice.[5]

Kenyan concerns at the misappropriation of valuable genetic resources and traditional knowledge[6] have chimed with international agreements, most importantly the Convention on Biological Diversity (1992), and with policies and model laws emanating from the Intergovernmental Committee on Intellectual Property and Genetic Resources, Traditional Knowledge and Folklore of the World Intellectual Property Organization (WIPO).[7] Since 2006 the National Environmental Management Agency has maintained an inventory of Kenyan biodiversity, as well as a system of conditional permits for accessing such material and for sharing benefits arising from its use.[8] More recently the Protection of Traditional Knowledge and Cultural Expressions Act (2016) has created a new class of intellectual property rights enabling communities to prevent the use of local herbal remedies, for example, without their consent or to license this for a fee or a percentage of any profits. This is intended to fill the gap created by patent law rules which allow traditional knowledge to be appropriated without compensation and then converted into products and processes subject to monopoly control.

Governing Through Problematization

In studying the processes by which reform of traditional medical practice and knowledge transmission is pursued, we are called by Dwijen Rangnekar to attend to the 'domestic political economy of law-making' (Rangnekar, 2014: 359). The strategic and discursive dimensions of these processes are visible in what governmentality theorists, building on the work of Michel Foucault, have termed 'problematization', that is, a mode of government which 'poses the obligations of rulers in terms of problems they seek to address' (Rose and Miller, 1992: 181).[9] This is an active process. Problems aren't simply found out there. Rather, they are produced through a combination of discourses and practical routines (Bacchi, 2012). They are defined by expert knowledges and official standards as objects in need of regulation. They have three significant dimensions (Rose and Miller, 1992: 178–9).

5 Copy of the Bill on file with author. The proposals have now been introduced under s74 of the Health Act 2016.
6 See IEA (2009: 6–7).
7 For an overview, see Nnadozie (2012) and Dutfield (2012).
8 Environmental Management and Co-ordination (Conservation of Biological Diversity and Resources, Access to Genetic Resources and Benefit Sharing) Regulations 2006; see further IEA (2009).
9 See also Foucault (1991). For a fuller discussion of problematization in the present context, see Harrington (2018).

1 Moral: setting out tasks and goals and prescribing fundamental values.
2 Epistemic: grounded upon knowledge about the nature of the problem and the target of regulation.
3 Linguistic: articulated in a distinctive language which renders the field thinkable.

Any activity is likely to be the object of not one, but multiple problematizations (Dent, 2009). Traditional medicine in Kenya is problematized in terms of threats to safety, health, resource sovereignty and national development.[10] Thus, an imperative to protect patients against unsafe treatment is defined by public health expertise, underpinned by an entrenched right to health,[11] and articulated in terms of hygienic practice. The state's task of defending resources against foreign 'pillaging' is expressed as a constitutional obligation 'to protect the intellectual property rights of the people'[12] and elaborated in the detail of statute law. Policies respond to this problematization by mobilizing 'technologies' (e.g. 'best practice' for record keeping and cleanliness; permit and consent mechanisms for accessing traditional knowledge) and calling new 'subjects' into being as vehicles of self-regulation (e.g. healers' associations; national research institutes).[13] This 'government at a distance' is steered by official agencies (e.g. the Ministry of Health; the Kenya Copyright Board), but also expert groups (e.g. university ethnobotany departments) and civil society organizations (e.g. medical professional associations) (Rose, O'Malley and Valverde, 2006). Given the dependence of countries in the global south on conditional aid, foreign and inter-state bodies also contribute to shaping problematizations through standard setting, training and legal obligations. I have already noted the influence of the WIPO Intergovernmental Conference on traditional knowledge legislation. The WHO Africa Office, for example, has developed tool kits which set out detailed processes for the formulation of national policies on traditional medicine, as well as model laws and codes of ethics (WHO, 2004). Such external interventions are not merely passively received by existing national institutions. They also serve to reconstruct states by calling for the creation of new ministries and agencies, and the development of expert groupings. Each of these bodies may be linked to external mentors and funders as much as to the rest of the national government apparatus, a process aptly described as the 'transnationalization' of the state by Sousa Santos (2006: 785).

It is clear from the foregoing that problematization is significantly achieved in and through discourse. While the role of coercion, corruption and open force

10 For an application of this framework to Vietnamese traditional medicine, see Wahlberg (2006).
11 Article 43(1) Constitution of Kenya.
12 Article 11(2)(b) Constitution of Kenya.
13 See generally Rose and Miller (1992: 813ff).

in governance must not be neglected, the latter also has a pervasively rhetorical dimension. Implementation of diagnoses and recommendations, as well as the creation of new governance subjects depends on their plausibility to electors, policy makers, judges, legislators and so on. This in turn depends on their ethical appeal (moral), the authority of experts promoting them (epistemic) and the form in which they are communicated (linguistic).[14] In each case we are concerned with strategic speech, whose effectiveness depends on its ability to move specific audiences in concrete situations. Tools of cultural criticism can be used to elucidate the purchase of different problematizations through examining their aesthetic properties and wider historical resonances. In the next section, I argue, using literary and socio-legal approaches, that a range of spatio-temporal images encapsulate and give force to the different problematizations of traditional medicine.

Chronotopes: Literary, Social, Legal

Chronotopes in literature include the threshold and the quest, giving expression to the 'intrinsic connectedness of temporal and spatial relationships' (Bakhtin, 1996: 84). The hybrid nature of the concept marks the fact that time is inevitably represented in space (e.g. the crossing of the physical threshold as the passage from one phase of life to another) and space is produced through time (e.g. the movement of the voyaging hero away from home) (Peeren, 2006: 28). Chronotopes contribute to the aesthetic appeal and moral force of literary texts, identifying them with specific genres. Paul Gilroy (1993: 4) identifies the recurrent image of the 'slave ship' as a unifying figure in the work of many African American writers. 'Storyscapes' of childhood focus the diasporic consciousness and authorial nostalgia of African fiction authors such as Chimamanda Ngozi Adichie (2003) (Ouma, 20143). Social practices too can be grasped as chronotopes whose moral significance depends on their aesthetic form. The queue outside a polling station moving slowly in space and time, may be understood alternatively as an emblem of democratic transformation or chronic maladministration.[15] Chronotopes are not simply products of imagination, but emerge from an iterative reaction of cultural ideals on physical forms and vice versa. For example, state borders, identified on maps and achieved through fences 'on the ground' may be valued for allowing the nation to develop in its own time, or challenged as an alien imposition (Klinke, 2012: 674).

Legal doctrine, policy arguments and law's institutional manifestations, as well as the representations of law in popular culture, are also filtered through spatio-temporal imagery (Valverde, 2015). For instance, the chronotope of the 'single-family detached' – childrearing parents living in their own home – has been at the heart of family and residential law in many countries (Valverde,

14 On these dimensions of rhetoric in law, see further Harrington (2017: ch. 3).
15 See further, Harrington (2020).

2015: 169ff). Its racialized nature can be grasped through juxtaposition with a rival chronotope: the separation of urban labourers from their rural families under colonial and apartheid laws. The peace and order of the country house, disturbed by a murder and restored by an intrepid detective, provides a legitimating image of British criminal justice.[16] Mariana Valverde (2015: 21) suggests that a distinction needs to be made between legal and social chronotopes. The former, I would suggest, are immanent in particular doctrines, for example the time-space 'envelope' created by a standard lease over defined property for a fixed term (Abbott, 2013). The latter originate outside the law, but often inform it, for example, the 'single-family detached' mentioned above. Both have important rhetorical effects, forming part of arguments about the application of detailed rules and proposals for law reform respectively (Harrington, 2017). Both add to and draw on a mutable body of common sense about the 'natural' time and space for specific legal interventions.

Law's chronotopes have an important affective dimension associated with the 'governance moods' which each calls forth (Valverde, 2015: 78). For example, while the country house mystery is tightly narrated in the confident expectation of a resolution, law and policy on cross-border bioterrorism is suffused with dread (Stern, 2002). Corresponding to the production of feeling, or 'pathos', in classical rhetoric, governance moods add to the persuasiveness of the problematization and the technologies proposed. In the case of bioterrorism, an atmosphere of dread will support rapid, dramatic interventions such as travel restrictions. According to Valverde (2015: 83) each chronotope also supports a distinct claim for jurisdiction. Thus, epidemiological modelling of smoking as an epidemic, spreading over time from developed to developing countries, characterizes tobacco control as a transnational matter, responsibility for which properly rests with the World Health Organization (Reubi, 2017). In the rest of this chapter, I will pick out a number of chronotopes which have informed and structured the recent problematizations of traditional medicine in Kenya mentioned above. For each one I will attend to its mutually reinforcing spatial and temporal dimensions, the mood evoked and the specific jurisdictional claim raised. My discussion is framed by an understanding of the strategic, agonistic and situated nature of these interventions. Law reform here is marked by rival moods, competing bids for authority and the quest for wider historical and cultural resonance. Accepting this state of contest, I note the hegemonic effects of certain chronotopes, their capacity to marginalize or obscure certain perspectives and interests.

The Tribe and the Globe

The British authorities expressed their understanding of traditional medicine in the Kenyan *Medical Practitioners and Dentists Ordinance* of 1910 which permitted

16 On chronotopes in detective fiction, see Valverde (2015: 165).

> the practice of systems of therapeutics according to Native ... methods by persons recognised by the community to which they belong to be duly trained in such practice; provided that nothing in this section shall be construed to authorise any person to practice native ... systems of therapeutics except amongst the community to which he belongs ...[17]

This provision effectively meant that local healers would not be allowed to integrate western techniques, instruments or medicines into their practice, thus bolstering the monopoly position of registered doctors. Like its counterparts across Eastern and Southern Africa, the Ordinance ascribes an inherently static and local character to traditional medicine (Osseo-Asare, 2014: 14). This chronotope of the 'tribe' played a key role in the wider system of 'indirect rule' across British colonial Africa. In effect, the 'tribe' was closed to the outside world save through the obligation to render tribute to the colonial power through a tribal leader who exercised authoritarian powers (Mamdani, 19964).

Colonial governance of traditional medicine was filtered through two further related chronotopes. First was that of Africa as a store of unknown and untapped remedies which properly belong to all of humankind, available for appropriation by those in a position to unlock their benefits. While western techniques were designated off-limits to African healers, colonial scientists were encouraged and facilitated in their quest for new medical resources. As Osseo-Asare (2014: 109) notes, the Berlin Conference of 1884–85 guaranteed safe passage for scientific parties along the Congo and Niger Rivers to just this end. The second chronotope of western medicine as a universally valid and progressively improving science provided the epistemic basis for the creation of a unified profession in European countries. Thus, the restricting of traditional healing to a static locality, as evidenced by the Kenyan Ordinance quoted above, enabled 'progressive' western medicine to exploit Africa as a store of untapped remedies in the interest of capitalist imperialism from the mid-19th century period of colonial conquest (Lawrence, 1994). Their normative effect was to marginalize local knowledge holders and subject Africa's biodiversity to the jurisdiction of colonial scientists and doctors.

Such essentializing moves do not fully accord with the reality of traditional medical practice then or in the present day. Historically many healers have travelled from their home area to learn their craft from more experienced practitioners belonging to another ethnic group (Rekdal, 1999). Equally, healers from beyond the locality, often far beyond, were and still are seen as being especially effective. For example, Tanzanian healers or those from, say, the coastal region of Kenya working in Nairobi advertise their specific origins prominently. Moreover, in the multi-ethnic slums of Kenya's growing cities, healers seek to build their reputations among people of all backgrounds (Iliffe, 1998: 191). Patients themselves are commonly unconstrained by 'tribal'

17 See further Iliffe (1998: 28–29).

categories or by the barrier between 'Western' and 'African' medicine in their pluralistic selection and combination of therapies.[18] However, the 'tribe' still figures in general political discourse, furnishing a still potent means for Kenyan leaders to define and rally their supporters.[19] It also continues to appear in official discourse about traditional medicine in Kenya. The National Assembly debates on the Protection of Traditional Knowledge and Cultural Expressions Bill, for example, were marked by frequent reference to ethnically denominated medical practices such as Kamba treatments for blood pressure,[20] the Luhya group's use of the neem tree,[21] and traditional surgeons among the Kisii.[22] As we will see later, critics also claim that the operation of the Act as passed risks rehabilitating competitive ethnicity over valuable resources.

The Village and the Matatu

The spatio-temporal figure of 'village' provides an important anchor for the problematization of traditional medicine as vulnerable and in need of legislative protection and modernization. It figures frequently as a point of departure in healers' own biographies. Thus, the proprietor of a large commercial herbal medicine business noted that on discovering his vocation he left his job as a pharmacist, visiting his native village in Central Province for extended training with a local 'medicine man' before returning to the city.[23] The village is here a chronotope of origin guaranteeing the authenticity of traditional medicine by virtue of its distance from the urban in time and space. As the leader of a nationwide healers' association put it, 'the genuine practitioners are those people out there … those people up country'.[24] MPs too have drawn on this image to identify what is at stake in legislative proposals to regulate practice. One remembered

> with a lot of sorrow that in my own village, there was an old woman … who used to attract very many couples to her home and they used to go for herbal concoctions …. It is a pity that [she] has since died with this knowledge with nobody to follow it.[25]

18 Founder of NGO for the promotion of traditional healing, interview 30 January 2013.

19 On the entrenchment of 'tribalism' in independent Kenya, see Atieno-Odhiambo (1987).

20 Mr Mulu MP, Kenya National Assembly Debates (Hansard), 12 November 2015, p. 24.

21 Ms Wakhungu MP, Kenya National Assembly Debates (Hansard), 12 November 2015, pp. 9–11. Neem, known in Kiswahili as Mwarobaini, is used across Kenya and indeed in many other countries.

22 Mr Tong'i MP, Kenya National Assembly Debates (Hansard), 12 November 2015, p. 29.

23 Herbal Medicines Proprietor, interview 29 January 2013.

24 Herbalist Association Leader, interview 31 January 2013.

Another called forth a more generic village with mythic temporality:

> In the olden days when there was tragedy in the village, people would visit the forest, rivers and lakes to seek intervention from the gods … Herbal medicine is a practice that goes on and has been going on since ancient days.[26]

These reflections conjure up an idyllic rural setting, embodying the past in its spatial dimensions.[27] The literary pastoral is often narrated by a speaker who has been removed from the locale, in our case urban-based healers and politicians. The associated mood of nostalgia gives it a political edge, since the idyll is represented as being threatened by outsiders. In the case of the village, and the authentic healing practices which it warrants, this threat is two-fold.

The first threat comes from 'fake healers', who feature in newspaper headlines and parliamentary interventions, but also in the more reflective comments of health officials. Such quacks and street vendors are said to be only interested in 'making a quick buck'.[28] This purely commercial ethos contrasts with that of 'genuine healers who are doing it for purposes of restoring health'.[29] It is also reflected in the newspaper advertisements and notices pinned to lampposts which list the products and promised remedies of entrepreneurial healers. Particular modes of using therapeutic resources are also taken to be a sign of quackery. This may involve heterogeneous mixing:

> There are some that have already borrowed from western medicine and they are injecting [but] the traditional healer in the village is not even aware of the injectables, because they are not a part of their culture.[30]

Or by contrast an oversimplistic approach to therapy:

> The ones in Nairobi, if you go to a chemist – they may give you a mix of one plant and say it is herbal medicine, for a million diseases. But those women out there [in rural areas], they know the right herbs.[31]

As both quotes show, the problematization of traditional medicine in terms of safety is achieved by contrasting urban markets with the pastoral world of rural

25 Dr Khalwale MP, Kenya National Assembly Debates (Hansard), 9 December 2009, p. 4442.
26 Mr Wamalwa MP, Kenya National Assembly Debates (Hansard), 9 December 2009, p. 4438.
27 For a useful summary, see Klinck (1994: 26–29).
28 Mr Wamalwa MP, Kenya National Assembly Debates (Hansard), 9 December 2009, p. 4438.
29 Senior Government Researcher on Traditional Medicine, interview 21 May 2013.
30 Senior Government Researcher on Traditional Medicine, interview 21 May 2013.
31 Herbalist Association Leader, interview 31 January 2013.

healing. Mobility of healers, vendors and medicines is the hallmark of the city. Thus, an investigative journalist opened her report on the reform initiatives being discussed here with the following vignette:

> Peter quickly launches into his sales pitch for the various natural remedies he is selling: oil for skin conditions, pills that will clean out the stomach, a liquid remedy which helps with digestion, a product that will purify blood .... Peter has carefully chosen his route, the majority of the passengers will alight at the hospital and clearly health concerns are on their mind. Several of them part with a few hundred shillings to try one of his products.
>
> (Gemson, 2013: 12)

The minibus taxi (or matatu) functions here as a further chronotope: a mobile, encapsulated space, populated by a rapidly changing and ethnically heterogeneous population of travellers, which is itself emblematic of urban entrepreneurialism in Kenya. The jurisdictional implications are clear. Quacks escape the spatio-temporal fixity and customary rules of tribe and village and are free to operate in the 'unregulated chaos'[32] of the city. They are in need of 'being visited properly by the law' according to a former health minister.[33]

The Community and the Patent

The chronotope of the village also functions as a synecdoche for Africa itself. Traditional medicine is routinely designated as 'African medicine'. The logo for a major commercial herbalist in Nairobi, for example, depicts a healer, seated under a palm tree, set against the map of Africa, with the phrase 'Back to the Roots'.[34] As we have seen this alignment points the potential customer back in time, serving as a guarantee of authenticity. But it also focusses and extends the colonial chronotope of the continent as an untapped source of remedies. As one MP put it, 'the knowledge of healers is unprotected and condemned in the open [and] the developed West will take advantage of it ... Africa is the only natural resource left'.[35]

The mood here is one of defensiveness and anxiety regarding a 'new form of colonial pillaging'.[36] In this vein, the threat of unregulated bioprospecting was a key focus of the 2009 National Policy for Traditional Knowledge, Genetic Resources and Traditional Cultural Expressions.[37] It has been made vivid by

32 Ng'etich (2011).
33 Professor Anyang Nyong'o, Kenya National Assembly Debates (Hansard), 13 August 2008, p. 2594.
34 'Dr Maina's Herbals Advertising Sheet', copy on file with author.
35 Mr Maina MP, Kenya National Assembly Debates (Hansard), 9 December 2009, p. 4452.
36 IEA (2009: 3).
37 See Government of Kenya (2009).

narratives of unwitting village healers disclosing valuable knowledge about the sources and uses of local medicines to ethno-botanists working for foreign companies seeking the impetus for new drug development and other commercial products. The most widely circulated of these concerns was the 'discovery' of rosy periwinkle in Madagascar as a source of treatments for childhood leukaemia and Hodgkins disease, which have earned immense profits for the Eli Lilly corporation (Osseo-Asare, 2014: 107ff).[38] In 2011 the Institute of Economic Affairs' review of law and policy documented two similar cases of appropriation in Kenya.[39] The German company Bayer had filed a patent on a process for the biosynthesis of acarbose, used for treatment of type II diabetes, in 1995. It was later confirmed that the process involved a type of bacteria (Actinoplanes sp.) originally taken from Lake Ruiru in Kenya (IEA, 2011: 6). In 2002–3 US biotech company Genencor reported to shareholders that it had licensed enzymes capable of fading denim jeans to Proctor and Gamble. The report included the image of a box of the detergent powder 'Tide' above a caption saying: 'See what we see in the soda lakes of Kenya'.[40] The enzymes had been discovered in a microbe, removed without authorization, from Lake Bogoria in the Rift Valley (IEA, 2011: 7).

Though the genetic resources in the two Kenyan cases had been acquired without the assistance of local healers, the ease with which they were extracted was a matter of concern to officials concerned with traditional medicine and to practitioners themselves.[41] The cases were referenced in the National Assembly debates during the passage of the Protection of Traditional Knowledge and Cultural Expressions Act 2016, which meets a timetabled constitutional obligation on the state to ensure that communities are compensated for use of their culture.[42] The minister introducing the legislation stated that it was intended to address a lacuna in Kenya's intellectual property law which had 'resulted in the widespread unfair exploitation of the traditional knowledge and cultural heritage for commercial and business interests and the continuous loss of important elements of traditional knowledge and traditional cultural expression'.[43]

One of only two such statutes in Africa to date,[44] the Act's provisions create an elaborate governance 'technology' in response to this problematization. At

38 As Osseo-Asare notes, this narrative retains its potency, notwithstanding evidence that Eli Lilly was able to source the flower in other countries and that it is a common weed rather than a rare plant (2014: 33).
39 Unlike the rosy periwinkle case, these Kenyan accounts have not been challenged.
40 Intellectual Property Lawyer, Nairobi, interview 1 October 2013.
41 Former Patent Inspector, Kenyan Industrial Property Institute, interview 1 July 2013; Prominent Healer, interview 22 April 2013.
42 Articles 11(3)(a) and 69(1)(c) Constitution of Kenya (2010). See also Mr Njuguna, MP, Kenya National Assembly Debates (Hansard), 12 November 2015, p. 12.
43 Mr Katoo MP, Kenya National Assembly Debates (Hansard), 12 November 2015, p. 3.
44 Similar legislation was passed in Zambia in 2016.

its core is a new or *sui generis* type of intellectual property right held by communities over traditional knowledge, including medical knowledge.

The spatio-temporal form of the right created by the 2016 Act can be contrasted with the patent which it is intended to displace or at least limit in the field of traditional knowledge. Patents are sharply defined, being enforceable within the national territory for a term of 20 years from the date on which the application was filed.[45] This legal chronotope is closely based on the social figure of the 'moment of genius',[46] when an individual makes an invention. Viewed thus, new knowledge originates within the person of an inventor and exists only from a defined point in time (Osseo-Asare, 2014: 10). This figure is reflected in statutory requirements for patentability, namely that the product or process concerned be novel and non-obvious, as well as being capable of industrial application.[47] The 'moment of genius' chronotope is also presumed by theories of intellectual property whether oriented to the rights of inventors or the need to offer clear rewards for research and innovation (Lee, 2015: 33ff).

As the National Policy recognized, the patent form itself enables biopiracy (Government of Kenya, 2009: 9). Its effect is to classify knowledge which is collectively held as part of the timeless common heritage of all mankind and, thus, available for appropriation without permission or compensation. Once the inventor, and the corporation which they work for, have transformed this into patentable knowledge, they are vested with authority to exclude others from using it without payment of a monopoly rent (Timmermans, 2003: 752). The response of the 2016 Act is to call forth a new governance subject, 'the community', whose informed consent must be obtained prior to any use or reproduction of its traditional knowledge.[48] These ownership rights are enforceable by an elaborate system of criminal sanctions and civil remedies,[49] as well as provisions allowing communities to enter 'authorized user agreements' with companies to share in the benefits of commercial exploitation.[50] This extension of intellectual property law has been an important theme in the work of the WIPO Intergovernmental Conference and in an influential report by Kenyan scientists and legal experts (Oguamanam, 2012: 158ff; Mutta and Munyi, 2010). The latter showcased the work of existing biodiversity management groups among the Mijikenda people of the coastal region and in Kakamega Forest in the west and their efforts to protect and profit from their

45 S.60 Industrial Property Act 2001.

46 This is well explained in the equivalent context of copyright and traditional music by Seeger (1992: 352).

47 S.22 Industrial Property Act 2001.

48 S.18(2) Protection of Traditional Knowledge and Cultural Expressions Act 2016.

49 Ss.37, 38 Protection of Traditional Knowledge and Cultural Expressions Act 2016.

50 Ss. 25, 34 Protection of Traditional Knowledge and Cultural Expressions Act 2016.

intellectual resources, for example by forming partnerships with research institutes.

By contrast with the patent holder, the 'community' which owns traditional knowledge under the 2016 Act is loose in form.[51] It is defined as 'a homogeneous and consciously distinct group' which shares any of the following attributes: common ancestry, similar culture, mode of livelihood or language, shared geographic or ecological space; or community of interest.[52] This eludes sharp spatial limits and is matched by a backward-looking temporality which refuses any clear point of origin for the community and its knowledge. The latter is defined as that which 'is generated, preserved and transmitted from one generation to another … distinctively associated with [the] community and integral to [its] cultural identity.'[53] This new legal chronotope is an important step in 'filling the gaps' left by orthodox intellectual property law.[54] But the complexity of its internal constitution poses new risks. The operation of the Act depends on the community decisions whether or not to enforce their exclusory rights, enter benefit agreements and so on. This will be difficult for some language groups in Kenya which number in the millions or which are spread over urban and a range of rural locations. Admittedly the Act does allocate limited decision-making power to individual 'holders' of traditional knowledge 'recognized' according to customary rules. However, holders may not speak for all or even a majority of the community. Indeed, as Forsyth has argued of similar legislation in the Pacific Islands, underlying assumptions about the homogeneity of communities tend to strengthen the powers of stronger members, often older men, at the expense of others who would perhaps resist the marketing of traditional knowledge (Forsyth, 2012: 4, 23). Moreover, the imprecise contours of the 'community' may be filled out in practice by the form of the 'tribe' which, as we have seen, has been established as a legal and social chronotope since the colonial period. This poses the further risk of ethnically denominated struggles over the valuable rights in traditional knowledge created by the sui generis regime.[55] Again it is worth emphasizing that the boundaries between communities and their knowledges are blurred.[56] Both also straddle colonially imposed borders, though this difficult jurisdictional issue is not significantly addressed in the 2016 Act (Deacon, 2017).

51 The Constitution provides no comprehensive definition, referring in different places to communities as cultural and linguistic, but also ethnic entities, see Articles 44(2) and 63(1). 'Marginalised communities', whose political participation and social welfare the state is under a duty to promote, are defined in much narrower terms than under the 2016 Act, see Articles 56, 204 and 206.
52 S.2 Protection of Traditional Knowledge and Cultural Expressions Act 2016.
53 S.6 Protection of Traditional Knowledge and Cultural Expressions Act 2016.
54 See further Gervais (2009).
55 See generally Lynch (2011).
56 See Antons (2013: 1404).

The Nation

The elevation of the 'community' generates a two-fold development of jurisdiction. Customary law and practice delimits the powers of action and duties of consultation among knowledge 'holders' within the community. It also defines knowledge and the context in which it is used as 'traditional'.[57] State law, in the form of the Act itself and the regulations which have yet to follow, sets out the framework for the community's relations with outsiders, for example, foreign bio-prospectors. In addition, it distributes functions, for example dispute settlement, the keeping of registers of traditional knowledge and the grant of formal approval to user agreements, as between county and national governments, and the Kenya Copyright Board.[58] The state is not simply the recorder and enforcer of the community's will, however. It also exercises residual jurisdiction, where for example no owner of traditional knowledge can be identified or where a dispute as to ownership cannot be resolved.[59] In such cases the national authorities may step in and issue a licence for the exploitation of the traditional knowledge to a private company. Given the blurred boundaries of who belongs to communities and what knowledge they hold, disputes are inevitable, widening the scope for state intervention. This is increased further by section 12 of the Act which allows state authorities to override the will of the community and grant a compulsory licence to a commercial concern, where the knowledge is not being sufficiently exploited. In the rest of this section, I argue that these provisions need to be read in terms of recent policy documents and international instruments and suggest that the Kenyan nation state is itself a legal chronotope.

In order to grasp the dimensions of this chronotope it is worth recalling the changing history of official attitudes to traditional medicine and traditional knowledge more generally. The early decades of independence from 1964 were marked by widespread hostility among medical civil servants and modernizing political leaders. First President Jomo Kenyatta denounced healers as conmen and parasites (Iliffe, 1998: 191). African nationalism was pursued in the health sector by removing racial barriers to practising and accessing biomedicine rather than through the promotion of indigenous healing practices (Ombongi, 2011). The late 1970s saw a relaxation of this position under the influence of the WHO's Alma Ata Declaration, which promoted the role of healers in the delivery of primary care.[60] A

57 Ss. 19, 30, 2 Protection of Traditional Knowledge and Cultural Expressions Act 2016.

58 See the brief summary in Deacon (2017).

59 S.30 Protection of Traditional Knowledge and Cultural Expressions Act 2016.

60 Declaration of the Alma Ata Conference on Primary Health Care 1978. https://www.who.int/publications/almaata_declaration_en.pdf (accessed 29 February 2020).

Traditional Medicines and Drugs Research Centre was established as part of the Kenya Medical Research Institute (KEMRI) in 1984.[61] The new stance was initially more verbal than practical and signalled above all else a symbolic re-appropriation of traditional medicine, as a 'national essence'[62] and something for Kenyans 'to be proud of', in the words of KEMRI's founder, Professor Kihumbu Thairu.[63] But it also marked the beginnings of a new focus on the potential for indigenous knowledge to contribute to economic development. In this regard Kenya was catching up with Tanzania and Ghana which had sought, admittedly with limited success, to create state-owned domestic pharmaceuticals industries based on indigenous knowledge (Langwick, 2010; Owoahene-Acheampong and Vasconi, 2010).

Policy and legislative initiatives, as well as academic commentary concerning traditional medical practice and knowledge over the last twenty years have been articulated in these developmental terms. The National Policy on Traditional Knowledge, Genetic Resources and Traditional Cultural Expressions, which provided the impetus for the 2016 Act, affirmed that 'no society can achieve its developmental goals if it ignores its rich cultural heritage imbedded [sic] in traditional knowledge' (Government of Kenya, 2009: 6).[64] Commercialization was one of the four key objectives of the 2005 National Policy on Traditional Medicine and Medicinal Plants which addressed obstacles such as: unsustainable harvesting practices; lack of funds for small scale investment; weak supply chains; and poor packaging and labelling (NCAPD, 2008: 9, 20ff). Compared with the 1980s and 1990s, there is now less international optimism about the potential for traditional medical knowledge to lead to lucrative new pharmaceuticals (Clapp and Crook, 2002). Attention has instead shifted to the massive market for herbal products and 'nutraceuticals' in Europe and North America. The Natural Products Industry Initiative established under the government's medium-term economic strategy Vision 2030 aims to meet this demand.[65] Traditional medicine does not directly serve the goal of self-sufficiency, as was the aim in Ghana and Tanzania after independence. Rather it positions Kenya as a competitor in the neo-liberal marketplace.[66]

These interventions contribute to the problematization of traditional medicine in terms of its potential contribution to development and the threats to this posed by neo-colonial exploitation on the one hand and domestic inefficiencies, on the other. Both aspects were well captured by Professor Julius

61 See NCAPD (2008: 1).
62 This is taken from Xu's (1997) study of struggles over traditional Chinese medicine in the 1930s.
63 Quoted in Ombongi (2011: 364).
64 This was echoed by MPs debating the Act, see for example, Mr Ali, Kenya National Assembly Debates (Hansard), 12 November 2015, p. 36.
65 Interview with senior researcher attached to the Natural Products Industry Initiative, 25 July 2013.
66 See Langwick (2010: 23–24).

Mwangi, himself a traditional practitioner, in his 2012 inaugural lecture as Chair of Pharmacognosy at the University of Nairobi. By allowing resources simply to be 'shipped out', Kenya was failing to grasp an opportunity to develop the industrial sector and neglecting its 'academic, moral and practical' duty to make full use of its 'green gold' (Mwangi, 2012: 15, 26). Mwangi's imperative is made explicit in the constitution which recognizes 'the role of indigenous technologies in the development of the nation'.[67] The state is the key governance subject within this problematization, the primary duty bearer for fostering development. Understood chronotopically, the state has to lead the territorially defined nation out of underdevelopment.[68] The governance mood is one of optimism, albeit tempered with a sense of vulnerability. Faith in progress, once characteristic of colonial science, has been appropriated by the independent state. The designation of traditional medicine as a resource for national development[69] under the stewardship of the state establishes a hierarchy of jurisdiction supported by international and national law. While Article 8(j) of the Convention on Biological Diversity obliges parties to respect the knowledge and practices of indigenous and local communities, this duty is subordinate to the 'sovereign right' of states to control their own resources recognized in Article 3 (Oguamanam, 2012: 148). Equally, while Kenya's Protection of Traditional Knowledge and Cultural Expressions Act 2016 carves out considerable scope for local and community control, provisions on lack of ownership and compulsory licensing restore state jurisdiction to a certain extent. If, as Chidi Oguamanam has argued, the spread of sui generis regimes betokens the emergence of a post-modern regime for traditional knowledge, that remains nested within a classically Westphalian ordering.[70]

Conclusion

This chapter identified a number of key chronotopes which served as a focus for contemporary and historical problematizations of traditional medicine in Kenya. In each case we saw a connection between spatial and temporal forms, and between these and the associated governance mood and specific jurisdictional claims which each grounded. The local and the traditional were mutually reinforcing in the pastoral image of the village and they contributed to a sense of vulnerability and a regulatory imperative to defend pure, safe and authentic practice. It was clear throughout that problematizations could be figured through more than one chronotope. Governance for colonial appropriation was realized by an articulation of the temporally static and spatially fixed form

67 Article 11(2)(b) Constitution of Kenya (2010).

68 As Branch and Cheeseman (2010) indicate, development has been the raison d'être of Kenya, like most other post-colonial states.

69 On the appropriation of traditional culture as a national resource for political and economic ends in Senegal, see Mills (1996: 70).

70 See Oguamanam (2012: 156).

of the tribe with the figure of Africa as virgin territory ready to supply the raw material for a dynamic, universal medical science. Our rhetorical perspective suggested that chronotopes may be more or less coherently realized and therefore more or less plausible in supporting specific problematizations and governance technologies. The 'community' called forth by the 2016 Act as the holder of sui generis rights is beset by uncertainty as to its spatial borders and its internal constitution. This complexity suggested potential difficulties in the operation of the new regime and its likely subordination to the nation state in the hierarchy of jurisdiction. The nation's pre-eminence is favoured by its historical role as the agent of development, whether state-led or neo-liberal, as well as its more clearly defined spatio-temporal limits. The latter was also a feature of the legal chronotope of the patent and its subject matter, by comparison with the fluid boundaries of traditional knowledge and the communities which own it.

The strategic value of chronotopes in legal and policy discourses lies in their persuasive appeal. They also have the hegemonic effect of making somethings visible and others invisible at the same time. While an essentialized view of the community would allow the claims of marginalized peoples to be promoted, it may also occlude genuine dissent within them. The view of Africa as a natural cornucopia suppresses the intellectual and practical contribution of individual healers and communities in identifying and utilizing medicinal plants over generations. Chronotopes cannot be grasped in isolation. They qualify and challenge each other in rhetorical struggles. The nation defends its natural resources against claims based on the common heritage of mankind. They define each other dialogically through relations of contradistinction or supersession. Village healing is constituted discursively in opposition to mobile medicine markets in the cities. Village healing is also the as yet unactivated source of the nation's longed-for industrial and commercial modernity.

The range of chronotopes was matched by the different governance subjects presumed by the different problematizations. Responsibility for safety will rest with individual healers, while the management of traditional knowledge is under the direction of a complex of state and non-state bodies, including communities. The governmentality framework adopted in this review suggests that the role of the state is not exhausted by command and control models. It also attempts to orchestrate without directing the regulatory work of other governance subjects. This effort is not always successful or uncontested as we have seen. It is a commonplace of the globalization literature that the state is challenged from below (locally) and above (internationally), that physical and normative exclaves are carved out from the national order and linked more directly to external sources of power and governance. Nonetheless the state retains a significant discursive role as the repository of popular anti-colonial ambitions and the aspiration to 'build the nation'. This subjectivization of the state had its international moment too. As Sundhya Pahuja (2011) has shown, the post-World War II order operated by the United Nations and the Bretton

Woods institutions enjoined newly independent states to achieve economic and political progress. They were governed, then and now, within the frame of another chronotope: the spectrum along which states are arranged and along which they can progress from failed, to underdeveloped to fully developed. Policy makers, scientists and herbalist leaders I interviewed also framed their efforts through this chronotope, making particular reference to Kenya's need to catch up with China as an exemplar of rapid industrialization including the modernization of its traditional medicine practices. These internal and external resources, I would suggest, still uniquely equip the state to provide a certain discursive coordination or 'imaginary unity' (Lemke, 2007) to the plurality of problematizations and technologies proposed and deployed in relation to traditional medicine.

References

Abbott, F., 2013. Seizure of Generic Pharmaceuticals in Transit Based on Allegations of Patent Infringement: a Threat to International Trade, Development and Public Welfare. In O.

Aginam, J.Harrington and P.K. Yu (eds), *Global Governance of HIV/AIDS. Intellectual Property and Access to Essential Medicines*. Edward Elgar, p. 131.

Adichie, C., 2003. *Purple Hibiscus*. Fourth Estate.

Antons, C., 2013. Asian Borderlands and the Legal Protection of Traditional Knowledge and Traditional Cultural Expressions. *Modern Asian Studies*, 47, 1403–1433.

Atieno-Odhiambo, E., 1987. Democracy and the Ideology of Order in Kenya. In Michael G. Schatzberg (ed.), *The Political Economy of Kenya*. New York: Praeger, pp. 177–201.

Bacchi, C., 2012. Why Study Problematizations? Making Politics Visible. *Open Journal of Political Science*, 2, 1–8.

Bakhtin, M., 1996. Forms of Time and of the Chronotope in the Novel. In M. Holquist (ed.), *The Dialogic Imagination: Four Essays by M.M. Bakhtin*. University of Texas Press.

Branch, D. and Cheeseman, N., 2010. Introduction: Our Turn to Eat. In D. Branch, N. Cheeseman and L. Gardner (eds), *Our Turn to Eat: Politics in Kenya Since 1950*. Lit Verlag.

Clapp, R.A. and Crook, C., 2002. Drowning in the Magic Well: Shaman Pharmaceuticals and the Elusive Value of Traditional Knowledge. *Journal of Environment Development*, 11, 79–102.

Deacon, H., 2017. Transboundary Co-operation and Regional Cooperation in the Protection of Traditional Knowledge in Kenya. *Journal of Intellectual Property Law and Practice*, 12, 226–235.

Dent, C., 2009. Copyright, Governmentality and Problematisation – An Exploration. *Griffith Law Review*, 18, 129–150.

Dutfield, G., 2012. From Traditional Medicines to Modern Drugs. In T. Bubela and R. E. Gold (eds), *Genetic Resources and Traditional Knowledge. Case Studies and Conflicting Interests*. Edward Elgar, p. 93.

Forsyth, M., 2012. Lifting the Lid on "The Community": Who Has the Right to Control Access to Traditional Knowledge and Expressions of Culture? *International Journal of Cultural Property*, 19, 1–31.

Foucault, M., 1991. Governmentality. In G. Burchell, C. Gordon and P. Miller (eds), *The Foucault Effect – Studies in Governmentality*. Harvester Wheatsheaf, p. 15.

Gemson, S.C., 2013. Herbal Medicine Industry in Dire Need of Regulation. *Daily Nation*, 19 February, p. 12.

Gervais, D., 2009. Traditional Knowledge: Are we Closer to the Answer(s)? The Potential Role of Geographical Indications. *ILSA Journal of International and Comparative Law*, 15, 551–570.

Gilroy, P., 1993. *The Black Atlantic: Modernity and Double Consciousness*. Harvard University Press.

Government of Kenya, 2009. National Policy on Traditional Knowledge, Genetic Resources and Traditional Cultural Expressions, submitted to the Intergovernmental Committee on Intellectual Property and Genetic Resources, Traditional Knowledge and Folklore, World Intellectual Property Organization, 16th Session, Geneva, 3–7 May 2010 WIPO/GRTKF/IC/16/INF/25.

Harrington, J., 2017. *Towards a Rhetoric of Medical Law*. Routledge.

Harrington, J., 2018. Governing Traditional Medicine in Kenya: Problematization and the Role of the Constitution. *African Studies*, 78, 223–239.

IEA, 2009. Biodiversity Related International Initiatives and National Policy Coherence for Development and Poverty Reduction in Kenya. *Trade Notes*, No. 23. Institute of Economic Affairs, Kenya.

IEA, 2011. *Biodiversity, Traditional Knowledge and Intellectual Property in Kenya: The Legal and Institutional Framework for Sustainable Economic Development*. Institute of Economic Affairs, Kenya.

Iliffe, J., 1998. *East African Doctors: A History of the Modern Profession*. Cambridge University Press.

Klinck, D., 1994. "This Other Eden". Lord Denning's Pastoral Vision. *Oxford Journal of Legal Studies*, 14, 25–55.

Klinke, I., 2012. Chronopolitics a Conceptual Matrix. *Progress in Human Geography*, 37, 673–690.

KWG-MAPS, 2011. *Kenya Working Group on Medicinal and Aromatic Plants: Training Report, Components A and B*. World Bank and Japanese Social Development Fund [copy on file with author].

Lambert, J. and Leonard, K., 2011. *The Contribution of Traditional Herbal Medicine Practitioners to Kenyan Health Care Delivery: Results from Community Health-Seeking Behaviour Vignettes and a Traditional Herbal Medicine Practitioner Survey*. World Bank.

Langwick, S.A., 2010. From Non-Aligned Medicines to Market-Based Herbals: China's Relationship to the Shifting Politics of Traditional Medicine in Tanzania. *Medical Anthropology: Cross Cultural Studies in Health and Illness*, 29, 15–43.

Lawrence, C., 1994. *Medicine in the Making of Modern Britain 1700–1920*. Routledge.

Lee, J.Y., 2015. *A Human Rights Framework for Intellectual Property, Innovation and Access to Medicines*. Ashgate.

Lemke, T., 2007. An Indigestible Meal? Foucault, Governmentality and State Theory. *Distinktion: Scandinavian Journal of Social Theory*, 8, 43–64.

Lynch, G., 2011. Kenya's New Indigenes: Negotiating Local Identities in a Global Context. *Nations and Nationalism*, 17, 148–167.

Mamdani, M., 1996. *Citizen and Subject. Contemporary Africa and the Legacy of Late Colonialism*. James Currey.

Mills, S., 1996. Indigenous Music and the Law: An Analysis of National and International Legislation. *Yearbook for Traditional Music*, 28, 57–86.

Mutta, D. and Munyi, P., 2010. Protecting Maasai and Mijikenda Healers' Rights. In IIED, ed., *Protecting Community Right over Traditional Knowledge Implications of Customary Laws and Practices*. p. 15. International Institute for Environment and Development.

Mwangi, J., 2012. Herbal Medicines: Do They Really Work? Inaugural Lecture. 14 March.University of Nairobi [copy on file with author].

NCAPD. 2008. *Seeking Solutions for Traditional Herbal Medicine: Kenya Develops a National Policy. Policy Brief No. 1*. National Coordinating Agency for Population and Development.

Ng'etich, K., 2008. Governing the Traditional Health Care Sector in Kenya: Strategies and Setbacks. In M. Sama and V.K. Nguyen (eds), *Governing Health Systems in Africa*. CODESRIA, p. 25.

Ng'etich, J., 2011. Searching for a Cure at all Costs. *Daily Nation*, 1 April, p. 8.

Nnadozie, K., 2012. Old Wine in New Skin: Traditional Knowledge and Customary Law under the Evolving Environment in Kenya. In T. Bubela and R.E. Gold (eds), *Genetic Resources and Traditional Knowledge. Case Studies and Conflicting Interests*. Edward Elgar, p. 183.

Oguamanam, C., 2012. *Intellectual Property in Global Governance. A Development Question*. Routledge.

Ombongi, K., 2011. The Historical Interface Between the State and Medical Science in Africa: Kenya's Case. In P.W. Geissler and C. Molyneux (eds), *Evidence, Ethos and Experiment. The Anthropology and History of Medical Research in Africa*. Berghahn. p. 353.

Osseo-Asare, A., 2014. *Bitter Roots. The Search for Healing Plants in Africa*. University of Chicago Press.

Ouma, C., 2014. 'Countries of the Mind' – Space-Time Chronotopes in Adichie's Purple Hibiscus. In O. Ougade (ed.), *Tradition and Change in Contemporary West and East African Fiction. (Matatu Vol45)*Rodopi, p. 167–186.

Owoahene-Acheampong, S. and Vasconi, E., 2010. Recognition and Integration of Traditional Medicine in Ghana: A Perspective. *Research Review*, 26, 1–17.

Pahuja, S., 2011. *Decolonising International Law. Development, Economic Growth and the Politics of Universality*. Cambridge University Press.

Peeren, E., 2006. Through the Lens of the Chronotope: Suggestions for a Spatio-Temporal Perspective on Diaspora. *Thamyris/Intersecting*, 13, 67–78.

Pharmacy and Poisons Board, 2010. *Registration of Herbal and Complementary Products. Guidelines to Submission of Applications*. Pharmacy and Poisons Board, Kenya.

Prince, R. and Geissler, P.W., 2001. Becoming 'One Who Treats': A Case Study of a Luo Healer and Her Grandson in Western Kenya. *Anthropology and Education Quarterly*, 32, 447–471.

Rangnekar, D., 2014. Geneva Rhetoric, National Reality: The Political Economy of Introducing Plant Breeders' Rights in Kenya. *New Political Economy*, 19, 359–383.

Rekdal, O., 1999. Cross-Cultural Healing in East African Ethnography. *Medical Anthropology Quarterly*, 13, 458–482.

Reubi, D., 2017. Tobacco, Non-Communicable Disease and Modernity. In C. Herrick and D. Reubi (eds), *Global Health and Geographical Imaginaries*. Routledge, p. 22.

Rose, N., O'Malley, P. and Valverde, M. 2006. Governmentality. *Annual Review of Law and Social Science*, 2, 83–104.

Rose, N. and Miller, P., 1992. Political Power beyond the State: Problematics of Government. *British Journal of Sociology*, 43, 173–205.
Seeger, A., 1992. Ethnomusicology and Music Law. *Ethnomusicology*, 36, 345–359.
Sousa Santos, B., 2006. The Heterogeneous State and Legal Pluralism in Mozambique. *Law and Society Review*, 40, 39–75.
Stern, J., 2002. Dreaded Risks and the Control of Biological Weapons. *International Security*, 27, 89–123.
TICAH, 2010. *Trust for Indigenous Culture and Health Final (Year 2) Report to the Rockefeller Foundation – Valuing Traditional Medicine* [copy on file with author].
Timmermans, K., 2003. Intellectual Property Rights and Traditional Medicine: Policy Dilemmas at the Interface. *Social Science and Medicine*, 57, 745–756.
Valverde, M., 2015. *Chronotopes of Law: Jurisdiction, Scale and Governance*. Routledge.
Wahlberg, A., 2006. Bio-politics and the Promotion of Traditional Herbal Medicine in Vietnam. *Health*, 10, 123–147.
WHO, 2004. *Tools for Institutionalizing Traditional Medicine in Health Systems in the WHO African Region*. World Health Organization.
Xu, X., 1997. 'National Essence' vs 'Science': Chinese Native Physicians' Fight for Legitimacy, 1912–37. *Modern Asian Studies*, 31, 847–877.

Index